D1479299

The Judicial Response to Police Killings in Latin America

Inequality and the Rule of Law

This book documents the corrosive effect of social exclusion on democracy and the rule of law. It shows how marginalization prevents citizens from effectively engaging even the best legal systems, how politics creeps into prosecutorial and judicial decision making, and how institutional change is often nullified by enduring contextual factors. It also shows, however, how some institutional arrangements can overcome these impediments. The argument is based on extensive fieldwork and original data on the investigation and prosecution of more than five hundred police homicides in five legal systems in Argentina, Brazil, and Uruguay. It includes both qualitative analyses of individual violations and prosecutions and quantitative analyses of broad patterns within and across jurisdictions. The book offers a structured comparison of police, prosecutorial, and judicial institutions in each location and shows that analyses of any one of these organizations in isolation miss many of the essential dynamics that underlie an effective system of justice.

Daniel M. Brinks is assistant professor of government at the University of Texas at Austin, teaching comparative politics and public law, with an emphasis on politics and democracy in Latin America. He holds a Ph.D. in political science from the University of Notre Dame and a J.D., cum laude, from the University of Michigan Law School. Professor Brinks's research has appeared in journals such as *Comparative Politics, Studies in Comparative International Development, Comparative Political Studies*, and the *Texas International Law Journal*. Among his many awards and accolades, Brinks has received Honorable Mention in the Gabriel Almond Competition for Best Dissertation in Comparative Politics (2006), the Helen Kellogg Institute for International Studies Visiting Fellowship (2006–07), the Eli J. and Helen Shaheen Notre Dame Graduate School Award in the Social Sciences (2004), the American Bar Foundation Doctoral Fellowship (2002–04), the Social Science Research Council International Dissertation Research Fellowship (2000–01), and a Fulbright Fellowship (2000–01, declined).

The Judicial Response to Police Killings in Latin America

Inequality and the Rule of Law

DANIEL M. BRINKS
The University of Texas at Austin

CABRINI COLLEGE LIBRARY
610 KING OF PRUSSIA ROAD
RADNOR, PA 19087

CAMBRIDGE
UNIVERSITY PRESS

85833308

CAMBRIDGE UNIVERSITY PRESS
Cambridge, New York, Melbourne, Madrid, Cape Town, Singapore, São Paulo, Delhi

Cambridge University Press
32 Avenue of the Americas, New York, NY 10013-2473, USA

www.cambridge.org
Information on this title: www.cambridge.org/9780521872348

© Daniel M. Brinks 2008

This publication is in copyright. Subject to statutory exception
and to the provisions of relevant collective licensing agreements,
no reproduction of any part may take place without
the written permission of Cambridge University Press.

First published 2008

Printed in the United States of America

A catalog record for this publication is available from the British Library.

Library of Congress Cataloging in Publication Data

Brinks, Daniel M., 1961–
The judicial response to police killings in Latin America : inequality and the rule of law /
Daniel M. Brinks.
   p.   cm.
Includes bibliographical references and index.
ISBN 978-0-521-87234-8 (hardback)
   1. Police shootings – Argentina.   2. Police shootings – Brazil.   3. Police shootings –
Uruguay.   I. Title.
KH619.4.B75   2008
344.805′232–dc   2007008792

ISBN   978-0-521-87234-8 hardback

Cambridge University Press has no responsibility for the persistence or accuracy of URLs for
external or third-party Internet Web sites referred to in this publication and does not
guarantee that any content on such Web sites is, or will remain, accurate or appropriate.

This book is dedicated to my family: my wife, Sandra, who was a constant source of support; my children, Derek and Aaron, who took every step of this journey with me, and Liam, who livened the final stages of the trip; and my parents, Ray and Gladys Brinks, who by their example awakened my concern for the dispossessed.

And it is dedicated to the families of the victims of police violence, who suffer not only the loss of a loved one, but also indifference, hostility, and further violence in their quest for justice.

Contents

Preface

As I began the research for this book, I approached the subject of police violence with some trepidation. Illegality and violence do not take well to transparency, and I anticipated some difficulty in producing information reliable enough to satisfy social scientific standards. And yet my personal experiences with the police during the Argentine dictatorship of the 1970s and the ongoing prevalence of state violence and impunity in the more democratic current period seemed powerful arguments in favor of addressing this issue in any discussion of the effectiveness of rights in Latin America. To complicate matters further, I believe we need to take seriously the notion of the legal system as a system with internal articulations among its various actors and institutions, and we must acknowledge the extent to which the legal system is articulated with its social, economic, and political context. Crafting responsive legal institutions in a context of social inequality and marginalization, on issues that raise powerful and conflicting emotions, is a complex, if not intractable, project. None of this is conducive to simple, elegant explanations.

As H. L. Mencken once said, however, "There is always an easy solution to every human problem – neat, plausible, and wrong."[1] As a result, I chose to use a broad brush on a large canvas to paint a more complete picture of how the legal system works, across a variety of contexts, to respond to police abuses. Although the substantive focus is relatively narrow – the prosecution of police homicides – the project covers six different jurisdictions, in five different cities, in three different countries. To explain legal outcomes in each

[1] According to Wikiquotes, this quote appeared in "The Divine Afflatus," *New York Evening Mail* (November 16, 1917) and was later published in *Prejudices: Second Series* (1920) and *A Mencken Chrestomathy* (1949).

jurisdiction I look not only at the judiciary but also at the social, economic, and political context in which it is inserted, at the procedural structure that governs prosecutions, at the police and prosecutorial forces on which it relies, and at the various social actors at work in these prosecutions.

One cost of this approach may be some loss of detail, as it is difficult to strike just the right balance between the Scylla of unsupported generalization and the Charybdis of too much undigested information. Another cost is the loss of theoretical parsimony, as the arguments get increasingly complex in the attempt to faithfully mirror a complex reality. As Mencken might have suggested, I clearly do not offer a neat solution, but I do claim to offer a faithful analysis of the real processes that are at work in these cases. I believe the payoff is a useful reflection on questions of larger theoretical interest, illustrating how structure constrains actors, context affects institutions, politics modify institutional design, and institutions interact with each other.

Whatever the payoff, it should be clear that I could not have completed this task without a great deal of help along the way. A proper accounting of all the intellectual and personal debts I accrued over the course of this project would likely dwarf the book itself; here I present only a sampling. To Guillermo O'Donnell, my advisor, I owe a deep intellectual debt. Any reader of this piece who is familiar with Guillermo's work will undoubtedly see his fingerprints on every page, when I cite him and when I do not. Scott Mainwaring must have read a thousand pages of early drafts and exhausted a gross of red pens. His comments were always detailed and incisive, never cutting. One of the greatest benefits of this project has been the opportunity to learn from him. Michael Coppedge and Andy Gould have been a pleasure to work with and sources of useful and timely advice. The comments of all four often pushed me to think in new directions, in ways too many to acknowledge. They will no doubt recognize many of their ideas and suggestions in the text, and rue my failure to adopt others.

Many lawyers helped me along the way. Juan Méndez generously put me in touch with his vast network of human rights colleagues across the continent and commented on early drafts of various chapters. While in the field I had the help of courageous (and stubborn) human rights lawyers who push and pull on the levers of the creaky and reluctant systems of Argentina, Brazil, and Uruguay: María del Carmen Verdú in Buenos Aires, Silvia Osaba in Córdoba, Ariela Peralta and Susana Falca in Uruguay, Maria Beatriz Sinisgalli at the Centro Santo Dias and the whole staff of the Ouvidoria da Polícia in São Paulo, and finally Marília Veloso, who drove me all over Salvador for an intense and exhausting few weeks, and then took me and my family into her home for several days of much needed rest and relaxation.

These lawyers are immersed in the daily reality I interpret here. Surely they will find in my conclusions a lot to criticize; I hope that they will also find some encouragement and useful information, from someone who is one step removed from that reality.

Of course, I could not have completed this research without the support of a number of extraordinary institutions. The Kellogg Institute for International Studies generously funded the preliminary research trip and has, over the years, made me welcome in that remarkable environment. The Social Science Research Council paid for nine months of fieldwork across six cities in three different countries through an International Dissertation Research Fellowship. The American Bar Foundation provided support and a stimulating intellectual environment during the crucial time of distillation and writing. Abroad, the Núcleo de Estudos da Violência of the Universidade de São Paulo – especially Beatriz Azevedo Affonso, Sérgio Adorno, and Paulo Sérgio Pinheiro – made São Paulo a slightly less imposing place and introduced me to many of the people I needed to know. The researchers of the Instituto de Ciencia Política, of the Universidad de la República in Montevideo, with their humor and knowledge of Uruguayan politics, made my all-too-brief visits to Uruguay as productive as they could be. The Coordinadora Contra la Represión Policial e Institucional (CORREPI), of course, in Buenos Aires and Córdoba, was the starting point for much of the information on which this project is based.

Last but not least, the final draft of this book owes a great deal to the numerous helpful suggestions of two anonymous reviewers and to the painstaking editorial help of Tracey Thomas. With this many talented and generous people and institutions helping me along the way, the only surprise should be that there remain as many errors as there undoubtedly are. They are, of course, entirely my responsibility.

Effectiveness and Inequality in the Legal System

Injustice anywhere is a threat to justice everywhere. We are caught in an inescapable network of mutuality, tied in a single garment of destiny. Whatever affects one directly, affects all indirectly.

Martin Luther King, Jr., Letter from the Birmingham Jail
(April 16, 1963)

Ana lives in one of the vast poor suburbs of Buenos Aires. Her son was beaten to death after he allegedly punched a police officer. She says they were trying to teach him a lesson but things got out of hand. At least four policemen – and probably several more – locked him in a room and beat him with heavy sticks until they fractured his skull and he died. The policemen who killed him got promotions even after they were charged with the killing. At the trial, the prosecutor argued that they should be acquitted because they were just doing their job, subduing an unruly prisoner. The experts called by both the prosecution and the defense agreed.

As the law permits, Ana got some lawyers from an NGO to participate in the trial, as sort of private prosecutors. These lawyers work for free in cases like hers. They called their own witnesses and brought in experts, and argued that these policemen should not be set free after brutally beating an unarmed twenty-four year old and leaving him to die without medical attention. The NGO also organized demonstrations, bringing in many of Ana's neighbors to march in front of the courthouse throughout the trial. Afterwards, one of the judges privately confessed to Ana's lawyers that they had intended to acquit the defendants, but thought that if they did, the people might burn down the courthouse. So, instead, the judges imposed suspended sentences of no more than three years on each policeman. Ana says what really bothers her is that they won't spend a single day in prison.

After the trial, Ana joined the NGO and became an activist. She led marches, attended other trials, met with other parents who had lost children, and worked to call attention to all the young people who die at the hands of the police. On a Friday night some time later, Ana told me, her son-in-law was sitting in a neighborhood pub when the bartender said there was a phone call for him. The caller, who implied he was with the police, said, "You better start checking the morgues, because we bought your son a ticket to hell." For nearly two days, Ana and her daughter and son-in-law, armed with a homemade, handwritten, habeas corpus petition, frantically searched for the young man, checking morgues and police stations. As it turned out, Ana's grandson had gone out of town, knew nothing about any threat, and eventually returned home, to everyone's nearly hysterical relief.

However, on the following day, a second phone call came in, on Ana's brand new cell phone. The phone was so new that few of her friends knew that number. This time the message was clear, and it was for her: "Stop messing around with the police, or the next time your grandson won't be coming home!" "No te metas con la cana. ¡Dejate de joder que la próxima vez va en serio!"

Ana asked me to protect her identity. Her daughter and son-in-law do not want anyone to go to the police or to the prosecutors to report the threat. They worry because it seems clear that the police know where their family members are at any given time, have access to their phone numbers, and could harm any one of them, but especially Ana's grandson. They would like Ana to reduce her activities and become less visible. She's determined to do what she can to make sure young people cannot be killed with impunity, but she's worried about her family.[1]

The focus throughout this text is on courts and criminal prosecutions. But at its core this is a book about rights and the lack of rights. It is about those who in practice have rights and those who do not, regardless of what their constitution might say. It is about courts, judges, prosecutors, and investigative police – those who protect citizens from abuse and those who do not. It explores the social foundations for the effective assertion of rights, the political foundations for the effective judicial protection of rights, and the institutional mechanisms that impede or facilitate the process by which formal rights are made effective. The book has implications for our understanding of what produces higher quality democratic citizenship, a citizenship

---

[1] Author interview with Ana, Buenos Aires, Argentina, January 16, 2001. Ana is not her real name. Also based on interviews with Ana's lawyers in November and December 2000 and on a review of documents relating to the case.

that comes closer to endowing all citizens with the full complement of rights guaranteed in constitutions and laws. The argument draws on and has implications for the literature on the relationship between law and politics, law and society, and law and democracy.

A. OVERCOMING RESISTANCE

The starting point for much of the analysis is the simple idea that legal rights seek to re-shape the distribution of power in a society: they shift rights/freedoms and duties/constraints away from where the market or the distribution of coercive resources might otherwise deposit them.[2] New legal rights aspire to be, as Max Weber once said, "a source of power of which even the hitherto powerless might become possessed" (1978 [1921]: 666–67). As Weber's own definition of power suggests, this implies assigning to those who are otherwise vulnerable to the unfettered will of another the capacity to carry out their own wishes *despite the resistance of the other*. When formal rights do indeed run in favor of the hitherto powerless, we should expect more resistance from the otherwise powerful. As these rights increasingly seek to change long-established patterns of domination and asymmetries of power, it will become increasingly difficult to up-end these relationships. This abstract idea becomes concrete in the details of many of the police killings I reviewed: the conflict often begins when the victim forcefully claims ownership of a (novel) right, and it ends with the ultimate negation of that right. Similarly, Ana's demands that police be more accountable challenge the existing order of police-suspect relationships.

Even as it contemplates that lived law will continue to reflect social power, this approach presupposes a certain degree of autonomy for the written law. It assumes that legal rights might arise that do not reflect the distribution of economic or coercive resources or other sources of social power,[3] and thus that the law and the state that enforces it are more than simply a condensation of relations of power (see O'Donnell [2004] and before him, of course, Poulantzas [1978]). Democracy ostensibly has this goal: in theory it assigns (mediated) lawmaking power to everyone equally, regardless of

---

[2] Coase, for example, makes this redistributive nature of rights clear in his treatment of the problem of social cost (reprinted in Coase 1988), but it is not news to students of the law that a right in favor of one individual imposes correlative duties on others.

[3] For a comprehensive discussion of the sources of social power, see Mann (1993). For purposes of this discussion, suffice it to say that social power is importantly but not exclusively constituted by and reflected in the state and its law, and that some parts of the law may purport to assign power in a way that is negated by other parts of the law.

wealth, social standing, the capacity to exercise lethal violence, or any other attribute beyond citizenship. A transition to democracy, therefore, can be expected to shift some measure of lawmaking power to new actors, producing new legal rights that clash with entrenched patterns of power.

Moreover, even when political influence perfectly reflects social power, new laws come about for a number of reasons unrelated to the "natural" distribution of power. Legislators as well as dictators very often enact laws that are meant to have more symbolic than literal effects. In many of the electoral democracies of the developing world, the commitment to universal citizenship rights is less than universally held. To put it broadly and imprecisely, especially but not only in the developing world, many laws and the institutions they conform have stronger ideational than material roots. These laws rest very lightly and uneasily on the surface of society.

The right examined in detail in this book, the right to be free from arbitrary police violence, is one of these "uneasy" rights. It seeks to upset long-standing relations of domination between the police, as representatives of the state, and ordinary citizens. It has its roots not necessarily in the distribution of economic or other resources but in the idea that, in a democracy, *everyone* is entitled to respectful treatment and due process of law, even those who have no social standing or choose to break the law and prey on their fellow citizens. It runs contrary to the normative expectations of many police forces, especially those that have long histories of violence and impunity like the police of Argentina and Brazil. Indeed, procedural limitations on police use of lethal violence even contradict the expectations of many of the people these limits are supposed to protect, as we will see. In this respect, this right is just one example among many: many core democratic rights, with their strong egalitarian bias, rest just as uneasily on the surface of deeply unequal societies.

To repeat, then, when law purports to change long-standing normative expectations or a deeply entrenched balance of power between the duty bearer and the rights holder (a balance sustained by many interconnected and mutually supporting resources) anyone purporting to exercise the right is likely to encounter strong resistance. But what form will that resistance take? If the original reasons for the law's creation persist, it is unlikely that the formal structure will be abolished outright. It is much more likely that the right in question will suffer, as James Scott puts it, from everyday, prosaic forms of resistance – not, this time, on the part of the relatively powerless (Scott 1986: 29–30) but on the part of the relatively powerful and, therefore, twice as effective. We should expect such rights to die by "small arms fire"

(Scott 1986), in a thousand small ways, rather than by a frontal assault and institutional change.

An example should make this clear. The ordinary low-ranking police officer does not, in the overall scheme of Brazilian or Argentine society, wield a great deal of social power. The police institution as a whole wields much more power, but not enough, since the end of the authoritarian period, to formally suspend constitutional guarantees. Still, in any confrontation between an armed police officer and an ordinary shantytown resident or criminal suspect, it is clear where the "natural," historical, pre-rights, pre-democracy (but state-supported) balance of power lies. It is in large measure the work of the legal system to change this balance of power, to moderate the behavior of those who exercise the state's monopoly on the legitimate use of force. The legal system, then, becomes one arena in which the resistance of the new duty bearers is played out.[4] Since they cannot change the formal rules of the game, this resistance is likely to come in the form of many small acts of sabotage, aided and abetted by the police corporation, rather than in a grand gesture of legal reform to eliminate due process guarantees.

In Ana's case, as we will see in later discussions of the Buenos Aires system, the initial trial of her son's killers was frustrated by the police's ability to sway judges and prosecutors in their direction, hide some information, and present expert witnesses to create an inaccurate picture of what took place. Ana was unable to completely overcome that resistance, despite the legal and political assistance of an NGO, and surely would have fared even worse without her lawyers. Her continuing claims were then suppressed by credible threats of violence against her family, threats backed by superior access to information about her and her loved ones' whereabouts and the implicit ability to replicate the near impunity of the first trial. All of this takes place without a frontal challenge to the formal rights structure that has been in place since re-democratization.

This entails that formal rights in favor of the "hitherto powerless" must be backed by a constellation of other legal, economic, social, and political resources, sufficient to overcome that resistance. It should be clear by now that even purely negative rights require a substantial social investment in a

---

[4] Note that the legal system is not the only arena, as this book will make abundantly clear. The struggle also takes place in legislatures, within the police corporation itself, on the streets, in the media, and in many other places. The analysis here takes us to many of those places, although principally to show how they impinge on legal processes. In any event, although the legal system is only one arena, and a peculiar one at that, some of the lessons to be derived from analyzing it are relevant to the entire process of constituting effective rights.

supportive framework of institutions (Holmes and Sunstein 1999). But the exercise of citizenship is not cost free for the individual even when such a framework exists. Rights bearers must have the resources to engage effectively with the best-laid supportive framework, including such expensive and scarce resources as transportation, knowledge of rights, access to lawyers and other professionals, free time, freedom from violent coercion, and, sometimes, social standing, a cultured accent, a Europeanized, non-indigenous appearance, and so on. Every legal system includes its own laundry list of the extra-juridical but very much "legal" resources that claimants must invest if they wish to effectively present a claim.[5] And once they get there, they must still overcome the resistance of those who oppose the claim. The more resistance the duty bearer exerts, the more resources the rights bearer will need.

Any society that seeks to extend universal effective citizenship, then, has a twofold task. Clearly, it is not enough to create a legal system that will equitably receive those claims of right that are brought to it and dispassionately decide them. It is necessary but not sufficient, then, to create efficient courts and to staff them with judges who understand the law and will enforce the rights inscribed in the legal system, along with all the other measures that legal reformers advocate. In addition, this society must endeavor to affirmatively endow rights bearers with the secondary, extra-juridical "legal" resources they need in order to engage the system and make an effective claim of right against the resistance of those who will oppose their claims. These resources range from education and income at the more general, agency-enhancing end of the spectrum to witness protection plans, free lawyers, and physically accessible courthouses at the more narrowly legal end. This second task requires, in short, sustained attention to what goes on outside the legal system itself, and in particular to the capabilities and resources of new rights bearers. As long as there is a severe imbalance between the legal resources of rights bearers and duty bearers, rights are likely to remain purely formal.

A society can ignore this imbalance altogether. It can simply pass universal rules and leave the rest up to private actions and resources, in effect pretending that the playing field is even. Anatole France's irony reminds us that the perfect equality of a citizenship that ignores the material circumstances of particular citizens is a recipe for actual inequality: "Another source of pride,

---

[5] These are extra-legal resources in the sense that they are not usually legally prescribed as an element of the claim. They are in a very real sense "legal" resources, however, in that they are a prerequisite for effective engagement with the legal system.

to be a citizen! For the poor it consists in...laboring under the majestic equality of the laws, which prohibit the rich and the poor alike from sleeping under bridges, begging in the streets, and stealing bread" (France 1922 [1894]: 117–18 [my translation]). The impartial application of facially neutral laws, in a deeply unequal context, tends to produce severely unequal results.

Most legal systems today, however, include various mechanisms that seek to ameliorate stark formal equality and redress the imbalance. One way to do this is through the use of procedural devices: Brazil's *ação civil pública* or India's Public Interest Litigation empower various actors to bring claims that are in the public interest; private class actions accumulate many small claims into one large one to produce the economies of scale that the wealthy and the corporate enjoy almost as a matter of course; contingency fees alleviate the need to fund legal fees in advance of recovery. Many states also create organizations to provide institutional support for private actions to vindicate rights, such as state-funded lawyers and other support institutions. Alternatively, states may create the legal and political space for claimants to organize into interest-based organizations, such as rights NGOs, to support individual claims. All of these devices by and large leave the enforcement action in the hands of private individuals, with more or less assistance from the state.

Occasionally, however, a society will constitute the state as a directly interested party in any action to enforce the right in question. Regulatory instances are one example of this. Presumably, the U.S. Environmental Protection Agency exists to protect the collective right of American citizens to a clean environment, yet it is often the sole entity legally empowered to act in this respect. The most dramatic example of giving the state ownership of the enforcement action is when the state criminalizes the violation of a right. Brazil has criminalized racial discrimination, for example. In theory at least, this places the state's entire prosecutorial apparatus behind the right, relieving individuals of much of the burden of enforcement. At the same time, in many instances, this limits the original rights bearer's ability to participate in the assertion of the right, screening and reshaping the claims that can be brought pursuant to that right.

When state power is truly, in fact as well as in law, placed behind the right, vindication of that right depends less on private resources, and thus social and material inequalities are less likely to translate into legal outcome inequalities. When a society depends on private resources for rights enforcement, social inequality is significantly more likely to leave its imprint on the outcome of the struggle to make formal rights effective. This simple equation brings politics into the very center of the question of legal inequality. Politics (mostly) determines how the state will direct its resources – which claims are valued and which are not, who deserves state backing and who does not. As a result, politics and political inequalities (mostly) determine the extent to which socio-economic inequality will translate into legal inequality. Poverty matters, in part, because political decisions allow it to matter.

To test this general idea, I first reduce this abstract model of rights and their enforcement to a concrete instance, the prosecution of police officers who exceed limits on the use of lethal force. I show how legal outcomes in many systems follow predictable patterns based on the socio-economic and political resources the victims and their survivors can bring to bear. I then chronicle the everyday methods of resistance the police use in the struggle to avoid the duties imposed by these rights. I evaluate the imbalance of resources between claimants and the police, and the institutional and social mechanisms that might redress that imbalance in each of five South American cities. I show how the criminal justice system, in its ordinary configuration, has structural flaws that keep it from putting the full weight of the state behind claims of police misconduct and how, as a result, inequality springs from over-reliance on private resources. Finally, I demonstrate how politics, mediated by institutional mechanisms of appointment or promotion and discipline, affects the support given by state actors, including judges and prosecutors, to these rights.

More broadly, this book reveals how deeply embedded the legal system is in its social and political context, even when it is specifically designed to have considerable autonomy. That embeddedness is both vice and virtue. More embedding – that is, more numerous and more effective institutional ties between the legal system and society – makes the system aware of social needs, responsive to social reality, and open to information about the situations that come before it. It allows the legal order to evolve in harmony with its social, economic, and political order. At the same time, unless they are consciously designed otherwise, more often than not these social ties import social inequalities into the system and reinforce social hierarchies instead of promoting universal citizenship. On the one hand, then, the analysis in this book exposes the manifold mechanisms that cause legal outcomes to reflect deeper social structures more faithfully than they reflect the pattern of legal rights lightly etched onto the surface of society. On the other, it shows that establishing and nurturing the right institutional connections can facilitate the task of using legal rights to overcome social inequalities.

The prosecution of rights violations against the police is a good test of this model. Those whose rights are violated are typically, but not always, weak. In comparison, the police are typically strong, especially in relation to those left on the margins of the formal society and economy, and most especially when social concern for crime reaches a fever peak. The rights in question, while not newly minted, are ostensibly meant to change long-standing patterns of behavior that go as far back as the origins of the state in Latin America. The judicial response to police violence thus brings into sharp focus many of the issues that are common to other attempts to use law to change social relations of power.

If the model is correct, we should expect to see the successful prosecution of rights violations only in those places that have solved this power imbalance by enabling the victims of police violence to overcome that resistance. We should see little or no effectiveness where the imbalance affects the entire class of victims and there is little or no attempt to solve it: when the victims are poor, the police are strong, and there are neither institutional devices that allow claimants to effectively engage the legal system nor political incentives for state actors to pick up the challenge. We should see more inequality in the outcomes, and average results that are dependent on the average level of resources in the victim class, when the state attempts to solve the imbalance with solutions that remain inside the legal system, depending on claimants to engage state structures more or less on their own. This is true when judicial institutions are strong, but there is little political support for proactive state intervention. Finally, we should see the best results, with high effectiveness and low inequality, in those places where state actors are mobilized to affirmatively engage with these claims and claimants, placing the state fully behind rights enforcement as a matter of fact as well as of law. This last result should obtain when the political conditions strongly favor the prosecution of violent police misconduct.

B. THE PROBLEM OF POLICE VIOLENCE

Legal protection from arbitrary killing by agents of the state is one of the most basic promises of the rule of law in a liberal democracy, and one of the promises of Latin America's transition back to democracy. The regimes that tortured and killed in the 1970s in countries like Argentina, Brazil, and Uruguay have been replaced with democratic regimes that hold elections and legally guarantee all the basic civil and human rights. Elected national leaders like Raul Alfonsín in Argentina and Fernando Henrique Cardoso in Brazil demonstrated a commitment to democracy and the protection of individual rights; others, such as Mário Covas in São Paulo, have done the same at the sub-national level. Argentina reformed its constitution in 1994 to grant constitutional status to international human rights treaties. Brazil drafted an entirely new constitution in 1988 that contains some of the most extensive protections of individual rights found in any constitution anywhere. And yet, in the darker corners of large cities and in remote rural areas, in the back rooms of police stations and in vacant lots, the promise that the law will protect individuals from state violence often rings hollow. With public safety as the justification, torture is the preferred method for extracting information, and criminal investigations sometimes begin and end with a bullet to the head.

In practice, then, many of the governments called into existence by the democratic transitions of two decades ago have a distinctively Hobbesian feel: in the name of protecting citizens from the depredations of fellow citizens, there are few if any restraints on the actions of the state, so that the hands of "that Man, or Assembly of men that hath the Soveraignty" remain "untyed" (Hobbes 1964 [1651]: 122). Over the course of the 1990s, the police in the state of São Paulo, Brazil, killed more than seventy-five hundred people. In some years, the São Paulo police killed, on average, one person every six hours. Nor are São Paulo's police the most violent. In Salvador da Bahia, in Northeastern Brazil, the per capita rate of police killings for a three-year period in the mid-nineties was three times higher than the rate in the worst years in São Paulo. Many other places show equally dismal results. In the second half of the decade, the police in Buenos Aires killed, on a population-adjusted basis, just as often as the police in São Paulo. There is information to suggest that in Venezuela, which is not a part of this study, the police killed twice as often as in Salvador.[6]

The phenomenon, however, is not universal; there are variations even within countries. In the Argentine province of Córdoba and in Uruguay rates of killing are very much lower. Uruguay has the lowest rates, reporting two or three deaths per year at the hands of the police, and Córdoba follows with about thirty killings per year. Adjusted for population levels, Uruguay's rate is about 0.1 per hundred thousand, and Córdoba's about 0.3, compared to more than 6 per hundred thousand for Salvador. Still, in many countries police violence is an everyday occurrence, and the phenomenon seems to be growing.

---

[6] The 2001 U.S. State Department Human Rights Report for Venezuela notes the government's claim that 2,000 criminals had been shot by the police in the first eight months of that year. That figure suggests an annual per capita rate of killings of 12.75 per hundred thousand, twice as high as Salvador's.

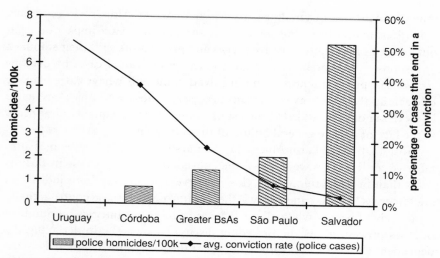

FIGURE I.I. Average annual per capita police homicides and conviction rates in Uruguay, Córdoba, Buenos Aires, São Paulo, and Salvador in the 1990s.

The courts, the principal mechanism for identifying and redressing rights violations in a liberal democracy, have largely remained at the margin of this virtual civil war in three of the five cities in the study. Conviction rates for police officers who kill are well below 5% in both Brazilian cities and about 20% in Buenos Aires.[7] But conviction rates climb as high as 50% in Uruguay and hover around 40% in Córdoba. The response by the courts to this situation suggests a problem if not exactly a paradox: precisely in those places where the police use lethal force most indiscriminately, the justice system punishes police homicides least often, as shown in Figure I.I.

Importantly, however, these aggregate results hide an injury to another central element of citizenship, liberal democracy, and the rule of law: equality before the law. Despite its high conviction rate, Córdoba shows the highest degree of outcome inequality of all the legal systems in this study: a police officer who kills a middle-class individual is more than twice as likely to be convicted as one who kills a lower income resident. The courts of Uruguay, in contrast, seem to hold a special place for the poor, whose cases actually produce a higher conviction rate. In São Paulo too, inequality seems to disappear; however, this is likely due to the fact that the victims are uniformly poor, so the court system rarely has the opportunity to show how it

[7] The data used in this analysis are more fully described in Chapter 2 and the Appendix.

might treat the case of a middle-class victim. In Buenos Aires, socio-economic conditions matter little, but political factors have a greater impact on legal outcomes, as politically sensitive judges and prosecutors shift their standard in response to the pressure brought to bear in individual cases by demonstrations or public attention. And in Salvador, the police have carte blanche to clean up the streets by any means necessary. Those who object are more likely than not to be added to the list of victims. Here, inequality disappears in the face of a more general failure of the rule of law.

Most analyses of Latin American court systems are plagued by measurement issues. How do we know if the courts are better or worse in Buenos Aires than in São Paulo, when close observers simply say both judiciaries are "in crisis"? How can we track the extent to which these courts actually protect civil liberties when all we have are aggregate statistics on numbers of cases processed? As the preceding discussion suggests, in designing the dependent variable for this study I begin at the level of the individual citizen and ask some very basic questions: how effective are my individual rights in this legal and political context? How likely is it that my rights will be violated; and if they are, what will the police, the prosecutors, the courts do about it? How much does it matter that I am white or black, middle class or poor, a young unemployed male or a middle-aged professional?

To answer these questions I gathered original information on over five hundred homicides committed by the police in Uruguay; in Buenos Aires and Córdoba, Argentina; and in São Paulo and Salvador, Brazil, and tracked these cases through the courts (see the Appendix and Chapter 2 for a more complete discussion of the data sources and sampling). This allows me to offer a more direct and more accurate measure of judicial performance: actual judicial outcomes in the form of conviction rates, rather than perceptions, formal rules, or other indirect measures.

Information about individual judicial outcomes is only the starting point, however, for examining the systemic causes of impunity and inequality. Why is it that Uruguay, with an outdated procedural code and a dilapidated judiciary, can do a better job of prosecuting police officers than São Paulo, with all its wealth and a relatively more modern court system? Why have numerous reforms, in Buenos Aires for example, not resulted in appreciable changes in judicial outcomes? Are judges in São Paulo or Buenos Aires simply authoritarian throwbacks to an earlier era, or are they hampered by institutional or other failures?

I approach these questions from a strongly contextual institutionalist perspective. I pay attention to formal and informal institutions. I push beyond the analysis of formal rules to examine how these rules work in practice, and how the social, economic and political context affects the way they operate. I explore the way institutional design interacts with political currents and socio-economic structures to modify actors' capacities and incentives. I show, for example, that the same institutional design will produce politically compromised courts in a politically hegemonic environment and strongly independent ones in a more pluralistic political context. I demonstrate that a context of exclusion and marginalization can frustrate the efforts of even high-performing courts and prosecutors. The results challenge, once again (see, e.g., Moser 2001), institutionalist approaches that limit their analysis to formal rules or assume that institutions produce the same results in any context.

I do not, of course, answer all the questions surrounding the failure of the rule of law in new democracies. Indeed, I do not answer all the questions surrounding the level of police violence observed in each society. Others have examined the police itself, its reform, and the difficulties in bringing it under civilian control, both in the United States and in Latin America (Skolnick and Fyfe 1993; Chevigny 1995; Geller and Toch 1995; Worden 1995; Lemos-Nelson 2001; Ungar 2001; Hinton 2006). My own focus is on the courts and their response to the phenomenon of police violence. It is undeniably true – in fact, it is the point of this book – that the courts are merely a small part of the apparatus that needs to be considered in reducing the number of police killings, and thus in making more effective the right to be free from arbitrary violence. More generally, it is equally true that the courts are but a small piece of what drives compliance with the law in each society. Is this an overly narrow focus, then?

I believe there are good reasons to focus on the courts' response to police violence. In the first place, as discussed earlier, exploring the obstacles to the assertion of rights by victims inside the criminal justice system is a good test case for what happens in other areas, as formal rights clash with social reality. The courts are the one place where we might expect the rule of law to be strongest, and the criminal process is the place where the state is supposed to be most clearly behind the enforcement action. If we cannot empower rights bearers here, inside the legal system, we have little hope of doing so elsewhere. Moreover, police impunity in all cases of misconduct is a problem that deserves attention in its own right. Any lessons we might derive to address impunity in the prosecution of torture cases, corruption, and so many other police abuses, are welcome. Finally, beyond anything this discussion may contribute to social science, I hope that it will expose some of the inhumanity currently being practiced in the name of public safety and contribute to a solution.

In addition, as will be discussed more fully later, this project is located at the intersection of several streams of literature, in an area that has not received sufficient attention to date. The literature on regimes and democracy in Latin America decries the lack of attention to questions of the rule of law and basic civil rights in the new democratic era of Latin America. Authors in the field of judicial behavior, which has focused on high courts in the United States, argue that more work needs to be done on comparative judicial behavior and more attention given to trial courts. Those who write about human rights violations have neglected the systematic study of judicial responses to those violations. The literature on judicial reform is characterized by a paucity of material pinpointing the places where the courts fail and evaluating the results of reform projects. This project illuminates each of these issues.

Over the last few decades, the literature on Latin American regimes has gone through various phases bringing us to the current concern with democratic performance. In the 1970s, scholars were concerned almost exclusively with the prevalence of authoritarian regimes, their causes, and their conduct (Linz and Stepan 1978; O'Donnell 1979). As more and more of these regimes began to fall in the 1980s, the literature focused on the causes and processes of transitions to democracy, and the effects of different modes of transition on the resulting regime (O'Donnell, Schmitter, and Whitehead 1986). Finally, as Latin America continues to be dominated by democratic regimes, the focus has changed to what scholars have variously called consolidation or institutionalization: issues of democratic stability and governance, especially the quality of democracy (Schmitter and Karl 1991; Valenzuela 1992; O'Donnell 1994; Karl 1995; Diamond 1996; Hartlyn 1998; Diamond 1999; O'Donnell 1999, 2001; Mainwaring and Welna 2003). One of the issues of quality that is repeatedly mentioned in these more recent writings is the failure of the courts or, more generally, the absence of the rule of law.

The rule of law is mentioned more and more often for the simple reason that it is one of the pressing issues facing the region. Diamond (1999) argues that the new democracies often fall shortest in terms of the rule of law. Shifter concurs: "Latin American democracy is most seriously stalled on two key fronts. The first is a drive for a legal system that guarantees both the equality of all citizens before the law and basic personal rights. The second has to do with the separation of powers and the imposition of effective checks on executive authority" (Shifter 1997: 116). Here I explore both of these "key fronts": the police are members of the executive and (technically if not always actually) subject to its control. Moreover, I look at questions of equality before the law in the context of the most basic of personal rights, the right not to be killed.

There have been many attempts to improve the level of individual rights and judicial functioning in Latin America. The recent wave of democratization was followed by significant legal reforms in most of the countries of the region, including the subjects of this study. Brazil, for example, adopted a new "citizen" constitution in 1988 that guarantees a plethora of basic rights, and Argentina made fairly extensive reforms to its constitution in 1994, enhancing the status of international human rights treaties. In addition, all these countries have implemented or at least considered a number of legislative reforms meant to "democratize" or "modernize" the law and its attendant institutions. Despite these efforts, journalistic accounts, the reports of agencies such as Amnesty International and Human Rights Watch, and articles by comparative political scientists all demonstrate that an effective rule of law still eludes many of the countries of the region (Stotzky 1993; Hammergren 1999; Méndez, O'Donnell, and Pinheiro 1999; Mainwaring and Welna 2003).

Moreover, this issue is central to the quality and stability of democracy. Guillermo O'Donnell (1993) argues that the legal system is an important part of the state and must also be democratic if the country as a whole is to bear that label. Indeed, O'Donnell (2001) has made the role of the legal system central to a truly comparative democratic theory. Larry Diamond agrees, arguing that one of the characteristics of liberal democracy is the requirement that "citizens are politically equal under the law . . . and protected by an independent, nondiscriminatory judiciary" (Diamond 1997: 12). The continued failure to ensure legality on the part of state actors and to protect citizens from rights violations erodes support for democracy (Mainwaring 2006) and threatens long-term regime stability (Diamond 1996).

Still, while most observers of Latin American politics point out the importance of the issue, there is very little work that combines close theoretical and empirical attention to the subject. The body of empirical work addressing something called the "rule of law" in Latin America is certainly growing. Many authors examine the reasons for the failure of judicial reform projects in various countries (Buscaglia, Dakolias, and Ratliff 1995; Dakolias 1995; Correa Sutil 1998; Frühling 1998; Jarquín and Carrillo Flores 1998; Hammergren 1999; Popkin 2000; Prillaman 2000; Correa Sutil 2001; Davis and Trebilcock 2001; Domingo 2001; Galleguillos 2001; Ungar 2001). These authors have offered important insights into the process of judicial reform, but they do not offer a systematic measure of judicial performance or show in what sense particular reforms have failed.

In fact, one of the clearest findings of this literature points exactly to this sort of diagnostic failure:

> The main difficulty that we encountered during the preparation of this study was the lack of useful data and empirical studies on how legal systems in the region actually work.... There are virtually no studies that examine how courts in different countries and in different areas of the law perform their functions. (Inter-American Development Bank 2003)

An ever-expanding list of authors tackles questions of judicial independence in useful and interesting ways (Caldeira 1986; Rhenan-Segura 1990; Buscaglia, Dakolias, and Ratliff 1995; Gargarella 1996; Larkins 1996; de Castro 1997; Correa Sutil 1998; Gibson, Caldeira, and Baird 1998; Larkins 1998; Prillaman 2000; Helmke 2002; Iaryczower, Spiller, and Tommasi 2002; Staats, Bowler, and Hiskey 2005). But this literature is relatively unhelpful in explaining how lower courts do their work and the pressures to which they are exposed. Because they look primarily at the highest courts, many of these works simply assume that whatever normative guidelines are established at the top will somehow filter down to the lowest levels (Bueno de Mesquita and Stephenson 2002, for example, do so explicitly). This project, on the other hand, highlights the manifold means of resistance lower level actors deploy in response to those guidelines.

Existing studies of equality before the law and the enforcement and protection of civil and human rights at the trial level usually avoid the close political and institutional analysis offered here. Adorno's sociological look at the question of legal equality in São Paulo (Adorno 1994, 1995) and a similar study which looks at the impact of race and ethnicity on judicial and prosecutorial decisions in the U.S. juvenile justice system (Poe-Yamagata and Jones 2000) do not focus on the political construction of legal inequality in any detail. My argument also offers a much more political account of the classic approach to access to justice (Cappelletti and Garth 1978–79; Berizonce 1987; Vanderscheuren and Oviedo 1995; Prillaman 2000; Correa Sutil 2001), pointing out the politically endogenous nature of the institutions that ensure access. Several of the contributions in Méndez, O'Donnell, and Pinheiro (1999) examine the reach of the legal systems to the poorest sectors of society from a more political standpoint but do not offer a comparative and systematic look at the institutional causes of legal inequality.

Most studies of police violence, on the other hand, focus primarily on actual violations with only a cursory glance at the judicial response (Geller and Karales 1981; Skolnick and Fyfe 1993; Geller and Toch 1995; CELS/HRW 1998; Holston and Caldeira 1998; as well as the many reports by human rights organizations). The studies that come closest to this one in terms of their focus on the judicial response to police homicides are Lemos-Nelson's (2001) study of Civil Police killings in Salvador, Cano's (1999) study of the role of the military justice system in the state of Rio de Janeiro, and Zaverucha's (1999) study of military justice in the state of Pernambuco. These studies all show that we cannot entrust the oversight function to institutions that are internal to the police itself. My own argument explains this finding and shows why taking the decision-making process outside the police institution may still not solve the problem.

A few existing theoretical approaches are cognate to mine, using political or social variables to explain the varying capacity of courts to make rights, especially newly declared rights, effective. Most of these studies were done in the United States (Rosenberg 1991; McCann 1994; Scheingold 2004), but at least one takes a more comparative view (Epp 2003). All of them explore court-led broad social policy change rather than the process of making existing rights effective for particular individuals, but their arguments have strong points of contact with mine. Epp rightly pays close attention to societal support structures for rights litigation, in an analysis that resonates with the arguments I present here. Rosenberg demonstrates, as I do, the failure of judicial pronouncements to "take" when political conditions are adverse. Moreover, he too highlights the resistance of non-judicial actors whose dominance is threatened.

But my argument adds to theirs and focuses attention on previously under-studied dynamics at the lowest levels of the courts. Epp's exclusive focus on organized civil society and broad policy change misses both the efforts of individuals in engaging with existing rights and the impact of institutional design on the capacity to engage with the courts. Rosenberg emphasizes the elite level, the actions of state and federal government officials and of the leaders of civil society organizations. I show that even with support at the state level, and even when courts do not purport to announce new rights, everyday resistance and social inequalities can frustrate court oversight. I show the sources of the occasional disconnect between apex courts and elite actions on the one hand, and trial court and street-level behavior on the other. I focus more closely on the imbalance of resources between opposing claimants and on the mechanisms that might redress some of that imbalance.

In short, all of these authors have made valuable contributions to our understanding of particular dynamics ultimately affecting the operation of courts, the police, and ultimately the rule of law. In this study, however, I add new empirical material, bringing to light new information on police violence and impunity. In addition, I introduce a theory that gives a prominent place to the influence of both politics and surrounding material conditions on trial court decision making. I test this theory systematically across and within three countries in Latin America. And I do so in one of the areas where it is most needed: the protection of citizens' lives from arbitrary state violence.

This is also the first project that looks at the legal system from the claimant's perspective, to discover how the legal system constructs legality in the daily lives of persons subject to state action. To pose this question is to raise at once all the piecemeal issues addressed in the literature. The failure of the courts could be and has been attributed to inefficiency and lack of resources (FORES and Colegio de Abogados de Buenos Aires 1999), lack of access (Cappelletti and Garth 1978–79; Vanderscheuren and Oviedo 1995; Garro 1997; Batista Cavalcanti 1999), lack of independence (Larkins 1998), poorly drafted laws (Faria 1988, 1996), the failure of social support (Holston and Caldeira 1998), an intentional government policy to repress the poor (CORREPI 2004), and more, and could be blamed on the police, the prosecutors, judges, elected leaders, and even "culture" more broadly.

The advantage of beginning with the outputs of the legal system and exploring the entire process that produces them is that we can see how these various actors and factors work together and influence each other. My research suggests that the cornerstone for legal failure is the disparity between the legal and political resources of claimants and those they oppose. For some claimants, all the obstacles just listed melt away, while for others even the smallest is fatal. If my approach is correct, the foundational variables will be contextual ones, while the institutional characteristics and idiosyncrasies of the legal system will matter primarily because of how they interact with underlying social and political inequalities.

C. THE DEPENDENT VARIABLE: LEGAL EFFECTIVENESS

The main phenomenon to be explained, the dependent variable for this study, is the responsiveness of the legal system to a claim of right, or what I have called legal effectiveness. In this section I first present a way to conceptualize and measure varying degrees of legal effectiveness across the cases in my study. Then I examine the process of adjudication, to see where inequalities might creep into the system, and present a simplified model of legal decision making that will help to structure the discussion of legal failures throughout the book.

In each jurisdiction, as noted, I will assess the effectiveness of the legal right to be free from arbitrary killing by agents of the state. Article 4.1 of the American Convention on Human Rights summarizes this right by saying that "every person has the right to have his life respected. This right shall be protected by law. . . . No one shall be arbitrarily deprived of his life." Despite significant procedural differences that I explore in each country chapter, this right is protected by a network of substantive laws and constitutional rights that are very similar in all three countries. Broadly speaking, everyone is entitled to due process and a fair hearing before being punished for a crime, and there is no death penalty in any event, no matter what the crime. The police, like everyone else, may not take a life except in self-defense or, under certain specified circumstances, to protect the public order. The penalty for a violation of this right varies from three years or less in the case of an involuntary killing, to about ten years in the case of an intentional killing, to life in prison in the presence of aggravating circumstances. In addition, various peripheral rights accompany this one, such as the right of those aggrieved by violations to petition the courts, and the right of relatives of the victim (and society in general) to see the violators punished.

Max Weber defined a right as no more than "an increase of the probability that a certain expectation of the one to whom the law grants that right will not be disappointed" (Weber 1978 [1921]). For a simple shorthand, we might call this increase in probability "Δp" (delta p). Delta p implies a change in expectations attributable to the existence of the law in question and perhaps to the implicit or explicit promise that the expectation will now be backed by the coercive power of the state. As quoted earlier, Weber's definition assumes that all rights are at least to some degree effective in becoming "a source of power of which even the hitherto powerless might become possessed" ([1978 [1921]: 666–67). The reality, of course, is otherwise: in many cases and many places, many remain powerless even after the creation of formal rights. When a right is ineffective, then, Δp approaches zero. The challenge is to estimate as closely as possible the value of Δp in the various cities in Argentina, Brazil, and Uruguay.

Delta p, however, varies not only across systems but within them. A highly effective legal system may have pockets of ineffectiveness reserved for unpopular groups, while a generally ineffective but more egalitarian one may treat these unpopular groups no worse and perhaps even better. For any given claimant, then, ineffectiveness can result either because rights are ineffective for all equally or because rights are denied to that sector of the population to which the claimant belongs.

In either event, there are two ways in which the effectiveness of a right must be supported. The first task, of course, is reducing the frequency of violations. Regardless of the effectiveness and efficiency of the legal system in providing redress, it is typically better for the individual to have his or her rights respected than to secure a remedy for a violation after the fact. This book has less to say about this aspect of making rights effective. The second is by providing redress or punishment for violations. While this is a second-best solution from the individual's perspective, from a societal or regime standpoint the existence of an effective mechanism to redress and punish violations is almost as important. And eventually, of course, the hope is that an adequate mechanism for punishing violations will reduce their number.[8] The focus in this book is on this second aspect, although I also present some important findings on the incidence and distribution of violations.

How does inequality enter this mechanism for redress? In the *Leviathan*, Hobbes said that the use of laws is to direct people and keep them on the path, "as Hedges are set, not to stop Travellers, but to keep them in the way" (Hobbes 1964 [1651]: 250). A well-ordered and well-functioning legal system acts as a series of signposts or barriers along a highway, marking the way to achieve valued social goals by setting universal conditions for passage. But I have alluded already to the fact that exercising rights in general, and engaging with the legal system in particular, implies the expenditure of certain resources for the rights bearer. When the system imports extra-legal particularistic conditions, as they all do to one degree or another, laws and legal instances work less as hedges set along the way and more like toll barriers set across the way. Individual laws and legal instances become obstacles before which one must surrender some toll or be refused passage.

The tolls are, by definition, characteristics of the actors or cases in question that are not legally prescribed conditions for extension of the right in question. The tolls could be cash for bribes or high-priced legal representation or less tangible means of exchange like social status or personal connections. Familiar examples are the use of race to deny rights that the law purports to make universal or even the disparate financial ability of criminal defendants to put on sophisticated defenses. I repeat: every legal system has some tolls, and securing a legal result always requires some investment that is not contemplated in the laws, no matter how minor. The only question is how high the tolls are and whether they are distributed in such a way as to ultimately produce unequal results.

Where this is true, then, Δp is noticeably composed of two values. One is given by the background level of effectiveness of the legal apparatus or

---

[8] I am aware, of course, that the question of deterrence is not a simple one, as the voluminous literature on the subject can attest. For the present, suffice it to say that when the likelihood of punishment approaches zero, we may expect, *ceteris paribus*, a greater number of violations than when it is considerably more substantial.

the state itself, and affects all equally, regardless of their resources. Even those who can pay the toll are often required to travel a poorly maintained and inefficient road. The other value is a consequence of the tolls that the individual holds or lacks: the increase in responsiveness of a system for certain and not other individuals. In a minimally functioning system, what separates users into those whose rights are made effective and those whose rights are not is the presence or lack of the toll. Indeed, a highly effective system that demands scarce and maldistributed tolls will be marked with more legal inequality than a poorly functioning system that cannot respond to anyone's demands.

Importantly, the tolls operate inside and outside the legal system, on both the initial violations and the response to them. The wealthy residents of gated communities in Buenos Aires and São Paulo have purchased immunity from police violence by removing themselves from the places where the state, and especially its police force, meets society (O'Donnell 1999). They contract private security and interact in private communal spaces like country clubs and golf courses. It is more than unlikely that one of São Paulo's elite *empresários* rushing through the city in his bulletproof chauffeured car, or flying over it in his helicopter, will meet a police officer with his finger on the trigger. On the other side of the toll barrier are the *favelados* living in São Paulo's shantytowns, whose view of the state is often limited to a police officer – more often than not, a police officer with a drawn gun.

Given the general crisis of confidence and the negative press that has attended most of the justice systems of Latin America, it is easy to imagine a virtual state of nature, where naked power rules and the economically dispossessed have no legal rights at all. In fact, the legal systems in Brazil, Argentina, and Uruguay are not completely unresponsive to the legal elements of a claim. Even when tolls are high and their distribution very unequal, the laws still (typically) matter. Paying the toll, for most, simply buys the right to travel the road, with all its shortcomings. Certainly, a very few are above the law altogether, enjoying rights but not duties, and some are beneath the law, feeling its obligation but not its protection. But the vast majority of the population inhabits a gray area.[9] They suffer the generalized delays, inefficiencies, and cost of the legal system, but they often can, after some delay and investing the right tolls, make the system work for them.

It is important to emphasize that this conceptualization does not define a completely lawless system. In fact, formal rights do matter, to different

---

[9] In addition to my own observations in the field, this discussion of tri-partite legal stratification owes a great deal to conversations with Guillermo O'Donnell.

degrees in different cases and in different systems. Outcomes must be phrased in formally legal terms, and possession of a formal right is important. As we will see in Córdoba and São Paulo in particular, formalism is one of the enduring characteristics of these legal systems, requiring an almost hyper-legal discursive style (for a discussion of formalism as a prerequisite for autonomy, see Lempert 1987). And the tolls are often sufficiently regularized and internalized that they acquire the status of informal institutions. The argument is simply that, while rights matter, they only gain effectiveness with the addition of something else, here called the toll, which can also respond to formal or informal rules. The analysis of individual-level data on judicial outcomes will allow us to map both the general level of effectiveness and the legal tolls present in each system.

But ultimately the more interesting task is explaining these aggregate levels of effectiveness and inequality. The question then becomes, how do these tolls enter the system? From unequal results observers often infer that conscious, animus-based discrimination in the decision-making process imports different rules of decision for different groups into the legal system. The toll imagery and the approach outlined at the beginning of this chapter suggest that legal exclusion for certain social groups may simply be a by-product of the system's universal demand for the investment of a resource that these groups, on average, do not possess. Next, I begin to answer this question, presenting a simplified model of legal decision making, and arguing that different tolls affect either of two dimensions of that decision-making process.

D. PROPOSING AN EXPLANATION

Simplifying the process of judicial decision making will allow us to explore the places where demand for particular claimant resources enters the system. In particular, this model of decision making is meant to highlight that judicial effectiveness depends on two separate processes. One is the construction of a procedural reality, and the other the construction and application of a rule of decision. Material resources enter primarily, though not exclusively, in the production of procedural facts, while political resources have their most direct impact on the creation of the rule of decision. At minimum, this conceptualization is useful because it highlights just how constructed both the facts and the actual rule of decision are in individual cases, and therefore how susceptible they both are to resource imbalances.

The model pushes to the forefront an important variable that is missing from most of the literature on both judicial decision making and the rule of law. Not all failures are simply the consequence of judges having

FIGURE 1.2. Schematic representation of adjudication in a murder case.

(or using) the wrong rules, the result of corruption and improper influences on the judicial rule of decision. It is at least as likely that the failures are the consequence of systemic blindness to information about certain classes of cases or certain classes of claimants. Finally, as we will see, the model graphically shows how normative shifts at any stage in the process can affect the capacity of subsequent actors to produce the correct result, even if the latter are applying the right rule of decision.

On its face, the process of adjudication is simply the application of rule r established by the rule-making authority (legislature, constituent assembly, authoritative judicial body, etc.) to a set of facts and circumstances that make up social object o, to determine where o falls within the categories defined by r.[10] An effective right, or more generally an effective law, is one that so guides decision making that the instances of o that come up for decision are placed in the correct categories as defined by r. An effective legal system, by extension, is one where this happens more often than not. Such a system translates formal rules into actual legal outcomes by ensuring that publicly binding decisions are made in accord with the categories created in these rules.

In practice, however, both r and o are unobserved, and the decision maker applies his or her understanding of the rule (r', "r prime"), to a re-creation of the social object to be judged (o', "o prime"). In a homicide case, to take a simple example, there is a continuum of possible versions of r' and o'. Whether the defendant is found guilty or not of murder will depend on where we place o' in relation to r'. We can depict this schematically, as in Figure 1.2. Note that if we place r' closer to the "not murder" end of the behavioral spectrum the category of "murder" *broadens*. This makes it easier for o' to fall in that category, and thus easier to convict the defendant.

In Figure 1.2, then, what might have been objectively murder is classified as not murder under a lenient (mis)interpretation of r and an exculpatory reconstruction of o. To achieve the "correct" result in this example we might

---

[10] The concepts coincide roughly with discussions of the law and the facts in judicial decisions. I have chosen to use r and o because, as we will see, it is not always clear that the "law" in any ordinary sense is being applied to the "facts" as we might ordinarily understand this term. I simplify the terms to their initials for convenience.

either shift r' to the left or o' to the right (or both). A shift away from the true position of o is what I will call an informational or information-gathering shift or failure. A shift away from r is a normative or processing failure because the information is processed according to the wrong rule or norm. In the Figure 1.2 example, the system has experienced a double shift, which combines to produce the wrong outcome. The focus of this project is on precisely these shifts and their causes.[11]

Some of these shifts are as random as the normative shift that occurs when a good judge wakes up in a bad mood. Others are more systematic but tied to individual decision makers: for instance, individual judges vary in sentencing strictness; some judges are explicitly pro-plaintiff or pro-defendant. Neither of these is, in and of itself, a systemwide phenomenon, but system characteristics such as politicized appointment processes, a weak appellate structure, or indefinite sentencing rules can create openings, making some systems more prone to these shifts than others. Outcomes in systems that evince lesser degrees of control over judicial decision making will show a greater dispersion in possible outcomes, but not necessarily a bias affecting any particular class of users (think of this as a greater standard deviation, which does not necessarily imply a bias). These shifts are problematic to be sure, since they detract from certainty, transparency, and predictability in the law, but they affect all users more or less equally.

More troubling is the effect of tolls that favor or disfavor a particular class of users across the entire system. Race-based animus in the Deep South, for instance, surely meant a normative shift for African Americans seeking to use the system to enforce their rights. The police in Salvador, in contrast, are favored users, who can count on impunity in the courts almost regardless of the characteristics of the crime or the victim. Not all such tolls are animus-based, substantive preferences for one group over another, of course. High filing fees and a lack of free legal assistance, for example, will import socio-economic tolls into the system, producing predictable informational shifts against the underprivileged. In any event, the problem here is no longer indeterminacy in the outcomes, which can be all too predictable, but a bias in the system. Analyzing the patterns in the outcomes of individual judicial

---

[11] This two-dimensional formulation is related to a notion Niklas Luhmann (1985, 1988) developed in connection with his "autopoietic" theory of law. He argued that legal systems are, first, "normatively closed." This includes the notion that any new rule or decision must be validated by standards that are internal to the system of laws, including what H. L. A. Hart (1961) called rules of recognition. But Luhmann also argued, second, that the law must be "cognitively open," which includes the ability to receive information from its environment. See Brinks (2003) for an elaboration of how Luhmann's theory might apply in this context.

cases will allow us to identify these biases and compare judicial effectiveness across social groups, across cities, and across countries.

From the characteristics that are associated with legal failures we can infer whether the dominant shifts in a given system are normative, informational, or both. The capacity to engage with the system and control the information that enters is the key to shaping procedural reality. Thus biases associated with socio-economic and similar "material" resources should spring from informational failures. In addition, of course, there are many resources of a more political or ideological nature that impinge on shaping the rule of decision. When these "political" variables, such as the criminal record of the victim or popular mobilization surrounding the case, matter a great deal, we can infer the presence of normative shifts. We can confirm these inferences by closely analyzing the process of decision making in individual cases, as I do in Chapter 3.

As we have seen, many scholars of the legal system are concerned with evaluating the system's independence or autonomy from political actors. The implicit subject of this inquiry is a normative shift: when outside actors interfere with the courts' decision making, they cause a shift in r' in a particular case. But the simplified model of legal decision making described in the next section suggests that any legal system's performance can be measured along two dimensions. The first, a familiar one to scholars of the legal system, is normative autonomy (a subset of which is judicial independence, but which might include other forms of undue influence on judicial decision making). The second dimension we might label informational autonomy, or informational competence. This dimension varies to the degree that the legal system not only is open to claims and information brought to it by many different agents (the classic concern of the access to justice literature) but also has the investigative capacity to seek out the information it needs from a variety of sources. Greater informational autonomy means that no one party can command a monopoly on the flow of information into the legal system.

I have argued (Brinks 2005) that true judicial independence has more to do with impartiality than with radical autonomy. Paradoxically, to have true independence, in the sense in which we value judicial independence, the courts must typically be subject to normative input from all competing sides in a dispute, as well as from lawmakers and other sources. Similarly, to achieve informational autonomy, the legal system requires something very much akin to the "embedded" half of what Peter Evans (1995) described as "embedded autonomy," in the context of the developmental state. The legal system needs multiple "institutionalized channels" for communication, "dense connecting networks" that tie it to society (1995: 12). If this embeddedness is only partial, if some actors or groups have the resources to operate these channels while others do not, or if certain actors can block these channels at will, then the legal system becomes dependent on those actors or groups for its information. Understanding these links and the resources they demand is the key to understanding how the tolls operate in a given legal system and how they produce normative and informational shifts.

The legal system, broadly understood as the set of actors, institutions, and organizations that make, administer, and enforce the law, has been described as an iceberg that goes far beyond the judiciary, incorporating many non-state actors (Galanter 1974: 134). The bottom tier of actors is the mass of potential claimants who must decide whether or not to engage the legal system at all (and, of course, those who must respond once a claim is brought to the system) and the crowd of witnesses and peripheral actors who decide whether or not to support claimants in their attempts. In criminal cases, the decision to engage the system is, obviously, more constrained for the defendant. But police officers decide whether or not to arrest, prosecutors decide whether or not to indict, and witnesses and affected parties decide whether or not to engage and cooperate with the system. In addition, as we will see, in Argentina, Brazil, and many other countries, the survivors of a murder victim can decide whether or not to participate in the prosecution of the case, thus becoming claimants working in parallel with the prosecution. Ana, in the anecdote with which I began this chapter, had to make a decision whether to invest her own resources into the prosecution. Her decision to participate is premised on her understanding of the way in which the police, the prosecutors, and the judges in her son's case will treat the case.

The struggle to define what I have called o', the event to be judged, is a contest between competing claimants. In civil cases, two non-state actors will compete, while, in modern times, a criminal case in theory pits the state against the defendant. Given that the event to be judged is constructed by the legal process, the balance of power between claimants in that process critically affects the judicial construction of o'. The socio-economic condition of the claimants, the context from which they are taken, and the state's response to that condition, then, will affect the resources these actors can bring to bear on the struggle to define o'. Ana and her family had to overcome physical and social distances in order to engage effectively with the prosecutor in her own son's case.

Furthermore, to the extent the state takes a hand in the proceedings (as in a criminal case, or by providing free legal assistance to certain classes of claims or claimants and not to others), broader socio-political considerations often determine the importance and legitimacy accorded to potential claims and, thus, to the resources expended by the state to develop these claims. Both the general political climate surrounding the prosecution in Ana's case and the specific political pressure brought to bear by demonstrations might affect the rule of decision the judges ultimately decide to apply. As a result, both the socio-economic and socio-political contexts in which the courts are inserted play a part in determining which claims and what information reach the courts.

Standing between purely social actors and the judiciary per se are various gatekeepers and facilitators that channel information to the legal system. In the civil arena, these are primarily lawyers, while in the criminal arena, the police are the predominant actors who receive information, screen it, and pass it on to courts and prosecutors (Macaulay 1979; Ross 1980; Kritzer 1990 all discuss lawyers' roles in screening civil claims in the United States). In Ana's case, the police heavily screened the information passed on to the courts to protect the identity of participants and skew the court's interpretation of the events. Prosecutors, who can serve the same selective access function, also failed to correct this bias. This forced Ana to work with an NGO to overcome the shortcomings of state involvement in her son's case – but the NGO has its own standards about which cases to engage with and performs its own screening.

The availability and nature of these institutional connections to society will crucially determine the informational autonomy of the legal system: systematic informational shifts should be more rare in systems with more effective and more varied sources of information and when contending parties have more equal resources. Under these conditions, more (and more balanced) information will enter the system. In the context of the prosecution of police violence, this means that informational shifts will occur in places in which (a) the state does not effectively investigate, and (b) there are fewer private resources for an independent investigation because victims come from a marginalized population and civil society organizations are relatively absent.

What then affects the placement of r', the rule of decision? I take the view, perhaps most forcefully and most recently expressed by Maravall and Przeworski (2003), that inducing compliance with norms, including the law, is primarily a matter of ensuring that individual actors' incentives favor compliance. I believe there is a "normative component" to rules (Brinks 2003, 2006), and it is possible, though Maravall and Przeworski deny this, that this normative component may induce, in some actors, compliance for the sake of the rule. At minimum, this normative element may lead some actors to overvalue incentives that favor norm compliance. But clearly the best way to ensure a general tendency toward compliance is to structure incentives so that they support normative behavior. We have known this at least since Madison said, "If men were angels, no government would be necessary. If angels were to govern men, neither internal nor external controls on government would be necessary" (Federalist No. 51, Hamilton, Madison, and Jay 1961: 322).

Each actor's preference as to the rule of decision, therefore, is affected by incentives generated from two different sources. Some of these incentives are endogenous to the legal process itself. Endogenous pressures are those that arise from the structure of the legal system, as a consequence of each actor's role in the legal process. Different legal systems assign different roles to the various actors in the process, thus affecting their normative tendencies. The investigative judges of the civil law tradition, for example, have a quasi-prosecutorial function and therefore have been criticized for being insufficiently impartial and too quick to convict. In the language I have used here, as a consequence of their role, the rule of decision of investigative judges is systematically shifted in favor of a conviction. This point simply recognizes that prosecutors and defense attorneys, for example, have very different perspectives on the law and that these perspectives are a consequence of their function within the legal process.

In addition, however, some incentives are exogenous to the legal process but impinge on individual actors by way of career incentives or social and political pressures. Thus, to understand why judges or prosecutors take a more activist approach in one system than in another, we must look not only to their role in the process but also to the incentives generated by the broader political context, as mediated by institutional design. Frontline prosecutors will be more sensitive to political demands for action or inaction in a police case if their careers depend on the benevolence of elected officials. Judges will be more or less strict in particular cases depending on whether they are susceptible to public demands for a certain response. In each instance, then, actors' preferences and capacities are a function of the interplay between the exogenous and endogenous incentives to which each of the actors is subject.

If we take seriously the notion that the legal system is, in fact, a system, we also need to explore how all the various actors impinge on each other, given what we have established so far. Epstein and Knight (1998, 2000) make a convincing argument that judges are strategic actors. If we look at the legal system as a whole, it becomes clear that it is not only judges who have the potential and opportunity for strategic behavior, but all legal actors. As a result, we should expect lower level actors to anticipate the actions of higher level actors and act accordingly. Prosecutors will not invest in prosecutions they expect to lose; claimants will not bring claims they believe will not be successful. Crucially, regardless of their interpretation of the rule, each claimant will seek to craft the facts in such a way as to produce the desired outcome, given the expected preferences of the key decision maker.

In this respect, we cannot overlook the fact that, while higher level actors are legally superior in creating and framing the rules that ultimately decide the case, lower level actors typically have the upper hand in the production of information. As a result, claimants with an upper hand in the production of information will introduce informational shifts into the system to ensure their preferred outcome. They will craft o' in such a way as to obtain their preferred outcome regardless of the rule applied by their normative superiors.[12] The police officers who killed Ana's son probably anticipated that an unvarnished account of a brutal beating following a relatively trivial provocation would exceed the court's capacity for lenience. As a result, they obscured the facts, hid the identity of some participants, and presented experts who emphasized the need to establish control over unruly individuals.

Note, in addition, that lower level actors may be able to use their informational ascendancy to blackmail higher level actors into shifting their rule of decision. In the case of the Buenos Aires courts, as we will see, the police can, and do, threaten to withdraw support in other cases if judges and prosecutors become too problematic. In Ana's case, it is hard to imagine that even a mildly skeptical court would not have seen through the meager defense presented by the police. But the strong pressure to maintain the willing cooperation of the police in all its daily operations is a powerful incentive to not look too closely at inconvenient facts; a crusading judge will find it increasingly difficult to carry out even routine tasks. In the following paragraphs I develop the consequences of this model of the legal system for the prosecution of homicides committed by the police.

---

[12] This informational dilemma is akin to the problem of hidden information described in the principal-agent literature (Kiewiet and McCubbins 1991: 25). While I have occasionally referred to lower level agents as subordinates of higher level agents, and while I have implied that the relationship is hierarchical, the police are not, in the true sense, agents of prosecutors, nor are the latter agents of judges. Higher level "principals" in the legal system do not establish the terms of the "contract," they do not select the "agent," and they cannot terminate the relationship. For the most part, they cannot choose whether or not to delegate, though they can occasionally choose to supplement the work of the "agent." If anything, the police are typically agents of the executive, while prosecutors are, in many courts including those of Argentina and Brazil, constitutionally guaranteed independence of action. In most cases, prosecutors tend to respond more to the executive, even when they are not included in the executive branch. Thus, while information plays a key role in setting the limits of oversight, many of the insights from the principal-agent literature simply do not apply in this context.

1. A Structurally Determined Normative Bias

Putting aside for the moment exogenous pressures on the actors, which will vary from case to case, in the ordinary criminal prosecution the actors' preferences as to the rule of decision can be expected to line up fairly consistently. We can make this visible by plotting the location on the continuum of factual situations where they would prefer to place r', the rule that marks the boundary between murder and not murder. In general, in the typical prosecution, the police are, after the victim, the party most interested in a conviction. Indeed, the system assigns them this task and depends for its effectiveness on their investigative zeal. Next to the police are the prosecutors, whose primary imperative is to prosecute cases to a successful conclusion, but who are more sensitive than the police to the nuances of the law and more prepared to abandon marginal cases. Again, every adversarial system depends on the zealous advocacy of the prosecutor. The final decision maker (who might be a judge, a panel of judges, or even a jury, but who is identified as "judge" in Figures 1.3 and 1.4) is in theory a neutral arbiter, falling somewhere between the prosecutor and the defendant in the zeal to convict. Thus, in practice, we find the police complaining that they arrest criminals only to have soft-on-crime judges let them go, and judges complaining that prosecutors are running wild and trying defendants in the press.

The line-up of actors' preferences on a continuum from most lenient to strictest construction of the law, therefore, typically looks something like Figure 1.3: claimants/victims want to draw the category of murder as broadly as possible, exempting as little conduct as possible from criminal responsibility; the defendants are on the opposite end of the spectrum; and everyone else falls somewhere in between, in fairly predictable order.

If the defendant is a police officer, however, and the conduct in question involves the way the police carry out their assigned task, the line-up changes substantially. Now the preferences of the police will be closer to the defendant's than to the victim's because a strict application of the law limits their freedom of action and exposes them to a greater risk of prosecution in the future. They now have to worry not only about their colleague, who is facing punishment, but about how the rule of decision applied in this case will affect their own ability to do their jobs, and about their own prospects in the event of a future prosecution. Of course, not all police officers are created equal in this respect. In most police forces there is a division of labor between those who do the security policing, and are more likely to find themselves in the defendant's seat in a future prosecution, and those who do the judicial investigation, and thus might distance themselves from the defendant. In general,

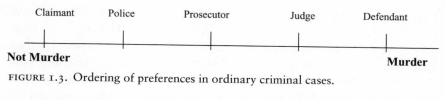

FIGURE 1.3. Ordering of preferences in ordinary criminal cases.

FIGURE 1.4. Ordering of preferences in cases involving police misconduct.

we might expect that, the closer the investigative arm of the police is to the frontline police force, the closer it will be to the frontline police officer who occupies the defendant's position in Figure 1.4.

Similarly, to the extent prosecutors and investigative judges are operationally indebted to the police, their preferences will be pulled closer to the police's, and hence to the defendant's. At best, the trial judge's preferences will be unchanged, though if the courts are heavily dependent on the police for many routine tasks, as well as for information, judges may well be pulled closer to police preferences. All else being equal, whether the prosecutor and investigative judge remain between the decision maker and the victim or squeeze in between the trial judge (if there is one) and the police will depend largely on the level of their operational dependence on the police. The more prosecutors and judges are indebted to the police in their everyday work, the closer their alignment with the police's preferences.

The victim's preferences, meanwhile, remain unchanged, leaving the claimant (in my cases this figure represents the victim's survivors) increasingly isolated, as shown in Figure 1.4. One of the most consistent complaints of victims and victim advocate groups in Police Violence cases is that the entire system seems to be lined up against them, that they must struggle against each of the other actors in the system. Figures 1.3 and 1.4 clearly illustrate the source of this complaint. The victims are likely to feel as if they are looking at the rest of the actors through the wrong end of a telescope. Everyone is grouped at the far end, conspiring to deny them justice.

The crucial importance of the victim's ability to be heard in the process is a consequence of this line-up of preferences. The state usually asserts ownership of the right to prosecute, so the typical claimants in a criminal case are the police and prosecutors on one side and the individual defendant on the other, while victims and their survivors remain largely outside the system. But when the system is left completely unbalanced, as in Figure 1.4, the ordinary state-supported internal actors cannot be counted on to perform their assigned task. For the reasons detailed in the next section, if prosecutors are aligned with the police – in fact, even if they affect a neutral stance – the outcome will tend to fall somewhere between the judge's preference and the defendant's, and vastly distant from the victim's preferred outcome. Even a strictly neutral judge is likely to reproduce the pro-defendant bias caused by the failure of other supporting actors. In short, without some affirmative corrective, the typical criminal justice system is structurally predisposed toward failure in these cases.

Exogenous pressures could in principle ameliorate the consequences of the endogenous incentives detailed earlier. Exogenous incentives are, as already discussed, a function of broader social and political pressures and the actors' susceptibility to these pressures. If prosecutors and judges expect that they will be held to account for failing to prosecute police officers, if there is a great social outcry with every police homicide, they will shift back toward the victims' position. On the other hand, strong social or political demands for repressive police tactics will move prosecutors and judges even closer to the defendant's preferred outcome. In each location, therefore, I will analyze the endogenous pressures produced by each institutional framework and the direction and likely impact of exogenous pressures, in light of contextual and institutional factors. The empirical discussion of the actual systems will identify whether exogenous pressures tend in the direction of stricter or looser enforcement of the law in police cases and the extent to which legal actors are susceptible to those pressures.

So far I have discussed only each actor's preferred rule of decision, while Figure 1.2 makes it clear that the strictest rule can lead to an acquittal if the procedural facts are exculpatory. In the next section I show how this line-up of normative preferences affects the construction of procedural facts.

2. Predictable Informational Shifts

Decision makers must have sufficient informational autonomy to adequately oversee the production of a procedural reality that will support a conviction under their preferred rule of decision. If they are overly dependent on one of the parties for this information, their decisions will invariably reflect the preferences of that party. Acting strategically, information-dominant parties can simply supply exculpatory information and suppress any other facts, producing a version of reality that can pass muster regardless of the actual standard applied.

In our cases, the police cannot formally change the legal standards decision makers will apply, but they can affect outcomes by rationing information in the particular case. I have so far shown all the actors on the same line, but they typically act sequentially, gathering information and feeding it up to the next level. Strategic investigators who prefer a not-guilty outcome and know where judges and prosecutors will place r' will seek to shift o' far enough to produce their preferred outcome. To the extent that they have a monopoly on the flow of information they will be able to produce an informational shift, refracting o' into the preferred normative classification. The stronger the control exercised by the police over the investigation, and thus over the construction of the procedural facts, the greater the likelihood of this informational shift.

If they are aware of the potential for an informational shift and are effectively deployed, other actors may seek to correct this bias. Judicial investigators who are independent in theory from the ordinary police are, in fact, present in some of the systems. But, as internal actors, they are still subject to those same endogenous and exogenous pressures, described earlier, to be lenient in cases involving police misconduct. The closer their preferred rule of decision comes to that of the police and the defendant, the easier it will be for police-supplied facts to meet their standards, and the less likely it is that they will expend significant resources to correct the problem.

In many cases, then, it will be up to the individual claimants to make up the informational deficit. They can do so by conducting their own investigations, rounding up witnesses and presenting them to prosecutors or judges, hiring experts to produce their own forensic reports, and, of course, coming into court to tell their own stories. Claimants gain prominence in the process when procedural rules, as in Brazil and Argentina, permit interested parties to appoint an attorney to act as a sort of Private Prosecutor. Depending on the strength of this figure and its attributes, a Private Prosecutor who owes nothing to anyone but the claimant may represent the best chance victims have of correcting this informational bias. But all of this requires a certain expenditure of resources and will tie even criminal justice outcomes to the resources of individual claimants. Claimants' resources will become less critical only when strong political pressures on internal state actors cause them to identify closely with the claimants, and thus to dedicate state resources to these prosecutions.

3. Concrete Implications of the Theory

Here I summarize the expectations that can be derived from this model, and that will guide the discussion in the coming chapters. As noted, bringing the state to bear on a claim of right entails a struggle between the purported bearers of rights and of duties. In police misconduct cases, we can expect the police generally to resist an expansive construction and strict application of their duty, and thus to seek to shut down the flow of information into the system. Similarly, endogenous factors predispose judges and prosecutors to leniency in police cases. In fact, the greater the dependence of judges and prosecutors on the police for their routine operation, the more permissive their rule of decision, and, *ceteris paribus*, the lower the conviction rate overall. This normatively driven lower conviction rate should cut across socio-economic lines, since it is largely unrelated to the capacity of claimants to produce their own version of events. Given this general tendency, prosecutors and investigative judges will seek to actively prosecute these cases only where there is strong exogenous pressure to do so and where the institutions to which they belong efficiently transmit this pressure.

The tighter the links between judges and prosecutors and their political environment (through appointment, advancement, and discipline mechanisms, primarily) the more susceptible these actors are to exogenous incentives. These incentives can cut either way, obviously: social and political approval of police violence will produce more permissive judges and vice versa. In either event, these links to the political context open the door to political tolls, so where the links are tighter, we should see higher inequality tied to the political construction of the case. Public demonstrations and political support for particular prosecutions, for example, should have a greater impact where these links are stronger. Socio-economic status may then take a backseat to other, more overtly political factors, since it is only imperfectly related to the politics of police violence.

On the other hand, more alternative, independent, and effective state-sponsored investigative channels should produce more convictions. But state resources generally follow social priorities, and state actors of all stripes respond to political incentives. As a result, where the political context is not explicitly favorable to the aggressive prosecution of police misconduct, these institutional ties to society will rely to a greater extent on individual initiative on the part of the claimant. Thus, where there are effective state institutions but a relatively non-supportive political environment, socio-economic inequalities in the claimant pool will lead to selective informational failures and sharp socio-economic distinctions in the outcomes. Indeed, the more effective those institutions, the sharper the inequality, since an investment of private resources buys access to a better mechanism of enforcement – the toll opens the gate to a better road.

E. IMPLICATIONS FOR THE RULE OF LAW

This analysis of the difficulties of bringing the criminal justice system to bear on the problem of police misconduct opens up some questions for the rule of law more generally. These possible lessons are worth keeping in mind as we go through the empirical material. If I am correct that the dependence of higher levels on information from below is a crucial feature of legal systems, then we can state something close to an axiom: a normative shift at lower levels of the system, so that the agents who produce information uphold a different rule of decision, will produce at least an informational challenge if not a shift at higher levels. The primary limit on the ability of an actor to force an informational shift is the level of informational autonomy higher level agents can achieve. And this autonomy is not the product of isolation but of its opposite, that is, of the diversity and effectiveness of alternative sources of information routinely available to decision makers.

This axiom, moreover, has a corollary: a single channel for generating and moving information up the system will be effective only if there is a high degree of consensus within the system on the norm to be applied. And as noted earlier, the more change in existing social patterns a right purports to produce, the higher will be the degree of resistance from lower level actors, and the more they will seek to ration information. Thus it is precisely at times of social and political transformation that it is most important to have a large number of information-producing agents with a variety of interests reporting to upper level decision makers.

This has broad implications for the rule of law, which presupposes the supremacy of the lawgiver at the top of the system, and especially for the rule of law in transitional societies. The ideal of universal democratic citizenship in new and socio-economically unequal democracies will require a change in entrenched social patterns, generating a great deal of resistance along the way. Given that resistance, one critical internal mechanism for ensuring the lawgiver's supremacy is the presence of alternative sources of information. Transparency enables top-down control.[13] Hence the special importance of mechanisms of horizontal and social accountability in new and unequal democracies (O'Donnell 1994; Mainwaring and Welna 2003; Smulovitz and Peruzzotti 2003; Peruzzotti and Smulovitz 2006). Their failure allows for the continued application of rules of decision at variance with state standards and the perpetuation of localized social relations of power.

---

[13] We should not forget, of course, that this control can serve democratic or authoritarian purposes, and that it is especially important for the latter – think of Foucault's description of Jeremy Bentham's Panopticon (Foucault 1980).

Moreover, regardless of the availability of horizontal accountability and other collective mechanisms, it is especially important that intended beneficiaries themselves have the capacity to engage monitoring systems effectively. The state and the various institutions that are designed to act on behalf of these intended beneficiaries may or may not share their goals, and may need extra prodding to do their work. Engaging with and navigating even the best oversight agencies, let alone prodding reluctant ones into action, as we saw, requires an investment of resources. And even then the battle is only begun. Once engaged, these venues are all arenas of contestation between those who claim rights and those who deny duties. In general, then, the rule of law will require a minimum level of citizen capability and a rough equality of resources among claimants, in addition to a variety of reporting and monitoring agencies. Greater equality, in a very direct way, reduces the likelihood that information about rights violations will be biased and maximizes the chances that lower level agents will act according to the normative guidelines laid down by upper level agents. Severe social and economic inequality is toxic to the rule of law.

In the following chapters I carry out the analysis outlined earlier. Chapters 2 and 3 are comparative chapters. Chapter 2 sets up the dependent variable, using mostly quantitative measures to analyze levels of effectiveness and inequality across and within the cases. Chapter 3 presents a first-order explanation for these levels of inequality and effectiveness, adopting a mostly qualitative approach to tie socio-economic tolls to informational failures and political tolls to normative failures. Chapters 4 through 8 examine each of the cases, using the framework described earlier to account for the presence of these tolls and the levels of effectiveness and inequality in each system. Each of the chapters concludes with some reflections on what the case can teach us more generally. Chapter 9, finally, presents a summary of the findings and some concluding reflections.

2

Charting Injustice in Argentina, Brazil, and Uruguay

In the 1970s the citizens of Argentina, Brazil, and Uruguay were *legally* powerless when confronting the security forces of authoritarian regimes that had explicitly suspended constitutional guarantees – at that time, demanding a badge number, in the classic expression of the power conferred by a legal right, was not only futile but dangerous. Today, those regimes have been replaced by formally constitutionalist liberal democratic regimes that explicitly guarantee due process and legal redress and forbid police violence and extra-judicial executions. If effective, these formal rights should produce an increase in the power of those who are most likely to be the victims of police violence. There is considerable evidence to suggest, however, that many continue to live in fear of the state and its security forces. Just how effective, then, are citizens' rights in São Paulo? How can we know whether the formal right to be free from arbitrary police violence, in particular, is more firmly rooted in Buenos Aires than in Salvador da Bahia? Whether a shantytown dweller in Córdoba has less effective protection in the courts than a middle-class resident of Buenos Aires? Whether Uruguay's courts back up this right with a more credible threat of prosecution than the courts of Salvador?

This chapter will compare judicial outcomes in the five locations that are the subject of this study. Uruguay has a unitary system and has more or less the population of the smaller cities in my study, so the analysis encompasses the entire country. In Argentina I will compare the federal and provincial courts of the Buenos Aires metropolitan area and the provincial courts of the city of Córdoba. Finally, in Brazil I present information on two cities, the state courts in the city of São Paulo and the state courts in the city of Salvador da Bahia in Northeastern Brazil.

As noted in the introductory chapter, the focus of this book – the dependent variable – is the judicial system's role in enforcing a claim of right. At

37

the same time, to focus exclusively on the judicial response is to elide the very condition that makes this response necessary. An after-the-fact legal remedy is a poor substitute for having the right respected in the first place, as seen most poignantly in connection with the right not to be killed. Thus, the effectiveness of a legal right is given first and foremost by the probability that it will not be violated. Any meaningful picture of legal effectiveness must include a look at the incidence of violations, even if that is not the primary focus of the analysis. Therefore, the first part of this chapter explores the incidence and distribution of violations in the various locations. For each location, I measure the average probability of being the victim of police violence, as well as the increased risk to members of particular groups – the poor, shantytown residents, or Afro-Brazilians, for example. This landscape of violations will become the context in which judicial effectiveness is measured, the challenge that the legal system must address.

At the same time, the distribution of violations could simply be the consequence of remoteness, the absence of the state, an accident of geography, or any number of other factors. As a result, to evaluate and explain the strength of the legal system in backing a claim of right, we must shift the focus to the state's response when an apparent violation comes to its attention. This response includes, though it is not limited to, a judicial one in the form of a criminal prosecution. To measure this response I estimate the likelihood that the state will successfully prosecute police officers who kill, placing its coercive power behind the claim of right. In technical terms, then, the twofold dependent variable for the study is the level of effectiveness and inequality of each judicial system, in response to police violence cases; and the primary focus of the analysis of succeeding chapters will be to explain why the courts respond more successfully in some locations than in others, and in a more egalitarian fashion in some locations than in others, given the level of violence they face.

The average level of violations and of the judicial response to violations enables broad comparisons across jurisdictions. But to gauge the effectiveness of rights for various classes of persons within (and across) jurisdictions, I go one step further, showing how the probability of a violation or of state enforcement varies for favored and disfavored groups within each jurisdiction. To measure inequalities in the probability of an initial violation, I compare the extent to which members of a particular group, say, shantytown dwellers in Buenos Aires or Afro-Brazilians in São Paulo, are under- or overrepresented within the victim population as compared to the group's share of the total population. To measure inequality within the legal system, I use the under- and over-representation of the target group among successful prosecutions, as compared to its share of the total victim population (i.e., the pool of potential prosecutions).[1]

For example, men typically make up at least 90% of the victim sample and approximately 50% of the total population, so the probability of a violation is almost twice as high for a man as it is on average. In São Paulo, however, the victim's gender has no impact on the outcome of a prosecution – men represent about 90% of the total victim population and about 90% of all convictions. In this case, the probability of a violation is, but the probability that a violation will be redressed is not, contingent on the victim's sex. In practical terms, low levels of enforcement with little inequality means that rights (and courts) are ineffective for everyone, more or less equally. If inequality measures are high, however, courts are more likely to respond to those who possess certain extra-legal goods or characteristics, regardless of the average level of effectiveness of rights. Under conditions of high inequality, a low average conviction rate simply means that favored groups are relatively rare within the victim population. It is the particular response, not the mean, that gives the effectiveness of a certain right for a given individual showing particular characteristics.

This chapter graphically demonstrates several things: first, levels and determinants of inequality in the distribution of initial violations vary independently from inequality within the courts. Thus, citizens are more likely to experience discrimination at the hands of the police than in the courts in nearly all the systems analyzed here, and the factors that mark the difference are not the same inside as outside the courts. Even the two locations with the most egalitarian court systems, Uruguay and São Paulo, show inequality in the distribution of rights violations outside the courts (albeit to a much greater degree in São Paulo). Second, high average levels of effectiveness in a particular court system may mask a high level of inequality. While Uruguay shows high effectiveness and low inequality, Córdoba shows high levels of both effectiveness and inequality; São Paulo, on the other hand, shows very low levels of effectiveness with low levels of inequality;[2] Buenos Aires is in the low middle on both, while Salvador's very low overall success rate leaves little room for inequality. Figure 2.1 classifies the judicial response in each location along these two dimensions.

The third conclusion we may take from this chapter is that, in three out of five cases – Buenos Aires, São Paulo, and Salvador – the courts are quite

---

[1] This is similar to the measure used by Geller and Karales (1981) to evaluate police violence in Chicago.

[2] São Paulo is a special case in this respect, as its low levels of inequality are primarily a function of excluding higher socio-economic classes from the victim pool. To some degree, it remains an open question how the system would respond to the claims of, say, middle-class victims.

FIGURE 2.1. Effectiveness and inequality in Buenos Aires, Córdoba, Salvador, São Paulo, and Uruguay.

ineffective, while in Córdoba the system is highly responsive primarily for those who possess the tolls. In São Paulo and Salvador one might question whether the right is effective at all, while in the Metro Buenos Aires area the probability of redress is still small but noticeably greater. In Córdoba, the middle classes have little to fear, but marginalized victims can expect both a high likelihood of a violation and little chance of redress. This pattern seems to confirm the impression of many (Méndez, O'Donnell, and Pinheiro 1999) that rights are generally ineffective, and do not reach the marginalized or underprivileged even in systems that for the well-off work relatively well. The sole exception among my cases is Uruguay, where the courts seem to respond even to those who cannot supply their own resources. In this last country, violations are much less frequent, and the courts react primarily to the legal characteristics of the event, rather than to various extra-legal factors.

This chapter will proceed as follows. In the first section – not as a dependent variable, but to set the context and illustrate the variance in background conditions – I compare the overall level of police homicides across the various cases. In this section I also examine the grounds of inequality in each location, the characteristics that make it more likely that certain individuals will see their rights violated, and I summarize and compare across locations. In the second section I describe the dependent variable for this project, following the same three-part outline as before but this time with respect to the actions of the judiciary. First I compare the likelihood that the courts will, on average, successfully prosecute violations across jurisdictions. Then I present a detailed examination of the extra-legal factors that affect the success of a prosecution in each location. I conclude with a summary of the combined impact of average levels of effectiveness and inequality factors, estimating the level of effectiveness of rights for members of different social groups across the locations in this study.

A. SOURCES AND TYPES OF DATA

One of the many difficulties in conducting a study of the problem of police homicides and the state response to them is obtaining accurate information about the overall universe of cases. In each location, therefore, I consulted the best available sources, using the work of NGOs, state oversight agencies, newspaper archives, and reports by human rights organizations. To obtain a more accurate gauge, I use both qualitative and quantitative information. The two cases at opposite ends of the spectrum in terms of levels of violations and judicial effectiveness, Uruguay and Salvador, are the most problematic from the point of view of quantitative information. In Uruguay the small number of cases makes it difficult to obtain statistically significant results, while in Salvador the absence of consistent monitoring of police violence by either state or civil society actors makes it very difficult to obtain quantifiable information despite the large number of cases. In both of these sites, to a greater extent than in the others, the quantitative information is extensively supplemented with the qualitative analysis of individual cases of police violence.

In each location, I obtained lists of persons who died at the hands of the police. The lists sometimes came from civil society actors, sometimes from state offices.[3] Using all the available information, as described in the Appendix, I purged the lists of any cases in which it was apparent that the victim had died in the course of a violent confrontation with the police. I then reviewed court documents and press reports and interviewed lawyers and family members of the victims to secure information about the incident itself, the victims, and the perpetrators. Most importantly, I established what treatment these cases received at the hands of prosecutors and courts. Using homicides obviates one of the most vexing difficulties for scholars of a legal system. Every homicide leaves a victim, and every homicide must, by law in these countries, trigger a judicial investigation. By beginning the inquiry with lists of victims of police homicides, then, I mostly avoid the selection problem that afflicts studies of legal outcomes, which for the most part cannot account for the many cases that never get to the courts in the first place.[4] Using these

---

[3] A more detailed description of the sources of data, the sampling methods, and the various screens employed to make sure the samples are comparable across cases is presented in the Appendix.

[4] I still miss, of course, the cases in which the police do not claim attribution. As described in the Appendix, this is a more serious problem in Brazil, where extermination groups with a strong police component are more common than in Argentina or Uruguay. But this means that I am mostly looking at the judicial response to official, acknowledged police violence, making the samples more comparable and my conclusions regarding Brazil, if anything, conservative.

lists as a sample of the universe of police homicides, I can make inferences about the frequency with which a police officer who kills someone in course of his or her duties is likely to face prosecution and ultimately conviction and punishment.

Comparing conviction rates across jurisdictions assumes that the underlying sample of cases in each jurisdiction is more or less comparable. A lower conviction rate could mean either that the courts in one place are too lenient or ineffective, or that the police officer defendants in that sample of cases are more likely to be innocent. I took several measures to ensure that I was comparing similar cases. As noted, using a combination of press reports, the police investigation, and where possible interviews with representatives of the victim, I first excluded cases of evident armed confrontations. This ensures that different locations do not produce different conviction rates because of different rates of armed and violent crime leading to shootouts with the police. Brazil, for example, does not have lower conviction rates than Uruguay in this sample because of a higher percentage of deaths arising out of armed confrontations. I also classified the cases, using all the available information about the characteristics of the event, into the various categories described shortly, and I make comparisons within categories, so I am not comparing domestic violence cases that happen to involve a police officer to cases in which a police officer shoots someone in the course of routine police activities.

Throughout the text, I use the following categories to organize the cases:

1. *Routine Policing*: intentional shootings in the course of routine policing operations, excluding armed confrontations.
2. *Execution*: the execution of suspected criminals after they have been reduced to custody, wounded, or otherwise incapacitated.
3. *Torture*: cases of torture ending in death.
4. *Death while in custody*: an intermediate category of deaths in custody that are at least partially attributable to an act by the victim himself or herself. A number of inmates died after setting fire to mattresses in their cells either as a suicide or as a protest. Moreover, family members blame the correctional institutions for inmate deaths when there is a suggestion that the guards staged the suicide, or contributed to the death by mistreating the inmates before the event, by egging them on, by failing to come to their aid during or after the event, or even by maliciously providing the materials used, and (especially in Córdoba) when prison conditions repeatedly led to suicides in a particular facility.

5. *Private Violence*: "private" homicides committed by police officers in the course of a crime, domestic dispute, or personal quarrel, that is, in events that are unconnected with their official duties.

6. *Bystander*: the death of an individual who was not the target of police action, but who was accidentally shot in the course of a police action.

Occasionally, I refer to categories 1, 2, 3, and 4, collectively, as "Police Actions," since they all take place in the course of carrying out police duties and involve some level of affirmative police action.

The nature of the cases I have chosen helps to ensure comparability. The law governing homicide is more discrete and straightforward than, say, the law regarding the constitutional separation of powers. A youth shot in the head while kneeling with his hands in the air was almost certainly murdered, while one who was shot as he attempted to kill a police officer was almost certainly killed in self-defense. There are borderline cases, but in the end the judgments are relatively clear-cut. To further address this concern, throughout the text I double-check my results against other sources of information to see whether alternative explanations are more credible. For example, since most agree that Uruguay has a lower level of human rights violations, it is unlikely that the conviction rate is ten times higher in Uruguay than in São Paulo because the Uruguayan police are ten times more likely to violate the law. Similarly, it is likely that my conclusions about the undisciplined violence of the Buenos Aires police are correct because they match the more qualitative conclusions of other close observers.

B. COMPARING VIOLATION RATES

1. Levels of Police Violence

As seen in Figure 2.2, the different cities vary considerably in terms of the absolute and per capita number of police homicides. In absolute numbers, São Paulo is the indisputable leader, amassing approximately seventy-five hundred deaths at the hands of the police over the course of the 1990s. On a per capita basis, however, Salvador leads all the cities in the study, with a rate of police killings three times that of São Paulo's, its nearest competitor. São Paulo and Buenos Aires finish the decade in a dead heat, in per capita terms, while Córdoba follows and Uruguay shows the lowest number in both absolute and relative terms. For comparison, police killings in Los Angeles, the U.S. city where Chevigny found the highest rate of police shootings, occurred at a rate of about 0.5 per hundred thousand, while in New York

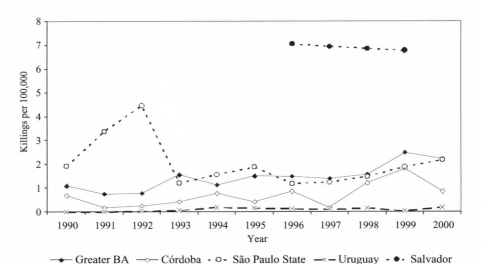

FIGURE 2.2. Police killings per capita in Buenos Aires, Córdoba, São Paulo, Salvador, and Uruguay, 1990–2000.

the rate was about 0.34 (Chevigny 1995). In Venezuela, in contrast, the incidence of killings may be as high as 12 per hundred thousand.[5]

Despite failings in the prosecution of violations dating from the dictatorship (Skaar 2002), Uruguay has acquired a deserved reputation for respect for civil rights and the rule of law. O'Donnell, as noted earlier, lists it as one of two countries in which the state has established a legal system that covers its whole territory and all social classes (O'Donnell 1999: 311). Because of this, Human Rights Watch does not even bother producing a report on rights violations in Uruguay. Amnesty International, while criticizing some other aspects of its civil rights performance, acknowledges that police killings are exceedingly rare in Uruguay. The U.S. State Department Human Rights Reports for the 1990s simply state, "There were no reports of political or other extra-judicial killings."[6] In fact, not only are killings by the police rare events but, in addition, most of those that occur are punished in the courts.

---

[5] As mentioned earlier, this estimate is based on the 2001 U.S. State Department Human Rights Report for Venezuela, which reports that the Venezuelan government claimed the police shot 2,000 criminals in the first eight months of that year. If accurate, this translates into an annual rate of killings of 12.75 per hundred thousand, twice as high as Salvador's.

[6] U.S. State Department annual human rights country reports are available from http://www. state.gov/g/drl/hr/c1470.htm.

In Uruguay, from 1992 (the first year for which there were complete sources of data) to 2000, my search revealed either two or three victims of police homicides each year (four in 2000), for a total of twenty-three deaths over eight years, and an average annual per capita rate of about 0.1 per hundred thousand. A total of thirty-two security officials were charged or named in connection with these incidents, one of whom was a defendant in connection with two separate deaths. This resulted in a total of thirty-three cases, one per defendant, per victim. Twenty-one of these officials were charged with an active role in the killing, one with inflicting serious injuries, four with a secondary support role, and three with failing to properly supervise their subordinates. Four were prosecuted for covering up the facts or interfering with the prosecution.

There was a much larger number of cases in both Buenos Aires and Córdoba. In the Buenos Aires metropolitan area, from 1990 through 2000, the Centro de Estudios Legales y Sociales (the Center for Legal and Social Studies, known as CELS for its initials in Spanish) reported 1,755 deaths at the hands of the police. Nearly 70% of these cases were attributable to the Buenos Aires Provincial Police, the largest police force operating in that metropolitan area. About 12% were attributed to the Federal Police, which has concurrent jurisdiction (for federal law enforcement) in the province of Buenos Aires, and exclusive authority within the capital city itself. The annual number of killings rose gradually over the decade, without any dramatic changes from year to year.

In Córdoba, organizations affiliated with the Coordinadora Contra la Represión Policial e Institucional (the Coordinator against Institutional and Police Repression, known as CORREPI for its initials in Spanish) reported a total of 107 deaths at the hands of the police over the same period, of which I retained 89 for analysis, after screening out those that did not meet the conditions set forth for sampling. The methods and criteria used by CORREPI and the CELS for gathering data are somewhat different, as described in the Appendix. Therefore it is likely that the Córdoba data underestimate somewhat the total number of deaths at the hands of the police in the province, although they are more likely to include only actual rights violations. Again, with some variations, the yearly number of cases was generally rising in Córdoba. The average annual rate for Córdoba and Buenos Aires during the 1990s was 0.7 and 1.5, respectively, per hundred thousand.

São Paulo is the largest city in Brazil. Approximately twenty million people live in or around the city proper, and another sixteen million in the rest of the state of São Paulo. It has a reputation for being among the most violent cities in Brazil, which has no shortage of violent cities. Police violence is also rife in São Paulo. The absolute number of deaths at the hands of the police is the highest of any city for which I have seen data – more than seventy-five hundred in the period of this study. Most of these deaths were the work of the state Military Police, which carries out the public safety function (the *policiamento ostensivo*). This is the largest police force by far, growing from about 70,000 in 1992 to over 81,000 in 1999. It is organized along strictly military lines. The Civil Police of São Paulo is a smaller force, numbering between 30,000 and about 40,000 for this period. It serves an investigative function and was responsible for only 5% of the total number of deaths, exceeding 10% only in 1998 and 1999.

Over the last decade, police killings in São Paulo follow a clear pattern: the number rises over a number of years, then abruptly drops (after 1992 and 1995) only to begin rising again in the following year. The number of police killings in São Paulo peaked in 1992, at a stunning 1,428. That was the year of the notorious Carandiru massacre, in which the Military Police killed 111 inmates of the São Paulo House of Detention. In addition to the initial violence, which claimed some lives, the police moved through the cell blocks shooting inmates, sometimes through the bars of the cell. Media images of naked inmates handling bodies in the yard of the prison – strongly reminiscent of concentration camp photos – temporarily focused attention on the problem. The resulting public and political backlash led to a drop of almost 75 percent in the number of shootings in the following year. Police killings have never returned to pre-1992 levels, but the numbers began climbing again in 1994 and are still growing. Even considering the immense population of the state of São Paulo – around thirty-six million – this ongoing pattern of violence produces an astonishing number of casualties. As Chevigny points out, in 1992 alone, in one state, the São Paulo police killed more people than the military dictatorship killed for political reasons in the entire country over fifteen years (Chevigny 1995: 145). Many countries in the midst of civil war or under dictatorial regimes do not experience this number of deaths.

Still, the dramatic numbers coming from São Paulo tend to obscure similar or even worse conditions in other cities. Taking the size of the population into consideration, the rate at which the police used lethal violence over the entire 1990s was only 33 percent higher in São Paulo than in Buenos Aires – 2.0 versus 1.5 per hundred thousand of population. And in the last half of the decade the rate for Buenos Aires was sometimes higher and sometimes lower, with a nearly identical average, as we saw in Figure 2.2. Even more striking, what we know about police homicides in Salvador suggests that the incidence of violations was considerably higher than in São Paulo. A review of press reports by the Justice and Peace Commission of the Archdiocese of Salvador counted 623 homicides by police officers between January 1996 and December 1999 in the Salvador metropolitan area (de Oliveira, Sousa Ribeiro, and Zanetti 2000), which has only 2.5 million people. The average annual rate of deaths per hundred thousand for these four years, then, was 6.9, three times higher than São Paulo's average.[7] In the end, then, São Paulo was not the outlier, although there remained marked differences in the rate of police killings per hundred thousand for all these locations: Uruguay was at 0.1, Córdoba at 0.7, Buenos Aires at 1.5, São Paulo at 2, and Salvador at 6.9.

2. Inequality in the Distribution of Violations

Since initial violations are rare in Uruguay, even on a per capita basis, the expectation that these rights will be respected is quite uniformly high for all the residents of Uruguay. Still, there are some tolls that raise the likelihood of a violation for certain individuals, as we see from an examination of who is over-represented in the victim population in relation to the general population. All of the victims were male, so that men appear in the victim pool about twice as often as they do in the general population. The unemployed represent 50% of the victims but only (on average for the period in question) 10.2% of the population.[8] We do not know the kind of neighborhood where some of the victims lived, but of the sixteen victims for whom this information is available two (12.5%) lived in shantytowns while only 5% of the total population is estimated to do so.[9] Eighteen of the victims lived in or around Montevideo, the capital, two in Salto, and the rest in various smaller towns in the interior, so that the cases are somewhat more concentrated in urban areas than is the national population. In fact, many of the incidents involve police activity in what are called "conflictive" areas of the capital (typically, lower class neighborhoods perceived as having a high incidence of criminal, and hence police, activity).

---

[7] This figure does not include the additional 85 annual victims of extermination groups (*grupos de extermínio*), even though all the accounts of these groups confirm a high participation by police officers (see, e.g., interview with Costa Ferreira, in de Oliveira, Sousa Ribeiro, and Zanetti 2000; Oiticica 2001). Including these numbers would bring the average annual rate to about 10 per hundred thousand.

[8] *Source*: Instituto Nacional de Estadística of Uruguay; figures available at www.ine.gub.uy.

[9] SERPAJ (1998: 202) reports studies finding that 151,541 of the country's 3 million people live in the precarious housing of a shantytown, most of them (122,000) in the capital itself.

The majority of the victims for whom this information is available were young but not disproportionately so: three were under twenty years old, another six between twenty and thirty, and three in their thirties. Comparing this distribution to the general population, 61% of the victims were younger than forty, whereas 67% of the total population of Uruguay falls in this age group.

Social classes up to the middle class are represented: five of the victims can be identified by their income or mode of employment as members of the lowest class, five of the lower working class, and four of the middle class; there is insufficient information to categorize the remaining seven. Fourteen of the victims (in fact, all but two of the ones for whom we can identify a motive) were shot because they were suspected of committing a crime or were thought to be resisting police identification or control; of these fourteen, only two were middle class. We can derive two principal generalizations from this data. First, an initial violation is more likely for men who attract the attention of the police by fleeing or resisting attempts at control, especially in conflictive areas of the city. Second, victims come from all social strata, but those who live in shantytowns are somewhat over-represented.

Who are the victims in Argentina? As is true in all the locations in the study, the data I collected in Argentina suggest a disproportionate targeting of young, lower class, unemployed males from precarious housing. The victims were overwhelmingly male: 94% of the victims in the Conurbano, the vast metropolitan area surrounding the city of Buenos Aires proper, were male, as were 85% of the victims in Buenos Aires City, and 90% in Córdoba. They were disproportionately young by a ratio of more than 1.5 to 1: in the Conurbano 91% and in the city 88% of victims were thirty-five or younger, while in Córdoba, 93% of the victims fell in that age group, as compared to 58% who were under thirty-five in the overall population of the provinces of Buenos Aires and Córdoba.[10]

Class and social marginality are also factors. In both cities, among those victims for whom I have this information, two-thirds were classified as either "lower class" (a classification based on employment, dwelling, and income information) or a slightly higher category my interviewees agreed to call "lower working class" (people who worked steady jobs but fell well below middle class). This classification was made by the advocates who knew them, although I classified some of the cases myself where I had the pertinent information. For a rough estimate of over-representation, consider that the

[10] *Source*: INDEC (Instituto Nacional de Estadística y Censos), Proyecciones de población por sexo según grupos quinquenales de edad, año 2000.

proportion of "lower class" victims is about three times the proportion of the population that was below the poverty line during the 1990s.[11]

Other, more objective, socio-economic variables also offer a basis for comparison. More than 38% of the Córdoba victims lived in the precarious housing of a *villa* (shantytown), while almost 19% of the victims in the greater Buenos Aires area did so. According to the Argentine sociologist Eduardo Blaustein, the percentage of the population of the Buenos Aires metropolitan area that lives in *villas* is only about 3.3%.[12] Victims were more than twice as often unemployed as the general population: 32% and 52% of the victims in Buenos Aires and Córdoba, respectively, were unemployed (not including those attending school), and the proportion is higher still in Police Actions.[13] This proportion is high compared to unemployment in both the Greater Buenos Aires area and Córdoba, which rose from 5% in 1991 to 13% in 1994 and averaged 16% between 1995 and 1999 for an overall average of about 13% for the decade.[14] Finally, half of the victims in Córdoba had an immediate association with crime (i.e., they were killed during or immediately after the commission of a crime, or had a known criminal record), while 37% of the victims in Buenos Aires fit this description.

In São Paulo we find a high level of violence that is sharply focused on the most vulnerable part of the population, so that the middle and upper classes are almost completely excluded from the victim pool. Race is also a factor in São Paulo, in contrast to the other cities we have seen thus far – primarily because of the more racially homogeneous population in those

[11] This variable does not, of course, correspond precisely with the indicators of poverty used by the Argentine census authority, so there is no comparable figure for the population as a whole. For a rough comparison, however, consider that the percentage of the population below the poverty line in Buenos Aires oscillated above and below 20% for the decade, with the numbers getting slightly worse toward the end (and spiking up above 50% after the 2001–02 crisis).

[12] The percentage of *villeros* in the population is estimated from a current article written by Eduardo Blaustein, and reproduced at http://www.piketes.com.ar/www/documentos/villas1.htm (last visited June 3, 2006). He reports that in 1976, before a major eradication effort by the military government, there were a total of 400,000 shantytown dwellers in Greater Buenos Aires. The eradication effort essentially moved them from the city to the outer rings of the Conurbano, but did not reduce the numbers appreciably. Figures are not available for Córdoba, so I use the same percentage there. This is likely to overestimate shantytown population in that province, and therefore to produce a conservative estimate of how over-represented shantytown residents are in the victim population.

[13] Employment information is missing for 30% of the Buenos Aires cases in my sample and for 21% of the cases in Córdoba.

[14] Unemployment information is taken from a United Nations Development Project publication (UNDP 1998: 129) for the early nineties, and from the Encuesta Permanente de Hogares available from INDEC for the second half of the decade.

other cities. In one of the *paulista* cases I reviewed, for example, according to the lawyers' files, a witness reported a police officer saying, in the wake of a deadly shooting, "If he's black and from the *favela*, we shoot first and ask questions later."[15] In another case, a witness reports the police saying "he's black, he's poor, he's from the *favela*; he must die."[16]

The available figures confirm this policeman's claim. In 1999 the São Paulo police ombudsman organization, the Ouvidoria da Polícia, reviewed extensive information on all the shootings reported by the police for the entire year (Ouvidoria da Polícia 1999). That year, blacks appear in the victim population 2.2 times more often than in the general population: nearly 55% of the victims were black, while only about 25% of the population of São Paulo is black (including those generally described as *pardos*).[17] The same study demonstrates that the police generally act in response to perceived criminality. The Ouvidoria reports that 44% of the victims were engaged in the commission of a crime at the time they were killed (the crime may or may not have been a violent one, of course), another 28% were *suspected* of having committed a crime, and the remaining 28% had no immediate link to an actual crime – they were approached by police simply to verify their identity, for example (Ouvidoria da Polícia 1999).[18]

An analysis of my own sample further opens a vista of inequality based on age, gender, class, and *favela* residence. Persons under thirty-five were 1.5 times more likely to appear in the population of victims than in the general population (93% of victims compared to 64% in the overall population).[19] Virtually all of the victims were male while the general population is only about 47% male. About 82% of the 167 victims for whom relevant information is available I classified as lower class based on their employment, income,

---

[15] "Se é preto e favelado, a gente atira primero, para perguntar depois." Statement recorded in witness interview files obtained from the Centro Santo Dias, São Paulo.

[16] "É preto, é pobre, é favelado, tem que morrer." Statement recorded in witness interview files relating to the case of Eneas da Silva, obtained from the Centro Santo Dias, São Paulo.

[17] Census data for 1991 cited by Sadek et al. (2000) suggests that 26% of the population of São Paulo is *parda* or black. Census data for 1980, cited in two separate studies by Adorno (1994, 1995) puts the figure at 24%.

[18] For this study, the Ouvidoria requested additional information on all the cases that came to its attention in 1999 from the police, the Medical Forensic Institute (Instituto Médico Legal) in São Paulo, and other sources. My own sample covers a longer time period but is based on a sampling of cases rather than the whole universe. The data from my own sample show essentially the same results on these variables.

[19] Total population numbers are from Instituto Brasileiro de Geografia e Estatística (IBGE), Contagem da População 1996, and Malha Municipal Digital do Brasil 1997. Data from the 2000 Census; national statistics (which are not disaggregated by city on the Web site of the Instituto Brasileiro de Geografia e Estatística) are similar.

or type of residence (e.g., whether they lived in a *favela*).[20] In the 91 cases in which there is information about the neighborhood where the victim lived, 64% of the victims lived in a *favela* (58.5% of the cases in the sample did not have residence information), while according to IBGE's 2000 Census, 10% of the population of São Paulo lives in *favelas*.[21] Seventy-two percent of the victims for whom this information was available were unemployed (10% of the cases did not have this information), while unemployment rates in São Paulo in the 1990s are around 5%. These groups are, therefore, significantly over-represented in the population of victims, as are Afro-Brazilians. The violence also appears to have been more circumscribed by crime prevention activities than it was, for example, in Buenos Aires, if we judge by the percentage of victims who were involved in a crime at the time, or who had a criminal record.

There is no readily available information on the distribution of deaths at the hands of the police in Salvador. We will see, however, as we go through individual cases, that most of them involved residents of Salvador's squatter neighborhoods, the *favelas* or *invasões* that surround the city. Moreover, homicides generally, including but not limited to police homicides, were again sharply targeted to residents of the periphery of Salvador, the shantytowns surrounding the metropolitan area. Ninety-two percent of the victims were men. Blacks and *pardos* together accounted for 97% of the victims. Between 80% and 85% of Salvador's population matches that description, meaning that whites are at least 5 times less likely than Afro-Brazilians to be murdered in Salvador. In some years, the police account for 20% of all homicides in Salvador, so we can use these figures to infer the patterns that are likely true for police killings. If, as is the case in other cities, police homicides roughly follow the patterns of homicides more generally, police killings in Salvador likely affect the marginalized population as much here as in São Paulo. At the same time, as we will see in the following discussion of Salvador's cases, the middle class is not exempt. Some of the most prominent

---

[20] As noted earlier, this variable is a composite of employment, dwelling, and income information. I do not have a similar figure for the population at large but the percentage of the population considered indigent in the São Paulo metropolitan area began the 1990s at about 6% and declined very slightly at the end of the decade after a spike to over 11% in the mid-1990s (Jannuzzi 2001). The percentage of the population living below the poverty line in São Paulo might be, if one sets the poverty line at twice the indigence level, somewhere around 18% by the end of the decade, with a high of nearly 32% in the middle of 1990s (Januzzi 2001: Table 4). By any measure, the poor are severely over-represented among the victims of police violence.

[21] Reported in the Folha de São Paulo, July 28, 2002, on the basis of an analysis of Census 2000 data for São Paulo (found at http://www.ibge.net/censo/noticias.shtm).

cases of homicide attributed to the police involve nurses and journalists, for example. And the number of middle-class victims even in the small number of cases I examine in Salvador exceeds the total number of middle-class victims in the larger São Paulo sample.

In short, Salvador shows the highest level of violations of any of the cities. The limited available information suggests that the violations especially target the disadvantaged, although, as we shall see, there are notorious cases against relatively middle-class people who dared speak out against police violence. While it is hard to estimate exactly, the pattern looks similar to São Paulo's but is more generalized: focused on the lower classes and the *favelados* but with considerably more spillover into slightly more affluent classes, and focused on suspects of crime and other "undesirables" but with more spillover into ordinary poor people who happen to be in the wrong place at the wrong time. In other words, Salvador shows an extremely high rate of violations and a moderately high degree of inequality in their distribution.

3. Comparing Violation Rates Across Locations

To make the comparison across locations, I standardize the measures by returning to the Weberian formulation set forth in the introduction: a right, when it is effective, should produce "an increase of the probability that a certain expectation of the one to whom the law grants that right will not be disappointed" (Weber 1978 [1921]). As is usual in discussions of discrimination and inequality, my discussion inverts Weber's formulation, focusing on the *detrimental* effect of *dis*favored characteristics rather than on the positive effects of favored traits. The probability of a violation is calculated simply by applying the rate of violations for the entire period under study, per hundred thousand of population, giving the likelihood that any average resident of the cities in question will be killed by the police over the ten years of this study. The effect of each toll, in turn, is calculated as the ratio of the percentage of persons with that characteristic in the victim population to the percentage of persons with that characteristic in the overall population. This ratio, in keeping with the Weberian formulation, produces a coefficient that, when multiplied by the likelihood of a violation, gives the probability that a citizen lacking that toll (that is to say, exhibiting a disfavored characteristic) will suffer a violation.

The formula for calculating the impact of a particular marker of inequality, the toll, is $(Vict_x/Vict_{total})/(Pop_x/Pop_{total})$ where $Vict_X$ is the number of victims with characteristic x, $Vict_{total}$ is the total number of victims, Pop_X is the number of persons in the relevant population with characteristic x, and

Pop_{total} is the total population. The toll, for example, will be greater than one for blacks and smaller than one for whites if being black increases the probability of a violation. If there is no effect of race on the probability of being targeted for a violation, the toll will be one. The greater the toll value, the greater inequality there is associated with that characteristic. The greater the combined effect of the toll and the background level of violence, the less effective a given right is for people exhibiting the relevant characteristic.

Thus, a right may be ineffective either because a violent police force violates everyone's rights equally, or because an otherwise relatively restrained police force targets a disfavored group for high levels of violence, or both. Calculating the tolls shows that there is considerable variation in both measures across the locations. Uruguay has the lowest average level of violations and the lowest socio-economic tolls. In Argentina, Córdoba has fewer violations but far higher levels of inequality than Buenos Aires, which has a higher overall level of violations but is more egalitarian. São Paulo in turn exhibits the worst combination – high levels of violations and high inequality.[22]

The tolls (think of them as risk multipliers) for shantytown dwellers, for example, are highest in Córdoba (11.7), which means that the violence in that city, though low overall, is highly concentrated among the very lowest classes. The Uruguayan toll for shantytown dwellers (2.66) means the probability of a violation is more than 2.5 times higher for this group than for the average Uruguayan citizen. At the same time, Buenos Aires and São Paulo exhibit levels of violations for *villeros* and *favelados* that are about six times higher than the average. A very high value of the toll for the unemployed in Uruguay (5.1) is surprising, but it is probably a result of collinearity between the sort of criminality that is likely to be targeted and unemployment. Inequality never disappears, of course, but there are marked differences across cities, some of which track what we might expect (Uruguay's noted egalitarianism), and some of which are more surprising – a level of inequality that is twice as high in Córdoba as it is in São Paulo or Buenos Aires, for example.

Calculating the combined effect of background levels of violence and the shantytown residence toll produces very striking comparisons. A shantytown resident in São Paulo is 52 times more likely, and one in Buenos Aires 32 times more likely, to be killed by the police than a shantytown resident in Montevideo. In Córdoba, because violence is so targeted toward the marginalized population of these precarious neighborhoods, a shantytown resident lives with exactly the same risk as one in Buenos Aires, even as the middle class

---

[22] Unfortunately, the quality of the data from Salvador does not permit including that case in this more quantitative analysis.

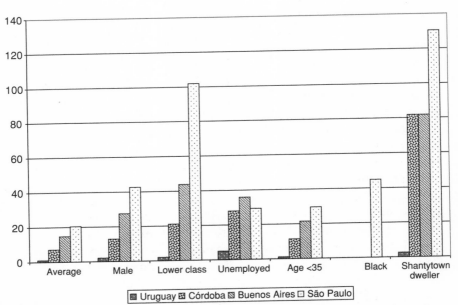

FIGURE 2.3. Likelihood of a violation per hundred thousand of population for various social groups in all locations.

can rightly perceive that its own risk is dramatically lower in Córdoba than in Buenos Aires. Age has a similar, although less dramatic impact. Persons under age thirty-five are 1.5 times more likely to be victimized than the average in Córdoba, Buenos Aires, and São Paulo, but no more likely than anyone else to be killed in Uruguay. The combined effect for this trait means that the probability of a violation for young people in São Paulo is 31 times higher than for those in Uruguay, and 23 and 12 times higher, respectively, for those in Buenos Aires and Córdoba.

Race is, as expected, a factor in São Paulo. Since there is no variation on this trait in the other countries, we cannot do a cross-country comparison, but the variation inside São Paulo is dramatic. A black person in São Paulo has a four times greater chance of dying at the hands of the police than a white person has. To provide a visual comparison of the risk to which different groups are exposed in each city, Figure 2.3 graphs the likelihood (per hundred thousand) of being killed by the police in each location, for members of different social groups.

One other category of persons, those suspected of a crime, cannot be ignored. In all countries, the police argue that they are merely fighting dangerous criminals. As we will see later on, and as many other studies have suggested (Ouvidoria da Polícia 1999; Amnesty International 2005), it is not true that the victims are typically dangerous criminals. But it is interesting to consider to what extent the police are using lethal violence as a routine policing tool, and to what extent the violence is more random, involving victims who have no connection to crime. Thus I identified the proportion of victims in each city's sample who were killed in connection with a crime (no matter how minor or unrelated to the actual shooting) or who had a criminal record. The percentage varies considerably from place to place – 72% in São Paulo, 60% in Uruguay, 50% in Córdoba, and 37% in Buenos Aires. Conversely, the percentage of bystanders killed by stray bullets in Buenos Aires (about 15%) is almost three times higher than in Córdoba and São Paulo, and five times higher than in Uruguay. In Córdoba, meanwhile, an astonishing number of the deaths (12%) resulted from domestic violence incidents or similar private quarrels.

Of the cases presented, then, São Paulo's police clearly target perceived criminality more than any others. The close targeting and very high level of violence suggests that the *paulista* Military Police use deadly force in a relatively disciplined manner as an almost routine instrument of crime control. The much lower level of violence and high percentage of criminal suspects in Uruguay suggests, on the other hand, a police force that is restrained overall, but whose excesses occur primarily in the course of repressing crime. Buenos Aires shows the lowest percentage of criminal suspects targeted, together with a high level of violations. Again, consistent with the reputation of the police force in this province, this suggests an undisciplined police force that is prone to violent excesses that are sometimes entirely unrelated to its mission as a law enforcement agency. Ordinary citizens, with no connection to crime, may be at greatest risk in Buenos Aires. Córdoba occupies an intermediate position, a consequence of a very high number of domestic violence cases in the sample, although the low level of violations means that, even so, Córdoba's police force is less deadly than the *bonaerense* for persons who have no involvement with crime.

One final reflection on this toll is necessary. The cases in the sample are selected to include a high percentage of civil rights violations. The mere fact that a victim was involved in some sort of illegal activity does not justify taking his or her life – these are precisely the individuals for whom due process protections are created. At the same time, the higher the percentage of victims with some criminal "taint," the more targeted police repression is toward criminal activity. If the number is low, it means that the police are killing people for reasons other than the suppression of crime. They may be shooting demonstrators, for example, or using lethal force in the course of private disputes or criminal activity, or shooting people in the course of the frequent document checks, or mistaking bystanders for fleeing suspects. All of these examples are present in the cases I examine, and they are more frequent in Córdoba and Buenos Aires than elsewhere.

In summary, then, the judiciaries in each of these places have different challenges to face. In São Paulo they are confronted with the routine application of lethal force as a mechanism of crime control, tightly targeted to the lower classes. In Salvador, the same practice is even more widespread and occasionally spills out of the lower classes. Córdoba shows a similar pattern to São Paulo's, in that violence is vastly more prevalent among marginalized sectors of society but the killings are far less frequent. Buenos Aires, especially toward the end of the decade, has achieved a similar level of violence to São Paulo's, but the violence appears to be more widely distributed – perhaps not among the truly middle class, but at least beyond the very poorest sectors. And in Uruguay, the problem truly seems to be exceptional rather than systemic. Against this backdrop, then, what do the courts contribute to the effectiveness of the rule of law? Given that their rights have been violated, who can expect that the courts will step in to redress, to the extent possible, that violation? That is the subject of the next section.

C. COMPARING THE JUDICIAL RESPONSE TO VIOLATIONS

This section details the dependent variable proper. The section's first part presents the average conviction rate in each jurisdiction, and the second part describes the extent and sources of inequality in the results. The main determinants of judicial outcomes can be broken down into three categories: one category addresses the socio-economic status of the victim, another indicates the strength of the prosecution's participation, and a third explores some of the political characteristics of the case. Each of these categories has a different impact in different systems depending on system characteristics.

The socio-economic condition of the victim is captured by variables such as income and shantytown residence. Variation attributable to these variables reflects the disparate resources claimants bring to the justice system – the family of a young, unemployed shantytown resident is likely to bring fewer resources to bear than the family of a middle-class youth. The impact of a non-governmental attorney in the prosecution of a case is an indicator of the strength of the prosecution. The more the presence of a non-state attorney contributes to the results, the more likely it is that prosecutors are not taking an active role in the prosecution of these cases. Finally, the

TABLE 2.1. *Conviction Rates by Type of Event and by City.*

	Type of Event		
	Police Actions	Private Violence	Torture
Conviction Rate			
São Paulo	6%	44%	–
	(210)	(9)	
Buenos Aires	18.14%	37.04%	52.94%
	(215)	(10)	(34)
Córdoba	37.88%	63.64%	60%
	(66)	(11)	(15)
Uruguay	52%	0%	–
	(27)	(2)	

Cells contain convictions as a percentage of total number of cases in that category and (total number of cases).

influence of variables related to the political construction of the case, such as the presence or absence of demonstrations, or the perceived blameworthiness of the victim, measures changes in the rule of decision applied by judges and prosecutors. The more that popular demonstrations affect the outcome of a case, the more likely it is that judges and prosecutors are responding to political pressure rather than to the strictly legal characteristics of the case.

1. Legal Effectiveness

There are stark differences across the cases if we simply compare conviction rates. Uruguayan prosecutions are quite effective, with a conviction rate of about 52%. Compare this to São Paulo, where the conviction rate is only 6% in Police Action cases. Table 2.1 compares conviction rates in the four jurisdictions in which the sample of cases is large enough and representative enough to justify tabulating.

The initial differences are obvious, but there are strong similarities as well. Uruguay has a surprisingly high conviction rate, Córdoba is a little behind, the Buenos Aires courts are half as successful as those in Córdoba, and São Paulo's are one-third as effective as those of Buenos Aires. Note that the problem is unlikely to be a general breakdown in the justice system as a whole. In all these cases (except Uruguay, where the one police officer accused of a double murder had not yet been apprehended), the Private Violence cases elicit a more effective response than do cases in which the police were acting in their official capacity. In the two locations in which the sampling picked up cases of torture ending in death, we see a similarly high level of effectiveness. Clearly, then, in every jurisdiction the courts can and routinely do convict police officers who commit especially heinous offenses, such as killing in the course of torture, and those who kill for private purposes, such as in a quarrel or a domestic dispute, or in the commission of an ordinary crime. Just as clearly, however, the courts everywhere but in Uruguay routinely fail to convict police officers who kill in the course of routine policing, even after we exclude from the sample those cases in which the police were responding to an armed aggression.

Nor is it likely that convictions are so infrequent in São Paulo, for instance, because the police are more often legitimately shooting violent criminals in actual armed confrontations. If the deaths were occurring in the course of armed confrontations that posed a legitimate danger to the police, we would expect at least a minimal correlation between the number of police killed in a given year and the number of civilians killed that year by the police. In fact, the correlation, for all the years available from the Ouvidoria da Polícia (1990–2002), is minuscule, at -0.042, and completely non-significant. There is no apparent relationship between the level of violence exercised by the police and the threat posed to the police.[23]

Salvador is not included in the preceding table for reasons that will shortly become clear, but the data suggest that Salvador's performance is somewhere below São Paulo's. Given the lack of systematic data, there are two ways to estimate the conviction rate in Salvador. The first is to review all the known cases of police homicide, assume that they are a representative sample, and use the percentage of convictions in that sample as a measure. But since, as we will see, this sample is in all likelihood strongly biased toward greater effectiveness, this is almost certain to overestimate the effectiveness of the system. The second is to take the number of known convictions and apply it to the total number of killings. Since there is no systematic information on convictions, this is likely to undercount the number of convictions and underestimate the effectiveness of the system. If we do both, on the other hand, we may at least be reasonably confident that the conviction rate falls within that range.

The conviction rate among the sixty or so cases I surveyed in Salvador is slightly higher than São Paulo's overall conviction rate. Among this small number of identified cases there are four confirmed convictions in cases involving children and three in cases monitored by the state witness

---

[23] The data are available at http://www.ouvidoria-policia.sp.gov.br/pages/tabelas.htm.

protection program, PROVITA,[24] for a conviction rate of about ten percent overall. But, again, the sample is clearly not representative, so this figure is likely to vastly overstate the true conviction rate, and it would be misleading to include it in Table 2.1. The sample is drawn from four sources: twenty-five (including twenty cases of "special interest") from the Center for the Defense of Children and Adolescents (Centro da Defesa da Criança e do Adolescente, known as CEDECA) fifteen cases in which at least one witness was in the official witness protection program, ten cases involving journalists (which were the subject of a newspaper's private investigation), and thirteen additional cases gleaned from newspaper reports, interviews, and other published reports. Of the ten cases involving journalists, many received the attention of international human rights organizations, and all of them were extensively reported in the media. What is missing from the sample is a representative number from among the hundreds of routine police killings that did not come to the attention of any special programs. Even in this select group of cases, then, targeted for special treatment by various state and non-state actors, the conviction rate is a mere ten percent.

The second measure suggests a conviction rate somewhere between one percent and zero for adults and two or three percent at the very most for children. Of just over twenty cases involving adults taken from published accounts and interviews, none led to a conviction. Ten cases involving journalists, which were investigated by the local daily *A Tarde*, led to no convictions. A search of *A Tarde*'s online archives using a variety of key words and phrases, including the names of all known victims, turned up no convictions either. PROVITA, the Bahian witness protection program, reports three convictions out of all the cases it has handled, of which 60% involved the police and another 20% involved extermination groups (Carvalho 2001: 104). Even if we attribute all three of these convictions to police defendants, this would mean a grand total of three convictions from among hundreds of police killings, for a negligible conviction rate in cases involving adults.

In cases involving children, Waldemar Oliveira, the director of CEDECA noted that, of 80 cases that took place in 1991, only one went to trial, and that one ended in an acquittal. CEDECA's list of 20 exemplary cases does include four convictions through 2001. In a later report actualized through 2005, however, CEDECA records a grand total of 84 indictments in cases taking place during the 1990s (not all of them, but a high percentage, involving

---

[24] The name PROVITA is taken from the name of the federal initiative, Programa de Proteção e Apoio às Vítimas e Testemunhas Ameaçadas, which in Bahia comes under the Departamento de Proteção a Testemunhas e Vítimas da Violência.

police officers). Two-thirds of these indictments are dismissed, leading to only 22 jury trials (Espinheira 2005).[25] If we assume that the annual number of children killed remained constant at about 80 per year, the evidence suggests that someone is charged with a crime in only about 10% of cases, and only a quarter of those go to a jury. Other than the convictions in the four "exemplary" cases, I have no information on the number of convictions that resulted, but even a 100% conviction rate in the cases that go to trial would produce an overall conviction rate of only 2.5% in cases involving children. According to this measure, then, the conviction rate would be negligible when the victim is an adult and less than 3% in cases involving children. Moreover, the only known convictions take place with the significant involvement of either CEDECA or PROVITA.

Other sources confirm the failure of Salvador's courts to police the police. One of CEDECA's lawyers, Maurício Freire, recounts that when the accused is a police officer, the courts presume that the victim was a criminal and deserved to die. He recalls that there was a police investigator (*delegado*) who had an excellent record in investigating ordinary crime,

> but when there was a death caused by an extermination group [with likely police involvement] he always said, "But *doutor*, the one who died was a thief, they're all thieves" ... Why did he say this? Probably because, if he wasn't involved, his colleagues were. If he investigated he would run up against his colleagues, at minimum. So he already had little interest in investigating. (Espinheira 2005: 50–51 [my translation])

A study by Lemos-Nelson shows that members of the Civil Police who kill a suspect are rarely investigated by the internal disciplinary system or the judiciary. She finds that in most Police Action cases the very first step in a judicial investigation, the *inquérito* or police report, is never completed. Since it is the *inquérito* that triggers judicial intervention, these cases do not even reach the prosecutor's office or the courts (Lemos-Nelson 2001).

Finally, evidence from the unsolved crimes unit suggests a high failure rate in police cases as well. Homicide cases that are not solved in the first fifteen days by the local police delegation are devolved to a specialized investigative unit in charge of homicides, the *Delegacia de Homicídios de Salvador*. In October 1998, the investigator in charge of this unit, a person with seven years' experience in that job, estimated that nearly 70 percent of the 1,000 pending cases on file in that *delegacia* involved the Military Police, often in cases that had all the indicia of an execution (de Oliveira, Sousa Ribeiro,

---

[25] The report contains only aggregate numbers, so I do not include these cases in the count of cases included in the sample discussed earlier.

and Zanetti 2000).[26] Of a thousand unsolved homicides, including about 700 cases with some indicia of police involvement, the *delegacia* had only about sixty suspects in custody at that time. Even in the extremely unlikely event that every single one of these suspects was a police officer, that would suggest an arrest rate of less than 10 percent in police cases – and arrests, as we saw, only infrequently translate into convictions. Based on all these measures, then, we can only conclude that policemen who kill enjoy nearly complete impunity in Salvador, with a conviction rate lower even than São Paulo's.

2. Legal Inequality

As noted, we cannot stop with an examination of the background level of effectiveness of a particular legal system. In the first place, for any individual within that system, the question is never the average response, but the particular response – how, exactly, is the system likely to respond to *my* claim, given *my* characteristics and resources? What determines the effectiveness of rights for a given individual in a given place, then, is the background level of response, as conditioned by the tolls that affect that individual, the markers of inequality. Moreover, one of the defining elements of the rule of law is the universal application of rules (Raz 1979; O'Donnell 1999; Holmes 2003), and therefore inequality in the application of the law is itself a problem for the rule of law, regardless of the average levels of performance of the system. What follows, then, is an examination of the kinds and extent of inequalities within each legal system. Where the data permit, these inequalities are measured numerically. Where the cases are fewer, in Uruguay and Salvador, a more detailed description of individual cases illustrates the differential treatment, if any, afforded to different claimants.

The case of Ismael Gamarra most clearly suggests the absence of socioeconomic and political biases in these prosecutions in Uruguay. Gamarra was forty-one years old at the time of his death.[27] He was widely known in the border town of Rivera to be a cattle rustler working both sides of the border with Brazil, and he had a police record that included prison time for

---

[26] The president of the Military Police Corporals' and Privates' Union of Bahia suggested that the figure could well rise above 70% (de Oliveira, Sousa Ribeiro, and Zanetti 2000). He defended his colleagues only by pointing out their lack of preparation and resources and arguing that the *Polícia Civil* committed just as many crimes.

[27] This account is taken from those appearing in *El País*, Uruguay's leading daily, and in reports published by the Peace and Justice Service of Uruguay (Servicio Paz y Justicia, known as SERPAJ).

killing a Brazilian police officer on the Uruguayan side of the border. He was also known to carry a weapon and believed by some to have occasional illegal dealings with the police arising out of his smuggling activities. In August 1996 the police announced that he had been killed in the course of an armed confrontation that had not been witnessed by anyone other than the policemen involved. A gun attributed to Gamarra was recovered at the scene. Far from outrage, the general feeling in the town of Rivera was that he had met his just deserts. With no witnesses and no public outrage to fuel aggressive judicial intervention, the case was ripe for a perfunctory dismissal on the basis of the police account of events.

Nevertheless, Gamarra's mother insisted that he had been murdered by the police to settle accounts, and she hired a young lawyer to talk to the prosecutor and the judge. Prompted by this one demand, the judge and the prosecutor decided to take a closer look at the events leading to Gamarra's death and carried out an extensive investigation, including a re-enactment of the crime. Digging up indirect witnesses and performing forensic tests on the weapon Gamarra had allegedly used in the exchange of gunfire, they concluded that the police version did not square with the evidence. Instead, the court determined that Gamarra had been ambushed by the police and that he had been brought down in a hail of automatic rifle fire when he turned his horse to flee. Moreover, the additional investigation uncovered witnesses who suggested that the *Comisario* (the head of the local police station) had been looking for Gamarra for days, perhaps to settle accounts relating to illegal dealings.

This aggressive investigation ultimately yielded a positive result. Three policemen were indicted in connection with the murder: the *Comisario* who commanded the raid, one officer, and one lower level policeman. The first two were charged with aiding and abetting, the latter with the actual murder. While state action was not completely spontaneous, as Gamarra's mother had to resort to a lawyer to trigger the investigation, it is noteworthy that a case with these characteristics was treated so aggressively. This is especially true since the investigation targeted the local police hierarchy, upon which the judge and the prosecutor surely depended for ordinary criminal investigations. Moreover, while the case was pending it became clear that town opinion was sharply divided on whether a prosecution should proceed. Local landowners in particular were opposed to the prosecution, defending the actions of the police. And yet the prosecution succeeded when the judge and prosecutor took out-of-the-ordinary measures to go well beyond the carefully packaged police version of events. Just how surprising this is will become clear in contrast to investigations in places like Buenos Aires, Córdoba, São Paulo, and Salvador.

Nor is this, for Uruguay, an isolated incident of judicial and prosecutorial activism. The case of Eduardo Albín is similar in that the victim was a socially marginal character and the prosecution was opposed by local economic elites, although Albín had no history of violence and his death prompted several strong popular protests. Albín was known as a *bagayero*, someone who sells often pirated name-brand merchandise or other cheap goods imported illegally into the country. On October 6, 1998, near the town of Salto, he was a passenger in a car that was coming from the Brazilian border when they were intercepted by an anti-smuggling police operation. Because they were carrying illegal merchandise, the driver turned the car and fled, while the police gave chase. At one point the smugglers attempted to lose their pursuers by entering a ranch that borders the road. Albín got out of the car to open the gate. His companion drove through, and Albín was shot and killed as he closed the gate.

Initial press reports carried only the police version. The driver, they said, had escaped in order to destroy the merchandise, leaving Albín behind, so that only the police had direct knowledge of the events. Citing police accounts, the newspapers reported that Albín had shot at the police several times with a .38-caliber pistol, recovered at the scene. A bullet hole in the jacket of one of the officers and another in the side-view mirror of the police car appeared to seal the matter. *El País* also reported negatively on the demonstrations staged by hundreds of *bagayeros* and their relatives, who insisted that Albín had been murdered while unarmed. The newspaper coverage explicitly noted the vagueness of the information on which demonstrators relied, and the fact that no one could provide specific evidence of wrongdoing on the part of the police. When the policemen's release pending the investigation prompted more demonstrations, the headlines again focused on the violence of the demonstrators rather than on any possible wrongdoing by the police.

Over the next ten months, however, the judge and prosecutor conducted what was described as an intensive investigation, sometimes accompanied by small demonstrations on behalf of the victim. Almost exactly one year later, the judge concluded that the victim had been unarmed, no shootout had taken place, and the police officers at the scene had planted the gun and shot holes in their own car and clothing. The prosecutor requested that the judge indict four members of the police force on a charge of intentional homicide. To the prosecutor's disappointment, the judge indicted one police officer for a non-intentional killing and two others for *encubrimiento* (obstruction of justice).

Clearly the judicial response in this case is less severe than the response in the Gamarra case. But so are the facts. This case involves a single, possibly accidental, shot in the leg that angled upward bizarrely to cause the death. Moreover, the incident came at the end of a car chase, rather than in an ambush with a fusillade of shots in the back of a fleeing victim. In the final analysis, the court chose a middle course, neither taking the police version uncritically, although there was plenty of opportunity to do so, nor simply responding to popular pressure, brought by the *bagayero* informal association, to throw the book at the police.

In these two cases, the key actors are the judges and prosecutors. In both, it would have been easiest simply to accept the police version, since there was plenty of support for the conclusion that the victims had provoked their own deaths by armed resistance to legitimate policing activity. There was also resistance to the prosecution by local economic elites: Gamarra's killers were championed by wealthy local landowners who disliked his cattle rustling, while Albín's supporters were strongly criticized by Salto's formal merchants, who believed the smuggling activity hurt their businesses. While there was some intervention by interested parties to pressure the legal system to prosecute the cases effectively, in both cases supporters of the prosecution are marginal social actors – in one the mother of an acknowledged criminal, in the other a group of participants in the informal economy. Even in the face of these factors, however, the judge and the prosecutor in each case chose the harder course, taking the time and the resources to personally conduct a careful investigation and ultimately to charge the police with exceeding the legitimate use of force. This performance would seem to warrant a positive evaluation of the Uruguayan criminal justice system's propensity to pursue police misconduct.

The inconclusive results in two high-profile cases, however, have succeeded in coloring some observers' perception of judicial effectiveness in Uruguay. One of these is the case known as "Hospital Filtro" and the other is the Berríos case. The Hospital Filtro case arose out of a violently repressed demonstration in support of a group of Basque separatists. The separatists, Spanish citizens who were being deported, were convalescing in the Filtro hospital after a long hunger strike. The demonstrators surrounded the hospital in an effort to prevent the police from driving the deportees away. The incident occurred as the police caravan ran directly into the densest part of the crowd, avoiding an easy alternate route. In the confusion, one demonstrator was shot to death and several others were wounded by police shotguns. When it occurred, in August 1994, the televised events shocked Uruguayan society, which values its freedom of expression and interpreted the actions of the police at the demonstration as a deliberate provocation. The individual police officer who shot and killed Fernando Morroni with a shotgun blast to the back was never identified, although people associated with the case have little doubt that his or her companions and supervisors could do so if they truly wanted to.[28]

After three years of investigation, two officers directly responsible for overseeing the crowd control efforts were convicted for failing to properly supervise the police operation and failing to prevent the killing. Three others were acquitted. The two convicted officers received one- and two-year sentences, respectively, which were subsequently suspended. The lawyer who represented Morroni's family argued that no one was punished for killing Morroni and that the supervisors' sentences were deeply unsatisfactory, as they focus on technical violations of police duties. The public feeling about this case was that the justice system ultimately failed to produce justice, for reasons that will become even more familiar as we look at the other countries: witnesses were fearful of the police, the prosecutor was not cooperative, and the police failed to identify the individual shooter.

The resolution of the case was disappointing overall, but the judge's performance was one positive aspect of an otherwise weak judicial action. The judge was the main force behind the convictions, writing a strong opinion that criticized the manner in which the police repression was conducted and highlighted the obstructions of the investigation by the police. Even Ariela Peralta, the lawyer who expressed deep disappointment with the results, praised the judge. While criticizing the prosecutor's performance, she noted that the judge had permitted the claimants broad input and participation in the case, despite the fact that there is no legal provision in Uruguay for such participation. She noted that the failure of justice was due to the inability to penetrate the wall of silence put up by the police, rather than a failure of the judge to take the case seriously. The failure here, then, was clearly an informational failure resulting from an informational disadvantage.

The Berríos case is the second high visibility case with a negative result. Eugenio Berríos was a former officer in Chilean dictator Augusto Pinochet's secret police. He went into hiding in Uruguay in 1991 with the apparent assistance of Chilean and Uruguayan military personnel, to avoid testifying in the Letelier case.[29] There is evidence that once in Uruguay he remained in military custody, although there has been no official acknowledgment of that fact. In November 1992, Berríos appeared at a police station, claiming to

---

[28] Interview with Ariela Peralta, attorney for Servicio Paz y Justicia (SERPAJ), a human rights NGO, Montevideo, December 2000.

[29] This case involves the investigation of the murder by Pinochet's secret police of an opposition Chilean diplomat, Orlando Letelier, and his assistant, Ronnie Moffit, in Washington, D.C., in the 1970s.

have been kidnapped and requesting some sort of protection. The police nevertheless released him back to two military officials. That is the last trace of him until about eight months later, when his long-buried body was found on a beach near the capital, with two bullets to the head. Suspicion focused on the police, military, and intelligence services of Uruguay and Chile. The former were obvious suspects because they were the last to see him alive and failed to protect him; the latter were presumed to be involved because of Berríos's connection to Chilean military secrets. Nothing, however, has ever been proven in the case, despite cooperation with Chilean investigators and a considerable forensic effort.

The Berríos and Hospital Filtro cases, together with the failure to prosecute rights violations committed during the Uruguayan dictatorship of the 1970s and early 1980s, complete the triad that is sometimes cited as an example of the inability of the Uruguayan justice system to penetrate the wall of impunity that surrounds the military and the police. These cases led Amnesty International, for example, to say in a 1996 report on human rights in Uruguay that "the vast majority of human rights violations committed in past years remained uninvestigated." This appearance of an ineffective Uruguay justice system is misleading, however, based as it is on these highly publicized but unrepresentative cases. While certainly the outcomes in these signal cases were less than satisfactory, in fact the routine cases in Uruguay are well handled and produce strong results.

Of these routine cases, in only five did the killers go unpunished: the two cases of Berríos and Morroni, where the killers are unknown; the case of a sixteen year old who waved a toy gun at a policeman; the case of a nurse who was hit by a stray bullet; and the case of two robbers killed after a shootout. Where the perpetrators are known, the acquittals are justified as the legitimate use of force. With the exception of the two robbers, the victims in these cases were middle class. There are no strong patterns associating the characteristics of the victims with judicial outcomes, although, if anything, there are more convictions in cases where the victim is a more marginal member of society – as in the cases of Gamarra or Albín, for example. Nor does the rank of the accused seem to affect the judicial outcome, as mid- and upper-level officers are jailed at least as often as the rank and file, although they appear much less often as suspects in a killing.

In conclusion, it is hard to pinpoint any extra-legal variable that affects judicial outcomes in an important way. Statistical analyses are nonsignificant, but this is likely a consequence of the small number of cases. If anything, the courts seem to go out of their way to conduct a thorough investigation in cases in which the victim was a social outcast and the local economic elites are opposed to the prosecution, as in the Gamarra and Albín cases. Conviction rates are higher in those cases in which the victim was a member of the informal economy or living mostly outside the law. Coupled with the strong participation of judges and prosecutors in these cases, this record demonstrates that the courts in Uruguay compensate for the inequality in the distribution of initial violations, ensuring, insofar as it is within their reach, that those who violate the rights of citizens of all kinds are punished.

In contrast to Uruguay, the number of cases in Buenos Aires and Córdoba allow for reasonable sampling and some statistical analysis. In the interests of efficiency and for easier comparison, I present them together here. Both Córdoba and Buenos Aires show the important effect of the presence of a Private Prosecutor to accompany the judicial investigation, while Córdoba shows a much higher level of socio-economic inequality, despite its higher level of average effectiveness. The following discussion highlights the most salient differences in judicial results between the two locations.

One determinant of judicial outcomes stands out in Buenos Aires, affecting the likelihood of a conviction in Buenos Aires but not in Córdoba: the perceived criminality or dangerousness of the victim. I coded all the cases in my sample according to whether the victim had some association with violent crime.[30] The results for Buenos Aires are compelling: if there is clear evidence that the victim had been involved in a violent crime that presented a serious risk to other members of society, then the victim's killing by the police is not punished even if there is abundant evidence that the case involves an extra-judicial execution carried out long after the threat is over. Of sixteen cases I coded as belonging in this category in the province of Buenos Aires, none led to a conviction. The same is not true in Córdoba, where one of only two cases in this category ended in a conviction.

These cases go unpunished even though they represent some of the most egregious violations: six of the sixteen cases in Buenos Aires are outright

---

[30] I used a dichotomy to classify these cases. In practice, of course, victims may be more or less tainted by a connection with violence, and the evidence of that involvement may be more or less firm. For purposes of this tabulation, I coded as "Violent Victim" cases only those in which there was solid third-party evidence that the victim had a close connection to a violent crime. Since the police attempt to characterize most cases in this manner, I decided not to rely on evidence that came from the police without corroboration. This category may be larger, therefore, than what these figures reflect, and it is possible that some of these cases might have led to a conviction. This informal exception is discussed at length elsewhere (Brinks 2003).

executions of victims who were offering no resistance, and one other is among the clearest cases of the execution of an inmate made to look like a suicide after the fact. In that case, the victim, who was involved in a bank robbery that turned violent, and who was a potential witness to police involvement in the crime, was taken into custody and shortly thereafter found dead in his cell. In short, in Buenos Aires (and, as we shall see, in São Paulo), persons who are perceived as engaging in violent crime essentially forfeit due process rights, earning an automatic death penalty.

Several other variables also strongly influence the outcome. First, the ability to enlist a lawyer who will police the legal process, pressuring the prosecutor and the judge to move the case forward, is almost essential in Buenos Aires and has a strong impact in Córdoba as well.[31] These attorneys, in most cases, have the ability to request certain investigative measures, to present evidence and argue the case in court, and generally to act as a prosecutor would, though of course without the backing of a governmental office. The conviction rates triple and quadruple in Buenos Aires and Córdoba, respectively, over cases that only summon individual mobilization in the form of a Private Prosecutor. Second, if the case also prompts popular demonstrations, it becomes much more likely to end in a conviction. Table 2.2[32] presents the impact of Private Prosecutors and demonstrations on the likelihood of a conviction in Police Action cases in each of these two cities.[33]

---

[31] All the jurisdictions in this study permit persons with an interest in the case to be joined as parties to the prosecution, although with prerogatives that vary somewhat from place to place and from time to time. These prerogatives are discussed in more detail in the context of the Codes of Criminal Procedure for each location.

[32] In each category, in Córdoba, Buenos Aires, and São Paulo, there are some cases with missing data. Since in many cases the information used to classify the victims – by race, or class, or type of neighborhood, for example – comes from court documents, cases that were not dismissed early on generate more information. The result is that whenever I exclude cases with missing data the average conviction rate is higher. Thus, the results are biased upward, and the conclusions about the extent of the failure of the system are conservative. This also explains the change in average conviction rates, depending on the variables included in the analysis.

[33] I discuss only the combined effect of a Private Prosecutor with popular demonstrations because the two go hand in hand in both locations. While there are many cases in which a Private Prosecutor is present but that do not include demonstrations, there are none in which we find demonstrations in the absence of a Private Prosecutor in Buenos Aires, and only 2 in Córdoba. For Buenos Aires, 50 cases with demonstrations showed the presence of a Private Prosecutor, while none of the 45 cases without a Private Prosecutor involved demonstrations. The other 20 cases with demonstrations were missing data on the presence of a Private Prosecutor. Given the general pattern, I imputed the presence of the Private Prosecutor from the presence of demonstrations. The results are similar but somewhat attenuated if we base the analysis on only the 50 cases that have complete information.

TABLE 2.2. *Impact of Private and Popular Mobilization on Conviction Rates in Buenos Aires and Córdoba.*

| | No Private Prosecutor | Private Prosecutor | | |
	No Popular Demonstrations	No Popular Demonstrations	Popular Demonstrations	Average (total *n*)
Buenos Aires	7.69% (*n* = 39)	15.63% (*n* = 32)	43.75% (*n* = 64)	26.67% (*n* = 135)
Córdoba	4.55% (*n* = 22)	20% (*n* = 10)	79.31% (*n* = 29)	41.27% (*n* = 61)

In 2×3 tables run separately for each location, the chi^2 for the difference in conviction rates across these categories is significant with $p. < .001$.

TABLE 2.3. *Conviction Rates by Socio-Economic Condition in Police Action Cases in Córdoba and Buenos Aires.*

	Lower and Lower Working Class	All Others	Average	Significance
Buenos Aires	25% (*n* = 100)	44.44% (*n* = 27)	29.13% (total *n* = 127)	chi^2 = 3.89 p = .048
Córdoba	32.56% (*n* = 43)	78.95% (*n* = 19)	46.77% (total *n* = 62)	chi^2 = 11.39 p = .001

Class affects outcomes more strongly in Córdoba that in Buenos Aires, as we see in Table 2.3. In Buenos Aires the conviction rate is indeed lower in cases affecting victims from the more popular classes, but in Córdoba the difference is even more marked, with a conviction rate that is two and a half times higher when a more affluent victim is involved.

In summary, justice in Córdoba is more effective as a general rule, but socio-economic tolls are much more important than in other places. In fact, middle-class victims and those with private support (in the form of a lawyer) and public support (in the form of demonstrations) see conviction rates there rise to levels not seen for any other group in any other system. For members of the popular classes, however, the courts here offer little more comfort than the courts in Buenos Aires – the difference in conviction rates for poor victims across these two systems is only 7 percent. In other words, the poor in Buenos Aires and Córdoba suffer from similar levels of legal poverty, to use O'Donnell's term, despite the higher quality Córdoba courts, and despite the fact that for the middle class the Córdoba courts are highly responsive.

In Buenos Aires, then, the socio-economic condition of the victim affects the outcome to a lesser degree, but private legal support to supplement the state's prosecution doubles the conviction rate. And when we add public support in the form of demonstrations to put pressure on judges and prosecutors, the conviction rate rises threefold over that. In addition, a victim's connection to violent crime is fatal to the chances of a successful prosecution in Buenos Aires. In contrast to Córdoba, then, the most important tolls in Buenos Aires are not economic. Instead, the process appears to require a relatively blameless victim, political mobilization, and a privately supplied prosecutor, suggesting a keen sensitivity to politics and indicating that the prosecutor's office is not adequately performing its function.

These results mesh with the experience of lawyers who practice in this area. In interviews with practicing lawyers, especially with lawyers who represent victims' families, a recurring theme is the importance attributed to their own participation as attorneys acting alongside the prosecutors and to the popular demonstrations they sometimes help organize. Moreover, this experience strongly supports the intuition depicted in Figures 1.3 and 1.4, showing the impact of endogenous factors on actors' preferences in these cases.

In São Paulo, as in Córdoba and Buenos Aires, I undertake a series of bivariate analyses to identify the effect of various factors on the likelihood of a conviction in police actions. Perhaps the most surprising result is the lack of significance of race in the courts. As we saw, race clearly plays a role in the selection of victims, but once the case reaches the courts, the treatment becomes more equal. In cases for which I have racial information, the conviction rate in cases involving white victims is 8 percent while for black victims it is 11 percent. The difference is not, however, statistically significant. The courts themselves, then, are less sensitive to the color of the victim than the police are in choosing their victims.[34] The victim's gender is similarly non-significant at this stage.

Class may well affect outcomes, but from this sample it is difficult to be certain just how much. There are five middle-class victims in the entire São Paulo sample, or a little over 2 percent. Four of these were innocent bystanders, not the target of police action at all. None of the innocent bystander cases led to a conviction, regardless of class. The single case involving a member of

---

[34] While these results run counter to popular perceptions of justice in Brazil, they are consistent with those of other studies carried out on the effect of race in the justice system. Fischer, for example, finds that class is a predictor of outcomes in murder prosecutions in Rio de Janeiro criminal courts, but not race (Fischer 2004), and Sadek et al. (2000) find race similarly non-significant in prosecutions for property crimes in São Paulo. Adorno (1995), however, comes to the opposite conclusion.

the middle class who was killed in a routine police action led to an acquittal. That leaves the two lowest classes, which are abundantly represented. If I isolate the most marginal of the victims – unemployed *favelados*, and those with a primary education or less – the conviction rate is considerably lower than it is for members of the lower working class (6% vs. 16%), although the chi² for a 2×2 table does not attain the .05 significance level. What is most striking about the socio-economic differences, however, is not so much the difference in conviction rates as the vast over-representation of the poorest sectors of society in the sample, a theme that was addressed earlier in this chapter. Almost 85 percent of the victims in the sample come from shantytowns and have less than a primary education, representing the most underprivileged residents of São Paulo. The rest are members of the lower working classes.

Calculating the impact of a victim's being from a shantytown is difficult because of the large amount of missing data and the fact that the data are not missing at random. The longer a case is in the legal system, the more information the case generates *and* the more likely a conviction. The conviction rate for cases in which the type of residence of the victim is unknown is just over 2%, while cases that have that information, regardless of where the victim lived, achieve more than a 15% conviction rate (chi² significant beyond the .001 level). If living in a shantytown is a legal disadvantage, therefore, *favelados* will be more likely to fail in their efforts to use the legal system and consequently more likely to fall into the missing data category. The conviction rate for all cases involving shantytown residents, therefore, is likely to be much lower than it appears when I calculate it using cases with complete information. Even among the selective sample for which I have information, however, the conviction rate for police officers who kill *favelados* is one-third lower (13.8% vs. 18.2%) than for those who kill people who are merely poor, although the chi² remains non-significant.

As in Buenos Aires, if the victim in São Paulo is classified as a violent criminal, the prosecution of the killer will fail: of the 78 cases in which the victim was so classified, none led to a conviction. But in São Paulo, criminality, even of a lesser degree, matters more. In fact, a pristine record on the part of the victim is almost a prerequisite for the conviction of his or her killer: only 2 of the 151 cases in which the victims had a criminal record of some kind (1.3%) ended in a conviction. As in Argentina, victims' survivors may legally retain an attorney to accompany the prosecution and participate in the trial. Despite the presence of a well-regarded public prosecutor (Bastos Arantes 2002; Sadek and Cavalcanti 2003), hiring a Private Prosecutor may be a necessary if not sufficient condition for a successful prosecution. In 33 out of 196 cases, the victim's family retained a private attorney to accompany the case. All but one of the eleven convictions in São Paulo are taken from these 33 cases, resulting in a conviction rate of almost 33 percent compared to less than one percent in cases without a Private Prosecutor. Despite its high performance in other areas, the vaunted Ministério Publico does not appear to work so well in this area, as claimants need to engage a private attorney if they wish to have any chance at all of a conviction.

In short, not only is the overall level of violations very high in São Paulo, it is also tightly targeted to the underprivileged. Members of the middle class, for example, need only fear being shot by mistake, and that is a rare event compared to Buenos Aires. The courts, on the other hand, are more equitable on most counts but very ineffective overall in Police Actions. Race, perhaps surprisingly, is *not* a factor in judicial outcomes for this sample of cases although, since Afro-Brazilians are disproportionately included in the victim population, they disproportionately suffer the (general) failure of the courts. Gender does not matter either. The victim's class and residence in a *favela*, as opposed to an ordinary neighborhood, seems to play a role, although there are significant data issues, and the difference is only significant at the .07 level. There is more impunity for the killing of twenty-somethings than for younger and older victims. And victims with a criminal record are truly unprotected – the conviction rate in these cases is a mere 1.3%. Finally, with a single exception, convictions take place only in cases in which relatives of the victim engaged an attorney to accompany the prosecution. The conviction rate for this group is about 33%, which is the highest of any identifiable group in the São Paulo sample.

What we know about police homicides in Salvador suggests that the incidence of violations is even higher, and judicial results are worse, than in São Paulo. Even well-documented high-profile cases in Salvador are marked by nearly complete impunity. In interviews and conversations with activists, the case of Heloísa Gomes dos Santos and her partner, Manuel Ferreira dos Santos, is often mentioned. Manuel was a former Military Police corporal. His son Valdemir dos Santos was killed for refusing to comply with an attempted extortion by a group of Military Police officers. Heloísa and Manuel appear to have brought all the necessary resources to the table as they pushed for an investigation and prosecution of the murder. They were (lower) middle class and employed. They carried out a very public campaign, bringing their complaints to the media, testifying before the legislature, joining various human rights organizations, even speaking to federal legislators. They identified by name the persons they thought were responsible for the murder – Eliomar Nascimento Machado, Antônio Fernando Barbosa Rodrigues, Luiz

Sérgio Lopes Sampaio, Paulo Roberto Conceição Terra Nova, and Edson Soares dos Santos. Heloísa in particular became a very public figure. In short, they marshaled considerable personal and political resources.

Soon after they began their campaign, Heloísa and Manuel received several death threats. On June 21, 1998, they were shot to death as they sat in their car in front of the hospital where Heloísa worked as a nurse. Since then, two other witnesses against these same policemen have been murdered, another has disappeared and is presumed murdered, and one is in hiding under the auspices of Bahia's witness protection program. There have been no convictions in connection with the murder of Manuel's son, the murder of Heloísa and Manuel, or the murder of the other three witnesses.

Another case of considerable prominence is the case of Robélio Lima dos Santos. On October 11, 1999, Robélio was apprehended after he and three others committed a bank robbery that resulted in one police officer being seriously wounded. Robélio was photographed by the press as he was handcuffed and placed in the back of a police wagon. In the photograph, taken from no more than six feet away, one can clearly see that he has only one wound in the pelvic region. Some time later he arrived at the Emergency Room of the local hospital. He was dead, shot in the chest with at least two different weapons. The four police officers who were in the car when Robélio was murdered were initially arrested for the killing. Despite the intervention of a United Nations rapporteur in 2001 (Jahangir 2001), these police officers have been released and at last check in 2003, no convictions had resulted.

A more ordinary case, one that received considerably less media attention, is the case of Sérgio Silva Santos, a physically handicapped youth who lived in one of the *favelas* around Salvador. On January 22, 1999, five police officers on midnight rounds decided to question a group of men standing around a street-side vending post. One of the police officers had drawn his gun as he approached the men, and he accidentally fired a shot, wounding Sérgio in the neck. The five loaded Sérgio in the police car, took him to a remote region, briefly debated what they should do, and executed him. Then they placed a gun in Sérgio's hand and prepared a report that said he had died in an exchange of gunfire with the police.

Eventually, confronted with the witnesses to the initial wounding, the victim's physical disability, and other damning evidence, one of the five disclosed what had actually happened and testified to the entire sequence of events. Despite all this, four years later the five were still employed by the police, remained free, and had not been convicted of anything. The judge's office reports that the difficulty in moving forward with the case lies in locating the witnesses to the initial event. This should come as no surprise, as on April

16, 2000, we read that "one of the main witnesses in the killing of the physically handicapped Sérgio Silva Santos...was beaten to death in Nordeste de Amaralina, the neighborhood where he lived" (*A Tarde*, April 16, 2000, p. 7).

There are many more stories like these, including the cases of no fewer than ten journalists who were killed in Bahia during the 1990s. The main Salvador daily, *A Tarde*, carried out an extensive investigation into these ten cases and was able to secure the names of suspects in every case, noting that politicians working with police officers were often the principal suspects. The daily concluded that "in traveling through the eight cities in which the crimes occurred, *A Tarde*'s reporting verified – in only 7 days of investigation – that the criminals enjoy impunity purely as a result of the omissions of the Courts and the Civil Police. There are witnesses and proofs for each of these crimes" (*A Tarde*, April 2, 2000).

Information from CEDECA follows the same pattern, with a possible exception for children.[35] CEDECA does not systematically track all cases of violence against children but rather selects particularly egregious cases involving poor children from marginal neighborhoods, and attempts to pressure the legal system to respond effectively in these cases. Their goal is to secure some exemplary convictions so that they can begin to change the perception and reality of impunity. The result is not a representative sampling of all cases of police homicides in Salvador. The sample involves a special class, children from poor neighborhoods, and the cases were selected for their shock value. In addition, these cases get special attention from an NGO and a specialized subset of the justice system.

Before the creation of a specialized juvenile justice system, police killings of children and adolescents were an open secret in Salvador. Many of the killings fit the mold of the so-called *grupos de extermínio* – a kind of social cleansing, carried out by or with the cooperation of the police, against petty criminals or other "undesirable" elements, often at the behest of small merchants. In 1992, for example, a group of Military Police officers had a confrontation in Liberdade, a peripheral neighborhood of Salvador, with a band of youth that apparently engaged in petty crime. The next day the police officers returned, out of uniform, and picked up two children they suspected of belonging to the gang. One day later, the parents found their children's bodies, savagely mutilated. The parents knew who had picked up the children,

---

[35] The following discussion of violence against children is based on a personal interview with Dr. Waldemar Oliveira, director, CEDECA, Salvador, Bahia, May 15, 2001, and on documents he provided (on file with the author).

and they were identified and charged with the crime. But the file on the case mysteriously disappeared from the court records, and the case has gone nowhere in ten years.

In another case, in 1991, a child from one of the *invasões* or shantytowns around Salvador tried to beg a ride from a bus driver. The driver refused to let him on, and as he drove away, the child threw a stone, hitting the bus on the side. The bus stopped, a policeman descended with his gun drawn and shot the child in the back as he ran away. This case never even triggered a formal investigation by the prosecutor's office and did not make it into the courts at all. In 1992, another policeman stabbed a child to death for hitting his dog with a stone. When representatives of CEDECA confronted the investigator in charge for his failure to open a formal inquiry, his only response was "when are people like CEDECA going to establish a center for the defense of the police?"[36]

The stories are chilling for many reasons, particularly because so many of the killings were almost casual, perpetrators did very little to hide their participation, the justice system did not investigate them, as noted earlier, and few if any are ever punished for these crimes. So far, then, Salvador's system demonstrates almost complete ineffectiveness. But the legal apparatus that attended these crimes in Bahia was reformed after the passage in 1990 of the federal juvenile justice statute, the Child and Adolescent Law (*Estatuto da Criança e do Adolescente*). This reform created the Specialized Childhood and Adolescent Criminal Division (*Vara Criminal Especializada da Infância e da Juventude*), a juvenile justice system that acts in the prosecution of crimes by or against minors. The investigators, prosecutors, and judges in this system work only in cases involving youth. They are supposed to be called in as soon as a child or adolescent comes into custody.

According to the director of CEDECA, since cases began to be processed by the new system, beginning around 1992 or so, there has been a marked difference in the way child homicides are treated. Whereas before it was difficult to find a police investigator, prosecutor, or judge who might show even a minimal interest in prosecuting violence against children, now the prosecutors and judges, who deal only with cases involving children, are much more aggressive. Today, a specialized investigative office (*delegacia*) opens formal inquiries in all reported cases. They are somewhat slow, they do not have a great deal of resources, the formal *inquéritos* often have errors, but at least they are done, and in good faith, according to CEDECA's director. Similarly, one of the two judges in this system noted many changes in the

---

[36] Interview with Dr. Waldemar Oliveira, director, CEDECA, Salvador, Bahia, May 15, 2001.

treatment of minors since the early 1990s, all of which permit monitoring children's safety from the time they come in contact with law enforcement.

As the system has become more aggressive in protecting the rights of children, a new problem has come to the fore. Since the police can no longer count on the benign neglect of the justice system, the rate of threats and violence against complainants and witnesses has vastly increased. Now, CEDECA's director reports, relatives of the victims come into his office in the initial days after the event, impelled by anger and grief at the harm to or loss of a child, asking the center to take some action to ensure that the perpetrators are held accountable. But often they call back some days later to withdraw the complaint, citing threats of violence against them if they persist: "His father has three other children to raise," said a mother recently. "Even the judge is afraid. We will trust divine justice; they will be punished there." Witnesses also cease cooperating with prosecutors and withdraw statements made initially about police participation in the crime. In short, those involved close down the flow of essential information to the system, preventing it from effectively prosecuting cases.

At the judicial stage in Salvador, then, nearly complete impunity marks a system with low effectiveness, and the fact that the system appears to fail for everyone from bank robbers to nurses suggests low levels of inequality as well. It now appears that children can command a more assertive reaction from the legal system, so perhaps we could identify them as a relatively more favored group, sharing in the benefits that accrue to "innocent" victims. At the same time, as we saw, a high level of secondary violence against complainants and witnesses keeps the level of effectiveness low even in these cases. One other group of cases that appears to have fared somewhat better, and will be discussed in more detail in the chapter on Salvador, comprises those cases in which key witnesses entered into the Bahian witness protection program. With these limited exceptions, it appears that the courts in Salvador do not contribute much to the level of effectiveness of personal integrity rights.

D. THE LIKELIHOOD OF A CONVICTION ACROSS AND WITHIN JURISDICTIONS

The challenge in reviewing all these disparate pieces of information about all these different systems is to put them in conversation with each other. In this section I summarize the findings on judicial effectiveness and legal inequality, placing all the systems in comparative perspective. Figure 2.4 presents the average conviction rate and the distance that separates the conviction rates

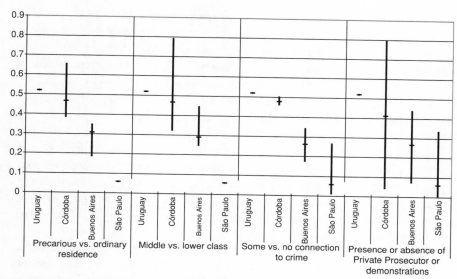

FIGURE 2.4. Conviction rates for various groups in Buenos Aires, Córdoba, São Paulo, and Uruguay. (In São Paulo there were no demonstrations. In that case, what is shown is the impact of retaining an attorney to accompany the prosecution. In Uruguay, conversely, there are no Private Prosecutors, and the graph indicates that demonstrations had no significant effect on outcomes.)

for various favored groups from the conviction rate for disfavored groups.[37] The vertical line connects the average conviction rate for persons in the favored category (e.g., those who do not live in a shantytown) with the conviction rate for persons in the disfavored category. The small horizontal line indicates the average conviction rate in that location. The longer the line, then, the more legal inequality there is associated with these extra-legal traits.[38]

By comparing the average conviction rate to the conviction rates for members of each group, we can also see whether members of a particular group are relatively rare in the sample of victims. If the vast majority of victims have the unfavorable trait (as is generally the case because they are also more often selected for the initial violation), then the conviction rate for these observations will be close to the sample average. Conversely, since the more favored groups are generally under-represented in the victim pool, the

[37] As before, Salvador is excluded from this calculation and the results are discussed separately.
[38] Where the differences are not statistically significant, as discussed earlier in this chapter, the value is left at the average for all groups. Where a group is as a practical matter missing, as middle-class victims are in São Paulo, the value is also left at the average.

conviction rate in their cases will be far from the average. The greater this imbalance (i.e., the closer to the bottom the small horizontal line), the more closely the poor performance of the system represents the ordinary experience of the average user of the system, while the positive response for a favored user becomes a more and more exceptional event.

If we simply look at the average conviction rates, as we did at the opening of this chapter, we find considerable variation, ranging from a 52% rate for Uruguay, down to 6% for São Paulo and likely much lower for Salvador, inversely related to the level of violations in each location. When we take certain extra-legal characteristics into account, however, a more nuanced picture emerges. In socio-economic terms, the courts of Buenos Aires are more egalitarian than the courts in Córdoba. Buenos Aires and Córdoba show a higher level of average judicial effectiveness than does São Paulo, but their results are much more unequal.

Córdoba is especially striking in this respect. Those citizens of Córdoba who do *not* live in shantytowns, and especially those who are members of the middle class, can anticipate a higher conviction rate than Uruguayan citizens – as high as 80%. In contrast, their neighbors with fewer resources will experience conviction rates barely exceeding 30%. The courts in Buenos Aires rarely punish police officers unless the case generates popular demonstrations and involves a private lawyer, but when this happens, the conviction rate approaches 50%. Uruguay, as noted, shows no statistically significant differences for individuals in what we might otherwise consider the disfavored classes, suggesting that in this area of the law at least the courts are as effective for those who live on the margins of society as for any others.

The variable with the strongest impact in all jurisdictions except Uruguay is the presence of a private attorney to accompany (or prod, or supplant) the prosecution. Accompanying the prosecution with a Private Prosecutor is virtually a necessity in São Paulo and Córdoba, and very important in Buenos Aires. With no lawyer intervening to prod the courts along, a conviction is 85 times more likely in Uruguay than in São Paulo, and 11 and 7 times more likely in Uruguay than in Córdoba and Buenos Aires, respectively. Indeed, a lower class claimant who cannot find a lawyer appears to be better off in Buenos Aires than in Córdoba. A Uruguayan police officer who kills someone who just committed a crime or had a criminal record is 39 times more likely to go to jail than his counterpart in São Paulo, and 3 times more likely to be convicted than his Buenos Aires colleague. Uruguayan police who kill shantytown dwellers are convicted at a rate 9 times higher than *paulistas*, twice as often as *bonaerenses*, and 20% more often than *cordobeses*. In São Paulo, in what may come as a surprise, the rate of convictions in cases involving white victims is not significantly different than the rate for cases involving Afro-Brazilian victims.

In Salvador, all the indications are that the involvement of third parties is also important, as we see from the cases in which CEDECA or the witness protection program was involved. Even in this sample, however, the conviction rate remains low, certainly not more than São Paulo's 6% and likely much less than that. And, as discussed earlier, observers are unanimous in suggesting that when the police are involved and the perception is that the victim was a *marginal*, impunity is the norm.

In short, demanding the badge number of an abusive police officer is a rational strategy only in Uruguay, although there are some teeth behind the implicit threat in Córdoba as well, as long as the claimant can pay the toll to open legal barriers. Some of these tolls, especially in Buenos Aires and São Paulo, have to do with the political construction of the case and affect the rule that will be applied at the moment of decision: if the case has achieved popular prominence, if the victim is perceived as untainted by crime, then the courts will respond. Others have to do with the legal resources that the advocates for the victim bring to bear. When they can contrive to have a private lawyer accompany the prosecution, the system is vastly more likely to respond, except, again, in Uruguay, where state actors carry the burden without such help.

Still other barriers have to do with economic resources. The most vulnerable members of society – residents of shantytowns, the poor, the unemployed – in Córdoba, Buenos Aires, São Paulo, and Salvador, are not only more frequent targets of violence, they cannot even count on the courts for redress after the fact. For them, democracy truly has not brought an increase in legal protection from the state, and the courts are no restraint on the power of Leviathan. In São Paulo, Salvador, and Buenos Aires, and in the shantytowns and lower class neighborhoods of Córdoba, as Hobbes once said, "Covenants being but words, and breath, have no force to oblige, contain, constrain, or protect any man, but what it has from the publique Sword" (Hobbes 1964 [1651]: 122).

Next, I turn to an examination of the processes that underlie these results, exploring the root causes of legal inequality in each legal system: why some systems – Salvador and São Paulo, most prominently – fail to respond at all; why others – Córdoba, in particular, but also São Paulo and Buenos Aires – rely so heavily on private investments; and why still others – Buenos Aires especially, but also Córdoba – require such a heavy political investment.

3

Informational and Normative Shifts
Across Jurisdictions

In this chapter I present a first-order explanation for the outcomes described in the previous one. In Chapter 1, I argued that to effectively protect a given right, a system must consistently apply the "right" rule to the "right" facts. In the course of interviews and conversations about this project, I often heard people attribute impunity for the police to the routine application by judges of an informal rule that simply gives the police a free hand in executing socially marginalized people (CELS 2004 is one example of this). If this diagnosis is correct, then the first-order explanation for low conviction rates is a repeated normative failure – judges who consistently fail to follow the law. The alternative first-order explanation is that judges are applying the right rule, but the system repeatedly produces an insufficient factual record – what I have called an informational failure. If this second hypothesis is true, then the blame for failure rests primarily with those charged with producing the "right" facts: the investigative police and litigants, including prosecutors, rather than judges. The solution would then be not more legal training for judges, but a more effective and more independent investigative force.

Throughout this book I argue that each system produces its particular pattern of effectiveness and inequality owing to a combination of these two failures. The legal system in Salvador da Bahia fails predominantly because it consistently applies a rule of impunity, producing both low effectiveness and (relatively) low inequality. São Paulo and Córdoba more often show informational failures than normative ones, driven by the resource disparity between victims and the police, and the failure of prosecutors to step into the gap. This results in high levels of inequality that are muted in São Paulo only by the nearly complete absence of middle-class victims. The courts in Buenos Aires, meanwhile, are more exposed to rule shifts in response to political pressures – both for and against a conviction, depending on the circumstances – thus producing moderately low levels of both effectiveness and socio-economic inequality. Uruguay, in relation to police violence cases at least, usually gets both things right, producing high levels of effectiveness and equality.

Even within the same system, however, different kinds of cases may be prone to different kinds of failures. Thus we see the courts carve out a "violent victim" exception to the law in both São Paulo and Buenos Aires. This chapter, therefore, is organized not according to geography, but according to the type of causal processes underlying the results in discrete classes of cases. At the end of the chapter I return to the geographical arrangement to summarize the results for each legal system.

Ultimately, however, this first-order explanation is insufficient. If we stop here, we are left wondering why judges in some systems systematically fail to follow the formal rules, or why judges in other systems are routinely presented with an inadequate factual record. As a result, in subsequent chapters I explore why, in certain systems and certain socio-political contexts but not in others, judges and prosecutors are willing to tolerate violent police conduct. Alternatively, if the problem is not normative but informational, I examine the elements of that legal system or its context that conspire to systematically produce informational failures.

Identifying what sorts of failures predominate in a given legal system is not a simple task. Informal rules, the building blocks of informal institutions, are not flagged by duly observed formalities at the time of their creation and then published for the world to see, and actors who follow informal rules that contradict formal ones do not often advertise that they are consciously flouting the law. As a result, informal rules are easy to confuse with mere empirical regularities (Brinks 2003, 2006; Helmke and Levitsky 2006), which could in turn be the result of repeated informational failures. Moreover, informational failures, by definition, will also be hard to detect. If the decision makers did not have sufficient elements at their disposal to determine that a given case in fact constituted an abuse of force and a violation of the law, then it will perforce be difficult for a researcher to make that determination in every case. The risk here is that the researcher will undercount the failures, just as the enforcement institutions undercount violations.

In this chapter I begin this admittedly difficult task by presenting case studies of individual prosecutions. I supplement these case studies with some analyses of patterns and statistical indicators that suggest the presence of either informational or normative failures.

The case studies serve several functions. First, a close examination of individual prosecutions makes more concrete the theoretical discussion of general concepts, illustrating informational and normative failures in actual prosecutions. Second, the case studies illustrate the processes that underlie the aggregate analyses presented here and in the previous chapter. Third, these case studies provide the foundation for the more detailed second-order explanations that will be presented in individual country chapters. In this way, they serve to connect the discussion of averages and differences with the institutions and structures that produce them. These case studies also serve a less academic function. In the clinical discussion of variables, institutional configurations, exogenous and endogenous incentives, and "cases" it is easy to forget that each of these cases represents a human being. The case studies in this chapter represent at least a small part of the stories of these human beings and those who work to redress the violations they suffered.

A. OPEN AND NOTORIOUS VIOLATIONS

I begin with the more shocking cases, notorious instances in which a rule of impunity dictated the judicial result. Since the hypothesized informal rule in this instance authorizes otherwise illegal practices, I present evidence that the relevant agents of social control, while observing this illegal behavior, fail to punish it. In effect, their conduct suggests that the behavior is normatively appropriate (Brinks 2003, 2006). Moreover, informational failures are primarily attributable to the resistance of one of the parties – in these cases, the police – who controls the system's access to information in order to avoid punishment. But when the rule of impunity is clear and consistently applied, there is little incentive for the police to hinder the production of information, so we should see prosecutions fail despite a relatively free flow of information about potential violations. Finally, while the production of information requires expending resources, a rule that exonerates the police in all or most cases should apply regardless of the legal resources the victims bring to bear, even if they hire private attorneys to supplement the prosecution's efforts.

1. A Nearly Universal Rule of Impunity in Salvador

While the investigative resources of the legal system in Salvador are truly deplorable, the fate of several well-publicized cases argues against an informational failure. The most striking is the case of Robélio Lima dos Santos, already discussed in the previous chapter. Robélio, recall, was photographed as he was taken away in handcuffs by the police, alive and with one pelvic wound. Upon arrival at the Emergency Room, Robélio was dead with multiple wounds. No convictions resulted even though it is clear to everyone that the police executed him while he was handcuffed in the back of the police wagon, on the way to the Emergency Room. The case of Sérgio Silva Santos is similar. Sérgio was first accidentally wounded, then executed to cover up the mistake. One of the participants has described in detail what happened, and yet there have been no convictions. Referring to the ten journalists who were killed in Bahia during the 1990s, the local daily concluded, as noted earlier, that the facts are readily accessible and impunity is purely the result of police and judicial complicity.[1] The lack of results in the presence of abundant information in each of these cases suggests that the formal rule limiting police use of lethal force is simply not enforced.

The failure of the police to hide their actions is itself evidence that they know and rely on this rule. Salvador police are especially casual and open about their killing, so long as it is within the course of their duties, and they appear to expect impunity. Witnesses and the relatives of victims report that police officers accused of a killing openly taunt and intimidate them, to the point that neighbors and family members discourage complainants from going forward, and the complainants themselves desist.[2] In fact, an editorial published at the time of Robélio's killing concludes exactly this: "Policemen do not act as these Bahian ones did if they do not feel protected."[3] The police officers in these cases are acting in accordance with an accepted and established rule of impunity.

The experience of CEDECA in Salvador is the exception that proves the rule. As described in the previous chapter, at the beginning of the 1990s a change in the juvenile justice system upset the expectation that killing street children would go unpunished. Before the change, information about these crimes was freely available. Parents and witnesses could contact CEDECA and complain, and CEDECA could try to publicize the cases without much fear of retaliation. But once it began to look like these children's rights might become more effective, upsetting the conventional balance of power in the streets of Salvador, the police started to take more extreme measures to impede investigations. In regard to child killings, the system converted from normative failures despite the free flow of information to informational failures in the context of normative success: the juvenile justice system would now apply the correct rule but has little opportunity to do so. The end result has been a slight improvement in outcomes but far less than what the advocates of reform had hoped. The precise contours of this apparent rule of impunity will become clearer in the more detailed chapter on Salvador.

[1] *A Tarde*, April 2, 2000.
[2] Interview with Dr. Waldemar Oliveira, director, CEDECA, Salvador, Bahia, May 15, 2001.
[3] *A Tarde*, October 13, 1999. Editorial: "Mais que mil palavras" [Worth a Thousand Words].

TABLE 3.1. *Comparing Conviction Rates in Violent Victim Cases in Buenos Aires, São Paulo, Córdoba, and Uruguay.*

	Conviction Rate (Total N)		
	Violent Victim Cases	All Other Cases	Total
Buenos Aires	0% (16)	26% (256)	24% (272)
São Paulo	0% (70)	11% (149)	7% (219)
Córdoba	50% (2)	44% (90)	44% (92)
Montevideo	80% (10)	30% (20)	47% (30)

2. A "Violent Victim" Exception in Buenos Aires and São Paulo

It should come as no surprise to find that the same legal system treats different cases differently. One such difference became apparent in the course of this study. The comments made by various contacts in São Paulo and Buenos Aires suggested the presence of an effective informal rule that permits the execution of persons perceived to be violent criminals. For ease of reference, I call this the Violent Victim exception.[4] To establish whether this rule existed, I coded all the cases to identify those that would fit within the parameters of the rule and compared judicial outcomes across the categories defined by the rule.

In practice, of course, victims may be more or less tainted by a connection with violence, and the evidence of that involvement may be more or less firm. The rule works more on a sliding scale, in which the level of prosecutorial and judicial resources devoted to a case goes down, producing a lower conviction rate as the cases approach the extreme. For purposes of this analysis, however, I included only clear-cut cases in this category, coding as Violent Victim cases only those in which there were third-party eyewitness reports, criminal records, or extensive news coverage that the victim had had a close connection to a violent crime – essentially kidnapping, armed robbery, or murder. Table 3.1 compares results in these cases to those from all other cases in the database.

In the first two locations there is clear evidence of this informal rule. In Buenos Aires and São Paulo, if the victim was involved at some point

---

4 This section presents research partially reported earlier in Brinks (2003).

in a violent crime that presented a serious risk to society, then the victim's execution by the police is not punished even if it took place after he or she no longer posed a threat. Not coincidentally, after Salvador these are the locations with the highest levels of violent crime. In Uruguay and in Córdoba, on the other hand, there is no evidence that this rule is driving the outcomes. If anything, the Uruguayan system shows a higher conviction rate in Violent Victim cases, although the difference is not statistically significant. In Córdoba there are simply not enough of these cases to ground a conclusion one way or the other.

A closer look at individual cases suggests that this outcome is not the result of an informational failure. The killing of a person believed to have taken up arms against society often goes unpunished whether or not all the information that might be needed to produce a conviction is present. In São Paulo, the case of Regiane Dos Santos makes this point most clearly. In March 1990, Regiane and her husband attempted to rob a home. The police arrived in the middle of the robbery, and she and her husband took the family hostage. In the ensuing exchange of gunfire, the police killed her husband and one of the hostages, a child. When this occurred, Regiane indicated her intent to surrender and turned over her gun to the owner of the house. The police entered the house at the invitation of the owner, took Regiane into the bathroom, and executed her.

The policemen were tried and acquitted in the military courts (before the transfer of jurisdiction to civilian courts, as discussed in the chapter on São Paulo). According to the attorney who represented Regiane's children and mother, the judges blamed Regiane for the death of the hostage and ignored the testimony of the owner of the house who said she had surrendered and relinquished her gun before they took her away to be killed. The civilian court of appeals affirmed the acquittal, demonstrating that this attitude transcends the military justice system.

In Argentina there are several similar cases. The best known is probably the "Villa Ramallo" case. In 1999, the police surrounded and incapacitated a car carrying four people away from a bank robbery. They shot the occupants in the car, executing all but one of them. One of those executed was a robber, but the other two were employees of the bank who had been taken hostage. All three men were killed in identical circumstances, unarmed and defenseless inside the car. Yet the prosecution proceeded (and succeeded) only as to the killing of the two hostages. The execution of the hostage taker, who was at minimum entitled to the benefit of due process, has not been pursued. In a similar case, police corporal Rubén Emir Champonois shot and killed two men in a car who were apparently fleeing a robbery. In the end, it turned out that one of the two was a music teacher, the owner of the car, who had been taken hostage by the other, the robber. Neither of them was threatening the police officer at the time they were shot. After a lengthy account by one of the trial court judges of the moral worthiness of the one and the criminality of the other, the trial court acquitted the corporal on the charges of murdering the robber (on grounds of self-defense), but convicted him of murdering the music teacher.[5]

In the end, in the Champonois case, the appellate court reversed the acquittal, suggesting in its opinion that the trial court had allowed pre-judgments about the "less worthy" victim to carry the day. It is noteworthy that the court of appeals, a court of cassation technically forbidden to re-appraise the evidence, found the trial court's factual conclusions so wanting in evidentiary support that it not only vacated the acquittal but convicted the defendant outright. It is also noteworthy that the reversal came over the vigorous dissent of one member of the appellate panel, who suggested that this was simply another instance in which the courts, bowing to public pressure, convict police officers regardless of the facts and the law.[6] Clearly, the results we have already seen suggest that this is not as frequent an event as this judge suggested. But this evaluation by a member of the judiciary is perfectly consistent with my conclusion that in Buenos Aires the rule of decision in a given case depends as much on the political construction of the case as on its legal characteristics.

In the final instance, the problem in these cases is that neither prosecutors, nor judges, nor juries (in São Paulo) are prepared to convict a police officer when they deem that the victim has, by taking up arms against society, placed himself or herself outside the social contract.[7] In these cases, it appears, legal decision makers simply look the other way if there is any evidence that might suggest a conviction is legally required. The main difficulty, then, in Violent

---

[5] Transcript of the verdict of the Criminal Court of San Isidro, September 5, 2003, in case No. 9193, against Rubén Emir Champonois (on file with the author).

[6] Transcript of the decision in case No. 15231 of the Court of Criminal Cassation (Corte de Casación Penal) of the province of Buenos Aires, on appeal by the prosecution from case No. 9193 against Rubén Emir Champonois (on file with the author). Both of these rulings come well after the time period of this study, but at the trial level at least they perfectly illustrate the process to which I am referring. The reaction of the court of appeals suggests not all judges share this view, but attorneys who worked on the case rejected the notion that this one opinion signals a major shift in attitudes across the judiciary. Author interview with attorneys from the police violence section of the Centro de Estudios Legales y Sociales, Buenos Aires, June 23, 2006.

[7] Sérgio Adorno, in a personal conversation with the author, suggested this way of describing the withdrawal of legal protection from those who are aptly labeled *marginais* – outlaws.

Victim cases in São Paulo and Buenos Aires, is the presence of a "competing" informal institution (Helmke and Levitsky 2006): the normative failure of the legal system, which applies an informal norm that is directly contrary to the formal laws that are supposed to determine the outcomes.

B. EFFECTIVE APPLICATION OF THE LAW: NORMATIVE AND INFORMATION-GATHERING SUCCESSES

1. Routine Policing Cases in Uruguay

In the previous chapter I discussed in more detail the investigation and prosecution of various cases in Uruguay to illustrate the lack of impact of socio-economic and other variables. Here I need only briefly review those cases, to emphasize how the information comes together in support of a prosecution. As we will see, even the cases we might have expected to pose the greatest informational challenges – cases in which the events take place far from public view – actually ended in successful prosecutions thanks to the efforts of judges and prosecutors.

The paradigmatic cases are those relating to Albín the alleged smuggler and Gamarra the alleged cattle rustler. In both of these cases, the events took place in isolated locations with few or no direct witnesses, the police resisted the prosecution and corrupted the factual record, and yet the cases led to a conviction. In each of these cases, the judge and prosecutor were not content with the information provided by the police. Rather, they took the investigation into their own hands, going to the scene, undertaking careful reconstructions of the event and then matching that information to the physical evidence, and requiring expert ballistic and other reports. When the information they generated did not match up with the police story, they re-examined the police officers and obtained additional testimony from both participants and circumstantial witnesses. Eventually, on the strength of their own investigation, they convicted the police officers.

The Uruguayan judiciary's investigative record is not perfect, of course. In the Berríos case, for example, the courts remain completely in the dark about what actually happened. So too in the Hospital Filtro case, the judge was unable to penetrate the veil of silence, where the circumstances suggest that fellow rank-and-file police officers protected those who had actually committed the crime. But even in that case the judge proceeded as to those who could be identified, the supervisors who should have prevented the violence. Other cases that failed to end in a conviction do not appear to have done so because of informational failures. For example, the judge acquitted a police officer who killed a minor carrying a toy gun. He concluded that the police officer reasonably (albeit mistakenly) believed he was being threatened. In short, there seems to be considerable evidence that the system in Uruguay is quite proactive in generating the requisite information, and that judges are willing to hold police officers accountable in many if not all the cases in which they kill someone.

2. When an Exception Becomes Formal

In all the systems examined, including Córdoba and Uruguay, the courts typically excuse police officers' actions when they harm third-party bystanders in the course of pursuing suspects. No matter how reckless a police officer may be in using his gun in a crowded area, the courts tend to regard the killing of an innocent bystander as unfortunate but not illegal – what we might call the "collateral damage" doctrine in an extension of the imagery that this is a "war" against crime. The rule is nearly universal. It applies in all the locations studied here, and the judges tend to make no secret of the fact that they are simply exonerating the police officer on this basis. They appeal to legal standards in making their determination, and their statements become part of the jurisprudence of the system. Neither higher courts nor the legislature have objected. In short, this exception is formal, not informal, leaving bystanders quite unprotected in all three countries.

Only in Buenos Aires do I find cases that test the limits of this collateral damage doctrine. I coded the cases to identify those in which the victim was not (apparently) the intended target of the killing. In Buenos Aires, of 37 cases that match this description only 4 (about 11%) have ended in a conviction. Of these four, two arise from the same event, and the other two are unrelated. An examination of the cases suggests a couple of limits. One seems to be that the initial use of force must actually be somewhat defensible, although there are several cases in which the courts exonerate police officers who kill a bystander when they use their guns in a crowded area against a fleeing criminal who is not responding with gunfire. For instance, Martín Porven, a sixteen year old, was shot 12 times when he happened upon a gunfire exchange between a police officer and a security guard and two thieves. Both security agents were convicted of his murder. However, from discussions with some of the attorneys involved in the Porven case, it appears that in this case the youth was intentionally targeted. If so, this is not so much a matter of a stray bullet (or, rather, 12 stray bullets) but of mistaken identity. This case is closer to the extra-judicial execution of an unarmed suspect, who just happened to be a passerby, than to a bystander shooting.

Another conviction resulted from a confrontation between two police officers and several unarmed "suspicious" youths loitering in front of a pizza parlor. In that case, one of the loiterers and Daniel Duarte, who simply happened by at the wrong time, were killed. The last case is that of Juan Suarez, a fourteen-year-old bus passenger, who was killed when a police officer on the same bus shot at an unarmed thief. These last two cases occurred when the police were using firearms against unarmed suspects. From these four cases in Buenos Aires, it appears that the latitude afforded to Argentine police in the use of their weapons in crowded areas, while not unlimited, is very wide.

In São Paulo, of thirteen innocent bystander cases, the only one that ends in a conviction is unrelated to police activity: it occurred when a police officer in a bar fight shot at his opponent and hit another patron. Bystander cases are the only ones in the São Paulo sample in which members of the middle class are among the victims, and the police are still acquitted. For instance, one middle-class woman was killed as she walked in a prosperous shopping area at lunchtime, when a police officer shot at a suspect running down the sidewalk. The case was quickly dismissed on the grounds that the shooter had been in hot pursuit of a criminal.[8]

Clearly, this exception applies regardless of the socio-economic resources of the victim. At the same time, several of my interviewees in both São Paulo and Buenos Aires suggested that this apparently class-blind rule has important implications for inequality. They argued that both the police and the courts consider marginal neighborhoods to be dangerous areas, and that they allow greater leeway for endangering bystanders in these contexts.[9] Thus, they argued, the law undervalues the lives of the poor by turning their neighborhoods into shooting galleries. But in my samples at least there is only some qualified evidence to this effect in São Paulo. The data from Argentina and Uruguay do not confirm this claim.

In São Paulo, eight of thirteen innocent bystanders in the sample were from a shantytown, a far higher percentage than a randomly drawn sample of the population would include, and a higher percentage even than what

---

[8] In the Córdoba and Uruguay data there are only one and two of these cases respectively, and none ends in a conviction.

[9] The result in the 1999 Amadou Diallo case in New York strongly suggests that this is also true in the United States: facially neutral standards permit behavior in areas considered dangerous that would never be permitted in an ordinary middle-class neighborhood. A black man in a dangerous neighborhood pulling a wallet out of his pocket in the vestibule of his apartment creates, in the jury's view, a *reasonable* fear that justifies the use of deadly force. It is hard to imagine this ostensibly neutral standard justifying the shooting of a suburban male standing in the door of his home.

we find in the intentional cases: shantytown residents make up only 20% of routine policing cases and 50% of executions. At the same time, the *only* middle-class people killed by the police were innocent bystanders – in other words, as far as police shootings are concerned, the only risk to a visibly middle-class person is from a stray bullet. And *none* of the cases, whether it involves middle-class victims or not, whether it takes place in a *favela* or on a crowded commercial sidewalk, ends in a conviction. The data thus support the perception that the police are more likely to shoot bystanders from a *favela*, but do not support the claim that this is the result of more lenient treatment by the courts, since the courts are equally lenient in cases involving more affluent areas and victims.

In Buenos Aires, on the other hand, the rule disproportionately affects the middle class. Shantytown residents account for only 2 of 22 cases in this category, while the middle class account for 18 (80%). No other kind of case draws so heavily from the middle class. In short, this is not a rule that either precludes the killing of middle-class victims or that disproportionately affects shantytown residents. If anything, the low incidence of cases affecting residents of the *villas* is more consistent with the observation that the Buenos Aires police rarely enter these places and therefore are less likely to shoot bystanders there.

C. SEE NO EVIL, HEAR NO EVIL, SPEAK NO EVIL: NORMATIVE AND INFORMATIONAL SHIFTS IN BUENOS AIRES

A tendency toward both normative and informational failures in one sense produces the worst combination, since it involves a failure of both requisite conditions for an effective judiciary, and yet it does not necessarily result in the lowest conviction rates. A system that applies extra-legal rules will produce the "correct" result whenever the actual rule applied happens to coincide with the law. As we will see, the judicial system in Buenos Aires is susceptible to normative shifts in response to political, public, or other pressures. Judges apply a strict rule of accountability when these pressures demand it, then relax the rule when police pressures outweigh public pressures for a conviction. As a result, we should expect the performance of the system to fall somewhere in the middle, between a high performing system and one that refuses to convict under any circumstances.[10] Also as a result of

---

[10] For the reasons developed more fully in the Appendix, the Buenos Aires area was treated as one case, even though it encompasses two different jurisdictions: the federal courts of the city of Buenos Aires and the provincial courts of the Conurbano.

this normative unpredictability, we should expect the police to work harder at concealing information about their violations than when a rule of impunity is clearly and predictably applied.

Just how difficult it is to generate trustworthy information about police homicides is evident in Buenos Aires. The most common complaints in connection with these cases in Buenos Aires are that the police doctor the crime scene, corrupt the record, intimidate witnesses, produce false forensic results, and generally hamper the incorporation of accurate and complete information into the legal record. While these claims are sometimes hard to confirm, they are often quite demonstrable, as when a gun found on a victim is later traced to the *comisario* in charge of the operation (the case of Luis Selaye) or when neighbors observe the body being removed from the trunk of a police car and placed at the location where the confrontation supposedly took place (the case of Gustavo Gallorini).

I entered markers in my database in all those cases in which court records or advocates for the victim provided detailed and specific allegations of informational tampering. According to these sources, the police in Buenos Aires added a gun to the crime scene in nearly 20% of all Routine Policing cases in my sample and in 55% of the cases in which the victim was simply executed, a situation that is under greater police control than when the police shoot a fleeing suspect or a demonstrator, for example. Similarly, the police staged a confrontation after the fact, by moving the body, shooting into the air or at their own cars, placing a gun in the victim's hand or otherwise altering the scene, in 45% of the Routine Policing cases and in 75% of the executions. Nearly 10% of the cases include some kind of falsified forensic report produced by police experts and introduced by the defense.

The police also take more drastic measures to impede an investigation. The harrowing story of Ana, with which I open this book, illustrates the level of intimidation claimants must overcome as they seek to impose some accountability for police misconduct. Many others, both lawyers and victims' relatives, described analogous police threats and violence. In fact, at the meeting where Ana related her story to me, two of the other four people present told similar stories of anonymous phone calls and blackmail. In one case the police threatened an entire lower class neighborhood with the complete withdrawal of police protection if residents did not cease protesting a certain killing. According to my interviews, the police threatened witnesses in 22 percent of the cases I sampled for Buenos Aires.

Nor are these empty threats. Ten percent of the cases in my sample involve a victim who was most likely killed because he or she was a witness in another case. Indeed, in its October 2001 opinion, the Supreme Court of Buenos

Aires itself accused the Buenos Aires police of killing and coercing minors who complained of ill treatment while in custody (Acordada No. 3012). The CELS also extensively documents stories in which witnesses have been threatened, injured, or killed (CELS/HRW 1998). Furthermore, according to my data, the police have also threatened lawyers for the victim's family in 8 percent of the cases, sometimes anonymously, sometimes not. One of the lawyers described how his car was firebombed in the middle of a trial against the police.

More generally, the police impede investigations simply by covering for colleagues. Officers within the police force cover for their colleagues by failing to cooperate in one way or another in 35 percent of the cases, according to the information I gathered. The purpose of all this obstruction, of course, is to craft the perception that the police are engaged in an armed war against crime and that the victims are killed in the course of that war. Published studies of police violence in Buenos Aires and São Paulo support my conclusion on this point (Chevigny 1995; CELS/HRW 1998). In commenting on a recent case, the CELS writes:

[This case] occurred in the context of an institutional pattern that promotes complicity and covering up these facts, forging proofs and attempting to present these murders as confrontations. In addition, it makes evident the refusal of those in charge of the Buenos Aires police to investigate these events, to adopt any preventive measures as to those charged until the courts require it, or to develop any policies whatsoever to reverse the increase in police violence. (CELS 2001 [my translation])

Does this pattern of misrepresentation and intimidation produce the desired police immunity from conviction? In numerous cases, advocates for the victims are persuaded that the full facts of the case – facts that would demonstrate that the killing was indeed illegal – remained unknown to the courts due in large part to police activity. A brief review of two specific examples makes it evident that the legal system in Buenos Aires is often handicapped by its inability to gather information about police homicides.

A typical case of pure informational failures is that of Gustavo Pérez. He and a group of friends were walking home after a party when they were approached by the police. All but Gustavo ran away. Some hours later, his body appeared next to the train tracks. The police claimed they had released him alive and well, and he then committed suicide by stepping in front of a train. The family believes he died of ill-treatment while in custody and was thrown on the tracks to cover up the crime. His injuries, they claim, are more consistent with a police beating than with a train accident. A number of circumstances suggest that he was most unlikely to commit suicide. And yet the courts dismissed the case for lack of evidence.

On another occasion, a police officer shot Luis Selaye after a chase, as Selaye knelt on the ground. A gun found next to the body was used to establish that Selaye was shot while violently resisting arrest. After the case was dismissed, however, a police officer admitted that the gun had come from the office of the officer in charge of the investigation – *Comisario* Patti, a notorious police chief with ties to the repression under the military government. In these cases and many others, the record presented a version of the event that is most likely inaccurate. These prosecutions failed because the investigation failed to produce a true version of the event in question.

At the same time, there is a Spanish saying that goes something like this: "No one is deafer than one who refuses to hear." In some cases at least, it appears that either judges or prosecutors intentionally create a weak record, blurring the boundary between normative and informational deficiencies. The case of Néstor Zubarán illustrates judicial complicity in creating a weak record. Néstor was shot in the back by the chauffeur to the then-chief of the Federal Police. The victim's family retained CORREPI lawyers to represent them, but the court consistently refused to take the evidentiary measures these lawyers requested and then dismissed the case, on the prosecutor's request, for failure of proofs. Clearly, the Buenos Aires judges are often at least partially complicit in their own blinding. In those cases, the role of the coverups and subterfuge seems to be simply to offer the courts adequate cover to rule in favor of the police without doing excessive violence to the appearance of justice.

Prosecutors also unquestioningly rely on police reports despite all the evidence of misrepresentations or limit themselves to investigating the criminal conduct of the victim. It is not uncommon for the prosecution to fail to call witnesses or even to call experts that exculpate the defendant, and then ask for an acquittal. Given the abundant evidence supplied by the CELS and others that the police routinely produce misleading investigations, it is hard to depict the passivity of prosecutors as completely innocent. Prosecutors in many cases could take the arguments of the victims' relatives more seriously and pursue the case on the strength of circumstantial or forensic evidence, as they routinely do in Uruguay.

What I think is an extreme example of prosecutorial cooperation with the defense occurred in the prosecution of *Subcomisario* Osvaldo Cutri for the killing of Gumersindo Ramoa Paredes, which I attended. I found myself increasingly confused as the prosecutor herself called a defense-oriented ballistics expert and carefully walked him through exculpatory testimony, then carried out a hostile cross-examination of a prosecution-oriented expert called by CORREPI's lawyers, and finally diligently worked to generate and highlight contradictions in prosecution-oriented eyewitness testimony. The defense attorney only rarely had to do much more than adhere to the arguments the prosecutor was already making. The confusion was finally clarified when the prosecutor argued in her summation that the defendant, unfortunately, had to be acquitted, since the evidence did not allow his identification as the shooter. She made this argument even though there was no evidence that anyone else had shot the victim, and indeed it was impossible that anyone else could have done so. Not even the judge, who ultimately acquitted Cutri on a technicality, accepted that argument. The lawyers who worked on that case, and many other lawyers, related similar experiences.

As the theoretical discussion in Chapter 1 (summarized in Figures 1.3 and 1.4) suggests, the lawyers I spoke to felt as if they were swimming against the current in these cases: the entire system is pitched against a conviction, so that even if one of the actors happens to be favorable – a certain judge in La Plata, or an aggressive prosecutor in San Martín – other actors inevitably hinder their actions. Any one of these – the judge, the prosecutor, the forensic experts – can effectively sabotage a prosecution by failing to build a strong case or by failing to take into consideration the elements contributed by other actors.

These cases of intentional blindness point up the concurrent failure of the legal system in Buenos Aires to apply the "right" rule. The default position is to give the police the benefit of the doubt, that is, to apply an exculpatory rule. The judge in the Cutri case, for example, treated the high-ranking defendant with the utmost deference while addressing witnesses from among the victim's relatives and friends as if they were the criminals. She questioned their credibility on trivial issues and had one of them arrested on an unrelated outstanding warrant. In other cases, the judges explicitly acknowledge the influence of outside pressures. Ana's lawyers, as recounted earlier, were told by one of three judges on the panel that a demonstration outside the courthouse actually changed an acquittal to a conviction, albeit with an insignificant sentence.[11] It generally takes some extraordinary pressure to move the system off that position and prompt an effective investigation.

Interestingly, this institutional inertia gives rise to the phenomenon Smulovitz and Peruzzotti (2001) label "societal accountability," by which social actors impose costs on state actors in an effort to make the system respond in a particular case. Of course, this account makes a virtue out of

---

[11] Similarly, another source showed me a judicial opinion in which a judge, in a squatters' rights case, expressly acknowledged the influence of popular demonstrations on his decision. The judge stated that he had been inclined to keep in custody an activist who was arrested for trespassing, but that since several large demonstrations had demanded it, he would release the defendant.

necessity. On the one hand, it is the story of the success of civil society in rallying around a cause and demanding a response from the state. On the other, it is the story of the failure of the legal system, which would not act without a massive outpouring of societal resources to push it into doing what it should be doing of its own accord.

In conclusion, the police in Buenos Aires strive mightily to distort the record, while state legal agents do little to redress the imbalance unless there is strong political pressure. The result is a tendency toward informational failures, built on an overly lenient, "better not to know" normative position on the part of judicial actors. This position can tilt in the opposite direction in response to extra-legal pressures, in which case the courts convict on the basis of less exacting evidentiary and legal standards, just as the appellate judge suggested in the Champonois case.[12]

D. GARBAGE IN, GARBAGE OUT: NORMATIVE SUCCESS FRUSTRATED BY INFORMATION-GATHERING FAILURES

The final category is one in which the courts process information according to the "right" rule but apply that rule to an incomplete or skewed version of the facts. The treatment of Routine Policing cases in São Paulo and Córdoba falls in this category. These two locations are marked by informational failures, just as Buenos Aires is, though failures are more frequent in São Paulo and less so in Córdoba. In contrast to Buenos Aires, however, in both locations there is considerably more effort on the part of the police and less complicity on the part of judges in the process of producing a biased procedural reality. As we will see in their respective chapters, courts in these two cities are more autonomous from both politics and police corporations. As a result, they are less prone to normative shifts in response to external pressures and have fewer qualms in ruling against the police when they are actually presented with the requisite facts.

1. Information Blackouts in São Paulo

A typical conversation in São Paulo on the subject of the courts and the police can go one of two ways. Some will say the police are merely killing dangerous criminals, and the courts are doing exactly what they should by exonerating them. Others will argue, however, that the justice system in São Paulo is

---

[12] Studies by Helmke (2005) and Iaryczower et al. (2006) come to the same conclusion with respect to Argentina's Supreme Court.

simply at the service of repression and lacks a commitment to effectively prosecute a violent police force – especially when the victims come from the popular classes.

Here I show that neither of these readings is fully correct. The evidence suggests that the police in fact often exceed the limits judges and prosecutors might be willing to tolerate. The low conviction rate results because the police manage to forge a procedural truth that prevents a conviction while allowing judicial actors to believe they have applied the law correctly. Ultimately then, the problem in São Paulo is not so much permissiveness on the part of the courts as a lack of sufficient information. At the same time, as in Buenos Aires but to a lesser degree, some part of that lack is surely attributable to disinterest on the part of prosecutors and judges.

Interviews with key participants in the system support this conclusion. There is a core of prosecutors and judges who take these cases very seriously, working hard to improve the judicial system's response to these cases. I spoke to several judges who are aware of reports published by the Ouvidoria da Polícia about police excesses and cover-ups. They use the initiative afforded to them by their greater control over the investigation (as compared to common law judges) to demand more thorough investigations in some of these cases than prosecutors would typically conduct. One judge related that he has become frustrated when prosecutors insist on requesting dismissal of cases that seem suspicious to him. In those cases he has used an extra-ordinary legal mechanism to send these cases back to the attorney general for review. I also spoke to several prosecutors who argued that their office is doing all it can to aggressively pursue cops who kill innocent civilians, pulling out case files to prove their point. These cases often involve criminality on the part of the police, leading the prosecutors to see themselves as going after a few bad apples, rather than viewing the violence as a pattern and practice of the police generally.

At the same time, it is clear that the system, somewhere, is failing in prosecuting the police. Nearly 65% of all the cases I collected in São Paulo were dismissed early on by agreement of the prosecutor and the judge, ostensibly because the available evidence was insufficient to establish that the incident involved the excessive use of force. Even the few cases that went to trial failed more often than not to produce a conviction – 60% of the tried cases ended in acquittals, compared to less than 25% in ordinary homicide cases.[13]

---

[13] The estimate is for cases in which a suspect is identified. Obviously, there are many cases in which no one is ever charged with the murder. Interview with Antônio Carlos da Ponte, prosecutor in the Primeira Vara do Júri, São Paulo, April 2001.

A look at the cases that went to trial confirms that their success depends on the quality of the information presented in court. In some, the case fails because the only witnesses are not seen as credible. In particular, *favela* residents are seen as living on the edge of the law and therefore cannot be trusted to testify truthfully against the police. For instance, Josevaldo Fernandes de Sousa was killed less than a block from the door of his shantytown residence. Five other *favelados* testified that Sérgio Chelas, a police officer, had accosted Fernandes at home, inquiring after a third person. Not receiving a satisfactory answer, Chelas waited a block away and shot Fernandes as he left home a few minutes later. At trial, apparently, the jury chose to believe Chelas's claim that all these witnesses were lying simply to get an honest cop in trouble.

In many more cases, witnesses simply fail to show up for the trial. While I do not have direct evidence of this in many of the cases I examined in São Paulo, there is sufficient evidence from other sources, as related here and in the São Paulo chapter, to conclude that a significant percentage of this absenteeism is due to police threats and intimidation. The rest is due to nothing more than the precarious living conditions that afflict those most likely to witness these events in combination with lengthy trial delays.

Two examples will make the point. In one case, the prosecutor failed to prove that policemen Alves dos Santos and Batista de Lira summarily executed José de Oliveira Rios, because he lost track of the two eyewitnesses to the event. Similarly, in 1984, the police removed two *favela* residents, Valdeci Antônio da Silva and Roberto Thomaz de Oliveira, from a gypsy taxicab run by an acquaintance. Their bodies were found hours later in an empty lot.[14] The officers who acknowledged killing them were brought to trial on September 18, 2000, before a São Paulo jury. The taxi driver could have confirmed that the victims were unarmed, were arrested without resistance, and were last seen handcuffed in the back seat of a police vehicle. But at the trial, the driver, also a *favela* resident, could not be found; the only witnesses were the two police officers. They told the jury that the two young men had shot at the police under cover of darkness and had been killed when the police responded by shooting into the overgrown lot where the bodies were found. The jury accepted their story and acquitted them on grounds of legitimate self-defense.

---

[14] According to the lawyers who worked on the case, the youths were executed after being mistakenly blamed for the shooting of a policeman's son. One thing that is remarkable is that this case made it all the way to the jury, because the judge and prosecutor were persuaded that this was a clear case of extra-judicial executions, and yet the prosecution failed.

A few cases, where it is clear that the prosecutor has failed to note information that would be available with very little more effort, fall closer to the Buenos Aires pattern of willful indifference. The case against the killers of Anderson Monteiro dos Santos was dismissed on the grounds that they had killed him in the course of an armed confrontation. The prosecutor failed to note, in his request for a dismissal of the case, evidence that the victim had suffered a severe beating before being shot. The case against the Military Police officers who killed Claudinei Andrade Santos was also dismissed, after the officers testified that Santos ran from a car they had been chasing, shooting back at them. The victim's friends and relatives insisted that he could not walk without crutches, but neither the judge nor the prosecutor felt this was enough to take the case to trial.

The case of Darcy Ferreira dos Santos and Fábio Mário Saraiva Rodrigues demonstrates how a record might be skewed by creating favorable testimony while the prosecutor ignores unfavorable evidence. The prosecutor's own description of the facts states that the victims entered a bar drunk and with weapons in hand. When they saw the police officer sitting at a table, it says, they started shooting, at which point the police officer drew his gun and killed them both. The ability of the lone policeman to successfully repel the aggression is somewhat surprising, since there were two attackers who allegedly started shooting first. But the owner of the bar claimed to witness the event, and he supported the police officer's testimony, and there, as is typical, the investigation stalled.

A closer look casts strong doubt on this version of events. The bar owner is the police officer's brother-in-law. The victims' relatives, who talked to the police but were not interviewed by the prosecutor, claim that the two young men left home only fifteen minutes before the shooting, were not drunk, and were unarmed. The details of the autopsy report are not discussed in any of the prosecutor's filings before the judge. If they had been, they would show that, in addition to one and two frontal wounds, respectively, each of the victims had a gunshot wound in the same spot in the middle of the back. At minimum, this final gunshot wound suggests an execution. A motive for the killing becomes clear when we learn that one of the two was on conditional release pending trial in the killing of a police officer. In short, in case after case, prosecutors and courts are presented with the police version of events and have very little contrary evidence on which they feel they can rely.

On the other hand, in those cases in which witnesses deemed credible by the courts are able and willing to testify against the police officers, there can be a conviction. The first example, the case of Júlio Cesar Antunes de Miranda, illustrates the work of a Catholic human rights center, the Centro

Santo Dias, and the jury, highlighting the latter's (minimal) willingness to convict when presented with the proper facts. In that case, two police officers chased after Júlio César when he allegedly fled from a routine identity check. They shot and killed him after he ran into a neighbor's backyard. The police officers claimed that Júlio Cesar had shot at them first and was killed in the subsequent exchange of gunfire.

The Centro Santo Dias represented the victim's child and father and was constituted as *assistênte de acusação* in the prosecution. At the trial, the father testified that police officers had told him the day before the shooting that if his son was outside after dark, they would execute him (he was suspected of car theft). A neighbor said she heard the victim pleading for his life and calling for his mother before the final shot was fired. When he died, the victim was wearing nothing but shorts, and the police did not produce the gun that he was supposed to have used. Moreover, a forensic test showed the lack of any gunpowder residue on the victim's hands, further suggesting he had not fired any shots. The autopsy report showed that the victim had one wound in the front of his body and two gunshots to the back.

The Santo Dias attorney participated fully in the trial and was given the opportunity to make a final argument to the jury. The combined arguments of the prosecutor and the Santo Dias attorney lasted just over three hours, plus another hour for a reply to the defense attorney's argument. Relying on eyewitness testimony and the autopsy, the prosecutor and the Santo Dias attorney argued that Julio César had been wounded while fleeing the police officers and then executed as he lay on the ground. After final arguments on all sides, the seven members of the jury voted on each of the following questions in relation to the officer identified as the shooter (the tally is in parenthesis):

1. Was the deceased the victim of a homicide? (yes, 7–0) If so,
2. Was the defendant the author of the injuries to the victim? (yes, 7–0) If so,
3. Did these injuries cause the victim's death? (yes, 7–0) If so,
4. Was the defendant responding to aggression? (yes, 4–3) If so,
5. Was it an unjustified aggression? (yes, 4–3) If so,
6. Was the aggression in progress at the time of the response? (yes, 5–2) If so,
7. Were the means of response necessary? (yes, 4–3) If so,
8. Did the defendant use these means in the appropriate manner? (no, 4–3) If not,
9. Did the defendant *intentionally* exceed the limits of legitimate self-defense? (yes, 4–3).

From the answers to questions 4–7, it appears that four of the seven jurors believed that the officers had acted properly in initially shooting Júlio Cesar, despite the lack of any evidence that he exchanged gunfire with the police. It is possible to read too much into an unexplained vote, but the pattern suggests that the jurors validated the officers' decision to use deadly force against a fleeing suspect simply because he disobeyed an order to stop – that is the only "aggression" in the record. At the same time, four of the seven jurors were unwilling to condone the subsequent execution, convicting the officer who shot Julio César as he lay wounded. For the cold-blooded execution of a young man who made the mistake of running away from the police, this police officer was convicted of "intentionally exceeding the bounds of self-defense" and sentenced to six years in prison, under a semi-open regime in which he can enjoy weekend passes and some work release.

In another of the Centro Santo Dias's cases, the police officer who killed twelve-year-old Eneas da Silva was convicted and sentenced to thirteen years in prison. Eneas was shot as he ran away from the police, who had discovered him leafing through an adult magazine. In that case, the prosecution survived a falsified autopsy report, a planted gun, false testimony from the police officer and his colleagues, and the intimidation and beating of eyewitnesses. At the trial, a second, accurate, autopsy report was introduced, the eyewitnesses testified despite the threats, and the trial court in the end chose to believe that the child who was killed was unarmed and had been killed in cold blood. In this case (prompted perhaps by media and international NGO attention to the case) the prosecutor ensured that there would be an adequate factual record to support a conviction by going so far as to exhume the body to conduct a second autopsy.

The final case study shows what happens when the state puts its resources fully behind a prosecution. During the course of an interview, Prosecutor Norberto Jóia reviewed a case file with me on a police shooting he was prosecuting.[15] The shooting involved two brothers, both members of the Military Police, one of whom had been imprisoned on charges of corruption. In the course of the judicial investigation of the corruption case, the main witness against this officer was called into court to give his formal testimony. Under the rules of procedure, of course, the defendant was notified when and where this witness was to come in to testify, so that his attorney could be present. As the witness walked away from the courthouse, a person jumped off the back of a motorcycle and killed him. A witness to the shooting provided investigators with a description of the motorcycle and the license plate number. The plate number was traced to the imprisoned officer's brother.

---

[15] Interview with Prosecutor Norberto Jóia, São Paulo, April 16, 2001.

Jóia described the extraordinary measures that were being taken to protect this second witness and increase the likelihood of a successful prosecution. Prosecutors entered the witness in a witness protection program. They sent him out of town, arranging housing and employment for him under an assumed name. When he did come in to testify, prosecutors arranged for transportation and security to ensure his safety. Forensic tests were being done by federal experts rather than by the usual state police experts. And no expense was being spared in tracing phone calls between the suspects before the killing, locating witnesses, and gathering all the available evidence.

This case is interpreted by the prosecutors as an attack on the very integrity of the system. In particular, what seems to gall the prosecutors is the fact that the suspects apparently took advantage of due process – their right to be notified and present when a witness offers testimony against them – to interfere with the prosecution and commit murder. Odds are this case will end in a conviction, though it had not yet been decided the last time I updated information. But the prosecution rests on nearly heroic efforts, which the prosecutors will not take in routine cases involving the police. This case demonstrates that the informational failures in São Paulo could often be overcome if prosecutors were more willing to take extraordinary measures in these cases.

There is other evidence of the proclivity of the system to informational failures. As in Buenos Aires, the police in São Paulo are adept at manipulating the record. One former police officer testified that the police will go so far as to put a gun in a deceased victim's hand and pull the trigger, then present the resulting gunpowder residue as evidence that the victim died in an exchange of gunfire with the police. Using the same approach as for Buenos Aires, I coded 25% of all the cases in São Paulo as showing evidence that the police added a gun to the scene. In my sample there is evidence that the police experts produced falsified forensic reports in 5% of the cases and engaged in other kinds of tampering in nearly 10% of the cases. The shooting is presented as a confrontation in 77% of all cases, while this can be confirmed by independent evidence in only 20% of the cases. At the Ouvidoria, I was told that the police in São Paulo often carry two weapons, the police-issued one that is registered and can be traced and another, typically with the serial number filed off, that can be used in questionable shootings or left as a decoy at the scene. Whether this is the reason or not, I often saw Military Police officers on the streets of São Paulo carrying two guns.

In summary, what we observe at the level of individual cases in São Paulo is a pattern in which either there is no information to contradict the police version or the information that is available is not deemed credible when contrasted with the testimony of the police officers involved. And yet, when there is sufficiently strong evidence to back a claim, the courts are willing to convict. At the same time, with some exceptions, judges and prosecutors take what is at best a neutral position, rarely expending a special effort to ensure that the case reaches the jury adequately supported.

2. Routine Policing Cases in Córdoba

At first glance, Córdoba seems to follow its own pattern. It has a vastly higher conviction rate than São Paulo, but results are much more unequal across socio-economic categories. Thus, it might seem odd to place these two cases in the same category. And yet a careful review of the cases suggests that the courts in Córdoba, as in São Paulo, can be quite serious about applying the law when the facts are laid out before them but they often fail to secure the critical information needed to convict. It is the poverty of information in cases affecting the underprivileged that produces the marked inequalities in Córdoba, not some sort of class-based animus. If this is right, São Paulo and Córdoba apply a more or less similar rule of decision, but São Paulo fails much more often than Córdoba to cobble together an adequate record.

An examination of successful prosecutions in Córdoba begins to outline the reasons for the remarkable diversity of outcomes. When the victim is an "honest citizen," the prosecutions proceed quite routinely. For instance, when Carlos Valenzuela, a working-class youth in his twenties, was shot in the early hours of the morning in the course of a routine police operation that went out of control, his case generated little attention and led to a conviction with little prompting from anyone outside the legal system. In fact, Córdoba activists who track police violence knew little about the case and had not taken an active role at all in connection with it.

This pattern is replicated in the cases of Sergio Bonahora and Ariel Lastra, which are almost identical and also led to convictions. Both of these youths, in separate incidents, were intercepted by the police while they were cruising the streets in the early hours of the morning. In both cases, police officers harassed and mistreated the youths and then shot them as they tried to run away. Sergio was shot in the back after jumping out of a police car and trying to run away. Ariel took advantage of a momentary confusion to try to escape, but one of the police officers chased him down and shot him in the back after he had stopped with his hands in the air. In both cases, the police tried to stage a confrontation, but the courts convicted them anyway. These cases generated some media attention but not the intervention of a private attorney.

In the case of Luis Gorosito, the conviction required the assistance of a private lawyer. Gorosito was suspected of being a thief and was killed in an operation following a robbery. A police officer named Cuadro was killed in the same operation, perhaps accidentally.[16] In any event, a case in which the police kill a criminal suspect after the death of a police officer is not, in most of the jurisdictions evaluated here, a prime candidate for conviction. His case did not trigger popular demonstrations or a great deal of media attention. Most of the witnesses to his execution were police officers who argued that he had been shot in an armed confrontation. And yet, on the strength of mostly forensic evidence, with the assistance of a private lawyer, the Córdoba provincial court chose to convict.

Lest we think the wheels of justice run too smoothly and of their own volition in Córdoba, we should take a look at two cases in which civil society intervention seems to have been determinative. Miguel Angel Rodríguez was the son of migrants from Salta, an impoverished province in Argentina, who lived in one of the poor neighborhoods that surround Córdoba city. He was only fifteen when a police officer, angry that the teenager had allegedly stolen a soccer ball, shot him in front of his house. By the time of trial, the police had raided the family's house, witnesses had been threatened, and one, an eighteen-year-old neighbor who saw the shooting, had been murdered. Despite all this, the prosecutor decided to charge the police officer with merely negligent homicide, a decision that triggered large demonstrations against the prosecutor. In the end, the court decided that the officer should be charged with intentional homicide, and he was convicted.

Sergio Pérez, the eighteen-year-old witness in the Rodríguez case, was first threatened and ultimately killed by César Cruz, a colleague of the defendant in the Rodríguez case. Cruz was also convicted of homicide despite attempts to make Pérez look like a criminal. These cases, involving residents of precarious neighborhoods, required mass demonstrations and had to survive egregious attempts to silence witnesses before they could produce convictions.

Given this difficulty, it is not surprising when cases arising in this context fail. Diego Ordóñez, Roberto Ordóñez Salazar, and Cristian Rodríguez all lived and died in the *villas* that surround Córdoba city, and all their murderers went unpunished. Diego was killed after a brief police chase involving him and a companion, both suspected of having participated in a crime. Although all the witnesses from the *villa* dispute this claim, the killing was presented as an exchange of gunfire. Diego's companion, the only witness to the actual killing, was charged with armed resistance, destroying his

---

[16] Cuadro was allegedly killed by Gorosito, although Cuadro's family and the lawyers who worked for Gorosito's family believe that the police officer was actually killed by his fellow officers.

credibility. Subsequently, the police harshly repressed demonstrations in the *villa*, and one peripheral witness was shot and wounded. Activists who worked on the case told me that circumstantial witnesses were afraid to testify. In the end, after a cursory investigation the prosecutor sought dismissal of the case on the grounds that the police were merely responding to aggression, even though it was clear that Diego had been unarmed and shot in the back.

In the other two cases there were more witnesses. Roberto Ordóñez Salazar had been arrested and handcuffed and was being taken out of the back seat of a police car when he was killed before a number of other people in the *villa*. The police argued that another individual, who was then charged with armed resistance, initiated the confrontation. According to witnesses, the police planted a gun at the scene to bolster the claim that there had been a confused armed confrontation in the course of which Roberto was killed. Despite the apparent openness of the crime and the presence of witnesses, the accused were quietly exonerated in the course of the investigation, and no charges were filed.

Both a lawyer who was active in the community and an activist who worked with the neighbors on this case suggested reasons for the inconclusive investigation. First, the witnesses were intimidated and were not forthcoming. Second, the police sent the family of the victim a lawyer to help them with the claim – which they, oddly, accepted – and this lawyer actually obstructed the criminal investigation while assisting the family with a modest claim for compensation. At the same time, the lawyer I spoke to partly blames the judge in charge of the investigation, saying that another judge might not have let the case go so easily.

Finally, fifteen-year-old Cristian Rodríguez was fleeing from police and tried to hide in a *villa*. A number of people saw the police catch up with him and shoot him while he was on his knees with his hands in the air. Three police officers were charged with the crime, but the case against them was ultimately dismissed. A lawyer who had some participation in the case related that the witnesses, all from the *villa*, had a very difficult time relating what they had seen in a way that would satisfy the judge. She said the witnesses were very afraid of testifying in court and of what the police might do to them once they went back to their neighborhood. As a result, they contradicted themselves on secondary issues and became incoherent when standing before the judge, the prosecutor, and the defense attorneys. The prosecutor and the judge ultimately accepted the police version over theirs, and the case was dismissed.

From the statistical analysis in the previous chapter we know that class has a strong impact on the outcome. All three of these cases show exactly how the social marginalization of the victim contributes to the informational failures of the legal system. In this type of case, the courts in Córdoba require credible witnesses and strong evidence before they will convict an accused police officer. Even lawyers who are sympathetic admit that witnesses taken from the *villas* are not very effective and end up being insufficiently credible. In this way, as in São Paulo, even a strictly neutral position by the courts can produce results that are heavily skewed against the undereducated, marginalized, and threatened residents of Córdoba's *villas*.

Thus far, the tally of cases shows several that failed when prosecutors exhibited a lack of interest and the few witnesses lacked social resources, while others succeeded when the facts were easy to establish or a private attorney intervened. The overall impression is that the courts hold these cases to a relatively high standard of proof, and when the cases take place among a marginal population, the evidence often does not meet this standard. More rarely, we see some acquittals that appear explicable only by a decision on the part of the judge to overlook the excessive use of force, as when a provincial judge acquitted the defendants on the same evidence used by a federal judge to convict in a companion case. In the background is the persistent impression that cases affecting the underprivileged are more tolerated by judges and prosecutors than they are aggressively prosecuted; these narratives, however, obscure the overall high success rate the Córdoba courts achieve in these cases, second only to Uruguay's.

Summarizing, then, when the evidence is clear judges often convict, and judges are able to find the information to ground a conviction in nearly half of all cases, hence a conviction rate that approaches 50 percent. In the majority of the cases that do not succeed, the evidence points to an information gap that the state's investigation fails to fill, rather than to the application of a rule of impunity. Clearly, however, when the case involves the more marginalized population of Córdoba, the courts are far less likely to be satisfied with the quality of the information. In these cases, the neutrality (if not indifference) of judicial actors combines with the lack of social resources of the main participants to produce an informational failure. In other words, the prosecutions fail primarily for lack of information, and they are far more likely to do so when the case involves the poor.

E. OVERVIEW OF NORMATIVE AND INFORMATIONAL FAILURES

Figure 3.1 summarizes the discussion of the investigative and normative performances of these systems. To illustrate the varying degrees to which the different systems suffer from normative and informational failures, I have made an admittedly impressionistic evaluation of the performance of the

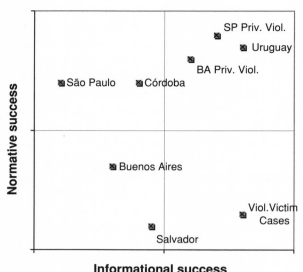

FIGURE 3.1. Rank ordering of legal systems on normative and informational dimensions.

cases on a more continuous measure of both dimensions, locating the cases on a graph. The cases are scored higher or lower according to their relative degree of success in solving the normative and informational problems discussed earlier. The scores are intended more as a visual summary of the information presented than as a precise quantification of the state of rights in each case. For comparison purposes, I also included special cases – particular categories of cases discussed earlier that appear to merit different treatment even within the same system. When no category of cases is identified, the graph refers to the treatment of Routine Policing cases. While there may be some debate as to the exact placement for each legal system, the rank order is clear from the evidence.

This graph reflects, for example, the difference in the potential for informational failures between Córdoba and São Paulo – while most of the cases that fail in both places do so for failure of proofs, this happens much more often in São Paulo than in Córdoba. And while courts in Uruguay do a creditable job of unearthing information and seriously pursuing murders committed by policemen in the course of their duties, they still occasionally fail in their investigations. On the other hand, while I classified Buenos Aires as suffering from both normative and informational failures, there are committed judges and prosecutors in Buenos Aires, and occasionally they wholeheartedly go after one of these cases, cobbling together the record that will support a conviction.

Similarly, São Paulo's judges are very professional as a whole, but some judges, often decried by their own colleagues, simply are not interested in looking too closely at these cases. And once the case goes to trial, the ultimate decision is in the hands of a jury, where there appears to be a high level of tolerance for police violence. In Salvador, on the other hand, the courts are aware of levels of violations in the aggregate, but the police still offer them plenty of cover in ruling on individual cases. They do this by keeping a tight lid on the flow of information out of the precarious neighborhoods where much of the killing takes place. In particular, any time an investigation appears to threaten the pattern of impunity, the police have little trouble imposing secrecy, by violence if necessary. The killing of Violent Victims, on the other hand, can be much more open than that in all three cases – Salvador, Buenos Aires, and São Paulo – where the exception seems to hold.

Two of the variables examined in the previous chapter offer support for these qualitative conclusions. The socio-economic condition of the victim should matter principally, as we saw in the individual case studies, because it affects the quality of the information being presented to the courts for consideration. Thus, the more socio-economic variables affect outcomes, the more the failures are likely to be informational rather than normative. These variables should matter more in Córdoba and São Paulo than in Buenos Aires and Salvador, with their normative failures, or in Uruguay, with its aggressive investigative posture. Similarly, the principal role of the Private Prosecutor is to contribute legal resources in the form of evidence and arguments for the judge's consideration. Hiring an attorney should matter more in systems that are less prone to normative failures, like Córdoba and São Paulo.

As seen in Figure 2.3, socio-economic variables have their strongest impact in Córdoba, more than doubling the likelihood of a conviction. São Paulo, with the lowest conviction rate, is also the place where the police most strictly avoid targeting the middle class.[17] Moreover, the two jurisdictions in which adding a Private Prosecutor has the strongest impact on the likelihood of a conviction are Córdoba and São Paulo. In Córdoba the likelihood of a conviction without a Private Prosecutor is 5%, no higher than the average for São Paulo, but it rises to 80% if a Private Prosecutor is involved with the

---

[17] In São Paulo, the middle classes are almost completely exempt from intentional police violence, so we cannot directly measure the impact their greater access to resources might have on a prosecution. There is, however, a substantial though statistically insignificant difference (13.8% vs. 18.2%) in the conviction rate in cases affecting the lower working class versus shantytown residents.

case.[18] In São Paulo, meanwhile, retaining an attorney quadruples the probability of a conviction, regardless of social class. In fact, when an attorney accompanies the prosecution, the likelihood of a conviction is higher in São Paulo than in Buenos Aires.

In sum, the impact of a Private Prosecutor in Córdoba and São Paulo is consistent with the more qualitative finding that, if only a legal claim is presented effectively, the courts are more likely to process it correctly in both of these places than in Buenos Aires. The much higher proportion of informational failures in São Paulo accounts for the difference in conviction rates. In Buenos Aires, socio-economic variables and Private Prosecutors matter, but not to the same degree. This suggests a somewhat lower level of informational failures, which combine with normative ones to produce a relatively low conviction rate. Uruguay shows an even higher level of success than Córdoba, and without the assistance of Private Prosecutors. In Salvador the principal problem seems to be a general rule of indifference and impunity, and informational issues take over only when the normative problem seems to be solved.

To understand the source of these patterns, I now turn to the second-order explanation. What accounts for the difference in the way these cases are processed in each location? Why informational failures in São Paulo and Córdoba, but not in Uruguay; why normative failures in Buenos Aires and Salvador, but not in the others? Why, furthermore, normative failures in the case of violent victims, even in systems that otherwise strictly apply the law? As explained in Chapter 1, neither purely institutionalist nor disembodied, acontextual rationalist accounts capture all the key variables. In the following chapters I carry out an in-depth look at each of the systems, to show how the various actors and their socio-political context interact to produce the outcomes measured in the last two chapters.

---

[18] Recall, however, that a high level of collinearity makes it difficult to separate the impact of a private attorney from the impact of demonstrations in Córdoba, as explained in the previous chapter.

4

Buenos Aires

Political Interference and Informational Dependence

> People are indignant with the police because they tried to pass off the three
> kids as thieves. This murdering policeman planted a knife on each of them
> to justify that he killed them because they tried to rob the service station.
> [They were actually killed for laughing at a police officer who had been
> assaulted by protesters.] If the kids had not been from this neighborhood,
> you can bet that the police would have claimed they were thieves, and the
> judge would have believed the story.
>
>   La Nación (January 6, 2002), quoting the cousin of one of the victims
>   (my translation)

The quote that opens this chapter aptly captures the essence of the judicial
response to police homicides in Buenos Aires. The police obscure the truth
and doctor the evidence, as nearly everyone knows or suspects. Despite this,
courts and prosecutors are all too willing to accept the police account, unless
there is some level of social mobilization surrounding the case. And so, in
the end, it is up to claimants with the support of collective actors to press for
an effective response. In the first two chapters I presented first the particular
pattern of effectiveness and inequality that marks each system and then the
nature of the prosecutorial failures that underlie this pattern. These patterns
pose two main questions for Buenos Aires. First, what institutional features
combine to produce both a strong normative bias in favor of the police as
well as repeated informational failures in the prosecutions that take place in
the Buenos Aires area? And second, why are the courts of Buenos Aires so
susceptible to collective demands that they seem to convict or acquit more
in response to political mobilization than to the legal features of the case?

  Discussing the legal context for police homicide prosecutions in the metropolitan Buenos Aires area poses unavoidable complexities. Homicides committed in the capital city and its metropolitan area could involve Provincial

or Federal Police forces, as well as a half-dozen other security forces. Legal claims concerning them could end up in one of two different legal systems. Events that take place in what is known as the Conurbano, outside the borders of the Ciudad Autónoma de Buenos Aires (the CABA), fall under the jurisdiction of the provincial courts of Buenos Aires. Events that take place within the borders of the CABA go to the National Courts of the CABA, which are a separate division of the federal judiciary.[1]

The Codes of Criminal Procedure applicable in these judiciaries were both amended during the 1990s, with consequent reforms of the relevant police, prosecutorial, and judicial structures. And yet both systems constitute one legal environment, since potential claimants might find themselves in one or the other depending only on what side of the city limits an incident occurs. Moreover, the two systems perform similarly on all the relevant variables in this study. In multivariate analyses of the determinants of successful prosecutions, interaction terms testing for differences in the impact of socio-economic variables or the Private Prosecutor turn out to be insignificant. One of the puzzles to be solved is precisely why outcomes change so little over time and from one system to another, despite all the legal and institutional differences.

To sort all this out, I will discuss the two systems together, comparing and contrasting as the discussion progresses. As we will see, a close analysis that goes beyond formal institutional arrangements shows that the aspects of the intended reforms that could have been most significant for improving performance in the cases at issue here were diluted in practice, and that what seem to be radical differences between the two systems are in fact erased.

A. FEDERAL AND PROVINCIAL CRIMINAL PROCEDURE

The basic lineaments of the criminal justice system flow from the Code of Criminal Procedure, which determines the course of a prosecution and thus many of the functions of the police, prosecutors, and judiciary. In doing so, the code, along with certain other institutional characteristics, will determine

---

[1] The constitutional reform of 1994 gave the city of Buenos Aires a status similar to that of the provinces, and the 1996 Constitution of the Autonomous City of Buenos Aires provides for the establishment of a city judiciary. Throughout the period of this study, however, negotiations to bring the federal National Courts under the aegis of the city had not been finalized, mostly due to the resistance of the judges who wished to continue within the federal system. For those familiar with the U.S. system, the National Courts of the CABA have a status similar to the courts of Washington, D.C. – they are creatures of the federal Congress but behave somewhat like a state judiciary.

the strength and direction of endogenous pressures on each of the actors (see the discussion in Chapter 1). The National Courts of the CABA follow the *Código Procesal Penal de la Nación* (CPPN), while the provincial courts of the Greater Buenos Aires area follow the *Código Procesal Penal de la Provincia de Buenos Aires* (CPPBA). Both of these codes saw fundamental reforms during the 1990s, the CPPN in 1992 and the CPPBA in 1998.

The procedural code with which both courts began the decade was patterned after a nineteenth-century Spanish system that, as Argentine jurists like to note, had already been discarded in Spain by the time it was adopted in Argentina. This system, which governed cases in the provincial courts for most of the decade, was a written, inquisitorial one. The initial investigation was entrusted to the police. The police handed over the results of this investigation to a judge, who began the process of *instrucción*, or pre-trial investigation. During the *instrucción*, the judge formalized the proofs by seeking documents, requesting any expert reports, calling in and questioning witnesses, carrying out crime scene reconstructions, and incorporating all the results in the form of summary reports into the *expediente*, the file.

In this system the judge played both the investigative and the deciding roles. The judge determined, on the basis of his or her review of the police report, what information was needed and how it should be procured, essentially taking on the task of building the case against the defendant. If the defense or the prosecutors believed some additional piece of information should be included in the file, they had to submit a request to the judge, who would decide if it was necessary and appropriate. Once the *instrucción* stage was complete, the parties would be given an opportunity to present written arguments about what they thought the evidence established and how the case should be resolved. Then the same judge who carried out the investigation against the defendant and determined what proofs were included in the record would re-examine the record and arrive at a final decision on the case.[2]

The New Procedure in the National Courts of the City
In 1991, following the path first taken by several provinces, prominently including Córdoba, the federal legislature radically reformed the CPPN to create an oral and accusatorial system for the federal criminal courts (Law

---

[2] The judge's dual function is the feature that marks an inquisitorial system as opposed to an accusatorial system. In the latter, the judge remains more of an impartial arbiter while the prosecutor and the defense vie over the reconstruction of the facts, building the record in an adversarial manner, then presenting it to the judge for decision.

No. 23,894, effective in 1992). The 1992 CPPN formally transferred responsibility for the initial investigation from the police to the prosecutors.[3] Prosecutors are now legally empowered to receive *denuncias* (criminal complaints) directly and are also charged with obtaining the proofs needed to build a case against the defendant. At the conclusion of the investigation, they must seek an indictment from the judge, by establishing that there is reason to believe the accused has committed the charged crime. Conversely, the judge needs the accusation of the prosecutor to produce an indictment. Thus the decision to prosecute is no longer solely the judge's, who retains oversight simply to ensure that defendants' rights are secure. This process takes place within the *Juzgado de Instrucción*. Once the investigative phase is complete, the *juez de instrucción* sends the file up to a tribunal that will preside over the oral trial.

The trial court, or *tribunal oral federal*, is composed of three judges. The case is presented by a trial prosecutor (the *fiscal de cámara*), who takes the information prepared by the investigative prosecutor (*fiscal de instrucción*) and ensures that it is presented in the appropriate manner to the trial court. Since the amended CPPN was meant to require an oral trial, the trial prosecutor is supposed to find the key witnesses identified in the investigative stage and make sure that they are available at the trial, as well as call up the documentary information included in the file so that it can be introduced at the appropriate moment. Ultimately, this information is supposed to be presented to the judges in a trial that caps the entire penal process, with live witnesses and arguments, much in the style of Anglo-American courts.

In practice, however, the new system looks much more like the old system than one might imagine from reading the new CPPN. In the first place, the prosecutor's office (Ministerio Público) does not have the resources to carry out its own investigations or to receive complaints and has therefore delegated these functions right back to the police. In addition, the old practice of relying primarily on the summarized, written information in the *expediente* dies hard. One study reveals that by the end of the decade, the *juez de instrucción* and prosecutors remained largely passive consumers of information produced by the police rather than – as the CPPN might suggest – actively engaged in investigating and producing information (FORES and Colegio de Abogados de Buenos Aires 1999a: 150–53).

---

[3] This describes the procedure for cases involving a crime punishable by three or more years' imprisonment. The process for lesser crimes is similar though more abbreviated and takes place in the *Juzgado Correccional*.

According to attorneys who practice in these courts, the oral trial often consists of the prosecutor's or the defense attorney's reading aloud directly from the file the summary version of witness testimonies gathered during the *instrucción*.[4] A more systematic study of the courts finds the same thing (FORES and Colegio de Abogados de Buenos Aires 1999a: 155). In a simple case, the oral trial may be conducted entirely in this way, though most often it ends up being a combination of live testimony and the oral presentation of written material from the record. For the convenience of lawyers and prosecutors, cases are also often resolved according to an abbreviated procedure that, again, largely resembles the old written model. In short, it is still primarily the police who carry out the bulk of the investigation; prosecutors and judges still rely heavily on the written record in judging the facts in question; and the final trial is substantially based on a recapitulation of what was produced during the *instrucción*.

Criminal Procedure in the Provincial Courts

The provincial procedure, in turn, followed the original written inquisitorial pattern for most of the decade, until it was reformed by Law 12,061 of December 1997 (effective in 1998).[5] The new provincial system also imposes an accusatorial model: prosecutors are in charge of the pre-trial investigation, the investigation is supervised by a judge (the *juez de garantías*) who intervenes only to protect the due process guarantees of the accused, a judge cannot indict unless the prosecutor requests it, and the cases are sent for trial to an oral tribunal after the investigation is complete. In the provincial system the trial courts for serious crimes also consist of three judges, and appeals are taken to a new *Corte de Casación*, which reviews for errors of law and trial-stage due process violations but does not review the facts. The new code also calls for the creation of a Judicial Police, which would be under the administrative and functional control of the prosecutor's office.

Again, however, reality has fallen short of the promise. Prosecutors have delegated the investigation back to the police because they simply have no resources to investigate on their own. The Judicial Police force has not been created, and, instead, an investigative division of the Provincial Police carries out this function, as we will see in more detail in the following section. Moreover, the code is not applied retroactively, so cases initiated under the old CPPBA continue under the written inquisitorial process. In sum, by the end of the decade, the practice of law had changed much less than the Code

---

[4] Interview with María del Carmen Verdú, January 2001, Buenos Aires.
[5] A detailed overview of the changes can be found in Mahiques (2002).

of Criminal Procedure, and in any event the changes in the provincial code came too late to affect cases in the 1990s.

B. SOCIAL CONTEXT

1. Socio-economic Context

As discussed in Chapter 1, the socio-economic context matters primarily because it affects the capacity of the claimant population to bring information to bear on the adjudication of their claims. In a secondary way, it matters insofar as it affects potential victims' capacity to influence the construction of public policies that are more favorable to these claims. The key indicators, therefore, are those relating to the victim population rather than to the population at large. At the same time, the more the victims come from a larger context of exclusion, the further they will be removed from the state, and the less likely they are to interact effectively with the legal system. And in the context of these cases, the more the victims are seen as coming from a large, threatening, criminalized urban population, the more difficult it will be to mobilize political resources on their behalf.

Although aggregate economic indicators differ radically for the Conurbano and the CABA – in the aggregate the city is wealthier but more unequal – the composition of the victim population in the police homicide cases that reach these courts is quite similar. In the Conurbano cases, fully 72% of the victims of homicides that occurred in the course of policing operations were either lower class or lower working class, while 15% of the victims for whom this information is available lived in a shantytown. No less than 60% had only completed their primary education through seventh grade. Thirty-three percent were unemployed. In the cases arising within the city, the percentage of victims from a shantytown is higher (30%), while only 57% were members of the working poor or lower and 45% were unemployed; 43% of victims in the CABA cases had only completed primary school. The claimants, of course, are the family members and survivors of victims and share their demographic profile. In sum, the majority of complainants and the at-risk population in both systems is likely to come from among the disadvantaged, whether the working poor or the unemployed, and the undereducated, with a large number coming from the shantytowns.[6]

---

[6] These percentages exclude cases with missing information. As discussed in Chapter 3, the victim data on these socio-economic variables are not missing at random. There are more missing data for the underprivileged for two reasons. First, the media and others are more

Moreover, this at-risk population is embedded in a society increasingly marked by poverty, inequality, and exclusion. Indices of inequality are quite high in Argentina as a whole. The mean Gini index of inequality reported for Argentina between 1989 and 1998 is 51 (compared to 43 for Uruguay and 59 for Brazil).[7] Within Argentina, the Buenos Aires area is marked by even higher inequality, as it has the largest shantytowns in the country and high indices of poverty and official unemployment, side by side with the most affluent neighborhoods in the country. On average, of course, the Conurbano looks considerably worse than the CABA, but the CABA also includes large pockets of marginalized population. The *villas* inside city limits are large, growing from about 50,000 people in 1992 to more than 110,000 in 2002 (*La Nación*, August 13, 2002). *Villas* surrounding the city are also huge, especially in various areas of Matanza and near the northern suburbs of San Isidro and Tigre. The pattern of inequality and exclusion in this area worsened during the 1990s: unemployment rose steadily, whereas poverty fell somewhat in the middle of the decade, only to rise again toward the end.

Two main consequences of the economic condition of claimants and their socio-economic context are relevant. One is a reduction in the supply of information from that context, the other a reduction in the demand for information on the part of the system. An attorney I interviewed made the first point most clearly. Gabriel Lerner, when in private practice, has intervened on behalf of the victim in a number of police homicide cases and otherwise represents precisely this class of working poor or unemployed individuals in criminal matters. He indicated that the principal problem he encounters in providing adequate representation to his clients is their lack of experience in interacting with the state as bearers of legal rights: "Marginalized youth cannot even imagine pressing a demand for a legal right. They don't have the capacity to address the justice system or even to process a transaction with the state."[8] He explained that many of them are in the informal economy, and many more have the greatest difficulty in understanding and meeting the

---

likely to remark on the status, employment, and educational background of middle-class victims. Second, if a case is not dismissed early on, it is more likely that I will have complete information about the victim. If class and resources have any impact at all, therefore, it is likely that the underprivileged are under-represented among the cases with complete information.

[7] A higher score indicates more inequality on a scale of 0 to 100; for comparison, the United States averages about 36, and Canada about 32. The data are from the All the Ginis database, by Branko Milanovic, available from http://econ.worldbank.org/projects/inequality (Milanovic 2005).

[8] "Para los muchachos marginalizados está fuera de su imaginación reclamar un derecho legal. No tienen la capacidad ni para dirigirse a la justicia, ni pueden hacer un trámite." Interview with Gabriel Lerner, Buenos Aires, Argentina, November 28, 2000.

demands of the legal system. They miss appointments and do not fully grasp what kind of information judges and prosecutors actually use in making decisions.

What is worse, Lerner noted a progressive deterioration in this respect over the last decades. The reduction in union participation, which was once a source of legal services and formalized interactions with state entities, and the rise in unemployment and informal employment together create an increasingly large population that has little or no experience making their way "downtown" to transact business with the state. A high percentage of the at-risk population, therefore, can be expected to relate poorly if at all to the legal system.

The communication problem is worst for shantytown dwellers. Blaustein, for example, notes that "the lack of communication between the two worlds [*villa* and non-*villa*] goes to the essence of the matter" (Blaustein 2003). According to lawyers who work there, conflicts among people living in these marginal areas are not referred to the legal system. They are either resolved informally or not resolved at all.[9] As one human rights lawyer put it, the northern suburbs of Buenos Aires are generally more affluent, but the people from the *villas* and needy neighborhoods are just as poor there as elsewhere, and this exacerbates their isolation from the neighborhoods around them.[10]

The exceptions to this lack of communication are periodic, confrontational mass events – like the *piquetes* and the interruption of traffic on major thoroughfares – in which popular demonstrations make political demands for material resources of one kind or another. The key point from the perspective of the interaction between the state and the population of these *villas* is that they constitute a nearly separate social reality within the larger polity. This population is unaccustomed to pressing rights claims through legal channels.

Lawyers are critical entry points into the legal system for those seeking to press a claim or defend a right (Felstiner, Abel, and Sarat 1980–81). Public opinion surveys confirm that the working poor and the *villeros* face special difficulties in interacting with lawyers and courts. Lower levels of education and income are associated with an increased perception that lawyers are hard to understand, ask for too much paperwork, and pay attention only to important cases (Fucito 1999a). Respondents from lower socioeconomic levels are also more likely to agree that lawyers steal from their clients (p. 871). Nor are these opinions simply the result of ignorance and

---

[9] Interview with Andrea Sajnovsky, Buenos Aires, Argentina, November 15, 2000.
[10] Interview with Andrea Sajnovsky, Buenos Aires, Argentina, November 15, 2000.

inexperience. Even among those who have had some contact with lawyers, lower socio-economic status is associated with higher indices of dissatisfaction with the services received. Since the most important source of information about lawyers is word of mouth (most respondents indicated that they selected their attorney on the basis of personal contact or recommendations), the higher indices of distrust and dissatisfaction greatly reduce the likelihood that people in this sector will easily reach out to an attorney for help with a perceived wrong.

The second consequence of these socio-economic facts is to reduce the demand by actors within the system for information about these claims. There are vast distances between the typical low-income, uneducated claimants in these cases on the one hand and lawyers, prosecutors, and judges on the other. These distances account for much of the suspicion with which claimants are greeted when they do enter the system. In one case that I observed, both the judge and the prosecutor noted at different times that the events in question had taken place in the dangerous context of the *villa*, where criminal acts were, in their view, commonplace. The judge also remarked repeatedly and with distaste on the fact that the witnesses who came in from the *villa* had shared a ride and that attorneys from CORREPI had arranged the ride. For a judge with apparently little appreciation for the economic necessity driving this conduct, this contact with other witnesses and with lawyers had tainted witness testimony, making it less credible. The intervention by CORREPI aggravated the situation by making it more political. By contrast, the fact that an expert who opined favorably for the defendant knew him personally went unremarked by anyone other than the victim's representative.

2. Socio-political Context

Just as the marginal condition of the typical victims and claimants affects the way they are perceived by actors within the system, it is also one of the factors creating a hostile political environment for these cases. In this section I evaluate the political and social support for the use of lethal force by the police and, conversely, the support for strict judicial control of police violence in the 1990s. Whether one subscribes to a strategic view of judicial behavior (Epstein and Knight 1998) or to an attitudinal one (Segal and Spaeth 2002), the legal system is never completely autonomous from its political system (Dahl 1957; Shapiro 1981). Many have noted that this is especially true for the Supreme Court in Argentina during the Menem years (Larkins 1998; Miller 2000; Helmke 2005), and, as we will see in this chapter, it is no less true for the trial courts of the Province of Buenos Aires (PBA) and CABA. The political context is, therefore, especially relevant here, if we are to understand judicial behavior in response to these cases.

As discussed in Chapter 1, the socio-political context affects the demand for complete information about claims of police violence in three ways. In individual cases, it is the source of exogenous incentives for prosecutors and judges to dig more deeply and prosecute more aggressively (or the opposite) (see, e.g., Epstein and Knight 1998). Indirectly, it also affects the supply of information by providing a supportive social environment for claimants who wish to pursue these claims against some institutional resistance. And perhaps more importantly, it can create social demands for systemic changes, thus affecting the configuration of the entire system (see, e.g., Dakolias 1995; Prillaman 2000, for examples of the importance of political support to judicial reform efforts). Unfortunately, the political construction of these violations, in the current Argentine context, creates a rather hostile environment for these prosecutions.

One of the constant refrains heard in Argentina in recent times is the concern over "*seguridad ciudadana*" ("citizen security," the preferred term for addressing issues of crime and personal safety). The papers editorialize about the "*ola de inseguridad,*" or wave of insecurity; parents complain that their children are not safe in the street; reports of kidnappings and violent crimes make headlines. The concern is especially acute in the Buenos Aires metropolitan area. Headlines remark on the higher level of violent crime in Greater Buenos Aires compared to the rest of the country. The Conurbano in general, and the *villas* in particular, are often presented as the source of much of this crime.

Ruth Stanley (2004) has done an extensive analysis of the rhetoric and politics surrounding the question of violent crime in Argentina. Her paper is replete with statements by elected leaders suggesting that the courts are ineffective in controlling crime and that the only way to combat the "wave of insecurity" is to shoot those who are threatening society with anarchy. Carlos Ruckauf, governor of Buenos Aires province at the end of the 1990s, has come to symbolize this approach to law enforcement. He has repeatedly made public statements about the need to fight crime with blazing guns (his policing approach is often described as "*meta bala*" – give them bullets, or mow them down). Hugo Patti, a notorious police chief associated with kidnappings and torture during and after the last dictatorship, and Aldo Rico, the leader of a military rebellion during the first civilian administration, have capitalized on this concern to seek and obtain political office at the municipal and provincial levels (Seligson 2002).

The *villas* play an important role in the popular imaginary as the locus and source of crime, and their inhabitants are portrayed as alien and criminalized (Stanley 2004). A statement from Ruckauf during the 1999 gubernatorial campaign highlights this perception:

It is necessary to enter into all the *villas* with all the [police] agents necessary to put an end to crime. The police are capable, it's simply necessary to give them instructions and combat decisions. But let us give them the norms they need: we can't have a situation where a policeman enters one of these places and kills someone and then some lawyer of the criminal appears and says it's the policeman who is the murderer. (Stanley 2004 quoting from *Página/12*, August 5, 1999)

The rhetoric suggests a war – and in war there is no due process. Indeed, Ruckauf is suggesting that the laws are too restrictive of police discretion and that the police should be even freer to shoot and kill those they perceive as being criminal. When the police kill inhabitants of shantytowns or suspected criminals, their acts are presented as the legitimate exercise of police powers in the course of open combat against crime. One consequence of this public discourse is popular support for the use of violent and repressive police methods. In a poll taken in 1999, 5.7% were more or less in agreement, 44.9% were in agreement, and 4.6% were strongly in agreement when asked if there was a need to shoot criminals (*"meterle bala a los delincuentes"*) (*El Cronista*, August 9, 2000, cited in Stanley 2004).

This general political environment at times becomes quite focused on judicial and prosecutorial actions. In a northern suburb of Buenos Aires, for example, when the policeman who killed a minor was arrested, there was a demonstration in front of the prosecutor's office demanding his release. When a judge sought to interrogate Patti in connection with the torture of two suspects, and Patti refused to obey the court order, the judge's insistence prompted widespread popular demonstrations in support of Patti. Then-governor Eduardo Duhalde later commended Patti as "the best police chief" in the country. Only rarely will a judge or a prosecutor score political points by aggressively pursuing a case of police violence, and, if anything, these attitudes only hardened from the beginning of the 1990s to their end.

The failure of the most comprehensive effort at police reform is a concrete illustration of the lack of a supportive political context for restraining police violence (Ungar 2001). In 1996, after a series of police scandals and in an attempt to bolster his presidential bid, then-governor Duhalde enacted a wide-ranging series of reforms. The reforms increasingly came under question, as "insecurity" became one of the leading issues in the 1999 gubernatorial elections. As we saw, during the course of the campaign, both Ruckauf, the eventual winner, and Patti made statements graphically advocating the outright killing of criminals. León Arslanian, the minister of justice and security who designed and spearheaded the reform, was forced to resign when even Duhalde backed away from supporting him. After winning the election, Ruckauf largely undid the reforms in response to public clamor for greater leeway for police action and a stronger hand against crime, and he continued to call for a policy of *meta bala*.

Importantly, social inequalities open up the political space for the continuation of repressive police practices and impunity. Increasing unemployment, urban migration, and the presence of large, socially marginalized urban populations feed the demand for more violent action on the part of the police. The *villas* and the large numbers of poor, unemployed urban males exteriorize and localize the problem of crime, magnifying the perceived threat and creating a large potential target for violent police action. At the same time, this perceived threatening population permits society at large to define the victims as someone other than "*la gente*," people like us. The discourse surrounding civil rights thus becomes a contest between "our" right to security and "their" right to due process (Stanley 2004). This is a contest with a predetermined outcome. This political discourse and the great social distances between the typical victims in these cases and all the relevant actors – prosecutors, judges, even voters who might bring political pressure to bear – create an atmosphere in which high levels of violations and impunity can coexist with a democratic system and generous formal rights.

This is not to suggest that the question of police impunity can never gain political traction in Buenos Aires. The frequent disclosures that the police are behind notorious kidnappings and murders, and have released state prisoners to rob for them, as well as periodic events like police complicity in the murder of a young woman, occasionally galvanize public reaction. Smulovitz and Peruzzotti (2003) describe this phenomenon of "societal accountability," in which a community organizes to demand a response from the state and the justice system. But this reaction has been more focused on perceived criminality and corruption in the police force than on due process and abuses in the course of policing operations. This distinction carries through to judicial outcomes, where Private Violence cases lead to twice as many convictions as Routine Policing cases.

The excessive use of force triggers a mainstream reaction only when the victim can be defined as one of "us." That is, it requires an "innocent" victim or visibly criminal actions on the part of the police. For instance, the death in custody of Walter Bulacio, a high school student arrested at a concert, has prompted annual mass demonstrations, benefit concerts, and the like. The killing of innocent bystanders – a schoolteacher in the Boca neighborhood of Buenos Aires in 2000, a music teacher in the northern suburbs of Buenos Aires in early 2001 – can prompt a popular outcry. The murder of three middle-class youths in Floresta in late 2001 led to a neighborhood revolt. And the disappearance of two youths in La Plata in 1990 and 1993, all too reminiscent of the "dirty war" of the 1970s dictatorship, prompted political and popular reactions that led to exhaustive forensic investigations and ultimately convictions. But the nearly daily killings and outright executions of marginalized youths do not cause an outcry.

More sustained political activity around this issue can be found in the peripheral areas of the city. Neighborhood groups and community activists in marginal neighborhoods around Buenos Aires repeatedly mobilize around individual cases they consider particularly egregious, focusing on the police station where the suspects work or the courthouse where the assigned judge is found. In my sample of cases, this sort of popular pressure is more likely in the blue-collar neighborhoods of the Conurbano, where 30% of the cases have prompted demonstrations of one kind or another. Only 13% of the cases in the CABA (which more often involve shantytown residents) generate the same response. These demonstrations range from a group of friends and relatives around the courthouse doors at the time of trial, to neighborhood-wide marches on every anniversary of the death, organized mass demonstrations around the time of key judicial decisions, and traffic interruptions on major thoroughfares. The Buenos Aires area courts are, as we saw in Chapter 2, responsive to these demonstrations.

In summary, police homicides are politically and socially construed as the response to violence and crime, and the victims are viewed as the enemy in an active war between the forces of crime and the forces of order. In turn, the population from which victims are drawn is at a relatively great distance from the state, in terms of both the socio-economic resources it can use to press individual claims and the political resources it can use to press collectively for greater protection from state violence. This victim population does have, and utilizes, the power of popular mobilization to prompt results in individual cases, but there is no organized movement with mainstream support for the strengthening of due process protections and increasing the restraint on police activities.

If anything, attempts to reform and restrain the police have foundered in the face of public demands for more effective policing – which is interpreted and presented by elected officials as a license to use "*mano dura*" or iron-fisted methods of law enforcement. Electoral formulas advocating increased police use of lethal force are far more common and more successful than those advocating restraint in law enforcement and greater protections for crime suspects. It is no surprise that neither individual victims nor their family members are adept at presenting their claims, nor is it surprising that the system has not been re-engineered to respond to this weakness. In the next section we see just how the investigative resources of the legal system work, given this social, economic, and political context.

C. THE SYSTEM'S SOURCES OF INFORMATION

There are both state and non-state channels that could potentially move information from this difficult social and political environment to the legal system. Foremost among the state entities are the police forces. Next in importance is the prosecutor's office, which is also legally empowered to receive complaints directly. Less important in this respect are the Defensor del Pueblo, an ombudsman agency that takes complaints of police abuses along with complaints about any other state agency, and possibly local and state legislators, principally through their Human Rights Commissions. Non-state agents include, most importantly, special-purpose collective actors such as CORREPI, COFAVI, CeProDH, and the CELS,[11] and individual actors such as attorneys who take these cases on behalf of individual claimants.

1. Police Forces Active in the Buenos Aires Area

The most important security and investigative force in Buenos Aires, in terms of number of agents, territory, and population covered is the Buenos Aires Provincial Police; this is also the force with the highest number of killings. *La Bonaerense*, as it is known, has a long and seamy history of corruption and violence (see, e.g., Dutil and Ragendorfer 1997). Attempts to reduce levels of criminality within the corporation by reforming it have, by and large, failed (Ungar 2001; Hinton 2006). The Federal Police force, on the other hand, has a reputation for being both less corrupt and less violent. The information in my sample, however, suggests that they both act similarly in generating or obscuring information about cases in which one of their colleagues is accused of homicide.

The previous chapter extensively documents police efforts to restrict access to information about these cases: the Buenos Aires Provincial Police

---

[11] CORREPI is the Coordinadora contra la Represión Policial e Institucional, COFAVI is the Comisión de Familiares de Víctimas Indefensas de la Violencia Social, CeProDH is the Centro de Profesionales por los Derechos Humanos, and the CELS is the Centro de Estudios Legales y Sociales.

threaten witnesses and lawyers, plant guns, rearrange the scene of the crime
to simulate a shootout, and similarly corrupt the record in 73% of the cases
in which one of their colleagues is a defendant. The number for the Federal
Police is identical: there is some indication of tampering with the evidence
in 73% of the cases involving a Federal Police officer. The social inequalities
discussed earlier apparently make it somewhat easier for the police to corrupt the record. In Buenos Aires, 87% of cases in which the victim was a
villero show evidence of tampering with the evidentiary record, while only
72% of all others do (the chi^2 for this 2×2 table is significant at the .032
level). A joint project by CELS and Human Rights Watch extensively documents similar efforts at obstruction on the part of the Federal and Provincial
Police forces in the first half of the decade (CELS/HRW 1998).

Significantly, when the agency to which the defendant belongs is a different one than the agency conducting the judicial investigation, the results are
radically different. Of twenty cases involving off-duty police officers providing private security services, only 20 percent show evidence of tampering. In
only one of eleven cases involving the Buenos Aires penitentiary service do
advocates identify problems of tampering with the evidence. Only two cases
of twelve involving the armed forces show this pattern, and those two took
place on an army base, where the military obviously controls the premises.
It is clear, then, that the police seek to actively limit or slant the information
that is produced and incorporated into the record in cases that involve their
own.

The structure of the criminal justice system gives the police considerable
latitude in this respect. The 1998 reform of the Buenos Aires Provincial Police
sought to separate the investigative and law enforcement functions, creating a
special division of judicial investigations (Provincial Law No. 12,155, enacted
August 11, 1998). Still, the new investigative police remain administratively
within the original force, and prosecutors complain that they are not truly
independent of their peers in the front lines. They are still subject to the same
hierarchy in terms of discipline, promotion, and compensation; the actual
personnel come directly from the law enforcement side, and they are often
housed side by side with their law enforcement colleagues. Prosecutors have
little influence over this investigative arm, which is supposed to be acting
under its supervision and control, and they have no in-house investigative
resources with which to generate their own information if the police resist
or produce tainted information.

Judges are similarly obligated to the police. This very same police force
carries out dozens of administrative functions for judges and prosecutors,
especially at the *instrucción* or judicial investigative stage. A walk through
any criminal court in the Conurbano or the CABA shows uniformed police

officers sitting at nearly every entry desk, answering phones, delivering official papers, shepherding witnesses around, driving judges' cars, and generally
serving as the hands and feet of the courts during the process of *instrucción*.
Witnesses who wish to describe incidents of police violence will find themselves, more often than not, doing so in the presence of a uniformed police
officer or, at minimum, with one standing just outside the door.

One lawyer described how, in the local prosecutor's office in Morón in the
Greater Buenos Aires area, police officers answer the phone, receive visitors
at the door, and answer questions about the progress of cases, thus serving
as the principal interface with complainants and their lawyers. To bring a
witness into court to present his or her testimony, he said, he had to negotiate
with the local police chief, essentially relying on his personal contacts with
the police. When that failed, he used threats of collective actions and media
denunciations. Prosecutors, on the other hand, never leave their offices, and
so, even though they are now technically in charge of the investigation, they
are merely passive recipients of the information the police wish to produce.[12]

In summary, the principal official conduit into the legal system for information about claims is the same organization that is being investigated in
these cases, and those who are supposed to supervise the investigation have
little capacity to bypass it. The reforms that transferred responsibility for the
investigation to the prosecutor have not yet changed this situation. Alternative sources of information from outside the police – the victims and their
families – are suppressed, often violently, or do not have the capacity to
engage the system effectively.

Any exogenous pressures that could be brought to bear on the police to
generate alternative sources of information from within the force have little
chance to penetrate. The internal discipline of both police forces is calculated to produce strict obedience and hierarchical control. One of the most
striking findings of a CELS/Human Rights Watch study (1998) is the extent
to which internal disciplinary systems are used to enforce obedience and suppress dissent. There are no due process protections for police officers accused
of relatively minor wrongdoings, and the few protections for those accused
of more serious wrongs are not observed in practice.

In the Buenos Aires police, it is a serious disciplinary infraction to anonymously report the wrongdoing of a superior officer, even if the accusation
is subsequently found meritorious. Reporting such wrongdoing to outside
entities such as the media or private individuals is punishable by up to sixty
days in jail, a penalty that can be applied summarily, without any judicial

[12] Interview with Javier Merino, attorney, Matanza, November 27, 2000.

proceeding, by the offender's immediate supervisor. Reports suggest that informal practices in the Federal Police mirror these formal rules of the Provincial Police (CELS 1997: 67). Clearly, then, internal criticism of police practices is drastically curtailed by these rules.

In addition, until 1997 the provincial internal discipline system included no provisions for receiving civilian complaints against the police. There are still none for complaints against the Federal Police. It is no surprise then, that this system is used primarily to enforce internal discipline and control, and that it appears to have little impact on the incidence of corruption, torture, murder, or other abuses, especially among superior officers (CELS/HRW 1998: 62–70), creating a militaristic internal discipline style (see, generally, CELS 1997: 60–66). In a burst of misguided hyperbole, the head of the Provincial Police aptly summarized the overall tenor of internal discipline: defending the force from allegations that it was continuing to torture arrestees, he said he would not tolerate torture and would personally shoot any torturers in the back (*La Nación*, October 18, 2000, p. 15). In short, "the disciplinary system makes it nearly impossible to report illicit acts that take place within the institution" (CELS 1997: 65), ensuring that little information about internal police matters can escape. More internal democracy in police corporations may well render the corporation as a whole more susceptible to external democratic control.

External sanctioning mechanisms are also ineffective. The 1998 CELS/HRW report concludes that "despite including institutions especially designed to control police entities, the control that the executive power exercises is, in general, irrelevant" (CELS/HRW 1998: 70). The Federal Police are completely outside the control of the government of the city of Buenos Aires, since they depend on the national government. And although the police are technically under the federal Interior Ministry, the national government exercises very little political control. In 1997 the chief of police expressed a principled objection to such control, on the grounds that it would permit political manipulation of police functions (CELS/HRW 1998: 71–72). The situation is somewhat different for the Provincial Police, which is subject to the Ministry of Justice and Security and was, in addition, placed under close civilian control (under a decree of *intervención*) in December 1997. But in this case even if there were a way, there is no will. As discussed earlier, during the 1990s, the provincial government was generally quite uninterested in creating a less violent police force (Dutil and Ragendorfer 1997).

In short, in both the CABA and the Conurbano the courts are largely dependent on the police for carrying out the judicial investigation. The entity that carries out that investigation is, in practice, the same one that is charged with law enforcement activities and thus has a strong interest in ensuring that the way it conducts these activities is not too closely scrutinized. Furthermore, if some individual police officers were motivated to report abuses of power, they would expose themselves to internal discipline and punishment, with few or no due process protections. There are no endogenous incentives, therefore, for the police to undertake active and aggressive investigations of incidents involving their own use of lethal force in the course of law enforcement activities.

Nor is there any outside check on this tendency. During the 1990s, political currents tended toward, not away from, the broader use of deadly force on the part of the police. Moreover, agencies of control that are more political have neither their own investigative forces nor any serious disciplinary powers. At the *instrucción* level, in turn, judges and prosecutors must tread carefully in exercising control over the investigative process because they are dependent on the police not only for investigative services but also for everyday administrative services. As a result, the police have a near monopoly on the supply of information regarding their own conduct, and oversight agencies have limited disciplinary capacity.

2. Non-state Investigative Agents

To offset the police investigative monopoly, victims must rely on alternative sources of information. CORREPI is probably the most important actor in the Metro Buenos Aires area for moving grievances about police homicides from the social arena – particularly from among the underprivileged – to the legal one. CORREPI is, on the one hand, well rooted in the popular neighborhoods where many victims reside and, on the other, legally empowered to deliver its outputs into the legal record itself. When it acts as a Private Prosecutor, CORREPI serves as an uplink from marginal sectors of society directly into the *instrucción* and trial stages of the legal process.

CORREPI was created in 1992 as an association of relatives of victims of police violence. It includes a number of lawyers who take on cases of police abuse, offering legal assistance to those affected. These lawyers not only comb newspapers for information about cases that might otherwise go unexplored and unreported, they also contact relatives of victims, offering them both social and legal support. The organization holds regular meetings of relatives of victims to plan popular mobilizations, talk about the progress of legal actions, and offer encouragement and support. CORREPI has branches in such places as Matanza, just outside Buenos Aires – a populous and largely poor urban municipality – and among the poor sectors of the northern suburbs of Buenos Aires, like the Tigre area and the shanty-towns beyond San Isidro, as well as in the interior of the province of Buenos Aires and in other provinces. Members and their contacts live in *villas* and poor neighborhoods. They have no shortage of experience dealing with the poor and uneducated and considerable credibility among them.

The lawyers involved do the sort of cause lawyering that the civil rights movement used in the United States. Recognizing the importance of generating exogenous pressures in addition to doing strictly legal work, these lawyers are involved in everything from conducting a parallel investigation, to protecting witnesses, to organizing (and marching in) demonstrations, to speaking to the media. Between cases they work on educating people about their rights, present papers at human rights conferences, and carry out other public education functions. Their primary formal point of purchase in the legal system itself is as the legal figure that is known as the *querellante* in the Argentine federal courts and the *particular damnificado* in the provincial courts (as noted, I have been using the more descriptive term "Private Prosecutor" to refer to this entire class of legal actors).[13] This figure allows persons directly harmed by the alleged crime to intervene in the prosecution, next to the state's representative.[14] The specific attributes of the Private Prosecutor vary somewhat from place to place. Until late in the decade, in the province of Buenos Aires the Private Prosecutor was truly a secondary figure, dependent on the goodwill of the prosecutor and the judge. She or he could not seek a conviction, for example, if the prosecutor refused to do so; could not independently introduce evidence that the prosecutor did not present; could not ask for a sentence greater than what the prosecutor had requested.

Some of these limitations remain in place, but in 1998 the National Supreme Court ruled that it was unconstitutional to deny the *particular damnificado* the ability to request a conviction when the prosecutor would not do so (in the case known as *Caso Santillán*). This expansion of attributions brings the provincial *particular damnificado* much closer to the federal *querellante*. The latter has all the attributes of an official prosecutor and gives the victim a much stronger voice in the proceedings. Even if the prosecutor

---

[13] A similar figure is the *Assistênte do Ministério Público*, configured in Art. 268 of the Brazilian Code of Criminal Procedure, more commonly referred to in Brazil as the *assistênte de acusação* or *assistênte do promotor*.

[14] There is nothing comparable to this in Anglo-American criminal procedure, although it is quite widespread in Latin America, being present in all the countries with which I am familiar except Uruguay. The limited role accorded victims in the sentencing process or in crafting plea bargains in certain American states is the nearest approximation.

argues in favor of an acquittal, for example, the judge is required to rule on the *querella*'s request that the defendant be convicted.

To return to the image of a cable uplink to the system: at one end of CORREPI is a broad and well-embedded network of social contacts in the milieu that is host to most of the instances of police violence. These contacts know the victims and their relatives, and they often know the police officers involved; they are, therefore, in an excellent position to know the "right" facts. At the other end is a lawyer acting as Private Prosecutor, with standing to accuse, present evidence, and demand a response from the legal system in legal language, arguing for the victim's version of the facts and presenting legal arguments in favor of a stricter application of the rule. One result of this uplink is the translation of victim knowledge into a procedural reality that is congenial to the claimant and cognizable by the system. Another is the presence inside the courts of a trained advocate for application of a victim-friendly rule of decision. CORREPI thus works on the facts and the rule from within the system, while at the same time mobilizing outside the system to create exogenous pressures in favor of a conviction.

Often, however, CORREPI's ability to persuade judges and prosecutors is limited by the suspicion with which it is viewed by these two critical decision makers. The trial court in the Champonois case, discussed earlier, for example, explicitly if obliquely discounted some of CORREPI's arguments as springing from its political orientation rather than from a dispassionate evaluation of the facts and the law.[15] This suspicion arises, in part, because its position comes closest to the victim's preference for a conviction at all costs, putting CORREPI at odds with both judges and prosecutors, as noted earlier in the discussion of the actors' preferences. Moreover, its political activities, important as they are in generating exogenous pressure to convict, give the organization a strongly political coloring in the eyes of judges and prosecutors. This tends to clash with the traditional civil law view that the law is above politics and should operate in an apolitical fashion (Merryman 1985).[16] The more "establishment" actors, therefore, tend to view CORREPI's actions as political and ideological, discounting its contributions unless they are virtually incontestable.

There are other non-governmental organizations with similar missions, including the CELS, CeProDH (Centro de Profesionales por los Derechos Humanos), the Public Interest Law Clinic of Palermo Law School, and

[15] Transcript of the verdict of the Criminal Court of San Isidro, September 5, 2003, in case No. 9193, against Rubén Emir Champonois (on file with the author).
[16] See Hilbink (2003) for a discussion of the implications of this judicial apoliticism in Chile.

COFAVI. Many of these are important in educating the public and officials and in shaping policy, affecting the context in which these cases are tried. They tend to intervene much less often than CORREPI in actual prosecutions, however, and when they do, they serve essentially the same function. As a result, they will not be discussed separately.

D. PROSECUTORS

Given that the Code of Criminal Procedure puts them in charge of the investigation, it should fall to the prosecutors to redress any deficiencies in the information supplied either by the police or by private claimants. But many of the complaints by advocacy groups like CORREPI were directed at the prosecutors' performance in exactly this area, in both the province of Buenos Aires and the CABA. In cases before the federal courts of the CABA, for example, lawyers evaluated more negatively the performance of the investigative prosecutor (the *fiscal de instrucción*), than that of the trial prosecutor (the *fiscal de cámara*) or the appellate attorney (the *fiscal de casación*). The former is charged with supervising the *instrucción* stage and preparing the file for trial. The latter two prosecute the cases at the oral trial on the basis of the file sent up by the *fiscal de instrucción*, and handle any appeals to the higher courts, respectively. These results are consistent with the analysis in Chapter 1, which suggests that endogenous and exogenous incentives largely determine prosecutors' responses in these cases.

Endogenous pressures bearing on prosecutors at the *instrucción* stage lead the prosecutors to be relatively uninterested in an aggressive prosecution of the police. As noted earlier, the police act as the eyes, ears, hands, and feet of the *fiscales* and judges working on the *instrucción*. The prosecutors at this stage are understaffed and dependent on the police for every aspect of their daily work. Thus it happens that, as one prosecutor put it, "if it does not exist in the file, it does not exist in the real world."[17] That is, since the police are the ones who build the file, they largely determine what exists in the real world for prosecutors. The level of dependence is so acute that even judges at the *instrucción* level feel powerless to insist that the police take actions they do not wish to take. One CORREPI lawyer described a case in the provincial courts in which he had, as Private Prosecutor, repeatedly requested a certain evidentiary measure from the judge who was carrying out the *instrucción*. After more than a year of CORREPI's repeated demands, the judge's secretary threw up his hands and said, essentially, "what do you

---

[17] Interview with Prosecutor Luis Domínguez, Buenos Aires, February 2001.

want us to do? Our hands are tied. We've asked the police to do it several times, and they just won't do it!"[18] While procedural reforms should have reduced these endogenous pressures, the limited practical effectiveness of the reforms has largely diluted their impact.

While the trial and appellate prosecutors who are more removed from the *instrucción* might be more interested in a strict application of the law, their dependence on information from below again hampers their actions. Trial prosecutors are not empowered to investigate, but only to try cases based on the information they receive. They are simply handed a completed file on each case by the investigative prosecutors, and they routinely work directly from that information in preparing for the trial. Thus, in the absence of a second source of information such as that from the Private Prosecutor, they merely pass on the skewed version of the facts they inherit. In short, the very structure of the system, in conjunction with the marginalization of the victims in these cases, ensures that, as a routine matter, the version of the facts presented at trial is very close to the police version.

Moreover, exogenous pressures from the prevailing political climate in the 1990s, readily absorbed by the structure of the prosecutor's office, made it unlikely that prosecutors would regularly invest extraordinary resources in police violence cases. The head of each of the prosecutorial forces is a political appointee, and rank and file prosecutors are strongly beholden to the internal hierarchy for their career advancement and in their daily activities. Both of the organic laws that govern these institutions begin by stating the hierarchical nature of the organization, noting that they are governed by the "principle of unity of action." Individual prosecutors are legally required to take direction from their superiors, even if their private legal judgment conflicts with those directives (*Ley Orgánica del Ministerio Público de la Provincia de Buenos Aires* [*Ley* 12,061], Art. 31; *Ley Orgánica del Ministerio Público de la Nación* [*Ley* 24,946], Art. 31). Thus prosecutors face strong internal controls that tend to foster top-down policies and unified action by the prosecutor's office. In the prevailing political climate, the organization as a whole has no incentive to devote the additional resources that would be needed to fully elucidate these cases in the face of police resistance. Individual prosecutors' conduct merely reflects this predisposition.

In summary, given the lack of independent investigative resources and the strongly hierarchical organization of the Ministerio Público, federal and provincial *instrucción* prosecutors in Buenos Aires are vulnerable to

---

[18] The judge's secretary in these systems is less an administrative than a judicial officer, carrying out many judicial functions delegated by the judge.

(endogenous) pressures from the police and (exogenous) pressures channeled through their own hierarchy. Both of these forces tend toward a hands-off approach to police violence. The consequences are clear: when a case involving a fatal police shooting lands on a prosecutor's desk neatly packaged by the police report as a response to violent resistance by the victim, the default position is simply to take that report as the basis for action. There is no reason in the ordinary case for the prosecutor or investigative judge to begin digging below the surface of the report in a search for inconsistencies in the evidence or gaps in the information. An overly skeptical attitude will ingratiate the prosecutor neither with his or her subordinates, superiors, or the public. Nor, as we will see, does the prosecutor face a strong demand from the judges in this respect.

E. THE COURTS

All the actors examined thus far bear primary responsibility for producing the information the legal system uses to adjudicate cases. Working together, the procedural reality they produce will tend to show a strong bias toward exonerating the police defendant and away from the victim's version of events. As we saw, this bias is a result of incentives that lead the police to cover up violations and lead prosecutors to be at best indifferent to them. The incentives produce what we might call normative failures on the part of the police and prosecutors, which are then translated into informational failures as these actors pass on misleading or incomplete information.

The legal system is always an arena for contesting opposed versions of the facts and the law. But the victims, who in the natural course of events would contest and seek to correct the bias, are incapable of doing so effectively in this case by virtue of their social position and lack of resources. The typical exception is when an external actor like CORREPI intervenes on their behalf. The procedural reality that results from this contest, often but not always won by the police, is handed up to the judges who use it in reaching the ultimate decision in each case. In the following pages, I first discuss the reasons why Argentine judges are so sensitive to external pressures and then examine the institutional mechanisms that lead them to rely far too much on this biased version of events.

As to the first of these issues, both the federal and provincial systems have seen important recent changes that have the potential to affect judges' sensitivity to exogenous pressures. The reforms changed the manner of designation of judges, their discipline and removal, and their career paths. The performance of Argentine judges under the former system contradicts some of the conclusions drawn by earlier scholars of civil law systems. These scholars, relying perhaps on an implicit comparison between the United States and continental Europe, claimed that the bureaucratization of the judicial profession in civil law systems produced politically compliant judges (Merryman 1985). In Argentina, as we will see, precisely the opposite is true. The U.S. model as implemented in Argentina produced highly subordinate judges, and the current reforms toward a more meritocratic, civil service-like career path might, if anything, improve the courts in this respect (Brinks 2005). Unfortunately, it is still too soon to tell for sure, as most of the changes came too late to affect performance in the cases included in this study.

The system that had been in place since 1853, when Argentina's original constitution was adopted, was identical in form to that of the United States. Federal judges at all levels were named by the president with the advice and consent of a simple majority of the Senate. As the system was applied, writes Virgolini, judges were selected on the basis of a "triple conformity criterion": conformity to accepted jurisprudential norms, including those concerning the proper limits of judicial action; conformity to norms of professional behavior, especially those concerning respect for hierarchy and seniority; and conformity to norms of social behavior, emphasizing conservatism and abstention from public political debate (Virgolini 1988: 47–48). The Buenos Aires provincial system was essentially the same.

In an attempt to secure greater judicial independence, both systems made a transition in the late 1990s from purely political appointments to selection by written examination, open to all who meet the formal qualifications, administered by a Judicial Council (*Consejo de la Magistratura*). Now both the federal and provincial councils are composed of a crosssection of political, judicial, and society actors and act in a more open and transparent way than the old system of discretionary appointments.[19] Di Federico, for example, notes that the federal council goes much further than any of its European counterparts in reducing the incidence of political considerations in judicial selections (Di Federico 1998). While Zaffaroni (1994: 161–62) criticized the council when it was in the proposal stage as merely a more fragmented political process rather than a truly merit-based one, in a personal interview he later conceded that it offers the best hope for reducing the politicization of the courts (author interview, Buenos Aires, September 21, 2000). Over time, therefore, we may expect that the lower courts in each of the systems will be

---

[19] In 2006 the legislature enacted amendments to the federal council's statute, reducing somewhat the presence of opposition representatives on the council. The following discussion addresses the composition of the council during the relevant time period.

much less politicized than they have been to date (Di Federico 1998; García Lema 1998; Ventura, Scoccia, and Arámburu 1999).

In both cases, however, the actual change did not take place until the end of the decade. The federal council was contemplated already in the 1994 constitutional reforms, but implementing legislation did not pass the Congress until December 30, 1997.[20] Under this legislation, the council must send the president a list of three nominees to fill judicial vacancies (for any positions below the Supreme Court). The president is required to choose from among those three, and the Senate confirms that selection by a two-thirds majority (Ventura, Scoccia, and Arámburu 1999). By December 2000, however, the council had sent the president only seven triads from which to select judges for appointments to ten positions (out of over 100 vacancies). Similarly, a 1994 provincial constitutional reform called for the creation of the Buenos Aires Judicial Council, setting a maximum deadline of two years during which the old appointment system could continue. The council was duly created in 1996 (Law No. 11,868) but has not performed according to expectations, and not enough judges had been named under the new system by the end of the decade to effect a significant change in the composition of the provincial judiciary. While each has accomplished much more since then, the councils' work clearly did not affect the performance of the courts during the time period of this study.

Pre-reform promotion and discipline mechanisms fostered the trial courts' political dependence. Until the constitutional reforms became effective, there was no formalized judicial career in either system, and any ascent from the trial to the appellate courts, or from there to the Supreme Court, required a new political appointment. As a result, even though the judges had tenure security, if they wished to advance their careers, they had to continue pleasing political actors.

Moreover, before the reform, judicial discipline for minor matters in both the federal and provincial systems was formally entrusted to the higher courts (the courts of appeal for trial judges, or the Supreme Court for appellate ones), and removal was by the familiar bicameral impeachment process. But in practice formal methods were almost never used (García Lema 1998: 83). Courts of appeal were reluctant to publicly sanction other judges, and, despite frequent complaints, the cumbersome nature of the impeachment process meant that it was rarely carried out to a conclusion. The mechanisms actually used for discipline and control were more

[20] It might never have passed had it not been for an extensive campaign led by Poder Ciudadano and other civil society entities (Fundación para el Debido Proceso Legal 2002).

informal. Zaffaroni, for example, details the historical pattern of total or partial removal of judges that accompanied changes of power from civilian to military administrations and back again (Zaffaroni 1994: 272). He notes that this subjection to political authority led to a pattern of judges who were "sterile and without commitment," arguing that judicial plasticity to political demands was enforced by partisan pressure applied to the highest judges, who in turn exercised internal discipline to secure compliance by trial judges.

In the province of Buenos Aires, responsibility for discipline over lower level judges has now been handed over to a specialized ad hoc jury, consisting of the president of the provincial Supreme Court, plus five practicing attorneys and five legislators chosen by lot (Constitution of the Prov. of Buenos Aires, Art. 182). The new jury takes the disciplinary process in serious matters away from the judicial hierarchy. Similarly, in the federal system, a division of the Judicial Council is now responsible for disciplining judges, although through the end of 2000 it had failed to institute proceedings in more than a handful of notorious corruption cases. Nor has the council eliminated informal mechanisms of hierarchical control. In recent years, appellate judges in both systems have responded to their new lack of formal disciplinary control by shifting to more public informal mechanisms. They have begun writing highly critical, harshly worded opinions reversing lower court judgments – and then releasing them to the press. Commentators note that these open criticisms are unprecedented.

In short, the appointment, discipline, and advancement process, for both of the systems and for most of the time under consideration, was unabashedly political. Control was exercised first through the power of appointment, then through informal mechanisms for discipline. Although the legislature held disciplinary authority through an impeachment procedure, this procedure was seldom used and does not appear to pose a credible threat. A judge could, if so inclined, carve out a politically independent path – indeed there are always judges with a reputation for independent action – but not too many judges were so inclined. The new system sets up a merit-based appointment and advancement procedure, but it does not fully eliminate informal mechanisms of control, and in any event by the end of 2000 it was still too soon to evaluate its effect on actual judicial conduct in the sorts of cases at issue here.

There is considerable consensus on the consequences of this institutional configuration. Most would agree that, with notable exceptions, both provincial and federal judges were politicized in the partisan sense of the term. Paradoxically, this politicization was demonstrated through an expressly apolitical rhetoric and a withdrawal from making "political" decisions. The result was, of course, that the executive, whether constitutional or de facto, was afforded a great deal of discretion in any question that could be construed as even remotely political.[21] Vega (1998) offers a rich historical account of Argentine courts' compliance with de facto governments. Helmke (2002) finds that the National Supreme Court is highly sensitive to dominant political players; Iaryczower and his colleagues find much the same thing (Iaryczower, Spiller, and Tommasi 2002, 2006).

The opinions of attorneys who use the system match these scholarly findings. In 1997, when the new appointment system was not yet under way, lawyers' opinions about the judicial appointment process and its results were abysmal, especially for the provincial judges of the Conurbano. Fucito, a sociologist who carried out extensive in-depth lawyer interviews and a survey on this issue, reports that lawyers used the following phrases to describe the provincial judiciary: "favoritism, farcical system, arbitrariness, by personal reference, political stamp, party affiliation, personal ties, and political loyalty as a result" (Fucito 1997: 1585, 1586).[22] In another survey, Fucito found that 51% of lawyers disagreed that judges have sufficient legal knowledge ("*conocimiento jurídico*"), and 10% had no opinion on the question (Fucito 1999: 1039).

According to Fucito, lawyers' opinions of the federal judges of the CABA were only slightly better. Federal trial court judges became infamous in the 1990s after President Menem expanded their numbers to meet the needs of the new oral procedures, appointing dozens of politically loyal judges. These judges became known as the "*jueces de la servilleta*," or napkin judges. Carlos Corach, the minister of the interior, reportedly scoffed at the threat of judicial action against the Menem administration, allegedly penning on a café napkin a long list of judges on which the administration could unconditionally rely. The list of anecdotes in which both higher and lower court judges engaged in blatant political favoritism is endless. We might expect the judiciary, then, to be sensitive to prevailing political winds even in such relatively low-profile cases as the run-of-the-mill police violence case. The results discussed in Chapters 2 and 3, showing the impact of popular demonstrations on judicial outcomes, bear this out.

---

[21] Hilbink develops this argument in more detail in her research on the Chilean courts (Hilbink 2003). While the Argentine courts varied on this measure more than did the Chilean ones, they do, at different moments, act in a very similar fashion.

[22] Fucito simply transcribes representative adjectives used in responses, listing "acomodo, sistema farcesco, discrecionalidad, recomendación, cuña política, camiseta partidaria, vinculaciones, y lealtad política como resultado."

In addition to their responsiveness to exogenous pressures, the courts are dependent on the police for what information they receive. Fucito's survey asked lawyers to agree or disagree with the statement that judges are out of touch with reality in deciding cases. Only 28% disagreed; fully 65% of lawyers agreed with this statement (and 15% expressed no opinion) (Fucito 1999b: 1040). For the earlier part of the decade, this should come as no surprise. In practice, the police carried out the investigation and brought the results into the judges' chambers. The written procedure reduced the complexities of oral testimony to a few summary sentences. Moreover, even though the code specified that the judge must preside over the questioning of witnesses, and even though official reports typically note that the judge was indeed presiding over them, this was almost never true, since judges simply delegated this function to staff members. Thus the judges using the written system decided cases on the basis of the recommendations of their staff, backed only by brief summaries of testimony produced by the same staff, on the basis of what the police had determined was the relevant scope of the investigation.

This arrangement set up a double information-filtering system. For most of the decade in the provincial courts, and for the few cases tried under the old code in federal court, the testimony on which a decision was based was first filtered by the police, who determined which witnesses would be brought into court for questioning, and then by judicial staff, who decided what was worth recording and preserving – and, as importantly, what was not. As a result of these filters, the production of a factual record tended toward a monolithic rather than a nuanced and controverted view of the events. And in police cases, as we saw, it was biased in favor of the police version. There were few checks on this bias: prosecutors, for the reasons discussed earlier, were unlikely to press for the inclusion of additional material that contradicted the official police version; and the courts were heavily indebted to the police for assistance in all aspects of their daily functioning. The new procedure has the potential to change this, but, as noted in the earlier discussion of the reforms, actual practices changed little with implementation of the new codes. The investigation continues to be the province of the police, and courts continue to look for the real world within the four corners of the *expediente*.

As if this were not enough, operational features of the Argentine judicial system exacerbate judges' informational dependence on the police. Judges at the *instrucción* level are among the busiest in the judicial system. One investigative judge complained that she received more than four thousand new cases every year, so that most of the cases were destined to remain unresolved, unless the case entered with a relatively complete police file detailing the circumstances of the alleged offense. This judge is in the federal correctional courts of the CABA, which investigate and try crimes punished by less than three years' imprisonment (of the cases in this study, only those in which the police officer is charged with negligent homicide fall in this category). From 1993, the year the new CPPN came into effect, to 2000, the annual number of new cases per judge fluctuated between approximately 5,200 and 6,700 (Portal de la Justicia Argentina 2003). Of these, only about half of one percent ended with a conviction and sentence (FORES and Colegio de Abogados de Buenos Aires 1999a: 150–51). The rest were archived (i.e., put on semi-permanent hold) or otherwise dismissed without a hearing.[23]

The investigative courts that deal with more serious crimes handle nearly as many, and more complex, cases. The number of new cases per judge in the ordinary criminal courts, the *Fuero Penal de Instrucción*, doubled between 1993 and 2000, from 1,366 to 2,772 (statistics from Portal de la Justicia Argentina 2003). The judges, like the prosecutors, do not have the staff that would be required to handle 2,000 new cases a year in anything but a routinized, mechanical fashion. Clearly they are not up to conducting an independent investigation when, as happens periodically, they are presented with a case in which a police officer is accused of homicide.

Judicial delays also disadvantage the victims of police violence. Many have remarked on the slowness of the judiciary in Buenos Aires in the typical criminal case, attributing it to inefficiency (FORES and Colegio de Abogados de Buenos Aires 1999a, 1999b) or overwork (García Lema 1998: 72). But police cases move even more slowly than the typical case. Under current rules – for obvious and good reasons – cases in which the defendant is jailed pending trial get top priority on the judicial calendar. Police officers, however, are usually released because they are charged with lesser offenses, such as an excess of self-defense or negligent homicide, or are first offenders, not deemed a threat to the community and not considered a flight risk. This occurs even though, in some cases, the same officers go on to kill again before coming to trial (Palmieri, Borda, and Ales 2004). In my cases, 76% of police officers with cases pending in the provincial courts and 90% of CABA defendants awaited their trial in freedom.[24]

---

[23] These numbers might suggest a complete abdication of the judicial function, but a vast proportion of these cases are the truly minor matters that do not generate substantive judicial decisions in any system – neighbor conflicts, petty property crime, and so on. Often the threat of judicial action is enough to resolve the conflict without an actual decision by the courts.

[24] This is drastically different than the norm for civilian accused murderers, who are routinely held pending trial, according to lawyers in Argentina.

As a result of this special treatment, police cases are placed on the less urgent track. More importantly, the fact that the defendant is free creates a strong incentive for engaging in what is popularly known in Argentina as *la chicana* – the use of procedural tricks to delay adjudication. These tricks include appealing every adverse decision, filing requests of all sorts in order to appeal the denials, delaying witness interviews and opposing evidentiary requests, and requesting far-off dates for every appearance. The time to adjudication in the provincial Buenos Aires cases in my sample ranges from a few days (for cases that are dismissed immediately) to nearly nine years, with an average of just over three years. Among cases that went to trial, the average delay rises to more than four years. These figures do not take into consideration post-trial appeals, which add approximately two more years before the decision is final. The courts of the CABA appear to work a little more quickly, with delays ranging from about one month to over seven years, for a mean delay of two years. But the lower average reflects primarily a larger number of cases summarily dismissed before trial, as the mean time to trial is nearly identical, at just over four years.

Delay contributes to the loss of independent information, since by the time the trial courts begin to look at a file, the facts are likely to be several years old, and it becomes increasingly difficult to challenge the official version preserved in the police report. Furthermore, the impact of delay can be expected to be greatest for the disadvantaged population from which the average victim is drawn. The lack of steady employment or a fixed address, as well as other informalities of the truly marginal population, mean that witnesses and complainants are more likely to disappear by the time a trial is finally scheduled. The results are apparent. Convictions are most likely among my sampled cases in the mid-range of delay: a substantial number of cases are dismissed outright at the very beginning, then there is an increase in successful prosecutions, and at the tail end of the distribution, nearly all the cases end in acquittals.[25]

The main difference in the informational dependence of judges from the beginning to the end of the decade is that in both jurisdictions the Private Prosecutor can now insist on the inclusion of additional materials in the file and on calling witnesses at an oral trial. Under this system, the decision maker is afforded the opportunity to observe the demeanor of the witnesses and

---

[25] I ran a logistic regression predicting convictions using only the length of time a case has been pending, plus the square and cube of that term. Graphing the predicted probability of a conviction over time results in a bell-shaped probability curve, with a low probability of conviction if the decision comes early or late, and a higher probability in the medium range.

see their testimony tested in cross-examination. The action of the Private Prosecutor at trial now adds a second stream of information that is not filtered by the police and is independent of the pressures brought to bear on prosecutors. Judges could use this information to begin to second-guess the version of events presented by the police and prosecutors. Unfortunately, the typical delays in these cases mean that memories have faded and witnesses are often reduced to confirming whatever their recorded testimony reflects.

Perhaps the strongest evidence of judicial informational dependence and the consequent autonomy of the police comes from the cases themselves. As discussed earlier, there is ample documentation of a pattern of obstruction and manipulation of the process on the part of the police. All the watchdog groups have raised the issue: CORREPI, CELS, and others have made it a constant refrain; the Supreme Court of the province of Buenos Aires remarked on the police's use of violence to silence youths who complained of ill treatment; and even the newspapers report on the problem. My database includes cases relating to 172 victims in the province of Buenos Aires and another 41 in the CABA. In three-quarters of these cases there is some indication of tampering with the record. And yet only seven persons have been prosecuted for covering up or obstructing the investigation in connection with these 213 homicides.

In theory, of course, judges are not powerless in response to the investigative failures of the police and prosecutors. Before the recent procedural reforms, judges were technically in charge of the investigation, and after the reforms, they were required to actually sit through the presentation of live testimony. Bringing judges into direct contact with witnesses and the Private Prosecutor should have reduced their reliance on a pre-packaged, pre-digested written record produced by lower level functionaries working with the police. In practice, however, the parties and the court still rely too much on the written record, and the police continue to control the production of information in both systems. As a result, the change did not do as much as it could have to eliminate the dominance of the police version of events at trial.

F. SUMMARY

Over the course of the decade and within the same general geographic area these cases encountered radical differences in institutional design. And yet these differences have had a negligible impact on actual outcomes, which remained uniformly poor despite institutional variation. This can be attributed to two factors that remained constant in the Buenos Aires system during the entire period of the study. The first is the dominant role of the police in the production of information, which maintained informational dependence and strong endogenous pressures toward acquittal in these cases. The second is the increasingly unfavorable political context, which created exogenous pressures for acquittals and limited institutional innovation that might have addressed the court's informational failures in these cases.

These two broad factors rest on and work through a variety of institutional mechanisms. Because they are both perpetrator and investigator, the police have the inclination and the capacity to hamper inquiries into these crimes. Judges and prosecutors are passive consumers of bad information because they are highly sensitized to a political climate that has been generally hostile to the prosecution of Police Violence cases, except in high-profile cases with sympathetic victims. Occasionally, social and political pressures push judicial actors toward a conviction, but then they run up against their limited independent investigative capacity. In those cases judges either rely on private investigative efforts or simply lower their evidentiary standards. In general, however, state actors acting without external prodding are either ineffective or counterproductive in these prosecutions.

Meanwhile, the social position of the typical victims makes it difficult for them, on their own, to generate either sufficient information or sufficient political pressure to overcome this state inertia. This is precisely why actors like CORREPI use both legal and political tactics, acting as Private Prosecutor and organizing demonstrations. The results of the quantitative analysis in Chapter 2 strongly validate this strategy: demonstrations matter, and so does the Private Prosecutor. Interestingly, in a simple bivariate analysis, the difference between having or not having a Private Prosecutor is more important in the CABA (32% conviction rate vs. 0%) than in the province (23% vs. 9%). This suggests, first, that the greater attributes of the *querellante* in the CABA over the provincial *particular damnificado* make a real difference. It also suggests that federal judges (as their reputation suggests) are more likely to convict if supplied with the legal elements they need to make a decision.

The passive response of the state and the consequent reliance on private resources should create special difficulties for the disadvantaged and lead to more socio-economic inequality in outcomes. This is especially true since the crucial Private Prosecutor figure is normally a privately paid attorney, dependent on the initiative and resources of an interested party. But CORREPI, the principal NGO acting in this capacity, has an ideological bias in favor of the marginalized and offsets their economic disadvantage in a large number of cases in the sample. This is one reason why outcomes in Buenos Aires are less responsive to socio-economic variables than a reliance on private resources would suggest. The other reason is that convictions respond to political pressures, which are importantly but imperfectly related to social standing.

In summary, the double normative and informational vulnerability of the system produces the low effectiveness and low inequality measured in Chapter 2. Buenos Aires claimants face relatively low levels of effectiveness that can often be attributed to a mischaracterization of the facts by the police. Individual efforts to redress this mischaracterization have only limited effects on the outcome because judges and prosecutors apply overly lenient standards – except in cases that acquire political prominence. The system's dependence on non-state investigative action produces a tendency toward inequality that is masked by two separate dynamics: some convictions are the result of political factors that are not directly correlated with socio-economic inequality but rather have to do with the socio-political construction of the case; and the most active civil society actors participating directly in the judicial process – CORREPI and a few others – work free of charge for the underprivileged, in this respect, at least, placing them on an equal footing with those who can afford to retain private lawyers.

5

São Paulo

Normative Autonomy and Informational Failures

> Então! Olhe pra você e lembre dos irmãos!
> Com o sangue espalhado, fizeram muitas notícias!
> Mortos da mão da polícia, fuzilados de bruços no chão.
> Me causa raiva e indignação
> A sua indiferença quanto à nossa destruicão!
>> Racionais MC's, "Júri Racional" (2006)

> Se eu fosse mágico?
> Não existia droga, nem fome, nem polícia.
>> Racionais MC's, "Mágico de Oz"
>> (1998)

The Brazilian rap artists Racionais MC's sing of society's indifference to those shot by the police. Their words accurately suggest that state violence in Brazil occurs in a social context that is largely indifferent to the deaths of the poor and marginalized. Only the most dramatic and bloody of these events make the news. It is no surprise, then, that they put the police squarely in the trio of ills they would eliminate if they had magical powers: no more drugs, no more hunger, no more police. All three have a deadly effect on the urban poor of Brazil. This chapter relates precisely this story – the dismal failure of an otherwise relatively functional legal system to respond to a violent police force, largely owing to the indifference of the general public. São Paulo presents a clear challenge to the notion that democracy comes all of a piece. Political rights are alive and vibrant in São Paulo, and yet the police routinely violate fundamental civil rights and, in practical terms, remain above the law. This is a problem for democracy under most definitions of the term, which insist that no one may be *de legibus solutus* (O'Donnell 2001) and that respect for civil rights is a necessary element of any modern democracy (Mainwaring,

Brinks, and Pérez-Liñán 2001). Observers have labeled this truncated version of democracy "disjunctive democracy" (Holston and Caldeira 1998).

The threat of a violent death at the hands of the police is a constant presence for many of São Paulo's marginal youths. Indeed, to the best of my knowledge, the absolute number of homicides attributed to the police in São Paulo vastly exceeds that of any other city anywhere in the world. Of the 7,500 people acknowledged by the police to have been killed in the state of São Paulo from 1990 through 2000, about half were killed in the capital city itself.

There is a popular Brazilian saying that goes "*Quem não deve, não teme*" (he who owes nothing, fears nothing). There is another saying that runs, "*Não deve, não teme, mas corre da PM*" – "Owes nothing, fears nothing, but runs from the police." Especially but not only for young black males, as we have seen, fear of the state and its agents is as strong today as it might have been at any time during the military dictatorship. In his book *ROTA 66* (1992), the journalist Caco Barcellos vividly brings that fear to life in dramatic recreations of some of the most notorious killings committed by the infamous ROTA force of the São Paulo police. The fear is undiminished by the illusory promise of protection offered by the law. The seriousness of this black hole in the midst of Brazil's democratic system makes it imperative that we begin to understand what drives the high levels of impunity documented in Chapter 3 for São Paulo.

As in the previous chapter, I will examine the endogenous and exogenous factors that produce informational and normative success or failure at the various levels of São Paulo's justice system. The dominant endogenous characteristic is the complete control over the supply of information to prosecutors, judges, and juries exercised by the police force as it investigates cases that affect its own agents. Meanwhile, the socio-political context is generally supportive of harsh and immediate police repression, opening up the necessary political space for a passive approach to these cases by prosecutors and judges. These exogenous factors channeled through career incentives trend away from a more aggressive stance, which might otherwise lead judicial actors to generate some of their own information and oversee police conduct more effectively.

The judicial apparatus is well designed to produce an independent and technically qualified judiciary, but judges appear little interested in police homicides. The prosecutorial corps is highly qualified and has been extremely active in promoting other social issues, but it is almost completely silent on the matter of police violence, especially in cases involving victims tainted by a connection to crime. The generally passive approach of the judiciary and prosecutorial forces, combined with the radical marginalization of the targeted population, leaves the Military Police with a stranglehold on the flow of information about police homicides up into the legal system. In fact, the dearth of information is such that even judges and prosecutors who are sympathetic to the cause of human rights and might otherwise be vigorous advocates for the victims are left with the impression that no rights have been violated, and hence struggle very little to deepen the investigation.

The same lack of information and the overwhelming concern with violent crime accounts for the apathy with which the rest of the population looks at these cases. And in contrast with Argentina, the most likely victims remain unlikely to mobilize in favor of a stricter application of the law to the police. The population that is most likely to find its young men among the victims lives under the constant fear of crime and shows a high level of support for draconian police methods.[1] The result is continuing and tolerated impunity, with no more than sporadic political impetus for changes that might address the problem more effectively.

A. THE BRAZILIAN CODE OF CRIMINAL PROCEDURE

Prior to Law no. 9,229 of 1996, known as the *Lei Bicudo*, any crimes committed by Military Police officers and punishable under the Military Criminal Code (which essentially mirrors the ordinary Criminal Code plus a series of infractions related exclusively to military discipline) were the exclusive concern of the military justice system. Under this system, a police officer accused of a crime faced first an investigation carried out by the Military Police, the *Inquérito Policial Militar*, or IPM. The investigating officer would turn over the IPM report (usually referred to simply as the IPM) to the *Promotoria Militar*, or Military Prosecutors, who carried out the pre-trial investigation, or *instrução*, and then took the case to trial before a military tribunal. This tribunal was made up of two Military Police officers who outranked the defendant plus one civilian judge from the military justice system. The tribunal represented a blend of lay and professional justice and acted more as an internal discipline system than as a true judiciary. The system was strongly criticized for its overt emphasis on internal discipline over human rights concerns and extensive delays.

---

[1] As noted earlier, we might question whether support for violent police action is inversely related to income, education, and other socio-economic variables. But it is clear that there is not a strong movement among the popular classes to restrain the police.

Enactment of the *Lei Bicudo* changed only the judicial aspects of this process, leaving the investigation in the hands of the Military Police. The new law transferred responsibility to civilian courts only for intentional crimes against life (*crimes dolosos contra a vida*), including torture and other attacks on physical integrity short of murder, but not including less serious abuses of authority or even negligent homicide (*homicídio culposo*).[2] As a result, the *inquérito* or initial investigation is still done primarily by the Military Police. In theory the police have sixty days to turn in the IPM to the relevant prosecutor, while in practice the report is often late. The Civil Police can also produce their own *Inquérito Policial* (IP) if they happen to learn of facts that suggest that a civilian crime has occurred. In fact, in most of my cases there was both an IPM and an IP. But typically the Civil Police intervene only when the Military Police claim that the victim committed a crime. Thus, the Civil Police IP is generally focused on the victim's alleged crime – resisting arrest or robbery, for example – while the IPM focuses on the actions of the Military Police.

In the event the IPM or the IP suggests that an intentional crime against life may have occurred, the case enters the civilian jury system. The IPM and IP are filed with the courts and with the civilian prosecutor, and the *instrução* stage begins.[3] The *instrução* stage is under the supervision of the trial judge, who evaluates the evidentiary and other requests made by both parties and determines what is appropriate. The judge also has the authority to ask for additional proofs, acting in this sense a little more like the traditional inquisitorial judges of the civil law systems than like a common law jury trial judge. The *instrução* stage can result in one of three outcomes: the prosecutor can seek, and the judge order, the dismissal of the case (*arquivamento*); the judge can summarily acquit the defendant (*absolvição sumária*); or the judge can set the case for trial (*pronúncia*). The first two are both decisions to drop the prosecution, although the first, technically, does not bar a reprosecution, while the second would invoke double jeopardy and prevent another attempt to prosecute the same defendant for the same crime.

---

[2] The original proposal presented by Representative Bicudo was much broader, but the strong lobby of the Military Police (with the support of many state governors) reduced it to this narrower scope.

[3] In practice, judges complain that the military justice system often retains the IPM long after it is supposed to be turned over to the *Tribunal do Júri*. Meanwhile the IP is labeled with the lesser crime of the victim and therefore does not go to the *Tribunal do Júri* either, but to the courts that have jurisdiction over robbery, resisting arrest, and the like. There it is quickly dismissed because of the death of the accused. As a result, the prosecutors and judges who are supposed to deal with police homicides often do not receive the file until months after the event.

At this stage, as in post-reform Buenos Aires, the prosecutor takes the initiative in pushing the case toward a trial or dismissal, although the judge must make the final decision. The prosecutor may limit his or her review to the facts alleged in the IPM and act solely on the basis of this report; may conduct his or her own investigation, bringing in the witnesses identified therein for further questioning and ordering additional forensic tests; or may send the whole report back for more investigation by the Military Police. Defense attorneys and the judge can also ask for the inclusion of additional information in the file and call additional witnesses. Witnesses are questioned in the judge's offices, and the resulting testimony summarized and set down by a judicial clerk or secretary. Documents and the results of forensic tests are also incorporated into the record.

At the end of the investigation, the prosecutor must file something like a formal indictment (the *denúncia*) requesting that the judge set the case for trial. The judge then evaluates the contents of the file for sufficient evidence that the defendant has committed the crime with which he is charged. If so, the judge will file a *pronúncia*, setting the case for trial. If the judge believes the proofs are insufficient, he or she may refuse to set the case for trial (*impronúncia*). If this is because in the judge's view the allegations describe merely a crime of negligence, for example, the case is remitted to the appropriate court for further processing; alternatively, the judge may order additional proofs before making a final decision or may simply dismiss the case.

Although the trial itself assembles all the characters with which most readers will be familiar – prosecutor, defense attorney, judge, and jury – the way it is conducted only vaguely resembles U.S. jury trials. Attorneys have much greater leeway in deciding the scope of the evidence and the manner in which it is presented. As in Argentina, even though the trial is indeed conducted orally, not all the witnesses are actually present and much of the testimony is incorporated by reading (or, even more remotely, by describing from memory) what was said during the pre-trial investigation. Moreover, attorneys typically use broad arguments about violence and crime and the character of the defendant. One prosecutor told me that he likes jury trials precisely for this reason: "juries judge the person as a whole, not just the narrow circumstances of the case."[4] In contrast with the greater activism of the judge at the pre-trial stage, during the trial itself the judge plays a very passive role.

The trial is very condensed and summary. Trials usually do not last longer than a few hours and run without major interruptions until their conclusion;

---

[4] Interview with Prosecutor Norberto Jóia, São Paulo, April 16, 2001.

it is extremely rare for a trial to be continued from one day to the next. As a result, trials often end late in the night – in one of my cases, the jury was finally dismissed after three o'clock in the morning; in one that I attended, we left the courthouse after one in the morning. When I mentioned this to a prosecutor, he suggested that it was not unusual. While there is no systematic information on this, it appears that at least as much time is devoted to the arguments of the attorneys as to actual witnesses. According to a standard commentary on the Code of Criminal Procedure, the prosecutor and defense get a total of two and a half hours each for closing arguments and rebuttals (Renó do Prado and Mascari Bonilha 2000: 234). For trials that may not last longer than six or seven or at most ten hours, this is a vast amount of time, showing the relative importance assigned to information that has been pre-processed by legal professionals versus the unadorned testimony of witnesses or documents.

At the end of the trial, the jury, the judge, and the attorneys all go into the jury room. There, the judge presents the jury with narrowly drafted questions that will determine the outcome of the case.[5] In addition to questions relating to guilt or innocence, the jury votes on questions that establish what the sentence will be, within the range established by law, based on the presence or absence of attenuating or aggravating factors. The questions move from the more general ("did a death occur?") to the more specific ("did this defendant cause the death?"), gradually guiding the process toward the final outcome. The jury votes by secretly placing small Yes or No cards in a basket; a simple majority determines the jury's answer. The results of each round are announced before the next round, so that the decision is built piecemeal, with information about the previous decisions made by fellow jurors.

No deliberation is allowed either in the jury room or during a trial. In contrast to the common law's tradition of juror deliberation, it is the height of misconduct and cause for a mistrial for one juror to make his or her voting intentions known or to attempt to persuade another juror. Like the secret ballot box, this voting method does not require jurors to identify, explain, or justify their decisions, giving them full freedom to act on their individual judgments about the case – and on their prejudices and preconceptions. Compared to the broad-ranging debate and presentation of information at the trial, the questions are designed to focus attention very narrowly on the elements of the crime, although the legal language often includes terms like

---

[5] This procedure is similar to the "special verdicts" occasionally used in complex U.S. jury trials.

"reasonable" or "excess of legitimate defense," which are intrinsically open to individual, subjective construction.

Once the jury has answered all the questions, the judge mechanically assigns a sentence on the basis of the jury's decision by applying the rules to the answers given by the jury. Simple homicide carries a penalty of 6 to 20 years in prison, while aggravated homicide (*homicídio qualificado*) can carry a penalty of 12 to 30 years, depending on sentencing factors. Thus, once the case is set for trial, the judge is almost completely uninvolved in the decision-making process. Prosecutors and defense attorneys manage the information presented almost without judicial interference, and the jury votes yes or no.

In 2001, I attended a murder trial that illustrates many of the less objective characteristics of a São Paulo jury trial. The emphasis from the opening of the trial was largely on the wave of violence afflicting society, with both the prosecutor and the defense attorney making broad appeals to the social context of the crime and emphasizing the jury's responsibility to care about the larger social questions, rather than focusing narrowly on the guilt or innocence of the accused. Even when the focus was on the accused, the inquiry ranged broadly over his character, prior conduct, and possible other criminality rather than, again, focusing narrowly on his guilt or innocence of the specific crime charged. Most shocking to U.S.-trained lawyers, the prosecutor relied heavily on the argument that the defendant was a drug dealer and had committed other crimes that had not been or could not be proven (and of which no evidence at all was presented). Further, the prosecutor emphasized the lawlessness of the *favela* where the crime occurred.

Most of the information presented at this trial was not live. Only one of the fact witnesses appeared in person to testify. The accused took the stand to give his own version of the story – although under the Brazilian privilege against self-incrimination, he was exempt from swearing to tell the truth and was not required to submit to cross-examination. The testimony of the remaining witnesses was incorporated directly by the attorneys, who simply described from memory what had been uncovered in the course of the *instrução*. In their closing arguments, attorneys made copious reference to witnesses who had not testified but had been questioned earlier in the judicial process. The prosecutor dwelt at length on what she said had been discovered in the investigation of a different crime that may have involved the same defendant. The judge never interfered with the attorneys' presentation of information to the jury. In fact, in the middle of final arguments, the judge simply left the bench for more than half an hour while the attorneys continued to argue their case. The arguments lasted at least as long as the presentation of evidence.

B. SOCIAL CONTEXT

1. Socio-economic Context

To evaluate the capacity of potential claimants to engage the legal system, we must view both their own socio-economic profile and the socio-economic environment from which they come. In São Paulo, conditions are sufficiently extreme that we should expect them to have a large impact on outcomes. São Paulo, like Buenos Aires, is the largest and most economically significant city in the country. Even more than Buenos Aires, it is marked by economic extremes, in a country already signed by inequality. In a study based on 1993 figures, Brazil ranks third in income inequality among a sample of 119 countries worldwide (Milanovic and Yitzhaki 2001). And Metro São Paulo, despite its wealth, includes large *favelas*, or shantytowns.

One of the clearest findings in my sample is how strictly selective the São Paulo police are in targeting lower class victims, while the middle class has almost nothing to fear. Out of 196 cases pertaining to intentional shootings occurring in the course of police activities per se (i.e., shootings, including outright executions, that occur in the course of routine policing activities), only one is known to involve a middle-class victim.[6] While I have less complete information about whether a victim lived in a shantytown or not, the proportion of victims who lived in a *favela* appears very high: out of 74 victims of the same routine policing shootings who can be definitely categorized as shantytown residents or not, 48 (65%) lived in a shantytown.[7] Nearly 75% of victims of intentional police killings for whom I have employment information were unemployed (I am missing data in about 10% of the cases). Indeed, as noted in Chapter 3, middle-class residents of São Paulo primarily have to worry about being caught in the crossfire, as 4 of 13 bystanders shot by mistake belonged to the middle class. Only 6 out of 219 cases of all kinds involved middle-class victims.

If, as Blaustein (2003) argues, the *villas* in Buenos Aires suffer from a lack of communication with the rest of Argentine society, the *favelas paulistanas* are even further removed from the formal world of the "asphalt," as it is

---

[6] In 49 of these cases there is no information regarding the socio-economic standing of the victim.

[7] In Chapter 2 I inferred shantytown residence from class, noting that among the lowest class victims for whom shantytown residence was known 85% lived in a shantytown. Applying the same proportion here to fill in gaps in the data leads to the same result: approximately 105 out of 160 cases with complete or inferred information – nearly two-thirds – involve a shantytown dweller.

known. In Chapter 2 I reported that a census-based estimate places about
10 percent of São Paulo's sixteen million people in a shantytown. Most
estimates place the *favela* population in the São Paulo metro area between
one and two million people, creating a separate and unequal universe within
the megalopolis.

The *favelas* in the state of São Paulo are characterized by territorial segregation, removal from the formal job market, a lack of state services and basic
infrastructure, and high indices of insecurity, violence, disease, and infant
mortality. And the *favelas* located in the São Paulo metro area are among
the worst of these (Rolnik 2001). Child mortality rates, despite decreasing
for São Paulo as a whole, increased in its marginal areas from 1980 to 1998
(Ferreira Antunes and Waldman 2002). NGOs that work in these areas often
find that residents need assistance with demonstrating their very existence
to the state, by securing birth certificates and identity cards.[8] Not all *favelas*
are the same – older, more established shantytowns tend to be less violent
(Gunn 1998), for example – but as a general rule, living conditions are dismal
indeed in the periphery of São Paulo.

Even more to the point, it is clear that in general *favela* residents in
São Paulo are excluded from ordinary and daily interactions with the state
and formal society. Lopes de Souza (2001) describes a process of increasing
territorialization or fragmentation of urban spaces. In his account, *favelas*
become increasingly isolated from each other because they are each under
the control of rival drug gangs. And they are isolated from the formal city
because the affluent classes expect and demand that "poor people, especially
favelados and blacks . . . be kept outside" middle-class public spaces (Lopes
de Souza 2001). For residents of the *favelas*, he says, the formal cities are a
no-man's-land where their security is not guaranteed. The incorporation of
favelados into the legal order of the state is minimal. Just as there is a parallel
legal reality in the *favelas* of Rio de Janeiro, as described by Boaventura de
Sousa Santos (1977), so too the massive *favelas* of São Paulo operate outside
the social and legal fabric of the city.

Nor have the lower working classes who live outside the *favelas* and make
up the other third of victims become more integrated into the fabric of the
city during the 1990s. As in Argentina, unemployment in general rose over
this decade – the monthly open unemployment figure trended upward, fluc-
tuating between 4% and 10% and ending the decade at about 9%. Absolute

---

[8] This is the origin of the *Balcões de Direitos* projects in, among other places, the São Paulo
and Rio de Janeiro metropolitan areas.

unemployment ended the decade above 16%.[9] And the majority of those who had jobs were missing the legal connection, through the *"carteira,"* or employment certification, to the state and formal economy. During the 1990s employment in the informal sector grew from 40% to 51% for the four largest metro areas in Brazil, including of course São Paulo (Ramos 2003, using data from IBGE monthly job survey).

The end result is a vast population that is urban but far removed from the state and its legal order, a prime example of what O'Donnell (1993) calls the "brown areas" of democracy. Their interactions with the state are for the most part limited to the police, who may or may not come into their neighborhood. Any communication with the legal system – contacting a lawyer, going downtown for free legal assistance, setting up a meeting with a prosecutor – is logistically difficult and conceptually foreign.

2. Socio-political Context

Over the course of the 1990s, the political leadership in the state of São Paulo appears to have shifted from right to left, from an emphasis on police effectiveness by any means necessary to an emphasis on police accountability. And yet this change coincides with accounts that attribute "massive support for illegal and/or authoritarian measures of control" to the population as a whole (Holston and Caldeira 1998: 267). Holston and Caldeira argue that "shooting to kill not only has broad popular support but it is also 'accepted' by the 'tough talk' of official policy" (p. 271). Caetano Veloso, in his song "Haiti," also describes São Paulo's "smiling silence when faced with the massacre of 111 defenseless inmates" (*o silêncio sorridente de São Paulo/ diante da chacina/ 111 presos indefesos*) of that city's immense house of detention.

Survey data support these observations. In several 1996 surveys in Rio de Janeiro, about 70% of those surveyed agreed with the statement that criminals (*"bandidos"*) do not respect the rights of others and therefore do not deserve to have their own rights respected (Murilo de Carvalho 1997). Fully 63% strongly agreed with this statement (*"concordo totalmente"*). Only among those with a university education did this percentage drop below 50% (to 46%). A lower percentage, 45%, agreed that the use of violence by the police to obtain confessions is sometimes or always justified. And while

---

[9] *Source*: Portal da Prefeitura de São Paulo (http://www.prefeitura.sp.gov.br), citing SEP, Convênio Seade-Diese, Pesquisa de Emprego e Desemprego.

46% flatly stated that those who lynch criminals (*"criminosos"*) are wrong to do so, 11% thought that they were right, and another 41% thought that their actions, while wrong, were understandable. These surveys consistently show more repressive attitudes among lower socio-economic classes, although it may well be that more educated respondents are simply more likely to give the politically correct answer.[10]

There appears to be consensus among operators and observers of the justice system that the population continues to accept the use of lethal force as an instrument to fight crime. I repeatedly heard public opinion described this way in the course of interviews with people such as Luiz Eduardo Greenhalgh, a Workers' Party (PT) national senator from São Paulo;[11] Hélio Bicudo, a former national congressman, the vice-mayor of São Paulo, the primary sponsor of the law subjecting the Military Police to civilian justice, and a member of the Inter-American Human Rights Commission;[12] Benedito Mariano, the first director of the Ouvidoria da Polícia;[13] Mário Papaterra, São Paulo's adjunct secretary of state for public security, a former prosecutor who was, when I spoke to him, the civilian in charge of the Civil and Military Police forces for the state Ministry of Security;[14] and Antônio Carlos da Ponte, a prosecutor in the jury division (which has jurisdiction over homicide cases).[15] Norberto Jóia, another prosecutor in the jury division, said roughly the same thing, although he framed it as a slightly less absolute rule, arguing that if the victim has a violent criminal past the police get the benefit of the doubt, while otherwise there is stricter scrutiny.[16]

Interestingly, all but Mário Papaterra attributed these attitudes to the population in general, but not to judges or prosecutors. Papaterra argued that many prosecutors are further to the right than many of his police officers. These prosecutors, he said, use the same metric as the rest of the population to determine who is entitled to full legal protection: a *marginal* may not be, but a *homem de bem* (an upstanding person) is.

[10] These surveys also suggest that civil and political rights more generally are weakly rooted in Brazilian society. They find, for example, that the majority of those surveyed could not name three civil rights to which they were entitled. In response to open-ended questions about rights, people were much more apt to name social rights, such as the right to health, work, or education, than basic civil rights like the right to freedom, equality, justice, physical integrity, life, property, or security.
[11] Interview with Luiz Eduardo Greenhalgh, São Paulo, April 30, 2001.
[12] Interview with Hélio Bicudo, São Paulo, March 27, 2001.
[13] Interview with Benedito Mariano, São Paulo, March 21, 2001.
[14] Interview with Mário Papaterra, São Paulo, March 23, 2001.
[15] Interview with Antônio Carlos da Ponte, São Paulo, April 2001.
[16] Interview with Prosecutor Norberto Jóia, São Paulo, April 16, 2001.

One of the roots of this support for violent police action in São Paulo is the fear of violent crime. In one São Paulo survey, Sérgio Adorno (1998) notes that 63 percent of respondents expressed a fear of being murdered. Increasingly common mass executions (*chacinas*) in the periphery of São Paulo place that population under constant threat, should they find themselves in the middle of a fight between rival drug gangs or even on the wrong side of a neighborhood dispute. Adorno concludes that the increase in violent crime in the city is not merely a matter of perception, media hype, or political exploitation of the issue. Violence is indeed on the rise in São Paulo, and it is one of the primary concerns of the residents, especially in marginal areas. Unfortunately, all too often this concern and the lack of faith in the justice system translate into support for violent and repressive police tactics.

This leads to one striking difference between Buenos Aires and São Paulo in connection with these cases. I have no record of any demonstrations, spontaneous or otherwise, connected with cases of routine police violence in Sao Paulo. On the contrary, lynchings are much more common, as the population rises up against a suspect and tries to beat him to death. In fact, people at the Centro Santo Dias suggested that complainants have to fight resistance even from their neighbors in order to pursue a claim for police abuses. This is in sharp contrast with the situation in popular neighborhoods in Buenos Aires where, more often than not, neighbors band together to support claimants and witnesses.

At the same time, while it may be true that there is a "pervasive cultural pattern that associates order and authority with the use of violence" (Holston and Caldeira 1998: 273), this pattern is not necessarily permanent nor always translated into political representation and public policies. A series of notorious events involving the police gained public notice in the 1990s. The killing of street children in the Candelárias incident in Rio in 1993, the massacre of 21 residents of the Favela Vigário Geral in 1993, the 1996 massacre of 19 landless peasants in Eldorado dos Carajás, and the televised murder, corruption, and brutality of the police in Favela Naval in 1997 all had grave repercussions in the Brazilian polity.[17] Public reaction to these atrocities may have helped to move the political mood toward tighter civilian control of the police in Brazil generally and in São Paulo specifically. According to Hélio

---

[17] Unfortunately, the continued rise in violent crime, including organized attacks by the Primeiro Comando da Capital, a prison gang, have led to increased use of the military in police activities and to renewed calls for a more effective response to crime. It remains to be seen whether "effectiveness" will continue to be measured by the body count.

Bicudo, the reassignment of jurisdiction over police homicides from the discredited military tribunals to the (less discredited) civilian courts and the passage of a law against torture can be traced to these events.[18]

As in Buenos Aires at the end of the decade, during the early 1990s, electoral formulas that emphasized civil rights protection lost to those that adopted explicit shoot-to-kill policies. Thus, Franco Montoro, the first governor of São Paulo after the dictatorship, preached a restrained police force and instituted various police reform measures. But he was followed in 1987 by Orestes Quércia, and then in 1991 by Quércia's secretary of security, Luiz Antonio Fleury Filho, a former prosecutor who studied in the Military Police Academy. Both of these governors hindered the implementation of Montoro's reforms and adopted an approach strongly reminiscent of the "*mano dura*" discourse we saw in Buenos Aires.

By the middle of the decade, however, elected representatives appear to shift policies toward a more restrained police in São Paulo. At the state level, Governors Mário Covas and Geraldo Alckmin, who took office in 1995 and 2001 respectively, did not follow the strong-arm rhetoric of Quércia and Fleury on policing issues. In 1996, under Covas's auspices, São Paulo became the first of several states in Brazil to create an Ouvidoria da Polícia, an ombudsman specifically designed to address police abuses. Covas offered strong institutional and political support for the monitoring activities of the Ouvidoria.[19] Alckmin de-prioritized the issue somewhat, but he did not completely back off on this support and did not adopt the law-and-order rhetoric of Covas's predecessors.[20] Thus from 1995 on, elected officials in São Paulo were less supportive of violent methods than those in the province of Buenos Aires at the end of the decade, and less so than governors at the beginning of the decade.[21]

---

[18] While Holston and Caldeira (1998) note that a significant proportion of the population actually supported the violent response, an even greater percentage opposed it, and discussion of the project to subject the Military Police to ordinary civilian justice revolved in large part around this event and the Candelárias murder of street children. The final impetus for passage of the law against torture was provided by the Favela Naval incident. Interview with Hélio Bicudo, São Paulo, March 27, 2001; interview with Judge Dyrceu Cintra, São Paulo, April 4, 2001.

[19] Interview with Benedito Domingos Mariano, first director of the Ouvidoria, São Paulo, March 21, 2001.

[20] Interview with Fermino Fecchio, director of the Ouvidoria da Polícia, São Paulo, April 2001.

[21] The municipal government does not have any significant policing responsibilities, but at this level there is also a shift to the left. The beginning of the decade finds Paulo Maluf (a well-known figure of the Brazilian right, governor of São Paulo during the military regime) as mayor, followed by his designated successor, Celso Pitta, also on the right. But at the end of the decade, *paulistanos* elected Marta Suplicy, from the PT, to the post.

In summary, it appears that political support for enforcing civil rights against police violence is weak in São Paulo society at large. It may be especially weak among the lower classes, according to poll results, although it is possible that more affluent respondents are simply giving the politically correct answer more often. On the part of elected officials, however, it has improved and was stronger at the end of the decade than at the beginning.

C. THE SYSTEM'S SOURCES OF INFORMATION

As in Buenos Aires, the legal system in São Paulo relies on state and private sources for information in processing cases. The principal state agent in cases involving the Military Police is the Military Police itself. Non-state agents include, most prominently, the Centro Santo Dias of the São Paulo archdiocese and several others. In this section I analyze their structures and their behavior in helping or hindering the prosecution of these cases.

1. São Paulo Police Forces

As in Argentina, in São Paulo the police stand as a barrier between the event in question and its re-presentation in a judicial proceeding. São Paulo, like the rest of Brazil, has two state police forces, the Military Police and the Civil Police.[22] The former carries out the public order function, known as *policiamento ostensivo*, which includes patrolling the streets, conducting traffic stops, responding to calls, and generally doing the crime prevention and repression work. The Civil Police force serves a purely investigative function and is sometimes described as a judicial police. By virtue of their function, officers involved in shootings are typically from the Military Police, while the Civil Police most often are the accused in cases of torture – indeed, many reports suggest that the use of torture is among the standard investigative methods of the Civil Police. Perversely, existing legislation ensures that both the Civil and the Military Police investigate their own crimes, giving them both ample opportunities to skew the investigation in a favorable direction.

São Paulo's Military Police have a violent past, extensively documented by America's Watch (e.g., in their 1993 and 1997 reports) and by Chevigny (1995). The Military Police were the author of all the violent incidents mentioned earlier – the murder of 111 inmates of the São Paulo house of

---

[22] There is also a Federal Police, but it is small, its actions are limited to federal crimes, and it does not appear to be very active in the São Paulo area. It does not appear even once in my database, perhaps because the source of the data is the Ouvidoria, which is a state agency.

detention, the killing of shantytown residents in Vigário Geral and Favela
Naval, the massacre of landless peasants, and the murder of street children
in Rio. The murders committed by one notorious task force, the Rondas
Ostensivas Tobias de Aguiar (ROTA), were numerous and violent enough to
be the subject of a book by the journalist Caco Barcellos (1992). The book in
turn resulted in Barcellos's forced exile to New York because of threats to his
life. Often, off-duty police officers even participate in death-squad activity,
in the employ of local merchants who find this an effective way to cleanse
the streets of petty criminals and other undesirables.

Early in the decade at least, there was open support by the officer corps for
violent police action. Chevigny documents the rewards paid by commanders
of the São Paulo Military Police to those who killed suspects (Chevigny 1995:
167–68). Although his investigation dates back to the early 1980s, Barcellos
presents a riveting and persuasive account of how the Military Police, time
and again, execute suspected criminals in cold blood and are rewarded for
their valor (Barcellos 1992: 143–45).

I interviewed Judge Antônio Carlos Malheiros, a judge with a long human
rights record who teaches human rights courses in the Military Police Officers' School.[23] He argued that he has noticed a change in the culture of the
Military Police, beginning about 1996 or 1997, toward greater respect for
suspects' rights. In each class of officers, he estimates, about 20% appear
truly interested in human rights and accept the notion that policing and
respect for rights can be compatible. About 75% listen silently. As to this
group, Judge Malheiros suggested that they may violate rights occasionally,
but with distaste, "*virando o rosto*" (turning their faces away); or they may
simply look the other way while others violate rights. Finally, in every class
about 5% actively voice the idea – to a judge, in a human rights class, no
less – that "*direitos humanos é bobagem; bandido tem que morrer, armado
ou não*" (human rights talk is nonsense; criminals must die whether armed
or not).

This may well be an improvement over the situation Chevigny reports
from the 1980s. But this evidence suggests that at least 5% of the active officers continue to convey to their subordinates the notion that the appropriate
response to suspected criminals is their execution, and another 75% are
willing to look the other way. When their subordinates carry out the killings
they have been explicitly or implicitly authorized to make, these same officers
will oversee the investigation. This is not a recipe for an aggressive, thorough
investigation.

[23] Interview with Antônio Carlos Malheiros, appellate judge, São Paulo, April 17, 2001.

While the Military Police are not ordinarily responsible for the judicial investigation of a crime, they are often the first to appear at the crime scene, and, of course, this is true by definition in the case of police homicides. In ordinary cases, they are supposed to identify and make initial contacts with witnesses and preserve the crime scene so that the Civil Police can take testimony and collect physical evidence. Under existing law, however, in cases involving a police shooting, they are also in charge of the *inquérito*, the complete investigation up to the pre-trial stage. Thus while in ordinary crimes there is a division of labor between the security and the investigative police, and definitely an arms-length relationship between the two, this division is voided in precisely the cases where it is most necessary – homicide cases in which a Military Police officer is the suspect. In these cases, the suspect and his colleagues not only control the crime scene but also are charged with the full investigation.

The Military Police has an internal disciplinary body, the *corregedoria*, as well as its own military justice system. But, as in Buenos Aires, this disciplinary body is mostly preoccupied with maintaining military discipline and strict hierarchical control, so that crimes against civilians are not treated with the same harshness as infractions that affect the discipline of the organization.[24] As in Argentina, this system makes it more difficult to resist internal pressures toward violent action. Also as in Argentina, whistleblowers are subject to punishment – and for officers with less than ten years of seniority, punishment can be applied summarily. This policy is often official, as when the Ouvidoria learned that the command of the Military Police had issued a *portaria*, or directive, prohibiting police officers from reporting alleged violations to outside agencies. Thus the informational functioning of the police in São Paulo is nearly identical to that in Buenos Aires: the organization committing the violation is charged with investigating it, and internal controls make it exceedingly difficult, especially for rank and file members, to blow the whistle on the corporation.

The result, again, is evident. In my data, it appears that the Military Police tampered with the factual record in as many as 85 percent of the cases involving one of their own, while the Civil Police did the same in all of the six cases attributed to one of their own.[25] Prosecutors and judges both mentioned the practice of planting a gun (nicknamed the "*cabrito*") by the

---

[24] Interview with Prosecutor Norberto Jóia, São Paulo, April 16, 2001. An in-depth study of training and advancement in the Military Police also notes the strongly hierarchical culture of the institution (Cardia, Adorno, and Pinheiro 1998).

[25] I should note that I am less confident of my judgment on this issue in São Paulo than I was in Buenos Aires, since in many cases here I had less contact with participants and relied

side of a victim's body to justify a shooting. As noted in the previous chapter, there are suggestions that the police will go so far as to place a gun in the hand of a dead victim and pull the trigger to produce a positive finding in gunpowder residue tests. This practice is sufficiently well known to be depicted in one of the opening scenes of the film *City of God* (Mantovani 2002). It is also the routine practice of the Military Police to remove the body of a victim, under the pretext of taking the victim to a hospital for assistance – no matter that the victim is far beyond any help. Often, victims are listed as dying in the hospital, even if they are dead on arrival. And quite often victims who leave the scene with a good chance of recovery arrive at the hospital hours later, too late for intervention or with the marks of in-transit beatings and execution.

Forensic evidence is also suspect, as in Buenos Aires. In several of my cases, autopsy reports contain false information, as confirmed by a second, independent report. The autopsies are produced by the Instituto Médico-Legal, which can be influenced by the police and is suspected of covering up police misconduct in connection with homicides and torture cases.[26]

According to prosecutors, witnesses in these cases are often threatened and intimidated.[27] There is clear evidence of this in nearly 25 percent of all the cases in my sample – about the same figure as for the Buenos Aires sample. Academic observers (Chevigny 1995) and human rights reports also remark on the harassment and intimidation suffered by victims who complain against the police (see, e.g., the 2001 U.S. State Department human rights report on Brazil, §1.a and 1.e; and the 2000 U.S. State Department report). This is what drove Barcellos, the well-known journalist and author, to exile in New York. Focusing the violence on the classes most limited in their access to attorneys, the media, and other mechanisms for redress is a virtual guarantee that the intimidation will go unpunished. And, in fact, there are virtually no reports of a prosecution for efforts to cover up violations. One prosecutor suggested, and one of the cases discussed in Chapter 3 supports this claim, that the Ministério Público would prioritize any case in which a victim was shot because he or she intended to testify against the police. But all the evidence – my own information as well as reports by the Ouvidoria and other human rights organizations – suggests that in routine cases witnesses are not sufficiently protected from police intimidation.

---

more heavily on claims made in court filings by one or another of the parties or on blatant inconsistencies between physical evidence and police accounts.

[26] Interview with Prosecutor Antônio Carlos da Ponte, São Paulo, April 2001.

[27] Interview with Prosecutor Antônio Carlos da Ponte, São Paulo, April 2001.

The bifurcation of the police, however, means that the relationship between judges and prosecutors and the Military Police is not as tight as in Buenos Aires. The Military Police can – and do, as we saw – restrict and falsify information about cases that involve their own misconduct. Still, the presence of the Civil Police as the main judicial investigative organization limits the capacity of the Military Police to blackmail judicial officers. In addition, there is very little of the daily interaction between street police and judges that we see in Buenos Aires. In fact, the relationship between the Military and the Civil Police in São Paulo is conflictive and competitive, and prosecutors and judges hold the Military Police in no high regard. Thus, the impact of the Military Police's control over information is mostly limited to the case at hand, shifting the information presented in an exculpatory direction, but not affecting the judges' normative stance in a significant way.

At the same time, however, the Civil Police is ill equipped to investigate its Military cousin. Judges criticize their investigations for being limited to the information that walks into police offices. In 2000 the judges of the *Primeiro Tribunal do Júri* in São Paulo conducted an investigation into the *inquérito* process.[28] They reviewed a sample of IPs and the quality of the investigation that went into them. They conclude: "The first and most evident problem verified is what we label investigative passivity." They show that the Civil Police rely on the Military Police to collect information on the occurrence and the nature of a criminal event. Despite the requirements of the Code of Criminal Procedure, they do not visit or preserve the crime scene, they do not take testimony from witnesses, and they do not collect physical evidence. Any physical evidence collected is invariably brought to the Civil Police by the Military Police officers who intervened in the first instance. Any witness testimony is, as a rule, due to the spontaneous appearance of complainants in the investigating officer's offices.

The judges' report offers several examples of this passive attitude: one murder occurred in March 1998, the file was opened in March 1999, and the first witness, the widow of the murder victim, was interviewed in August of the same year – fully seventeen months after the event. Another Military Police report gives the names of those who were with the victim when he was murdered, yet the Civil Police did not attempt to contact those witnesses until five months later. One victim was in the hospital for eight days after the attempt, but by the time the Civil Police tried to interview him, he was

---

[28] This discussion is based on an internal report of the investigation given to me confidentially by an anonymous source within the court. It is available for review from the author on request.

nowhere to be found and the case had to be dropped. Another victim was in the hospital for sixty-seven days, but the prosecutor was forced to rely on medical records and the recollection of treating physicians because the Civil Police never bothered to conduct their own examination. The result, the judges say, is the loss of information, the disappearance of witnesses, and, ultimately, the dismissal of an increasing proportion of cases because the proofs are inadequate.

In short, institutional design gives Military Police investigators both the incentive and the capacity to subvert the record and strangle the supply of information in individual cases; however, it also limits their capacity to pressure judges and prosecutors to treat them with lenience. Especially in view of their traditional rivalry, the Civil Police could in theory be used to investigate the Military Police and provide independent information about their actions. But the Civil Police are as a practical matter dependent on the Military Police for much of the information they produce and thus unlikely to be effective guardians.

2. Other State Agencies

The most important alternative state agency for receiving information about police violence in São Paulo is the Ouvidoria da Polícia. The Ouvidoria was created in 1996 by the Covas administration. It does not have legal standing to file claims on behalf of complainants, but it has the authority to demand information from other state agencies such as the police, prosecutors, and the courts. It has played an important role in bringing to light and disseminating to the mass media information about the conduct of the police, including information about police homicides. The Ouvidoria also follows the progress of individual cases, pushing prosecutors to explain delays and decisions. In this latter context, the Ouvidoria is not an investigative agency, but it does receive information from interested parties. It has a toll-free phone line and accepts anonymous complaints. It is proactive only in that it canvasses newspapers for reports of violence involving the police and then follows up with a request for the police report on the incident. But it does not contact victims or complainants directly, unless they reach out first.

The Ouvidoria's main impact, therefore, has been on the socio-political context. Perhaps the most important example of this was the production of a report in 2000, which examines in full detail the homicides committed by São Paulo police in 1999 (Ouvidoria da Polícia 1999). In preparing that document, the Ouvidoria sought the police and prosecutorial reports and requested autopsy reports on all the deaths. The report offered compelling evidence that the high number of killings claimed by the police could not be explained away as the result of confrontations between the Military Police and armed and dangerous violent criminals. Among the more telling details are the following: there were three police guns for every one civilian gun involved in these events; more than 50% of the victims had been shot in the back; more than half of the victims had no criminal record at all; 36% of the victims had been shot in the head; and fully one-quarter of the victims showed signs of physical abuse in addition to the gunshot wounds, suggesting a beating and subsequent execution. Both judges and prosecutors mentioned this report as raising important questions about the way the events are presented in the IPMs and as prompting them to take a closer look at the police narrative in these cases.

The Ouvidoria also provides annual reports to the state legislature with policy proposals intended to curb the high levels of violence by the police, including new training programs and new operational policies. Over time, then, the Ouvidoria may well change the way police violence is interpreted by state officials, as well as changing some of the institutional arrangements that lead to the current high levels of violence.

Lawyers who represent victims, on the other hand, sometimes appear frustrated by the Ouvidoria's lack of enforcement capacity. As one of them put it, the Ouvidoria is like a dog that barks but does not bite. This is in part because it has no legal standing to appear in individual cases of police abuses, and in part because the Ouvidoria does not second-guess prosecutors. Once a prosecutor has acted, whether recommending the dismissal or the prosecution of a case, the Ouvidoria closes its files on the complaint. Its mission is to oversee police activities, not judicial ones, and so its policy is that a matter in the hands of prosecutors or judges is beyond its jurisdiction. Without in any way discounting the importance of this agency, therefore, it is clear that in individual prosecutions its effects are purely indirect. The sole exception is its capacity to receive and memorialize information from complainants who take the initiative of contacting it. In a couple of instances, the Ouvidoria has taken the sworn testimony of a witness and then offered it to the responsible prosecutor.

Elected officials are another link between the state and the victims in these cases. But since the creation of the Ouvidoria, legislators acting on constituent complaints have worked through that agency. When they receive a complaint they refer it to the Ouvidoria for follow-up. Their actions are thus increasingly filtered through and subject to the Ouvidoria's capacities and limitations.

3. Non-state Agents

The Centro Santo Dias de Direitos Humanos is undoubtedly the most important civil society actor on this issue in São Paulo. Under the leadership of
Cardinal Paulo Evaristo Arns, a noted human rights defender, the Archdiocese of São Paulo established the center in 1980, named after a Catholic
worker murdered by the São Paulo Military Police while he was leading a
strike in October 1979. From the beginning, its primary mission has been to
work on behalf of the victims of police homicides. Over the last twenty-plus
years, the center has acted on behalf of the victims in over three hundred
cases of police violence (not limited to murder), offering legal assistance in
both civil and criminal actions. In the former, it files claims for compensation,
and in the latter, it acts as the Private Prosecutor or *assistênte de acusação* on
behalf of relatives of the victims. The *assistênte de acusação* or *assistênte do
promotor* is the substantial equivalent of the federal *querella* in Argentina: it
can press charges even over the objection of the prosecutor, pursue appeals,
present witnesses, argue to the jury and the court, and generally participate
as a second prosecutor.

In this capacity, and motivated by its direct relationship with the survivors
of the victims, Santo Dias can prompt greater zeal from prosecutors, and,
when prosecutors fail to act, perform the required tasks itself. After sixteen-
year-old Enéas da Silva was killed, for example, the official autopsy report
showed that he had been shot in the chest, consistent with the police account
of a violent shootout. The case was ripe for dismissal. After speaking to
his family and other witnesses, however, the center and other national and
international NGOs pushed for a more rigorous investigation. It was largely
through their actions that da Silva's body was exhumed and a second autopsy
performed, showing that he was shot in the back of the head and not in
a frontal exchange of gunfire. Ultimately, the case ended in a conviction,
which would have been unthinkable without the pressure from these NGOs.
In addition, the center's attorneys can call witnesses, obtain expert reports,
and generally bring information into the courtroom that would otherwise
not come to light.

Santo Dias and individuals connected with it have also been instrumental
in changing the official rules and in staffing the state agencies that deal with
this issue. Hélio Bicudo, who sponsored the legislation that would bring killer
cops into the civilian justice system, served on the center's Board of Directors
from the very beginning. The center lobbied extensively for the formation
of the Ouvidoria da Polícia. Benedito Mariano, one of the key figures in
the development of the center, was the first director of the Ouvidoria. His

successor, Fermino Fecchio, is also a Santo Dias alumnus. As directors of the Ouvidoria, Mariano and Fecchio devoted significant attention to proposals for new rules and procedures governing the police.

While it fills the same niche in the legal ecosystem, channeling demands and information from society to the courtroom, Santo Dias differs from CORREPI in both structure and action. Rather than a grassroots organization with an extended lay membership, it is a church-run organization with a small staff of lawyers and their assistants. The staff does the typical work of lawyers, filing papers and requests with the courts and meeting with clients who come into the office. The center does not organize and participate in political demonstrations in the streets of São Paulo or at the doors of the courthouse, although it has organized conferences and public acts in support of human rights, published studies, and lobbied for public policy changes.

In further contrast to CORREPI, the center does not appear to suffer the suspicion and distrust of judges and prosecutors. Several reasons can be offered for this. First, of course, Santo Dias is identified with the Catholic Church, an organization with a great deal of legitimacy in Brazil. More important, Santo Dias prefers to use traditional legal arguments and methods to affect the construction of the rule of decision in a given case. It limits its political activity to lobbying for a change in the formal rules, rather than using demonstrations to pressure judges in the case at hand. As a result, it is viewed as a more mainstream human rights organization than its Argentine counterpart with its Marxist rhetoric, confrontational politics, and courtroom-door demonstrations.

The contrast between the center's actions and CORREPI's is fully consistent with my diagnosis of the problem in São Paulo and in Buenos Aires. Its emphasis on traditional legal advocacy rather than political methods supports the claim that the São Paulo judiciary is less sensitive to political pressures. In its more diffuse work, the center's focus on reforming laws and structures suggests that it has some confidence in the faithful application of the rules to particular cases. The center's results also support this diagnosis. Before 1996, while the cases were subject to military justice, center attorneys saw a very low conviction rate even in cases in which they fully participated: "even with an abundance of proofs and the confession of the military police officers, the rule was the absolute absence of any punitive action" (Mariano and Toneto 2000: 14). After these same cases were transferred to the civilian courts, "the situation changed, to our great satisfaction." In the civilian system, the cases received "more prompt and just adjudication" (ibid.).

In my sample, the vast majority of convictions represent cases decided in the civilian system in which the Centro Santo Dias was an active participant.

Adding a Private Prosecutor to the case raises the conviction rate from practically zero to 32 percent. In other words, judges and juries in São Paulo do respond when presented with a well-supported case. This suggests that, while in the military justice system the problem was the practical application of an informal rule of impunity, in the civilian courts this is no longer a problem. At the same time, the fact that its success is rarely if ever replicated when center attorneys do *not* participate suggests that something other than the rule of decision is wrong with the civilian system in the absence of a Private Prosecutor. The problem, in short, is the misrepresentation of the event, which begins with a biased IPM and carries through to prosecutors, judges, and juries.

There are other entities in the São Paulo area that work on the problem of police violence in the context of human rights more generally. Examples are the Commissão Teotônio Vilela and the Human Rights Commission of the Brazilian Bar Association (the Ordem de Advogados do Brasil, known as the OAB). The Commissão Teotônio Vilela and the OAB intervened in the prosecution of Ubiratan Guimarães, the Military Police colonel in charge of the Carandiru massacre.

These NGOs do the important work of putting together human rights reports, bringing media attention to bear on the problem and lobbying for change, and participating in the prosecution of high-profile cases, but they rarely intervene directly in routine criminal prosecutions of rights violators. In that sense, they are more like the CELS in Buenos Aires. Their work is primarily bent on changing the legal framework, the socio-political context, and the social construction of these cases; it is less concerned with the judicial construction of facts and arguments in individual cases. Even their work in landmark cases is oriented toward rule change, not individual outcomes.

D. PROSECUTORS

The prosecutor's office, known as the Ministério Público in Brazil, has more than earned its good reputation in the years since the 1988 Constitution gave it additional independence and attributes. The question then is why it does not intervene more aggressively in the prosecution of police homicides, which at times represent 20 percent of all homicides in São Paulo. The answer has more to do with exogenous than endogenous factors. Endogenous pressures for impunity are less important for prosecutors in São Paulo than they were in Buenos Aires: the presence of the Civil Police and greater institutional strength means that prosecutors could, if they chose, take a more confrontational stance with the Military Police without fearing retribution in the investigation of their other cases. On the other hand, while the relative independence of the leadership of the organization renders it less subject to direct exogenous pressures, the political context still gets translated into organizational imperatives and thence into career incentives. As a result, despite its strength in other areas, individual prosecutors and the organization as a whole take a passive and reactive approach to police homicides. Given the procedural structure of the *Lei Bicudo*, so long as they remain passive, prosecutors will receive most of their information in these cases from the Military Police, becoming unwitting partners in impunity.

Article 2 of the São Paulo state prosecutor's organic law guarantees its "functional and administrative autonomy" (*Lei Complementar* No. 734 – November 26, 1993). Even the politically appointed head of the organization, the *Procurador Geral de Justiça*, owes his or her selection as much to the profession as to elected leaders. The *Procurador Geral* is named by the governor from among three candidates selected by the secret vote of all career prosecutors in active practice. Thus, while the executive has a say in the ultimate designation, the list of candidates is prepared by the entity itself. Members of the governing body of the Ministério Público are similarly elected by all active prosecutors (Art. 26). Among other things, this governing body selects the members of the admissions committee, proposes candidates for advancement by reason of seniority or merit, and disciplines or removes prosecutors subject to disciplinary proceedings (Art. 27).

The procedure for selecting frontline prosecutors emphasizes technical merit. Applicants who survive the pre-qualifying test sit for a full-length written exam, followed by a psychological evaluation (*exame psicotécnico*), an oral examination, and a personal interview. An admissions committee selected by existing prosecutors administers the entire process. Those applicants with the highest scores who are approved as to character and fitness are admitted and given their choice of appointments in the order of their test scores. According to an in-depth study by the Núcleo de Estudos da Violência (NEV) of the University of São Paulo, despite some shortcomings (especially in terms of legal education), this rigorous admissions process generates a high-quality prosecutor corps (Cardia, Adorno, and Pinheiro 1998). Moreover, once they have passed the two-year probationary period, prosecutors have the same guarantees as members of the judiciary: life tenure, salary protections, and the right to exercise their independent legal judgment (in contrast with Argentine prosecutors, whose judgment is subordinate to that of their superiors). Prosecutors consider judges to be their peers and are always striving to present the two positions as equals (when they do not claim superiority to the judicial corps).

By law, prosecutors are guaranteed advancement on the basis of seniority and can advance more rapidly on the basis of merit. There are some criticisms of the selection and advancement process, of course, both by practicing prosecutors and by academic observers. For our purposes, the most interesting critique offered in the course of the NEV study is directed at the career-advancement criteria. The prosecutors interviewed for the study argued that, although merit criteria are reasonably well spelled out in legislation, in practice they are extremely subjective. The use of subjective criteria for promotion generates a high degree of internal politics and the advancement of those who are ideologically or personally close to the governing body of the institution (Cardia, Adorno, and Pinheiro 1998: 206–208). Thus, even though prosecutors are guaranteed freedom of action in individual cases, career incentives produce a normatively coherent organization – with some exceptions – in which frontline prosecutors act in ways consistent with prevailing internal political currents or suffer the consequences.

These internal political currents are not necessarily inconsistent with liberal democratic values, including a reduction in police violence. The same NEV study concludes that, after the constitutional reforms of 1988, "the institution was quite influenced by the constitutional changes, so that its actions became oriented toward social interests and independent of the government and political leaders" (p. 207). Others reach similar conclusions (Bastos Arantes 1999; Batista Cavalcanti 1999; Bastos Arantes 2000; Sadek and Cavalcanti 2003). In more general terms, however, NEV investigators conclude "the central preoccupation of the institution is the political struggle – internal and external – to confer *status and power* on the Ministério Público" (p. 208, emphasis theirs).

This and other studies of the São Paulo Ministério Público note that there is an ongoing internal struggle to define the proper scope and focus of action of the organization. A repeated criticism is that the organization continues to be somewhat isolated from social reality, overemphasizing legal-technical formalisms. But from its most public actions, it appears that the Ministério Público has determined that the way to elevate its status and increase its power is to tackle issues of high relevance and broad support, especially among the middle classes, such as high-profile political scandals and corruption, environmental issues, and consumer protection (Mello de Camargo Ferraz 1997; Paulina 1999; Pereira da Silva 1999; Bastos Arantes 2000). Over the last decade, for example, the Ministério Público has successfully prosecuted for corruption dozens of officials at the state and local levels, including both Paulo Maluf and Celso Pitta, former mayors of São Paulo

(Sadek and Cavalcanti 2003), and has intervened on behalf of the environment and consumers in many prominent actions.

However valuable the actions of the Ministério Público may be in these areas, and however proactive the institution is in areas that garner a high institutional priority, its undoubted successes do not translate into effective action in the prosecution of police homicides. Reducing the number of these homicides does not appear to rank as a compelling social interest. So little political capital is to be derived from an investment in controlling police violence – especially violence in the course of policing as opposed to corruption – that police homicides do not receive sustained attention from the institution as a whole. Career-oriented prosecutors, hewing more or less closely to institutional priorities, naturally de-emphasize these prosecutions.

Pereira da Silva argues that São Paulo prosecutors fall into two ideal-typical categories, *promotores dos fatos* and *promotores de gabinete*: "facts" prosecutors and "office" prosecutors (1999: 103–20). The latter fit the description earlier presented of Buenos Aires prosecutors: they rarely leave their desks, they limit themselves to reviewing the facts that come into their office, and they find the real world within the four corners of the file. The former are the sort that I have suggested are needed in the face of the informational deficit generated by police resistance to prosecutions: they are proactive, they conduct investigations, they go out into the community and meet witnesses, and they act extra-judicially as well as within traditional legal venues. Whether because they adapt their behavior to the imperatives of the institution, or because the best prosecutors will naturally gravitate to the areas that are selected as high priority, the institutional incentives suggest that we will find "office" prosecutors working police homicide cases. The result is a prosecutorial organization that, despite its strengths in other areas, is mostly passive in connection with police homicide prosecutions.

Interviews with judges and prosecutors support this conclusion. One prosecutor suggested that police violence is not an institutional priority. It is up to the individual prosecutor on his or her own initiative, he said, to take a strong stance in these cases, and he or she receives little institutional support. He argued that police homicides are especially difficult to prosecute – as I have suggested here – because of the difficulty in assembling proofs, and that without systematic institutional backing, prosecutors are unlikely to devote the requisite time and resources to these cases.[29] A trial judge also remarked that he noticed a marked difference in the way these prosecutions are treated

---

[29] Interview with Prosecutor Antônio Carlos da Ponte, São Paulo, May 2, 2001.

by the prosecutor's office: in sharp contrast to ordinary murder cases, the least qualified attorneys are assigned to police cases, they prosecute these cases with the least enthusiasm, and they give the defendant the benefit of every doubt.[30] Prosecutors follow the same forms in these cases, he said, but in a markedly different manner (*"formalismo igual, jeito diferente"*).

In short, despite its considerable merits, the São Paulo Ministério Público continues to depend largely on the Military Police for information about cases involving members of that organization and limits itself for the most part to passively receiving information about these cases. The result is that prosecutors can say, with all sincerity, that "today, what we see are minor excesses, the police are more contained, institutional policy has changed...executions are extremely rare"[31] – this, despite the abundant indications that the police routinely execute suspects and abuse the use of lethal force in their activities. For now, suffice it to say that even judges disagree with this assessment, and at least one judge has had to resort to direct appeals to the *Procurador Geral* in cases in which he considers that the acting prosecutor is all too uncritical of the version of the facts presented in the *Inquérito Policial Militar*.[32]

Some of my interviews suggest that prosecutors take a more lenient position in these cases than do judges. Judges, understandably, tend to attribute much of the courts' ineffectiveness in controlling the police to prosecutorial rather than to judicial neglect. But so do various human rights activists, as well as former prosecutor Mário Papaterra, as noted earlier. One judge who made this comment relied on a sort of learned habits or informal norms argument. It is difficult to switch, he said, from lambasting criminal suspects with purple prose about crime and a disintegrating society to attacking the very police who are, in theory, holding this crime wave back from honest citizens. It may well be true that prosecutors who deal with ordinary murder are ill equipped, rhetorically and psychologically, to deal with police killings. But their passive, ill-at-ease posture in these prosecutions is aided by the low institutional priority for these cases, stemming from social approval of police violence, and by the police's capacity to strictly ration the information on which their judgments are based.

In summary, in terms of endogenous pressures, the prosecutors are not purely dependent on the Military Police for information in the majority

---

[30] Interview with Judge Luis Fernando Camargo de Barros Vidal, São Paulo, April 23, 2001.
[31] Interview with Prosecutor Norberto Jóia, São Paulo, April 16, 2001.
[32] Interview with Judge Luis Fernando Camargo de Barros Vidal, São Paulo, April 23, 2001.

of their cases, and thus there is no reason to suppose that their normative preferences will line up closely with those of the police (and the individual defendant) in these cases. Indeed, they may well remain somewhere between the judge and the victim rather than between the judge and the defendant in the line-up of preferences. Exogenous factors, however, while more remote and generalized in comparison to Buenos Aires, still get translated into career incentives that promote a passive institutional stance on police homicides. This stance permits the Military Police to retain a virtual monopoly on information about individual cases involving their own personnel and thus to take the lead role in constructing procedural reality in these cases. The result is the routine misconstruction of the facts at the prosecutorial level.

E. THE COURTS

It is hard to find anyone who will say anything positive about the Brazilian courts. Articles about them tend to have titles like "A Crise do Poder Judiciário no Brasil" (Faria 1996). Authors like to repeat a quote from Teresa Caldeira's research, in which a Brazilian in a poor neighborhood says of the justice system *"é uma piada!"* – "it's a joke!" (Chevigny 1995; Holston and Caldeira 1998; Caldeira 2000). Despite this apparent consensus, I believe these criticisms underestimate the quality of the judiciary in the Metro São Paulo area. While my belief is based in part on impressions too subjective to serve as a measure of judicial merit, there are some objective indications that, in a more comparative framework, the average *paulistano* is not as poorly served as these critiques suggest. Criminal cases move more quickly than in Buenos Aires, and judges are less overworked, more independent, and less corrupt than their *porteño* peers. Even the vaunted successes of the Ministério Público necessarily depend on the courts, since this is ultimately where the decisions are made on the legal proposals put forth by prosecutors.

In connection with police homicides in particular, endogenous pressures to conform to the police version of the facts are less strong in São Paulo than in Buenos Aires, and there is little evidence that the judges shift their interpretation of the laws against police violence to meet political pressures in individual cases. However, exogenous pressures, even though diluted by the autonomy of the institution, make it likely that most judges will not take an aggressive stance in these cases, facilitating the informational dependence that renders them ineffective. Juries in turn suffer from the same informational deficit and are, in addition, more likely to reflect societal prejudices against the claimants in these cases.

The Judges

On the negative side, the judicial organization is very hierarchical and dominated by an elite core of senior members, who are sometimes criticized for
enforcing a rigid and formalistic view of the law and who give the entire
institution a strongly conservative bent. On the positive side, this judiciary
enjoys a rigorous selection process that ensures high legal-technical quality
among judges, a high measure of judicial independence from political powers, and freedom from corruption. Even the excessive formalism is a guard
of sorts against the informal pressures that distort judicial decision making in Buenos Aires. In connection with police homicides, however, these
exogenous characteristics ensure that the average judge will behave more or
less as the prosecutors do: they will not consciously modify legal standards
to accommodate social pressures for an "effective" response to crime, but
neither will they go out of their way to level the playing field, assuming
instead that their job is simply to apply the law to the facts presented to
them.

In purely objective terms, the trial judges who deal with police homicides
in São Paulo have a relative advantage over their colleagues in Buenos Aires.
Judges' workloads in São Paulo's jury trial system are much lower than that
of trial judges in Buenos Aires: the *Primeiro Tribunal do Júri* in São Paulo,
which boasts that it is the largest jury system in Latin America and carries
out most of the trials in my sample, decides more than a thousand cases per
year. It works out of an impressive, modern and massive building designed to
project the full power of the state, dwarfing any judicial building in Buenos
Aires. It has ten active courtrooms and trial judges (*juízes plenários*), and
about half that number of pre-trial judges (*juízes sumários*).[33] Between 1993
and 2000, the years for which I was able to obtain data, the number of
cases entering this court and distributed to its ten trial judges went from
1,560 to a peak of 4,008 in 1996 and then back down slightly to 3,980
(i.e., from about 150 per trial judge to about 400 per trial judge).[34] This is
surely a more reasonable number than the Argentine trial courts face, with
their annual influx of over 5,000 new cases for the *jueces correccionales* and
nearly 3,000 for judges who try more serious cases.

Despite a growing backlog, the time to trial is not excessive. On average,
from 1993 through 2000 the judges resolved 39 percent fewer cases than

[33] The latter carry out a role that is substantially similar to that of magistrates in the U.S.
federal system, overseeing many aspects of the trial-preparation process.
[34] *Source*: Internal report prepared on the author's behalf, at the request of one of the judges,
by support staff of the *Primeiro Tribunal do Júri*. On file with the author.

the annual number of new cases, with a consequent rise in the number of pending cases over the course of the decade. The court began in 1993 with about 8,000 pending cases and ended 2000 with a little over 11,700. But, as noted in Chapter 3, the cases in my sample that began in the civilian courts and were not dismissed at the pre-trial stage took, on average, less than 2.5 years to go to trial.[35] Despite universal complaints about the slowness of the Brazilian courts, this is only about half of the mean delay in the Buenos Aires courts.

More than these functional aspects, however, it is the selection and advancement mechanism for judges that gives São Paulo's courts their character. The selection process in particular – essentially the same as for prosecutors – is very rigorous.[36] It begins with a qualifying exam, which about 10% of applicants pass. This selective group goes on to a more individualized second round that consists of an in-depth written exam focusing on technical legal issues, followed by an extensive psychological evaluation that can take up to three days, then an oral examination, and finally a personal interview. Between 1990 and 1997, only an average of 2.6% of applicants passed this hurdle and entered the judicial service. Judges who survived it criticize this system as excessively focused on the ability to recite accepted formulas and legal technicisms (Cardia, Adorno, and Pinheiro 1998). Despite these criticisms, this study concludes that the entry process is essentially meritocratic and open to all, with a clear emphasis on legal preparation and technical merit.[37]

According to the NEV study, the advancement and promotion system is more problematic: the interviewed judges describe the structure of the judiciary as authoritarian, dominated by a few of the most senior judges who sit on the highest courts (Cardia, Adorno, and Pinheiro 1998: 242). Legally, the decisions of higher courts are not binding precedent for lower courts. This suggests that trial courts are quite free to decide as they see fit. But career incentives and other pressures tend in the opposite direction. Even the Association of Judges for Democracy, which defends this freedom of

---

[35] In contrast, the mean delay for cases that began in the military courts and were transferred to the civilian courts after 1996 is nearly ten years.

[36] By constitutional imperative, one-fifth of appellate judges enter laterally, from the prosecutorial corps or the private bar. The following description applies to the career judges that make up the entire trial court bench and most of the appellate bench.

[37] In reality, it is the prevailing definition of merit that is criticized. The "progressive" critics of the system argue that legal education, and the resulting profession, is overly focused on memorization of sterile legal standards, rather than on a more socially conscious "living" law.

decision for lower court judges as a way to democratize the judiciary, agrees that higher court opinions "although non-binding, are as a rule respected by all judges" (Associação Juízes para a Democracia 1999). It argues that this is because the opinions of the highest courts simply reflect the distilled wisdom of the lower courts, which are therefore simply following their own reflection. This may be partly true, but a more prosaic explanation surely also plays an important part.

My own explanation points to the de facto impact of promotion and discipline mechanisms. As do prosecutors, judges can advance at a slow pace on the basis of seniority or much more quickly, through merit-based promotions. The standards for evaluating merit, however, are subjective and ill defined. The primary qualification for merit-based promotions or reassignments, the study finds, is avoiding *de*merits and remaining in the good graces of supervising judges (Cardia, Adorno, and Pinheiro 1998: 298–302). These supervisors are the judges who sit on the appellate court immediately above the judge in question. For trial judges, then, advancement requires simply following and liberally citing with approval the opinions of this immediately superior appellate court. Precedent may not be binding, but it is certainly politic.

Those interested in the highest courts engage in a similar although more personalized political campaign, which emphasizes allegiance to and personal connections with senior judges in the highest courts. In short, the upper echelons of the judiciary have both the information and the sanctioning capacity to ensure a fairly high level of normative consistency within the judiciary. This routine adherence to precedent is inconsistent with the traditional view of the civil law (Merryman 1985). It is, however, consistent with Shapiro's analysis of how French courts operate in practice (1981: 135–48), and even Merryman (1985: 46–47) concedes the practical impact of previous decisions.

If, then, lower courts tend to follow higher courts, what is the ideological stamp these upper echelons seek to impose? While the subjective nature of the promotion process renders it essentially a political one, the politics are internal to the judiciary, not necessarily tied to broader social and political currents. The judges at the top, who exercise this control over lower court judges, are quite insulated from elected political powers and momentary social currents. The courts even have budgetary autonomy, although some argue that they are in practice less autonomous than the Constitution would suggest (Cardia, Adorno, and Pinheiro 1998: 237). Other than their natural affinity as members of an elite class, then, there is little incentive for judges to take direction from the executive, or even from societal demands. Although they are surely not impervious to either of these forces, they also need not follow them slavishly.

As a result, among the many jeremiads detailing the "crisis of the judiciary" in São Paulo, one does not find allegations of political subjection comparable to those in Argentina. Faria, a long-time observer and critic of the Brazilian judiciary, notes only that the courts are likely to be tied to dominant economic interests, attributing this to the class make-up of the courts.[38] Sister Michael Mary Nolan, a São Paulo attorney with a long-standing association with the Centro Santo Dias and many years of working with the homeless, the landless, and underprivileged criminal defendants, agrees. She argues that judges in Brazil generally seek out and use technicalities to frustrate the claims of the underclass, but she attributes this to a general conservative bent in the judiciary and not to outside pressures in particular cases.[39] In summary, then, these institutional features tend toward the creation of a judiciary that is hierarchical, conservative, and (likely) allied with dominant economic classes; that emphasizes legal technicalities over equity-based claims; with judges who are reluctant to take risks that might incur the disapproval of higher courts.[40]

This judicial profile colludes with the posture of the police and prosecutors to produce a low conviction rate. As we saw, these cases come into court with an exculpatory version of the facts inscribed in the police report, which is unlikely to be corrected by prosecutorial activism. Individual judges with a progressive bent have the capacity to insist on a more complete investigation, because they still have many of the attributes of the civil law judge, controlling and directing the pre-trial investigation (*instrução*). And the fact that precedent is not legally binding frees them to do "justice" regardless of the conservatism of higher courts. Indeed, even less-than-progressive judges are likely to be independent of political powers and subject to close appellate control, and therefore not inclined to tolerate illegality to suit the demands of law enforcement. At the same time, the structure of the judiciary is such that we are not likely to find many judges willing to go out on a limb on behalf of claimants who are associated with the lower classes and with criminality. Thus, the dominant trend to faithfully apply the rules to the facts as presented by the police report and the prosecutor is completely consistent with

---

[38] Interview with José Eduardo Faria, São Paulo, July 1999.
[39] Interview with Sr. Michael Mary Nolan, São Paulo, April 24, 2001.
[40] More recent demographic analyses of the judicial corps in São Paulo and other states suggest this may be changing, at least at the trial court level. Judges have become much more representative of society as a whole, in terms of gender, socio-economic status, and the like (Sadek 1999).

institutional incentives, and likely to produce a large measure of impunity for a police force that closely controls the flow of information.

Acquiescing in an exculpatory construction of the event is a safe course of action for a judge, as it is highly unlikely that anyone will successfully challenge the judge's construction of the facts. First, most of the dismissals are done at the request of the prosecutor and therefore will not generate an appeal (although a Private Prosecutor, if present, may still appeal the dismissal). Moreover, even if there is an appeal, the judge has considerable control over the facts that are placed in the record and thus can present the appellate court with selective information – for which he or she need only mine the IPM – to support the preferred outcome. Finally, stating and applying a controversial rule of law is a more political step, and more likely to incur the displeasure of higher courts, than simply acting on the basis of facts presented by the police, even if later a higher court considers that the judge should have gone beyond these facts.

The Jury

This account of judicial incentives and capacities explains the high percentage of cases that are dismissed by judicial decision at the pre-trial stage on the basis of the IPM – more than 80 percent of all the cases. But if, in the view of judges and prosecutors, the case warrants a trial, judges must turn over the ultimate decision to a jury. Brazil is one of the few countries in Latin America with a long history of jury trials. These trials go back to a law dated June 18, 1822, creating a jury to decide defamation claims. In the federal Constitution of 1824 the right to a jury was extended to civil and criminal cases generally, but in 1967 the military regime limited jury trials to their current reach: intentional crimes against life (Renó do Prado and Mascari Bonilha 2000). At present they remain reserved for intentional crimes against life (*crimes dolosos contra a vida*), the category of crimes that was removed from military jurisdiction by the *Lei Bicudo*.[41]

Unlike oral trials in Buenos Aires, jury trials in Brazil are not a new development, and patterns of behavior are well established. The panel of seven jurors is drawn on the day of the trial from a pool previously assembled through voter rolls, large corporations' employee lists, and telephone directories. The judges, prosecutors, and lawyers I spoke to on this issue all seemed satisfied that the jury selection method produced a relatively representative cross section of society (though it obviously over-represents people with telephones and those employed in the formal sector). Unfortunately, as

---

[41] The 1988 Constitution permits but does not require extending jury trials to other areas.

discussed earlier, this means that the jury is not likely to be overly sympathetic to claims that the police exceeded their limits in repressing crime. At trial, the attorneys will encourage the jury to evaluate the case based on the totality of the circumstances, including the high levels of crime, the character of the victim, and the dangerous nature of police work. As a result, jurors may well be shifting the rule to create more space for impunity, in an exercise in jury nullification. In the opinion of prosecutors, as discussed at length in Chapter 3, this shifting certainly takes place if the victim was a *marginal*, and had a criminal record of some sort. In short, many of the cases, especially those involving a violent victim, fail because the jury is simply unwilling to convict.

But the problem of crafting a record that will support a conviction is more basic. The nature of the trial and the realities of prosecuting these cases ensure that the exercise will add very little new information. As discussed earlier, much of the evidence is simply taken from the written record. As one judge put it, the jury is served a "done deal" (*"prato feito"*) that comes directly from the file. And the file, as we have seen, is based substantially on the IP or the IPM prepared by the police.

Moreover, what new information does come in at the trial is also likely to be skewed in the direction of an acquittal. The few witnesses who might be called to testify in these cases are often illiterate or have criminal records. As we saw in Chapter 3, many will be missing altogether. One prosecutor complained that the high mobility, lack of permanent employment, and social marginalization of these witnesses made it difficult to actually locate them and bring them in for the trial. More important, the same prosecutor complained that witnesses are often intimidated by the police and too afraid to tell the truth or to appear at the trial.[42] On the other side are the police defendants, their colleagues, and even forensic experts, all reputable witnesses who will argue that the victim died in the course of a violent confrontation. The case is thus presented to the jury as just another instance of the police's battle to hold back the ever-present wave of violent crime. In the end, even after surviving prosecutorial and judicial scrutiny, 60 percent of the few cases that actually go to trial end in an acquittal.

F. SUMMARY

In São Paulo, the police are in charge of investigating their own violations and enjoy a radical advantage in presenting these cases as merely the response to violent assaults on society. While governors in São Paulo have been more

---

[42] Interview with Prosecutor Norberto Jóia, São Paulo, April 16, 2001.

supportive of police reform and less prone to repressive discourse in the second half of the decade, social support for violent police tactics appears stronger in Brazil than in Argentina. The lack of exogenous pressures for a more effective response to police violence reduces career incentives for prosecutors and judges to be more aggressive in making up the informational deficit themselves. As a result, judicial decisions – whether by judges or by juries – are based on a radically skewed version of the event, which offers ample support for an acquittal despite judicial application of a rule that is quite faithful to the law.

São Paulo's abysmal conviction rate in police homicide prosecutions contrasts sharply with the picture of a progressive and effective Ministério Público and an independent judiciary. The analysis in this chapter suggests that the police target a population that is radically marginalized and unable to bring its own economic or political resources to bear in support of their claims. The police then craft an investigation that shifts procedural truth drastically in the direction of exoneration. In a social climate of fear and concern over crime, prosecutors never look beyond this police-crafted reality, instead representing the cases as the legitimate use of lethal force in response to violent attacks on society. As a result, police violence is socially and judicially interpreted as a legitimate response to the wave of violence afflicting São Paulo, allowing impunity to reign despite generally healthy and strong institutions.

Judicial decision making, meanwhile, is more insulated from conjunctural and political pressures in São Paulo than in Buenos Aires. Endogenous pressures on prosecutors and judges to take a lenient view in police cases are much more attenuated in São Paulo: the presence of a separate investigative police means that prosecutors are less dependent on the Military Police. Similarly, a more insulated institutional arrangement protects judges from exogenous political pressure. At the same time, however, the perception that violent crime threatens the fabric of society generates considerable public support for a violent response to crime. Coupled with a general conservative bent in the judiciary, this means these cases are far from institutional priorities for either judges or prosecutors. As a result, state actors generally do not assign to these cases the resources that would be needed to successfully prosecute them.[43]

---

[43] The case discussed in Chapter 3, of two police brothers who conspired to kill a witness in a corruption case, dramatically illustrates the resources that would be needed to ensure a greater likelihood of success: witness protection plans, special escorts, forensic evidence, and the like.

In São Paulo, as in Buenos Aires, the passive posture of state actors means that claimants must rely on their own resources to overcome the information deficit created by the police. However, the victims are so universally underprivileged that instead of inequality we see a nearly complete lack of effectiveness, built on the inability of the system to see past the police report. Their vulnerability to harassment and intimidation, lack of material and educational resources, and lack of contact with the state ensure that these marginalized victims cannot successfully redress the informational deficit. NGOs such as the Centro Santo Dias can dramatically improve the information available to decision makers by intervening as Private Prosecutors. But the limited reach of this and similar organizations means that aggregate levels of impunity remain high. The Centro Santo Dias, for example, has intervened in more than three hundred cases since its creation in 1980. In the same period, the police in São Paulo have killed almost twenty thousand people. Although critically important in the cases in which it intervenes, the center's impact on aggregate outcomes is barely noticeable.

In Buenos Aires the dominant impression was that judges and prosecutors avert their eyes in cases that involve the police, so as not to see too much. In São Paulo, a more apt image is of judges peering through a microscope, while the police carefully select the pieces of information they place on the slide.

6

Uruguay

Strong Results from a Weak System

> We cannot defend our democracies if we abandon respect for due process. When a society puts security before human rights, or when public order is put over and above the civil liberties of citizens, then that democracy has adopted the tactics and principles – or lack of principles – of its enemies, and has been partially defeated.
>
>   Statement attributed to Sophia Macher, of the Peruvian Truth and Reconciliation Commission, in an April 2005 Brief to the Canadian House of Commons by the International Civil Liberties Monitoring Group

Uruguay has not yet put security above civil liberties. The case of Uruguay gives us considerable leverage in searching for an explanation for judicial effectiveness, since it gives us cross-system variation to expand the within-system variation I have been exploring in places like Buenos Aires and São Paulo. In sharp contrast to Brazil and Argentina, Uruguay actually protects the victims of police violence. It also varies from these other jurisdictions on a number of potential explanatory variables. Whereas São Paulo presented a case of strong institutions and weak results, Uruguay shows strong results with quite weak institutions. The answer to this paradox lies in the context in which these institutions are embedded: a more congenial political atmosphere creates incentives for judges and prosecutors to be proactive in these cases; and a less marginalized victim population allows these judicial actors to penetrate the veil of darkness that typically surrounds these cases in Brazil and Argentina. A society that, for various reasons, has not placed security over due process combines with a less remote state to produce an effective judicial response to police excesses.

Interviews with human rights lawyers in the country and an exhaustive search of human rights reports and newspaper archives reveal no more than twenty-three persons killed by a police officer in the course of his or her duties during the 1990s. Even given Uruguay's small population, the odds of being shot by the police are twenty and fifteen times greater, respectively, in São Paulo and Buenos Aires, and sixty times higher in Salvador da Bahia. Conviction rates echo these results: they approach 50 percent, besting the performance of all the other cities in this study. Even Córdoba, its nearest competitor in judicial effectiveness, shows a markedly higher level of class-based inequalities in judicial outcomes. These results are entirely consistent with Uruguay's reputation as a country with a high degree of respect for human rights and a working rule of law. O'Donnell lists it as one of two countries in which the state "long ago . . . established a legal system that, by and large, functions across its whole territory, and in relation to most social categories" (O'Donnell 1999: 311).

While these results are consistent with Uruguay's reputation, they contrast with the actual state of its institutions. We might expect a functioning legal system to rest, however partially, on a well-funded, efficient judiciary, and on laws that are modernized and rationalized. Indeed, as we saw, these are the dominant (implicit) hypotheses among judicial reformers in Latin America: courts, the argument goes, either need more resources, or they need to spend them more efficiently, or they need more modern laws – especially procedural laws (for an overview of these approaches to enhancing the rule of law see Salas 2001). Uruguay defies each of these commonsensical intuitions, building a functional legal system out of shrinking budgets and ancient codes.

In terms of funding, Uruguay's courts lag far behind Argentina and Brazil. As of January 2003, after the strong devaluation of the Uruguayan peso, trial judges earned between $15,000 and $17,000 per year. Supreme Court justices earned about $24,000 per year. Even before the devaluation, during the 1990s, they earned less than half what their peers earned in Argentina. On average throughout the 1990s, Uruguay spent about 1.4% of its budget, or 0.35% of GDP, on its judiciary (Bittencourt 1997 for 1985–96 figures, FORES and Colegio de Abogados de Buenos Aires 1999b for 1995–99). Argentina spends twice that percentage (of budget and GDP) on state and federal judiciaries (FORES and Colegio de Abogados de Buenos Aires 1999b). In the state of São Paulo, Brazil spends about 5% on its courts, more than three times as much as Uruguay.[1] The courts' smaller share of

[1] As with Argentina, to properly compare expenditures in Brazil's federal system to those in Uruguay's unitary system requires combining the spending on courts of state and national governments. In 2000 the Brazilian federal judiciary received about 5% of the total funds directed to the three federal branches, while the state of São Paulo spent about 6% of its total budget on the judiciary (*source*: *Orçamento do Estado de São Paulo* [São Paulo State Budget], 2000, available at www.planejamento.sp.gov.br, and *Orçamento da União* [Federal Budget],

the total budget is reflected in the average expenditure per case. In the early 1990s, Uruguay spent $256 per case filed and only $93,000 per judge, per year, while Argentina spent $760 per case and (because of a lower ratio of judges to administrative and other personnel) $760,000 per judge (FORES and Colegio de Abogados de Buenos Aires 1999b). Clearly, spending more did not buy a better performance in Argentina, at least in connection with the prosecution of rights violations by the police.

Moreover, while it is true that Uruguayan courts make do with less, they are far from being paragons of efficiency. The complaint heard most consistently among users of the system is that the courts are slow, inefficient, and costly for the user. Criminal court judges in Uruguay resolve an average of seventy-one decisions per year, while judges in Argentina, for example, attend to over two thousand new cases per year, deciding hundreds more than their Uruguayan colleagues. Given their lower workload, the time taken to resolve cases should be shorter even than it is. In criminal cases, the average delay from the filing of an indictment (*sumario*) to the final resolution of the case at the trial level is over two years in the capital, and just under two years in the interior (Poder Judicial various years). This does not include the time involved in the initial investigation (*pre-sumario*). While there is more than one reason for this, the fact that up to 85 percent of the prison population in Uruguay at any given time is being held in preventive detention awaiting trial (Bayce 1996) testifies to the courts' lack of efficiency.

Nor is Uruguay working with the latest procedural rules. Argentina and Brazil have joined the majority of countries that reformed their criminal procedure laws to move away from the cumbersome written inquisitorial system to a more agile and adversarial oral procedure. Uruguay has failed to do so, despite the 1997 passage of a law mandating this change. The courts have resisted implementation of the new law, arguing that they lack the physical capacity and financial resources to accommodate the necessary changes. These changes are supposed to improve the ability of the courts to get in touch with reality, move cases with agility, and act with more flexibility, but they have yet to be implemented in Uruguay. In short, it appears that, in terms of organizational strength, funding, and resources, in terms of normative modernization and efficiency, the Uruguayan courts are, at minimum, no

2000, available at www.planejamento.gov.br). To get a rough measure of total expenditures on courts in the state of São Paulo, I calculated a weighted average of federal and state expenditures, using the share of the federal budget proportional to São Paulo's share of the total population of Brazil. Given São Paulo's disproportionately high level of economic activity within Brazil, it is likely that this significantly understates spending on courts in São Paulo.

better off than the Brazilian and Argentine ones we have examined already, and possibly worse off. And yet these courts clearly obtain better results in the cases we are examining here. How do we account for this apparently anomalous result?

As with the other case studies, I will first examine the socio-political and socio-economic context and the institutional framework within which the prosecutions take place. From the interplay of environmental and institutional factors I will derive the exogenous and endogenous pressures on the various actors within the system, and explore the impact of these pressures on the actors' informational capacity and normative preferences. We will see that, as in the other cases, the key to the courts' performance lies in the capacity and motivation of judges, prosecutors, and interested parties, set off against the incentives and capacity of the police to restrict their access to information.

The Uruguayan judiciary does not include an independent judicial investigative force. As much here as in Buenos Aires or São Paulo, judges and prosecutors rely on the police to conduct investigations. As a result, as we saw in previous cases, the decision to undertake an in-depth independent investigation in a Police Violence case requires an out-of-the-ordinary expenditure of effort and resources on the part of judges and prosecutors. Uruguay differs from the other cases, however, in the access judicial actors have to alternative sources of information (that is to say, in the reduced capacity of the police to drastically curtail such access) and in the external pressure for judges and prosecutors to make use of that access. The result is a higher conviction rate, because more information is available than in Buenos Aires, São Paulo, and Salvador, for example, and lower levels of inequality, because the system is less dependent on private resources in generating that information than in Córdoba.

A. THE URUGUAYAN CODE OF CRIMINAL PROCEDURE

The procedural code delineates actors' roles and responsibilities and, along with certain other institutional characteristics, will determine how dependent they are on each other. The critical questions are the same here as in the other jurisdictions we have already examined – do the police investigate their own crimes? Do judges rely on the police for information, or is there a judicial investigative police? Do claimants get an active voice? Who is the ultimate decision maker in the case? Interestingly, the formal institutional answer to each of these questions, in the abstract, does not bode well for the successful prosecution of police crimes in Uruguay.

Uruguay has retained its traditional procedure in criminal cases. Despite an attempted reform in 1997, the basic rules of criminal procedure are set forth in a 1980 *Código del Proceso Penal*, established by a *"decreto-ley"* (*Decreto-Ley* No. 15,032)[2] of the recent military regime. This code abolished the *Juzgados de Instrucción*, purely investigative tribunals, and transferred responsibility for the investigation to the *Juzgados de Primera Instancia en lo Penal*, ordinary criminal courts. Within these courts, prosecutors are solely responsible for deciding whether the state will accuse. If the prosecutor requests a dismissal (*sobreseimiento*) at the initial stages, or refuses to proffer the equivalent of an indictment (*acusación*) at the end of the investigation, the judge must dismiss the case. The judge cannot modify a charge or impose a more severe sentence than the prosecutor has requested.

At the same time, however, the prosecutor is beholden to the judge for the development of the evidentiary record on which his or her case depends. What in the common law system we might consider the prosecutorial function is, in essence, split between the judge and the prosecutor, forcing these two to work closely with each other. The building of the factual record is fully in the hands of the judge. While the prosecutor and defense attorneys can request measures of proof, the judge has the final decision on whether or not to take these measures. The Uruguayan code also does not permit claimants to participate directly as a party in a criminal prosecution (except in defamation cases). There is no figure similar to the *assistênte do promotor* we saw in Brazil or the Argentine *querella* or *particular damnificado*, and the judge has no obligation to request any measures of proof an interested party might request. In addition, the code does not provide for the creation of a purely judicial investigative force, so that the court must rely on the police for the logistics of the investigation.

As we saw, in Argentina procedural reforms have transferred responsibility for the investigation to the prosecutor but left the final decision with the judge, while in Brazil the judge has substantial control over the investigation but turns over the final decision to a jury. Under Uruguay's code of criminal procedure, the judge is primarily responsible for both the investigation and the final decision on the case – the hallmark of the inquisitorial model. The danger of an inquisitorial model is, of course, that by virtue of his or her quasi-prosecutorial role, the judge tends to adopt a stance that is more prosecutorial than judicial. Having conducted the investigation, the judge tends to become more invested in and more confident of the information

---

[2] A *decreto-ley*, or legal decree, is a decree initially enacted by the military regime that has been expressly ratified by the legislature after the transition to democracy.

thus produced. As we will see, this actually helps to overcome the police's informational advantage in these cases, although it simultaneously raises due process concerns.

There is no trial, as such, in Uruguay. When the investigation is complete, the parties submit written briefs and the judge decides on the basis of the written record of his or her own investigation. This is not to say that judges never see witnesses and defendants. As in Argentina, a precondition for beginning the investigative stage is the oral declaration of the accused in the presence of the judge. Moreover, it is the judge's responsibility to question witnesses, and in Uruguay practice usually follows the rule, with questioning taking place in the judge's chambers and at least in his or her presence (Cisa 1994). Judges here rely much less on their staff, coming in direct contact with the parties and the witnesses much more often than in Argentina. The average ratio of non-judicial support personnel to judges is about two to one, less than half of what it is in Argentina (Bayce 1996).

The legislature approved a new code of criminal procedure in 1997 (*Ley* No. 16,893, December 1997) in an attempt to modernize criminal procedure and make it more congruent with Uruguay's international obligations.[3] But the new text, despite its advantages in many respects, was immediately criticized by both those who said it went too far and those who argued it did not go far enough. This left it with little support in the legislature. The Supreme Court, which was itself none too supportive of the change, took the opportunity to point out that if the courts were now to begin conducting oral proceedings, they would need new courtroom facilities. Since then the legislature has failed to appropriate the necessary funds to make the new procedures possible, and the new law remains a dead letter. The effective procedural code is still the code of 1980, with its roots in the military regime.

In summary, the investigative function is entrusted to the judge, who relies on the police to carry out most of the actual tasks required by the investigation. In the absence of an independent investigative force that answers directly to the courts, judges rely on the police to do much of the legwork in these investigations. The prosecutor is responsible for the accusation but depends on the judge – and the police – for evidentiary measures, as do defense attorneys. The same judge who presides over the investigation makes the ultimate decision on the merits of the case.

---

[3] Uruguay is signatory to a UN convention that requires that the investigative, prosecutorial, and judicial functions be separated, something that is clearly violated by the existing inquisitorial arrangement.

These formal arrangements, indicating a close working relationship between the judge and the police, would posit (as in Buenos Aires) a more lenient judicial attitude toward police defendants. Moreover, because claimants are unable to participate directly, their influence is more diluted. In short, endogenous pressures to be lenient with the police are likely to be high, and the center of gravity of the entire system should tend toward the defendant in a police case. But the results in Uruguay make it clear that we cannot stop with an acontextual institutional analysis. In addition to these endogenous factors, we must consider the exogenous pressures transmitted to judges and prosecutors, as well as the capacity of claimants to interact with these judicial actors. The next section examines the social, economic, and political context for the first clues to the ability of the courts to examine police conduct in these cases.

B. SOCIAL CONTEXT

1. Socio-economic Context

The socio-economic context from which claimants are taken matters primarily because it conditions claimants' ability to influence the legal system on their own behalf. The social composition of the victim population in Uruguay is similar to that of Buenos Aires and Córdoba. Fully half were unemployed, and two-thirds belonged to the lower working class or below. As in other places, most of the incidents in Uruguay occur in what the media and the police call "conflictive," typically lower class, neighborhoods. Here as in each of the locations of this study, the most frequent targets of police violence and rights abuses are young males from among the underprivileged (as discussed in detail in Chapter 2). What is different in the Uruguayan case is the broader context in which these victims are inserted and the distance between the claimants – victims' immediate survivors – and the state.

Historically, Uruguay has experienced lower levels of inequality than its Latin American neighbors. Data for the 1990s show a more even income distribution in Uruguay than in any other country in Latin America (CEPAL 2003); Uruguay's average Gini is 43, compared to 51 for Argentina and 58 for Brazil (Milanovic 2005). Brazil, one of the most unequal countries in the world, has always had vastly higher levels of income inequality than either of the other two. Urban households below the poverty line are also a smaller percentage of the population in Uruguay (about 6% by the end of the decade) than in Brazil and Argentina (about 13% and 25%, respectively). Uruguay has no equivalent to the 1.5 million *favelados* in São Paulo or to the vast *villas* in Buenos Aires. Its most impoverished urban residents are still closer to formal society than those in Buenos Aires and São Paulo.

But a focus on income inequalities alone misses the point. Observers often remark on Uruguay's noticeable ethos of egalitarianism. This ethos may be a consequence of the smaller population, narrower gaps in material conditions between the underprivileged and other sectors, or the long history of (not yet dismantled) social welfare policies (see, e.g., Castiglioni 2005 for an analysis of state reforms in response to the Washington Consensus). While warning of a more dismal future, the Uruguayan sociologist Rubén Kaztman notes that Uruguay has historically enjoyed a very high level of social integration. He says, "This level of integration can be seen in the functioning of its institutions, in the absence of important social distances, in the fluid and symmetrical communication between persons of different social extraction, as well as in the many ways in which social solidarity is expressed when called upon" (Kaztman 1997).

In other words, despite indices of poverty and income inequality that are still high, though somewhat better than those in Argentina, not only are social distances reduced, but the more social democratic state in Uruguay maintains a stronger presence across social strata. Rubén Bayce, another Uruguayan sociologist, argues in a comprehensive study of access to justice that no one is too far removed from the justice system: "The total number of people specifically dedicated to the administration of justice ... configures a very high number ... on a per capita basis. ... Uruguay has the fifth highest rate of judges per capita in the world, one of the highest rates on the planet in police per capita ... which makes Uruguay one of the countries with the greatest social control capacity, enforcement and guarantee of justice" (Bayce 1996). While it would be wrong to imagine Uruguay as an egalitarian paradise, it is clear that contacting both the state and its administration of justice personnel is neither an unfamiliar idea nor an insurmountable logistical task. The legal system is well within the reach of almost any citizen.

2. Socio-political Context

Perhaps the most important factor contributing to the successful prosecution of police violence cases in Uruguay is the favorable political context. This creates sufficient exogenous pressure on judges and prosecutors to overcome unfavorable endogenous incentives. Despite an important rise in crime rates, including violent crime, there continues to be no support for draconian and repressive policing tactics. A decade-long study concluded that while murder rates remained stable from 1990 to 2000, armed robbery increased almost threefold, from just fewer than 17 per 10,000 inhabitants to nearly 45 per 10,000.[4] In fact, if one trusts official statistics, Uruguay's homicide rates are nearly identical to Argentina's.

Moreover, Uruguay shows much the same pattern of concern over crime as all eight countries included in the 1996 Latinobarómetro: 87 percent of respondents felt that crime had increased, and Uruguayans were second only to Venezuelans in the percentage of respondents (8%) naming crime as the principal problem in the country. The level of concern about crime is as high in Uruguay as in Argentina, but the social and political response to this concern is palpably different in Uruguay. I searched in vain for political platforms and public statements by elected officials comparable to Ruckauf's, Patti's, or Rico's "*mano dura*" and "*meta bala*" arguments. Opinion polls and interviews show nothing comparable to the "*marginal tem que morrer*" (criminals must die), or "*bandido bom é bandido morto*" (the only good criminal is a dead criminal) heard in Brazil.

Moderate statements are common even when we might expect the opposite. In July 2000, an armed robber shot and killed a taxi driver. The taxi drivers' association released a statement in response that read, in part, as follows: "We ask ourselves: what could lead someone to kill for a few coins, other than the most atrocious poverty, the greatest degradation of the basic values of a human being, the lack of employment, of a just wage, a fraternal education [*educación solidaria*], and dignified living conditions? ... We are convinced that this is one more murder committed by the reigning economic and social model, and that those who promote policies that marginalize and exclude the immense majority are just as responsible for this crime as the individual who pulled the trigger ending the life of this worker" (*La República*, July 12, 2000). This opinion, attributing crime to social conditions and the solution to social change, is widespread.

As in São Paulo, elected leaders also shifted from less to more concern for civil and human rights from the beginning to the end of the 1990s. Of the three Uruguayan presidents over the course of the decade, Luis Alberto Lacalle, Julio María Sanguinetti, and Jorge Batlle, the first two de-emphasized human rights accountability for the abuses of the previous regime (Skaar 2002), but they never openly called for greater latitude for the police under democracy. Sanguinetti and Lacalle, who between them governed during the entire decade, were not especially strong advocates of

---

[4] See Anuario Estadístico 1990–2000, and Anuario Estadístico 2003, showing an ending rate of 44 armed robberies per 10,000.

human rights, but neither were they advocates of the *"mano dura"* approach to crime.

Batlle, elected at the end of the decade, is an old-fashioned liberal with a rhetoric of social responsibility on crime issues and a more proactive stance on the human rights question. Batlle immediately took steps, for example, to uncover information in some of the most notorious cases associated with the latest dictatorship (Skaar 2003). In 1999, Batlle, then a candidate for the presidency, argued that crime was a response to social problems, which the government could and should resolve (*El Observador*, "Batlle pide atacar las causas del delito," March 13, 1999). A year later, at a funeral honoring two police officers killed in the line of duty, Batlle returned to the same theme: these violent events, he said, "lead us to reflect that we not only need a capable and well-paid police force, but that it is also essential to take strong measures in the formative area, in the educational area, to resolve problems of marginality that are the ones generating, in most cases, these situations and circumstances that are so sad and so irreparable" (*La República*, December 19, 2000, p. 22).

Meanwhile, the electorate steadily moved to the left, as evidenced by the ever-greater success in local and national elections of the Frente Amplio, a coalition of left-of-center parties. In São Paulo, the electoral success of the left was divorced from public opinion regarding the use of lethal force and due process guarantees for criminals. In Uruguay this does not appear to be the case. Despite a temporary hardening of opinions against lawbreakers in 1995 (*El Observador*, November 19, 1995, pp. 32–33), polls generally show that Uruguayans hold a more social democratic view of crime and the proper response to crime: 46% blame social conditions, only 35% moral decay; and 48% oppose the death penalty compared to 43% in favor (Latinobarómetro results reported in *El Observador*, May 19, 1996). Bayce, relying on a series of polls by Gallup, Factum, Vox, Equipos, and Marketing, also reports less support for repressive measures: in 1995, he shows only 31% favoring the death penalty, while 61% were opposed (Bayce 1996: 101).

Unfortunately, there are no polls directly addressing the question of the use of deadly force by the police. But whereas in Argentina and Brazil there was no dearth of statements by elected officials or the public in favor of using lethal force as the solution to crime, I was unable to find any such statements reported in the press in Uruguay at any time during the 1990s. Moreover, some of the polls reported by Bayce indirectly suggest disapproval: in 1989, 46% opposed while 36% favored a *"mano dura"* approach (the reference is to a repressive style of policing); in 1990, only 10% favored the use of "more repression" to control crime; in 1993, only 20% agreed that *"más vigilancia"* (more vigilance) was needed on the part of the police, and only 8% agreed that more "*persecución*" (which here translates as "prosecution") was needed. In 1995, an absolute majority of respondents (54%) stated that the solution to crime does not lie in repressive measures, whether harsh or soft, but rather in addressing the social causes of crime (Bayce 1996).

When I asked Juan Faropa, who runs a police training program established with UN and local funding, why the police in Uruguay kill so much less than the police in other countries in the region, I expected to hear something about superior training, more civilian control, or even lower levels of violent crime. Instead, he said only "our society would not tolerate it. People will tolerate moderate levels of violence [moderate beatings, for example, which have been a persistent problem in Uruguay] but not killings."[5] The legislative history of a series of proposals to extend the police's right of self-defense and protect police officers who use their guns while on duty backs up this assessment: every one of those proposals, introduced at different times in the course of the decade, usually after a police officer has been shot, failed.

The fact that police shootings are so much less frequent in Uruguay also helps to focus attention on these cases. The press devotes considerable space to the stories, usually running more than one article on each case, with follow-ups on successive days and continued reporting as the courts decide whether or not to indict. In Buenos Aires and São Paulo, in contrast, as we saw in preceding chapters, if the incident is reported at all, it is usually a small story that simply repeats the initial police position. The Uruguayan press, in contrast, often highlights the response by the minister of the interior, who is the civilian head of the police and usually a prominent member of the governing party, giving the story a decidedly political bent.

The result of this political environment in Uruguay becomes evident in the aftermath of these events. After a police officer killed González Ortiz, nearly two hundred neighbors approached lawyers from the group Servicio Paz y Justicia to press for a legal response. The Hospital Filtro case generated repeated mass demonstrations. When a police officer killed Nuñez Sellanes, the public mounted a demonstration in front of the local police station that lasted all the following day, according to press reports. These three cases involved "innocent victims," youths with no previous connection to crime. As we saw, such a victim can prompt demonstrations in Buenos Aires too. But public reaction in Uruguay is not limited to the "worthy" middle-class victim. The death of Albín, the *bagayero* shot after a car chase in the midst of a smuggling operation, might have gone unnoticed in Argentina or Brazil.

---

[5] Interview with Juan Faropa, Montevideo, December 19, 2000.

But in Uruguay, as we saw, Albín became the subject of extensive popular mobilization demanding justice.

At times even those public officials we might expect to be most defensive about these cases speak out in favor of a prosecution. When Valente Gómez was killed after a car chase, the minister of the interior promised he would get to the bottom of the incident, initiating his own internal investigation of the events and supporting a prosecution (*El País*, July 6, 1998).

In summary, the demographic profile of the victim pool in Uruguay is similar to the profile of victim populations in Buenos Aires or Córdoba, but the social and political context is quite different. Uruguay shows less inequality overall, the state is more accessible, and the pools of marginal residents are smaller. Victims are not as far removed from the rest of society, and their deaths prompt greater popular outcry. Even the underprivileged are likely to have some access to and contact with the state besides routine encounters with the police. Moreover, the political reaction to crime is not a call for giving the police more latitude in the use of deadly force, but rather a focus on resolving the perceived social causes of crime. As a result, claimants have more personal resources to overcome police attempts to restrict information. In addition, as we will see shortly, they are met halfway by judges and prosecutors responding to exogenous pressures that favor the aggressive prosecution of police officers accused of murder.

I now turn to an examination of the police, to uncover the incentives and opportunities the police might have to resist these demands, both by restricting access to information and by putting pressure on judges and prosecutors. After that we will look at the role of civil society actors and the structure of the prosecutor's office and the judiciary to determine whether there are institutional reasons why we might expect judges and prosecutors in Uruguay to be more responsive to exogenous or endogenous pressures.

C. THE SYSTEM'S SOURCES OF INFORMATION

1. Police Forces in Uruguay

In Uruguay as elsewhere, the very first investigation of the crime scene is carried out by the first police officers on the scene, and they are typically the same ones who would be prosecuted if the shooting was unwarranted. In addition, like Buenos Aires but unlike São Paulo, Salvador, and Córdoba, the investigative police are part of the same police structure as the frontline police officers most likely to use lethal force. As a result, the courts cannot count, a priori, on an independent investigation. Furthermore, on other issues at least, the Uruguayan police have proven as resistant to oversight as the police forces in the other locations we have examined. They are not likely to adopt an aggressive investigative stance when the result will be at best an embarrassment to the corporation and at worst personal criminal responsibility. At the same time, the police corporation as a whole is under far less social pressure to use any means necessary to curb violent crime. The end result is a police force that will participate in a cover-up when excesses occur, but is less willing to use lethal force as a routine means of law enforcement.

Uruguay has a national police force, which is part of the executive branch under the jurisdiction of the Interior Ministry. As in Argentina, the same police force serves the security and investigative functions, although various subdivisions are charged with specialized tasks, such as responding to narcotics or smuggling. In contrast to the infamous ROTA in São Paulo or certain strike force units in Argentina, there do not appear to be any units with an especially violent record. Only a few of the officers charged with homicide in the 1990s belong to a special unit at all. The police officers who killed Albín, the presumed smuggler, were part of an anti-smuggling task force; the officers involved in the Valente Gómez case were part of the *Radio Patrulla*, a radio-dispatched force. The defendants in the Hospital Filtro case were *Coraceros* and *Granaderos*, two elite forces in the Uruguayan police, essentially acting as riot police. But the majority of the defendants are members of the ordinary police force.

The *Policía Técnica* is the division in charge of the technical aspects of crime investigation. They carry out DNA, ballistic, and other tests and produce the expert reports requested by judges. They are even, occasionally, referred to as the "Judicial Technical Police," but they, like all the other divisions of the Uruguayan police, report ultimately to the minister of the interior, not to the judicial branch. Judicial investigations are typically a joint effort of this force, which is concerned with matters requiring more advanced techniques, and the ordinary police, which secure the scene, take witness statements, and produce a report.

While their reputation for misdeeds does not match that of the Buenos Aires police, there have been notorious instances of police corruption and crime reported in the media. In the 1990s in particular groups of off-duty police officers became known as the "*poli-banda*" or "*super-banda*" after they committed a series of sophisticated robberies. The problems did not end after the "*super-banda*" was disbanded.[6] These continued problems,

[6] See, for example, "A Black Week: Four Police Cases with Police Officers Committing Crimes" [La Semana Negra: Cuatro casos policiales con policías delinquiendo], Posdata, February

together with notorious problems of corruption in controlling smuggling at the border with Brazil, attest to the fact that, while it may be less lethal, this police force is no more transparent to civilian oversight than its counterparts in Argentina and Brazil.

Part of the problem is the militaristic and hierarchically disciplined nature of the force. In May 2000, an anonymous police officer gave an interview detailing his fall into corruption (*La República*, May 7, 2000 [monthly edition]). Throughout the 1990s, his colleagues and his superiors had gradually embroiled him in ever-greater instances of corruption. Tellingly, he says, "If you try to be clean, everyone turns against you. . . . If you, a rank-and-file police officer, denounce a superior you get a disciplinary hearing and the superior gets nothing." In short, it does not appear to be any easier for Uruguayan police officers than for their Argentine or Brazilian colleagues to report wrongdoing on the part of their colleagues and superiors.

In short, the key institutional variables show very much the same results for police in Uruguay and in Buenos Aires: in cases of police violence, the police force must investigate itself; the police are the principal source of information for the system in all cases; and internal hierarchical control over legal and illegal conduct is quite strong, rendering the corporation opaque to external oversight. All of this suggests that the police have both motive and opportunity to engage in the sort of information rationing we have seen already, especially in Buenos Aires and São Paulo. We would predict, therefore, a similar pattern of obstruction.

Perhaps the major difference between the Uruguayan police and the others is this: while the police are not overly susceptible to oversight – and thus show relatively high indices of crime and corruption – they do not face the same demands for a violent response to crime. Indeed, whenever they exceed certain boundaries on the use of force, they are likely to lose the support of their civilian leadership and face criticism from the population. It is surely not the case that a police officer who commits murder can say he is being prosecuted for doing what society asks him to do, as police officers claimed in São Paulo, for instance. In the absence of external pressure to this effect, there is unlikely to be any internal pressure on street-level police to use their weapons. What we might expect, however, are efforts to whitewash the killings that do occur, to avoid embarrassment and criticism, and efforts to distance the corporation from the more egregious killings.

18, 2000; "Thirty-seven Police Officers Prosecuted This Year" [Este Año Procesaron a 37 Policías], *El Observador*, May 24, 2000.

The data from actual cases match this prediction. We see the same pattern of cover-ups and falsified proofs in Uruguay as we do in other places. In the Albín case, the police planted a gun on the victim and used it to shoot holes in their own clothing and in their own car. In the Hospital Filtro case, the police simply closed ranks around the individuals who pulled the trigger, so that their identities were never established. In the Gamarra case, the police chose a remote location to ambush the victim and prepared a false police report to cover up the killing with the full collaboration of the local police chief. In the case of González Ortiz, the police prepared a report that claimed that the victim struggled with the police officer over the gun and was killed accidentally, despite eyewitness accounts that say the victim was prone when the police officer placed the gun against his neck and pulled the trigger. It is not, of course, a surprise to find that the police attempt to cover up when they commit a crime, but at least we can rule out as a possible explanation the theory that the police in Uruguay are more transparent to external control and simply will not tolerate illegal behavior on the part of their colleagues.

Thus far, the results are contrary to what we might have expected. Given the higher success rates in Uruguay, and the ability of the police in other systems to deprive the system of the information it needs, in Uruguay we might have expected an independent Judicial Police, or at minimum one that is better controlled or more transparent than that of Argentina and Brazil. But, in fact, problems of corruption within the Uruguayan police are quite as intractable as in Argentina or Brazil, suggesting that the police are similarly opaque to outside oversight. Moreover, they are still the main source of information, and they still belong to the same corporation as the perpetrators and so can be expected to prefer an acquittal and obstruct any investigation. Sociologist Bayce argues, as I have for each of these countries, that "the true Achilles heel of the Judicial System [in Uruguay] is the Police, not the Judiciary" (Bayce 1996: 99). The difference between the outcomes in Uruguay and those in other places, therefore, must lie in the ability of the system to overcome this pattern of obstruction by the police.

2. Civil Society Actors

First we must ask whether some part of this coping ability can be attributed to the claimants themselves. As we saw, while indices of poverty are similar overall, claimants are more diverse in Uruguay and tend to have greater political and economic resources. The Procedural Code, however, denies them the ability to participate as a Private Prosecutor – a critical tool in Buenos Aires and São Paulo for redressing power imbalances between claimants and the police. Still, there are collective actors in Uruguay who work on claimants' behalf from outside the legal system. Spontaneous gatherings and demonstrations in response to specific events also play an important role in focusing media and judicial attention on the cases. These ad hoc gatherings are not usually organized by special-purpose NGOs, although they may ultimately resort to them. The cases I have examined suggest proportionally more spontaneous civil society activity in Uruguay than in São Paulo and Salvador, although we see similar phenomena in Argentina.

The principal non-state organized actor dealing with issues of police violence and human rights is the Servicio Paz y Justicia (SERPAJ). Although it does not focus exclusively on police violence, SERPAJ also tracks such incidents, offers a forum for those with complaints, and provides free legal representation to those who wish to pursue a legal claim. It has had an important role in some of the cases discussed here, especially the Hospital Filtro case. Its role in the prosecution of that case is illustrative of the cooperative relationship between judges and claimants, in sharp contrast to the adversarial relationship of CORREPI, for example, with the Argentine judges. Recall that evidentiary measures are entrusted to the judge's discretion, and SERPAJ is prevented from intervening directly in the case. Nevertheless, the judge encouraged Ariela Peralta, an attorney who works with SERPAJ, to bring witnesses and documentary evidence to the court's attention, which the court readily accepted into the record. The judge also ordered police agencies to produce information that SERPAJ requested. Overall, Peralta reports, the judge was very receptive to her participation in the case, although she was conscious at all times that her activity was entirely subject to the judge's goodwill.

While the results in the Hospital Filtro case were positive, SERPAJ (and claimants in general) have no recourse at all should the judge choose to leave them out of the process entirely. Under the existing code, they cannot accuse if the prosecutor chooses not to, and they have no legal right to argue the facts or the law, although judges occasionally allow interested parties to file some sort of brief. As a result, collective action of this sort is a much weaker tool for influencing legal outcomes in Uruguay than similar avenues open to civil society in Argentina and Brazil. While claimants might have additional resources, therefore, they act at the sufferance of judges and prosecutors. To find the answer to Uruguay's greater efficacy, then, we must move up the ladder another rung or two and examine the conduct of prosecutors and judges.

D. PROSECUTORS

I have already established that exogenous pressures are likely to be in favor
of more aggressive prosecutions, while endogenous pressures exerted by the
police on individual prosecutors in a given case will run in the opposite direction. How these opposing forces will balance out for individual prosecutors
depends on how open the institution is to exogenous pressures, and how
able it is to enforce normative homogeneity within its ranks.

Prosecutors are part of the executive branch, subordinated to the Ministry of Justice. They are named by the executive with the advice and consent of the Senate and, once appointed, enjoy the same tenure protections
as judges. Tenure protection gives them considerable individual freedom of
action, but career incentives make them susceptible to internal control. They
rise in the ranks and obtain more desirable geographic assignments on the
basis of seniority weighted by performance. These performance evaluations
are carried out by their immediate superiors (*Ley Orgánica del Ministerio Público y Fiscal* [1982], Art. 32), who also have disciplinary authority
over them. Once appointed, Uruguayan prosecutors are, therefore, subject
to the displeasure of the hierarchy as much as any prosecutor is in Argentina
and probably more so than prosecutors in Brazil. Interviews with attorneys
confirm that prosecutors face considerable internal pressures to conform.[7]
The head of the agency, moreover, the *Procurador General*, is a political
appointee named by the president with the advice and consent of the Senate. Unlike in São Paulo, where the executive must select its nominee from
a list produced by prosecutors themselves, the Uruguayan executive is free
to select a congenial *Procurador General*, subject to Senate confirmation. In
contrast to Brazil, these appointments are typically viewed as appropriately
partisan.

The result of this arrangement is a prosecutorial corps with job security
but considerable incentive to respond to their politically appointed top leadership. Individual prosecutors are shielded from external political pressures,
but their advancement is subject to the pleasure of their superiors. Their
superiors, in turn, are influenced by the political stance of the appointed
head of the office. Thus directives from the top are likely to conform to
political trends, while the internal discipline and promotion regime should
produce a high degree of compliance among frontline prosecutors. In other
words, the prosecutorial force is open to exogenous pressures at the top and
transfers these pressures efficiently to prosecutors down the ranks. In the

---

[7] Interview with Ariela Peralta, Montevideo, December 14, 2000.

favorable political context of Uruguay, this allows for the transmission of exogenous pressures to produce positive results in police homicide cases.

As noted in the discussion of the Code of Criminal Procedure and the police, endogenous pressures run counter to these exogenous ones. Not only do these prosecutors, like all others, work with the police daily to incarcerate defendants who often fit the same profile as the victims, but they also depend on the police for information in all their cases. They can ill afford to antagonize the police. But in Uruguay prosecutors also work closely with the judge to develop the evidentiary record. Because the code effectively splits the prosecutorial function, judges and prosecutors collaborate very closely as they collect information during the *sumario* stage. According to reports, relations between judges and prosecutors are much better than the quite conflictive relationship between prosecutors (and judges) and the police. One consultant, for example, has identified the improvement of relations with judges and prosecutors as one of the most important current problems for the police (González 2003). Prosecutors hold the police in disregard as being ill prepared and ineffective, while the police distrust prosecutors because they lack policing experience.

In the end, therefore, exogenous pressures dominate endogenous pressures, and prosecutors retain an adversarial stance with respect to the police. Although they are far from zealots, Uruguayan prosecutors are more likely to respond with a serious investment of resources when the needs of a case demand it than are their counterparts in Buenos Aires or São Paulo. This matches the perception of human rights attorneys who, in discussions of concrete cases, do not complain of obstructionism by prosecutors (with the possible exception of the Hospital Filtro case). Attorneys do, however, rank the conduct of judges more favorably still, and we turn to them next, to understand the source of their engagement.

E. THE COURTS

Scholars who simply tabulate the formal institutional characteristics of the judiciary place Uruguay near the bottom of the Latin American pile in terms of independence (see, e.g., Skaar 2002), and for good reason. The justices of the Supreme Court are subject to a two-thirds vote of the General Assembly (a combined meeting of the bicameral legislature) for appointment. They serve a term of only ten years and can be reappointed after a five-year hiatus. Additionally, since there is no constitutionally guaranteed budget, the Supreme Court presents a proposed judicial budget to the executive, merely as a guideline in the preparation of the budget proposal to the legislature.

Both judges and independent observers agree that the executive largely disregards the Court's requests, drastically trimming its proposal before sending it on. Thus, the Court is beholden both to the legislature for its composition and to the executive and legislature for its funding. Individual justices who aspire to a second term must not offend the legislative leadership, who will approve their re-appointment. If formal institutional design has anything to do with independence – and it should (see, e.g., Epstein and Knight 1998: 17; O'Brien and Ohkoshi 2001; but see Herron and Randazzo 2003) – we would not expect the Uruguayan courts to exercise much independence at all.

And yet informed observers agree that Uruguayan courts are far more independent in practice than nearly all their counterparts in Latin America, perhaps even more so than the courts in Costa Rica and Chile. Staats and his co-authors, for example, after reviewing and tabulating indicators derived from expert and public opinion data, place Uruguay in the very first place, followed by Costa Rica and Chile (Staats, Bowler, and Hiskey 2005: Table 3). Uruguayans themselves, while they complain that their courts are slow and inefficient, uniformly maintain that their judges – at all levels – are honest and independent. While it is beyond the scope of this work to fully account for such a high level of independence given the seeming lack of institutional guarantees, we can draw a partial answer from the political context and the informal institutions this context fosters.

As noted, appointments to the Supreme Court must be approved by a vote of two-thirds of the General Assembly (*Constitución de la República Oriental del Uruguay*, §XV, Art. 236). The Constitution also has a "safety valve" in the event of a deadlock: if the legislature fails to fill a vacancy within ninety days, the most senior appellate judge on active duty is automatically named to the Court. Going back as far as 1942, neither the Blancos nor the Colorados, the two dominant parties in Uruguay, had a two-thirds majority, giving each party veto power over the other's judicial candidates.[8] They did, however, jointly control at least two-thirds of the General Assembly until the 1994 election (when their combined share dropped to just over 64%). In response, the parties worked out an express informal agreement to alternate candidacies for the Supreme Court. As vacancies arose, each party in turn named a justice, and the other party supported the nomination, producing the two-thirds majority.

[8] I am grateful to David Altman for generously sharing his data on legislative partisan composition in Uruguay.

Given a five-member court, this arrangement meant that the parties alternated court majorities with each nomination. Moreover, the justices' relatively short tenure (ten years) meant that vacancies arose, on average, every two years. Under this agreement, the parties had three choices: (1) losing control over the Supreme Court by operation of the "safety valve" clause, (2) naming highly partisan candidates who would either upset the juridical order every two years or spell the end of the informal arrangement, or (3) naming qualified and independent candidates who might produce legal continuity, a neutral forum, and a more stable and independent institution. The parties chose the third option. While individual judges are inevitably associated with the party that named them, this association is understood as an ideological affinity rather than as overt partiality to the interests of that party or to the executive, and the Supreme Court is strongly believed to be free from partisan political meddling in the outcomes of cases.[9]

The Supreme Court dominates the careers of lower court judges. The consensus opinion in Uruguay is that lower court judges are also honest and independent, but those who transgress institutional boundaries face established disciplinary mechanisms, controlled by the Supreme Court. The Supreme Court appoints lower court judges, without legislative intervention, by a simple majority vote. It also promotes judges to appellate positions, though these nominations are subject to confirmation by the Senate. After a two-year probationary period all judges have life tenure and salary protection, but the Supreme Court exercises a disciplinary function, removing judges by a four-vote super-majority. Similarly, the Supreme Court must approve any promotion by four out of five votes. From appointment to promotion, every aspect of a judicial career is subject to close control by the highest court.

Judges typically begin their careers in rural courts of general jurisdiction and ascend by moving closer to the capital and from less prestigious courts (such as the criminal courts or the juvenile justice courts) to more prestigious ones (civil trial courts, and ultimately appellate courts). Historically, Cisa argues, seniority was the greater part of the advancement equation,

---

[9] After the 1994 election, however, the old cooperative code fell apart. The two traditional parties lost their combined two-thirds control, and the Colorados, who were either the largest (1994–99) or second largest (after 1999) party in Congress, have not reached a similar agreement with the Frente Amplio, the newly dominant force in Uruguayan politics. As a result, the last few justices to reach the Supreme Court have done so by virtue of seniority. The consequences of this pattern for judicial independence are hard to predict, although on its face it does not appear to be a threat. If anything, it might further de-link justices from the political realm.

with little regard for merit (Cisa 1994: 87). To address this perceived imbalance, the Supreme Court in 1993 created an advisory committee to evaluate applications and propose candidates for promotion. The committee is composed of one Supreme Court justice, an appellate judge designated by the association of judges, a practicing attorney designated by the bar association, and a law professor named by the national law school (*Acordada* No. 7192 [June 9, 1993, renewed in 2000]). Committee members serve for two years and can only be re-elected once. The committee receives survey forms filled out by members of the bar association plus a report from each judge's immediate jurisdictional superior, evaluating judges' capabilities. While the Supreme Court is free to disregard the recommendations of the committee, attorneys believe that the committee carries considerable weight, especially for candidates in less visible posts.[10] This new committee essentially creates more veto players, especially for the early stages of promotion.

The Web site of the Supreme Court is careful to state:

The Judicial Power is organized so that each of its organs is independent in the exercise of its jurisdictional function. There is no hierarchical relationship among judicial organs in relation to the exercise of its jurisdictional function. A Court of Appeals may not give instructions to a Trial Judge or Justice of the Peace regarding how to resolve a matter. The apparently hierarchical line existing between different judicial organs – the fact that one may appeal the sentence of a Justice of the Peace to a Trial Judge, or of a Trial Judge to a Court of Appeals – is not, in reality, the exercise of the attribute of a hierarchical superior.[11]

Formally, then, trial judges are framed as independent actors, exercising their judicial judgment free from interference. This image is promoted by judicial protestations regarding the internal independence of trial judges from their immediate superiors, and by the fact that, as in many civil law countries, the jurisprudence of the Supreme Court and the courts of appeal is not binding on lower court judges. Nevertheless it is clear that a judge's career path provides powerful incentives for conformity. The Supreme Court does assert administrative authority over lower court judges in its Web site. Judges must please not only their immediate superiors but also the members of the Supreme Court, and, to a somewhat lesser degree, the members of the bar association, if they wish to be promoted or assigned to a desirable location. In fact, two of the persons I interviewed spontaneously mentioned career incentives as a factor in maintaining a generally conservative judiciary that

---

[10] Interview with Renzo Gatto, Montevideo, December 2000.
[11] Quote from http://www.poderjudicial.gub.uy (obtained February 6, 2004).

is cautious, resistant to change, and very orthodox in its interpretation of the laws.[12]

According to human rights attorneys, these characteristics make it difficult to prevail on claims that rest on such innovative notions as the domestic applicability of international human rights law or new interpretations of existing laws. These are indeed serious obstacles to the prosecution of the human rights violations of the previous regime, which are not only difficult to frame within the ordinary penal code but are further protected by an amnesty law. These career incentives are surely at least partially responsible for the rather dismal record of Uruguay's judiciary in pursuing these human rights cases (Barahona de Brito 1997; Skaar 2002).[13] At the same time, in an ordinary murder prosecution, even a police officer defendant will be impartially subjected to the conventional rules, according to these and other lawyers.[14] Judges' very orthodoxy and exposure to scrutiny make them more reluctant to bend the rules in favor of the police, whatever their sympathy for the police.

As in São Paulo, then, we have well-qualified if cautious judges who are likely to be receptive to direction from superior courts. What this means for their willingness to take up claims against the police depends, of course, on whether their superiors are in favor of these prosecutions and will in fact transmit exogenous pressures in favor of police prosecutions. On the subject of human rights prosecutions relating to the abuses of the previous regime, Skaar (2002) argues convincingly that the Supreme Court, appellate courts, and Presidents Sanguinetti and Lacalle and other political leaders were all hostile. She persuasively argues that one judge in particular, Judge Reyes, was transferred to punish him for his overly activist role in investigating disappearances that took place during the dictatorship.

[12] Interview with A. Peralta, human rights attorney with SERPAJ, Montevideo, December 2000; interview with Hebert Gatto, attorney, author, columnist and former professor of political science, Montevideo, December 2000.
[13] While it may be true that the abuses of the prior regime have been off limits, these cases clearly have a different political import than instances of police violence during the democratic period. After the transition to democracy in 1985, Sanguinetti pushed through the legislature what was essentially an amnesty law. Groups on the left sought to invalidate the law by means of a plebiscite but ultimately lost the referendum (for details on transitional justice issues, see Barahona de Brito 1997 and Skaar 2002). The amnesty law was therefore backed by the president, by both of the dominant parties, and – by virtue of the plebiscite – by a majority of the population. The plebiscite in fact produced a dominant social consensus to leave the past alone that has endured (at least until Batlle's election). Importantly, even victims of the prior regime and their survivors seemed to acquiesce – until the early part of the decade of 2000, there were almost no cases filed by individuals seeking redress for those violations.
[14] Interview with Susana Falca, criminal defense attorney, Montevideo, December 2000.

Police cases, however, do not raise similar political difficulties. On the contrary, because the minister of the interior is in charge of and closely associated with the police, police abuses are deeply embarrassing to the ruling party. And there is no indication that the two main political parties – or by extension, the judges they have appointed – are willing to turn a blind eye to police shootings. This is especially true since, as Faropa indicated, the population simply will not tolerate killings. As a result, a judge will be expected to carry these cases to a just conclusion. In terms of incentives, then, exogenous pressures run in favor of a prosecution, and the judicial hierarchy is fully capable of transmitting these pressures to individual judges. The case of Judge Reyes suggests that there is a powerful disciplining mechanism at work but not that this discipline would be exercised to restrain judges from investigating police wrongdoing.

But what of judges' informational dependence? As we saw, in the ordinary course of events, judges in Uruguay depend on the police for information, and in the other analyzed systems this dependence was fatal. Even if we grant, therefore, that Uruguayan judges might be more motivated than those in Brazil and Argentina to dig deeper for information about these cases, how do they overcome their informational dependence? The most important part of the answer to this question has already been set forth in the discussion of the socio-economic context: the inequality of power between the police and the claimants is simply not as pronounced in Uruguay as it is in Brazil or even Argentina, and so the police are less able to impose silence on claimants and witnesses, even when the victim is a member of the underprivileged class.

Moreover, in response to pressures to convict, judges and prosecutors rely on fact-finding techniques and legal theories that do not require as much police assistance. The most important of the former is the re-enactment of the crime, which gives judges the capacity to come to conclusions that are independent of the police report. Even when these techniques offer slender objective evidence, so that a jury (as in São Paulo) or an independent panel of judges (as in Buenos Aires) might resist convicting, the dual-role investigative/adjudicative judges can simply act on the basis of their convictions. Ironically, then, the inquisitorial nature of the judicial process in Uruguay contributes to a higher conviction rate in these (and possibly in ordinary) cases. Alternative legal theories are also available, although they often do not result in a very stiff sentence. In the Hospital Filtro case, for example, the court opted for a legal theory that did not require identifying the actual shooter. Unable to overcome police obstructionism, the judge used this theory to indict and convict the officers in charge of the operation for failing to prevent the killings.[15]

Finally, judges in Uruguay have far smaller caseloads than their peers in Brazil and Argentina and, importantly, far fewer cases of this nature to deal with. Thus, they can spend the additional time required to investigate a homicide committed by a police officer without falling far behind in other cases. Justice is not swift, however. The initial indictment or dismissal delays anywhere from a few days to a full year after the incident, while the cases in my sample that went to trial all took between three and four years to do so.[16] Interlocutory appeals (appeals that challenge intermediate rulings before the final disposition of the case) can eat up about two years.

The cases we have already discussed illustrate this process. In the case of Gamarra, the cattle rustler killed in an ambush, the judge heard the complaints of Gamarra's mother, ordered a re-enactment of the crime, and showed that Gamarra could not have been killed in the exchange of gunfire described by the police. The same happened in the Albín case when the judge re-enacted the shooting. In both instances, despite active police resistance to the investigation, the judge ultimately convicted the officer after speaking directly to interested parties and witnesses. Crucially, there is little indication in Uruguay that witnesses in these cases fear for their lives, and none of the cases in the data set involve the killing of a witness to cover up other instances of police violence. Indeed, there is no evidence that complainants, lawyers, or judges have been threatened, despite the higher likelihood of a conviction.

Uruguay demonstrates, in addition, a markedly different attitude toward police obstructionism. In São Paulo, Salvador, and Buenos Aires, despite exceptionally high levels of tampering with the evidence and outright violence against complainants, there were virtually no prosecutions for obstruction of justice. In Uruguay, on the other hand, we find several prosecutions for obstruction of justice and the prosecution of superior officers when the

[15] Interestingly, civil court judges in São Paulo – who have fewer ties to the police and prosecutors – have done something similar. In the face of a lack of cooperation and information in cases for damages arising out of police shootings, they either shift the burden of proof to the police, to show the shooting was justified, or impose a legal duty on the state to protect the lives of those in its custody or control. The result is a radically more positive outcome in civil suits for damages than in the criminal prosecutions, even in the very same case.

[16] The word "trial" is a misnomer in Uruguay. As we have seen Uruguay still follows the written, inquisitorial model of penal justice. The length of time thus refers to the time from the events to the decision taken after full evidentiary review, in cases that survive an early decision to dismiss.

actual shooters cannot be identified. This suggests, at minimum, that the level of informational dependence and the tolerance for an information blackout is not as high. In short, while the police are the main investigative arm of the judiciary, judges (and prosecutors) are more highly motivated to investigate and have access to alternative sources of information, thus breaking the police monopoly and permitting the successful prosecution of at least half of these cases.

F. SUMMARY

In summary, exogenous pressure on all actors in the system – the politics of police prosecutions – runs in favor of more aggressive investigations and prosecutions in Uruguay. The police are, as in the other locations, often resistant to a full investigation. Judges and prosecutors, on the other hand, while independent of partisan political pressures in individual cases, respond to broad social and political demands to take these cases seriously. While the police can and do resist efforts to prosecute by restricting and slanting the information they produce, they cannot overwhelm and impose silence on claimants to the same degree as the police can in São Paulo or even Buenos Aires. Judges and prosecutors, working together on criminal investigations, are able to overcome their informational dependence not only because claimants have more resources but also because they have fewer cases of this nature and more time to carry out investigations.

Ironically, the inquisitorial nature of Uruguayan criminal procedure gives judges greater latitude in overcoming an information blackout, since they need persuade only themselves. The more the police obstruct the judge's efforts to investigate, the more likely it is that a frustrated judge will conclude they are hiding illegal conduct. Even though the claimants do not have a right to present evidence, judges and prosecutors are receptive to their claims and actively seek out supportive information, bringing that point of view into the system anyway. This active state intervention shifts the balance of power away from the defendant without relying on the personal resources of the claimants.

Uruguay is an interesting case, therefore, for what it teaches us about the impact of the broader economic and socio-political context on institutional functioning. Indeed, politics matters for a host of reasons, not typically captured by standard models of strategic action on the part of courts (see, e.g., Vanberg 2001). It matters because it affects the selection of justices (Dahl 1957) and the decisions of strategic judicial actors (Epstein and Knight 1998), to be sure, but also because it encourages prosecutors to be more active, the police to be less resistant, the media to be more supportive, and claimants to be more aggressive. Importantly, it matters because it places state resources at the service of private claimants, sharply reducing the potential for results that are conditional on their socio-economic status. And it matters in ways that are not clearly predicted by formal institutional analyses. It is not only the formal institutional arrangement that matters (O'Brien and Ohkoshi 2001) but also informal institutions that can last as long as fifty years (see Helmke 2002 for a similar example in the Argentine context).

But we cannot lose sight of the distribution of wealth and degree of social exclusion either. Reduced social inequality allows rights bearers to more effectively engage the machinery of rights protection in ways that go beyond the standard account of law and society research (e.g., Galanter 1974; Felstiner, Abel, and Sarat 1980–81). They overcome procedural disadvantages and police resistance to meet judicial actors halfway and jointly produce the information the criminal justice system requires. Moreover, when the poor are not perceived as an Other, but as full members in the political community, their concerns begin to matter to social activists and politicians alike, and therefore to judges and prosecutors. The alternative is surely one of the worst consequences of the recent urbanization and informalization process in Latin America: the massive accumulation of urban poor who increasingly live in segregated communities, work in the informal sector, and participate less and less in the associational life of the rest of society. Such segregated sectors are increasingly viewed as the repository of crime and violence, inhibiting both the extension of rights to the marginalized and the effective exercise of those rights that are extended.

By focusing on context, I do not mean to suggest that formal laws and institutional design do not matter at all. On the contrary, it is the design of judicial and prosecutorial careers interacting with a favorable political climate that creates incentives for these judicial actors to invest extraordinary resources in these prosecutions. And some institutional features that would be nefarious in a different climate or in different kinds of cases actually lead to positive results in prosecuting police officers who exceed limits on the use of force. The permeability of judges and prosecutors to broad social demands leads to impunity in Buenos Aires but to more convictions in Uruguay. The ability of an inquisitorial judge to meet less exacting evidentiary standards redresses the police's greater control over the production of information in cases of police violence, leading to more convictions. But it also leads to convictions on flimsier evidence in cases across the board, when we might want the system to meet a more exacting standard of proof.

We cannot, therefore, take these results to suggest that we should always ensure that judges are highly responsive to public opinion, although some level of responsiveness is surely appropriate in a democracy (see, e.g., Fiss 1993). Nor, especially, should we always endorse the quasi-prosecutorial investigative judge. Judicial reformers appropriately point out that collapsing the investigative and decisional functions weakens due process by eroding the impartiality of the decision maker. This is very troubling in the ordinary case, where the imbalance of power typically runs against the criminal defendant and an inquisitorial court has the potential to overwhelm the defendant's capacity to respond. Even in police cases, where it solves an undue informational advantage, the courts could seek other ways of addressing the same concern without raising due process issues.

Uruguay, then, crafts its positive results in the prosecution of police officers through the cooperation of interested judicial actors and capable claimants, by creating a judiciary that is sufficiently independent in practice, and by offering political support for these prosecutions. The system is open to information about these cases and successfully configures a record that will support a conviction, especially given a somewhat more lenient standard of proof. The result is a series of convictions that do not depend on the socioeconomic or other personal investment of the claimants and a high conviction rate that is unmatched in any of the other jurisdictions examined here.

7

Córdoba

High Levels of Inequality in a Strong System

La ley se hace para todos
Mas sólo al pobre le rige.

La ley es tela de araña
En mi inorancia lo esplico:
No la tema el hombre rico,
Nunca la tema el que mande,
Pues la ruempe el bicho grande
Y sólo enrieda a los chicos.
    José Hernández, La Vuelta
    de Martín Fierro (1878),
    vv. 1091–92

On average, rights in Córdoba are respected and enforced at almost the same rate as in Uruguay. The per capita level of police killings is comparable to Uruguay's and drastically lower than the levels in the other three locations, and the average conviction rate is about 45 percent, again very similar to Uruguay's. But if we scratch just below the surface, Córdoba's results are deeply disturbing. This jurisdiction shows the highest level of socio-economic outcome disparity of any of the systems examined here. The probability of a conviction when a police officer kills a middle-class person is nearly three times higher than when the victim is of lesser means (see Chapter 3). Conviction rates are twenty times higher if the victim's survivors are able to retain an attorney to work with the prosecutors and can organize public demonstrations. The courts' positive response is more closely conditioned on an investment of private resources here than in any of the other places we examine. In this chapter I discuss the roots of this high level of inequality, without losing sight of the fact that Córdoba does achieve an impressive conviction rate overall.

The close look at the cases in Chapter 3 suggests that the problem in Córdoba is, generally, one of information gathering rather than information processing: prosecutorial failures happen when claimants, or the prosecution acting on their behalf, fail to build a record that will satisfy the ultimate decision maker. It also strongly suggests that, in these cases at least, judges hold these cases to a rather high standard of proof. The analyses in Chapters 2 and 3 further demonstrate that these failures overwhelmingly affect the lower classes. In other words, we have already established that the Córdoba legal system consistently fails to secure sufficient information in cases that affect the underprivileged.

In this chapter I show that the immediate cause of this failure is the interplay between a rule-oriented judiciary and weak prosecutorial performance. As in Uruguay and São Paulo, judges in Córdoba are willing to convict, applying a substantive rule of decision that does not excuse arbitrary police conduct. The fact that they are technically proficient, risk-averse, rule-oriented legal operators is both their strength and their weakness. They will follow the law to the letter even if the defendant is a police officer, but they will also demand high-quality information in order to convict. At the same time, unlike prosecutors in Uruguay (but like those in São Paulo), unless prodded, prosecutors do not actively take on the task of developing information when the police fail to do so, thus placing a greater burden on individual claimants. As a result, procedural truth is systematically skewed away from a conviction except when affected individuals have the resources to develop and bring to bear information, either directly or by pressuring prosecutors and investigators. The causal process underlying judicial failures in Córdoba, then, is akin to the process in São Paulo – the problem is not a normative failure (judges who excuse police violence) but an informational failure (judges who will not convict because of the shaky record built against the defendant).

The difference in aggregate results might raise questions about this conclusion. Uruguay and Córdoba are similar to each other in average conviction rates but radically different in terms of inequality. São Paulo, meanwhile, is near the bottom of the list in terms of conviction rates. How is it that the same process of informational failures coupled with normative consistency can lead to such different results in Córdoba and São Paulo? The answer is consistent with the analysis carried out throughout the book. More of the victims in Córdoba than in São Paulo have the resources to engage the legal system effectively, and even the disadvantaged there are not quite as marginalized. This prevents the police from imposing such an absolute information blackout in Córdoba. Moreover, public pressure is more frequent and both prosecutors and judges are more sensitive to these pressures in Córdoba than in São Paulo, ensuring a more aggressive pursuit of particular cases in Córdoba. More often in Córdoba than in São Paulo, then, cases will receive the special attention needed to overcome lax police investigations, but these sporadic interventions leave a clear pattern of uneven results, as we have seen.

Uruguay, on the other hand, relies far less on individual resources and mobilization. This is primarily the result, as we saw, of a more proactive judiciary, acting in response to somewhat more favorable socio-political conditions. In fact, because the judges still follow the old inquisitorial model, it is likely that the Uruguayan courts are willing to convict on the basis of a factual record that might not support a conviction in Córdoba. As a result, the Uruguayan courts produce positive results even when the individual victim belonged to the lower classes, thus generating lower levels of legal inequality than in Córdoba. I now turn to an analysis of the contextual and institutional variables that lie behind this pattern of effectiveness and inequality.

A. THE CODE OF CRIMINAL PROCEDURE IN CÓRDOBA

How does the Code of Criminal Procedure in Córdoba assign responsibility for fact-finding and final decision making? Córdoba was an early innovator in Argentina, introducing oral and public trials as early as 1940. In 1987 a constitutional reform added a series of protections and guarantees for the accused, reinforcing or establishing many due process protections. Importantly, for example, the provincial constitution now calls for the exclusion of coerced confessions and other evidence obtained in violation of the law, including evidence that was discovered as a result of an initial illegal procedure.[1] This reform also began the process of restructuring the relationship between prosecutors and judges, which culminated in the procedural reform of 1991 (although these reforms did not become fully effective until 1996).

Just as the military government did in Uruguay, the procedural reform in Córdoba removed the investigative function from the judges of the *Juzgados de Instrucción* (investigative courts). Rather than sharpening the inquisitorial nature of the system by transferring this function to the trial judge, however, in Córdoba the new code transfers this responsibility away from judges, to

---

[1] While these rules may seem rather basic, they are by no means uniform in Latin America, especially historically. And in the United States, the cognate rules known as the exclusionary rule and the "fruit of the poisonous tree" doctrine are judge-made rules, the limits and constitutional necessity of which are occasionally called into question. The Córdoba Constitution puts these questions beyond debate.

the prosecutors, setting up an adversarial system. Under the current Code of Criminal Procedure, an investigative prosecutor (*fiscal de instrucción*) is in charge of the investigation (Art. 321). The prosecutor can request the assistance of the Judicial Police, who form part of the prosecutor's office, reporting ultimately to the attorney general. The investigation phase remains under the supervision of a *juez de instrucción*, but in Córdoba this judge's primary function is not to build a case against the defendant but rather to safeguard the interests of the accused while the prosecutor carries out the investigation.

Once this phase is done, the *fiscal de instrucción* may recommend that the case be elevated to trial. If the *juez de instrucción* concurs, the case is sent up to a trial court (the *Cámara Criminal*), which in murder cases is usually composed of three judges.[2] The prosecution is at this point taken over by the *fiscal de cámara*, or trial prosecutor. Affected parties can participate at both the investigative and trial stages. The code gives them standing to participate as what I have called the Private Prosecutor, although here they are called *querellantes particulares* (Art. 7, and Arts. 91–96). There is no intermediate court of appeals for these serious cases; appeals go directly to the Supreme Court (the *Tribunal Superior de Justicia*). In short, on paper at least and in contrast to Uruguay, Córdoba has everything we might ask for in a modern and democratic code of criminal procedure: extensive protections of due process rights for the accused, oral hearings, an adversarial rather than inquisitorial structure, and even a Judicial Police. The investigative function, carried out by prosecutors and Judicial Police under judicial supervision, is formally independent of both the security police (who typically commit the violations) and the final decision makers.

We will see, in the discussion of each of these actors, how they actually carry out their assigned roles. Given this structure, our expectation is for these roles to vary considerably from the standards set in Uruguay. We might expect prosecutors to be more aggressive in cases involving the police, since they are less subject to police pressures. Judges, too, who are freed from investigative responsibilities and are primarily charged with protecting defendants' rights, should be more neutral, neither adopting a prosecutorial stance (as in Uruguay) nor bowing to police pressures (as in Buenos Aires).

As we will see, however, the weakness of the Judicial Police tends to erase much of the advantage gained by placing this force directly under

---

[2] Córdoba has recently begun experimenting with a jury system, but none of the cases in this study were tried by a jury.

the control of prosecutors. Endogenous pressures on prosecutors essentially revert to what they were in Buenos Aires, where the police conduct their own investigation, or in São Paulo, where the Civil Police shares many of the same weaknesses. Police and prosecutors in Córdoba shift to the right of the judge and become, once again, the weak links in the process. Judges, however, remain insulated from endogenous pressures and are subjected to at best ambivalent political attitudes toward police violence. As a result, they retain a neutral attitude that favors those with more resources to invest in a judicial intervention.

B. SOCIAL CONTEXT

1. Socio-economic Context

The socio-economic context creates difficult challenges for the legal system in Córdoba. The metropolitan area in particular has a high degree of inequality and a large marginalized population. The shantytown population in this area grew from just under 50,000 in 1991, to 73,000 in 1994, to 103,000 in 2001.[3] On average, then, the most marginalized represent about 5% of the population of the metropolitan area, but to this we must add a population classified as "unsatisfied basic needs" (*necesidades básicas insatisfechas*) that can be as high as 30% in some of the peripheral areas of the city. More than 80% of the population in some of the neighborhoods surrounding Córdoba belongs to "low" or "marginal" classes.[4] The victim population is disproportionately taken from these classes. As many as 38% of the victims come from shantytowns – that is, shantytown residents are eight times as likely to be victimized as the average inhabitant of the Córdoba metro area, so that their risk of being killed by the police is essentially identical to that of shantytown residents in Buenos Aires. About two-thirds of the victims are members of the lowest classes.

Studies repeatedly show that the lower socio-economic sectors in Córdoba have limited access to the justice system. An active group of legal sociologists in that city has undertaken several studies aimed at uncovering just how removed these populations are from the legal system. In contrast to the findings Bayce (1996) reports for Uruguay, these studies show considerable

---

3 *La Voz del Interior*, February 23, 2004, reporting on three studies conducted by Conicet (Consejo Nacional de Investigaciones Científicas y Técnicas) and SEHAS (Servicio Habitacional y de Acción Social).
4 For population data on the Córdoba metro area and an analysis of geographic inequality in that area, see Bressan, Fernández, and Atea (2003).

inequality in access and use of the legal system. Based on extensive polling, they find the legal aid system is "little visible, scarce and fragmented" (Vilanova 2000: 273). Access to legal services is actually shrinking throughout the 1990s, and "in a context of increasing inequality, broad sectors of the poor population...are completely unserved" (Vilanova 2000: 279). Lista and Begala find that the poor typically fail to regularize their legal relationships (employment, housing, etc.) in legal documents (Lista and Begala 2000: 413). Bergoglio reports that, while 50.7% of middle- and upper-class respondents have had some contact with an attorney, only 28% of lower-class respondents have ever contacted one, for any reason (Bergoglio 1997), even though litigiousness rates in Córdoba are as high as in the United States (Bergoglio 2003: 63).

Lista and Begala supplement this observation with the finding that, among the lower classes, the more contact respondents had with the legal system the more negative was their opinion of its operators (Lista and Begala 2000: 421). Members of the lower socio-economic strata do not believe that justice system operators are interested in making the system better serve their needs or that they can themselves effect changes in the system.[5] This is not surprising, as operators of the legal aid system work to the rules (*"a reglamento"*), repeating and reinforcing "asymmetries found in social relations" (Vilanova 2000: 275; Bergoglio 2003: 63). The most common improvement to the legal system this population would like to see is, simply enough, the creation of legal aid offices located in the *barrios* or neighborhoods where they live.

A widely held belief in the inequality of the legal system is one consequence of legal marginalization. Attitudes toward the legal system vary widely by class in Córdoba (Bergoglio and Carballo 1997). As in Buenos Aires (but seemingly more so) the poor in Córdoba distrust all the actors associated with the legal system – lawyers, police officers, and judges (Lista and Begala 2000). While on average the population has more confidence in the judiciary in Córdoba than in Buenos Aires (Bergoglio 2003), an overwhelming majority believes that the courts are permeated with inequality: 95% of the poor (and 69% of the middle and upper class) believe that the laws benefit some groups and not others; 94% of the poor (and 85% of the middle and upper class) believe that criminal laws are not applied in an equal fashion (Bergoglio

---

[5] Interestingly, this sector of the population believes collective action is necessary to force a judicial response in individual cases (Lista and Begala 2000: 427). The results discussed in Chapter 3 suggest that they are correct in this regard, as cases that trigger popular demonstrations have a much higher likelihood of a conviction.

and Carballo 1997: 50, Table 5). The latter belief is amply borne out by the results of this investigation, reported in Chapter 2. In summary, Córdoba has a large population living at the margin of society, in informality and out of touch with a legal system that fails to reach out. More than half the victims are taken from this class.

2. Socio-political Context

There is not a great deal of available data on the levels of social support for *mano dura* public safety policies in Córdoba. Polls show a slightly higher concern for crime than in Buenos Aires (polling by Centro de Estudios de Opinión Pública, April 1999, reported in *La Voz del Interior*), but there are no polls directly addressing the use of lethal force by the police. The issue of public safety did not dominate politics in Córdoba the way it did in Buenos Aires province for much of the decade. Leaders' platforms do not include the aggressive statements we found in Buenos Aires in the middle and end of the decade or in São Paulo at the beginning of the decade.

The Union Cívica Radical held the governorship during almost the entire decade, until 1999 when the current governor, De la Sota (Justicialist Party), was elected. Eduardo Angeloz, a member of the Radical Party, was governor from 1983 until 1995, when he resigned in a corruption scandal. He was succeeded by Ramón Mestre. Angeloz was later tried and acquitted, a result that many observers attributed to the fact that he had named most of the judges who sat in judgment over him. Both Angeloz and Mestre were more or less in the center of the Radical Party, itself a centrist party, and neither of them used strong law-and-order rhetoric, although neither of them was a vigorous human rights advocate either. During the José Manuel De la Sota administration, public safety became more of an issue than it had been, but the main policy proposals (at least in his first term) centered on community policing rather than more repression.

In some instances, the leadership's reaction to the use of lethal force by police suggests less support for police officers who kill and attempt to hide the facts. To simulate a confrontation in the case of Sergio Bonahora, for example, a gun was taken from a local precinct and placed next to the body. Long before the case came up for trial, the *comisario* or local police chief from whose precinct the gun was taken was forced to retire, on suspicion that he participated in the obstruction of justice. Still, this is the exception, not the rule. Overall, political leaders in Córdoba have not distinguished themselves by exerting pressures too far in either direction on the issue of police abuses.

Although organized, sustained movements in favor of greater police restraint or greater protections for criminal suspects are weaker here than in Buenos Aires, the public does bring pressure to bear in favor of a conviction in individual cases. For example, in the case of Miguel Angel Rodríguez, when the prosecutor proffered an indictment charging merely manslaughter, public demonstrations ensued demanding a murder charge. There have also been demonstrations in favor of prosecutions in the so-called *Precinto 5* case. This event involved inmates who suffocated in a jailhouse fire started when the youthful prisoners set their mattresses on fire. It is widely believed that the police goaded the youths into setting the fire and then failed to offer any assistance. In fact, I have found popular demonstrations in 33 percent of the cases in the Córdoba sample – the highest percentage of cases involving popular mobilizations of any of the locations studied. Significantly, the percentage of mobilizations is the same even in cases involving victims with a criminal past, but it is ten points higher in cases involving the middle class. In summary, then, the political leadership is mostly neutral, awaiting public reaction before taking a stance, while public pressure is more common here than in either Buenos Aires or São Paulo.

C. THE SYSTEM'S SOURCES OF INFORMATION

1. The Investigative Police

The Córdoba Judicial Police have a classically Argentine organizational history, in which formal rules precede by many decades the organizations they purportedly call into being. The Judicial Police are first mentioned in the Procedural Code of 1939, authorized and regulated by statute twenty years later, in 1958, but not even partially implemented until 1985. In 1985, supervision over the investigative division of the Provincial Police was effectively transferred to the judicial power, and then re-assigned to the prosecutor's office (the Ministerio Público) as a result of the procedural and constitutional reforms of 1987. But virtually nothing was done to sever the operational ties between this erstwhile division of the Provincial Police and its former parent until mid-1996. At that point, an agreement by the governor, the president of the Supreme Court, and the attorney general created the structure that permitted prosecutors and police to work together within geographically organized units linked to particular courts.[6] Still, as of February 2004 Córdoba

---

[6] This brief institutional history is adapted from the Web site of the Judicial Police, www.justiciacordoba.gov.ar/site/Asp/PoliciaJudicialHistoria.asp, last visited August 30, 2006.

continued to work on proposals that would take the offices of the Judicial Police physically out of Provincial Police precincts.

Moreover, according to an assistant prosecutor interviewed in Córdoba, a number of factors hinder their full independence from the Provincial Police even in their current configuration.[7] In the first place, investigators' offices are physically located within the precincts of the ordinary police and only in the capital city. Investigators travel to the interior of the province only if the local police call them in on a technical issue. Second, the "Scientific Police" investigators who report directly to the Ministerio Público carry out purely forensic activities, leaving everything else to the Provincial Police: "Our eyes and hands are the [Provincial] Police," she said. "The police are a piece of work. They won't carry out search orders [when they don't like the case]." And finally, the tendency, at least so far, is to recruit investigators from among police ranks. From the perspective of human rights attorneys, this means that in the end the Judicial Police are no different than the regular police: "The Judicial Police work inside the police stations. They end up being regular cops."[8] The result, once again, is a less–than-optimal investigative force in cases involving the police.

The police itself, meanwhile, follow the by-now familiar pattern of obstruction and violence. In cases involving shantytown residents in particular, witnesses have been killed, as in the case of Miguel Angel Rodríguez, or charged with a crime, as in the case of Diego Ordóñez. In other cases arising in the *villa*, the witnesses are threatened and intimidated until they are too frightened to testify, as in the case of Roberto Ordóñez Salazar or Cristian Rodríguez. When the information in question is not an expert report or forensic test, the police ensure that the investigation goes virtually nowhere. And the tactics are, of course, most effective against the most vulnerable members of society.

In short, Córdoba has taken some important steps toward creating a Judicial Police, and we should expect slightly better results from these investigators than prosecutors get from the police in Buenos Aires. But the Judicial Police are still far from constituting an effective, independent investigative force that might overcome the sandbagging of the ordinary police. The continuing importance of the ordinary police to the everyday functioning of the Judicial Police and prosecutors exposes the latter to the same informational dependence and pressure to look the other way as seen in São Paulo and Buenos Aires. The burden of producing adequate information remains

7 Interview with Norma Parrelo, *asistente fiscal*, Córdoba, February 28, 2001.
8 Interview with Silvia Osaba, attorney affiliated with CORREPI, Córdoba, February 20, 2001.

largely with affected individuals. And when those individuals come from the marginalized classes, they are often unable to overcome violence and intimidation in order to participate effectively in the construction of an adequate record that might be used to convict.

2. Civil Society Actors

As in Buenos Aires, CORREPI is a frequent participant in the cases that I reviewed for Córdoba. As in Buenos Aires, there are also other attorneys who take on these cases and are not formally affiliated with CORREPI. As established earlier, the role of these attorneys is dictated by the legal framework, which is essentially identical to the legal framework in Buenos Aires, giving them full participation in the investigation and trial. Their intimate connection with victims' families gives them access to information that is often beyond the ken of prosecutors and investigative police. In the *Precinto 5* case, for example, CORREPI, working with relatives, rescued physical evidence that was about to be destroyed by the Provincial Police. In other cases (the cases of Roberto Ordóñez Salazar and Cristian Rodríguez, for example, both of which took place in a *villa*), they located witnesses and brought them downtown to talk to prosecutors. In short, the participation of Private Prosecutors is as important procedurally in Córdoba as it is in Buenos Aires.

The principal difference lies in the impact of these prosecutors on outcomes. As already anticipated, and as we will see later in more detail, judges in Córdoba are more likely to strictly apply the law in these cases. A Private Prosecutor, therefore, is more likely to find a positive reception if he or she can substantiate the case against the defendant. The results discussed in Chapter 2 show this quite clearly. Without a Private Prosecutor, the conviction rate is actually higher in Buenos Aires (7%) than in Córdoba (4.55%). But Private Prosecutors working on a case in Córdoba quadruple the conviction rate, to 20%, even in cases that do not trigger popular demonstrations. Doing the same in Buenos Aires only doubles it, to 15%. This not only demonstrates that judges are receptive to legal argument and proofs, but it also strongly suggests that the prosecutors are a critical weak link in these prosecutions.

D. PROSECUTORS

As noted earlier, prosecutors have greater responsibilities and greater latitude in undertaking an investigation in Córdoba than in Uruguay and, therefore, can affect judicial outcomes to a greater degree. The structure of the institution, confirmed by local interviews, suggests that exogenous political pressure enters the institution at the top and freely travels downward, to influence frontline prosecutors' decisions in individual cases. In addition, the weakness of the investigative police renders prosecutors vulnerable to endogenous (police) pressure to take a lenient stance in police cases, though perhaps less so than in Buenos Aires, where they are completely dependent on the police for information. Given the neutral approach of the political leadership, endogenous pressures ordinarily carry the day, producing lackluster investigations except in highly visible cases, in which the prosecutors' responsiveness to public pressure suddenly induces more vigorous action.

The head of the office is the attorney general, known as the *Fiscal General*. Although the Constitution places the Ministerio Público inside the judicial branch, during the 1990s the attorney general was named by the executive, with the consent of a simple majority of the Senate (*Ley Orgánica del Ministerio Público*, Ley 7,826, Art. 7).[9] The attorney general serves for only five years, but can be re-appointed for additional terms. There has been some debate in Córdoba as to whether the prosecutor's office is truly independent and akin to a fourth branch of government, or whether it remains administratively subject to the courts (Centro de Estudios y Proyectos Judiciales 2005: 140–47). In any event, given the initial appointment mechanism, a short tenure, and the possibility of re-appointment, the leadership can be expected to reflect dominant political forces at the time of their appointment and to remain subject to political influence thereafter.

Under Article 4 of the same law, lower level prosecutors are expressly admonished that they "owe obedience" to their hierarchical superiors. Article 13 notes that:

a prosecutor that receives instruction regarding the exercise of his functions shall comply with them, though he may express his personal opposition. If he considers the instructions contrary to law, he shall inform the Attorney General by written report giving his reasons. If the Attorney General ratifies the questioned instruction, the prosecutor must obey and the Attorney General will assume responsibility for the act.

This stringent hierarchical structure contrasts sharply with the commitment (formal at least) in São Paulo or Bahia to freedom of judgment on the part of individual prosecutors. In São Paulo, the organization as a whole tends to respond to internal imperatives, and individual prosecutors have career incentives to conform but strong ideological justification for charting their own courses. This produces more continuity of policy and more

---

[9] The Senate itself disappeared after 2001, when the bicameral legislature became unicameral.

consistent organizational priorities. In Córdoba, in contrast, the head of the agency is open to political pressure, and adherence to hierarchy is an important goal of the organization. As a result, individual investigations readily respond to social and political pressures for or against more aggressive action. Indeed, local attorneys complain that these reforms have politicized the prosecutorial function to a greater degree than before.[10] Córdoba's institutional arrangements thus tend to encourage sharper fluctuations in prosecutorial attitudes in response to short-term external pressures.

When there is no public pressure to act and the political leadership takes a neutral stance, we can expect a lackadaisical approach by prosecutors. We have already seen that prosecutors are dependent on an investigative force that is tightly bound to the police, when, indeed, they do not depend directly on the Provincial Police. As a result, there is some (endogenous) pressure on prosecutors to take a permissive view of cases involving the police and not much reason to expend resources on a case. But, in cases that attract public attention, we can expect exogenous pressures to be more important given the dominant hierarchical nature of the institution, its openly political leadership, and the presence of an (albeit weak) Judicial Police.

This pattern, a default position in favor of laissez-faire combined with responsiveness in cases in which there is public demand for vigorous action, is clearly visible in the aggregate data discussed in Chapter 2. The conviction rate goes from a paltry 4.55% in cases without either a Private Prosecutor or a demonstration, to nearly 80% in cases with both. Its impact is visible in the following illustrative cases. In the case of Miguel Angel Rodríguez, detailed in Chapter 3, the prosecutor decided to charge the police officer with negligent rather than intentional homicide. This decision triggered a series of demonstrations after which the defendant was charged with the more serious offense. Similarly, prosecutors initially closed the case of Vanessa Ledesma, a transgendered activist who apparently died from a beating by the police, but they re-opened the investigation after a series of demonstrations and after the case received the attention of international human rights organizations.

Before concluding, I should temper my largely negative depiction of Córdoba's prosecutors. Córdoba does have a conviction rate that is nearly as high as Uruguay's. Since prosecutors play a crucial role in the investigative process, these prosecutions could not have been successful without their participation. Weak as it is, the presence of the Judicial Police helps free prosecutors to pursue these cases. Moreover, public reactions to police excesses are sufficiently vocal and common so that prosecutors are prodded into

---

[10] Interview with Silvia Osaba, Córdoba, February 20, 2001; Ortiz (1991) makes the same point.

action more frequently than in Buenos Aires, São Paulo, or Salvador. At the same time, it seems quite clear that the prosecutors need to be especially motivated to undertake a serious effort in these cases. At times, their lack of enthusiasm means judges take a more accusatorial role than the prosecutors themselves. Without the assistance of a private attorney and the prodding of public demonstrations, their record is worse than that of prosecutors in Buenos Aires in similar conditions, and no better than the average in São Paulo.

E. THE COURTS

When asked about the quality of their courts, many lawyers in Córdoba begin with a discussion of the long history of legal development in the province: they boast that they have the oldest law school in the country, which has been teaching law since the 1790s, and they refer to the many eminent jurists who have come from Córdoba, including Dalmacio Vélez Sarsfield, the drafter of the Argentine Civil Code. Although they are not immune from criticism, Córdoba's courts have a good reputation in Argentina as a whole. Domingo Sesin, a justice on Córdoba's Supreme Court and the director of the Center for Judicial Studies and Projects, claimed with some justification that "the advances of Córdoba's Judiciary with respect to strengthening the technical capacity of our judges are more than well known, and its reforms are permanently discussed at the national and Latin American levels" (quoted in Centro de Estudios y Proyectos Judiciales 2005: 5). A study that surveys all the provincial courts placed Córdoba in the group with the highest marks for judicial independence. It did so even though Córdoba lacks a judicial council (*consejo de la magistratura*) with binding nominating authority, one of the technical innovations that are currently seen as necessary to safeguard judicial independence (FORES and Colegio de Abogados de Buenos Aires 1999b).

At the same time, there is no shortage of local critics on the question of the independence of the courts – especially after Angeloz, who was governor for the first twelve years after democratization and had named most of the sitting judges, was acquitted of corruption charges. Human rights attorneys often identify individual judges whom they believe are strong, independent judges but argue that the rest are for the most part subject to the reigning political powers.[11] One attorney described the judicial situation in Córdoba as follows: "The provincial judges are very Radical, while the federal judges are

[11] Interview with Silvia Osaba, Córdoba, February 20, 2001; interview with Amalio Rey, Córdoba, February 23, 2001; interview with Juan Carlos Vega, Córdoba, March 2001.

all Menemistas [after President Menem, who expanded the federal bench at the trial and Supreme Court levels and is widely considered to have packed the courts with unconditional supporters]." Vega, a frequent critic of the judiciary in Córdoba and Argentina in general, charges that judges in Córdoba (as in the rest of Argentina) have always been subservient to the executive power and are now in danger of becoming slaves to public opinion (Vega 1998: 391 and personal communication). But even he concedes that many judges act according to the law, regardless of political pressure.

Given this split in opinions, it would be hard to definitively assign Córdoba's judiciary a particular level of independence without extensive analyses of judicial rulings. Moreover, nearly all the interviews suggest that there is considerable variation from one judge to the next. For our purposes, however, the key question is more limited: whether judges are vulnerable to exogenous and endogenous pressures to rule for or against the police in homicide cases. The question of endogenous pressures is easier to answer. The fact that judges are free from responsibility for the investigation – they are less involved in the investigation than any other judge in our study – means they are also free from dependence on the police. Even the prosecutors with whom they work closely are one step removed – by virtue of the Judicial Police, such as it is – from the Provincial Police. Since this informational dependence is the main source of endogenous pressures, we can be confident that, in a case involving a police homicide, judges are not overly concerned with offending the defendant or the officer's colleagues.

The appointment and career structure of the judiciary suggests that judges might be more sensitive to external pressures, however. Under the Constitution, judges are appointed by the executive with the consent of a simple majority of the Senate. There is no formal judicial career per se, but career judges are common. To advance professionally by moving up to the Supreme Court or to a more prestigious seat, judges must be re-appointed by the governor and re-approved by the Senate.

We saw in Uruguay that the inability to command a two-thirds majority in the Senate led to a more independent court. In Córdoba, the party that controlled the executive also controlled the Senate from re-democratization in 1983 until 1999. First Angeloz and then Mestre certainly had a majority that would have permitted them to act arbitrarily in the designation of judges. At the same time, Córdoba is by no means a one-party province. The Radical Party controlled the Senate from 1983 to 1999 and was the dominant force in the 1980s. But in 1999 the *Partido Justicialista* (also known as the PJ, or the Peronist Party) took control of the executive and tied for control of the

Senate when De la Sota won the governorship and the PJ won 43% of the seats. In the years leading up to this victory, the PJ was a strong force in the province, typically holding around 40% of Senate seats. In the 1990s, then, the Radicals lived under the ever-present threat that the Peronists would hold power next.

Whether out of fear of losing power (see Hirschl 2004 for such an argument) or out of conviction, in 1992 Angeloz put in place an independent judicial advisory committee that looks much like a judicial council. The committee was established by law in 1991 (*Ley* 8,097, October 24, 1991, effective 1992) and was composed of seven members: a judge of the Supreme Court, a prosecutor, one representative from the Chamber of Deputies, a member of the Council of Political Parties representing a party with no parliamentary delegation, one delegate from the Federation of Bar Associations of the Province of Córdoba, a member of the bar association from the jurisdiction where the candidate practices law (or sits as a judge, if currently a member of the bench), and a full professor at Córdoba's law school. In short, the committee brings in a number of major actors who would not otherwise have a voice in the selection process and potentially broadens the political spectrum that weighs in on appointments.[12]

Judicial selection under the committee became an open and public process. Candidates presented themselves for consideration and submitted a file with their qualifications and references. The committee evaluated the formal qualifications of the candidates, conducted a personal interview, and created a short list of candidates for each position, listing them in no particular order. The executive selected a nominee from the list, and the Senate approved the selection. Although the list was not legally binding on the governor, both Angeloz and Mestre routinely accepted the committee's recommendations. The current judicial council has taken a step further, listing the candidates in order of merit. As his predecessors did, Governor De la Sota has (with important exceptions that come well after the end of the decade) routinely accepted the recommendations, typically selecting those candidates identified as most meritorious by the selection committee. Under either arrangement, the members of the committee have been satisfied that the executive, despite having the constitutional latitude to disregard the recommendations, has not done so.[13]

---

[12] This gubernatorial advisory committee was replaced by an actual *consejo de la magistratura* in 1999 (Law No. 8,802, published in *Boletín Oficial*, December 28, 1999) with a roughly similar composition.

[13] Interview with Nelson Filippi, defensor del pueblo [state ombudsman], Córdoba, and a member of the advisory committee from 1992 through 1994, March 1, 2001.

The advisory council muted the overtly political tone of judicial nominations in Córdoba. At the same time, since its power was merely advisory, the
committee surely had to gauge whether the candidates it proposed would
prove acceptable to the governor. The institutional and political backdrop,
then, produced an ameliorated political system of appointments, tempered
by the presence of open and public proceedings, an advisory council, and,
in the 1990s at least, the persistent threat of an opposition victory at the
polls. Judges who wished to advance their careers had to submit to this same
system for every new appointment and thus could not afford to offend any
of those who weighed in on the recommendations. To the extent the nomination process marked the political bent of the judiciary, the close ties between
the Radical Party and Córdoba's economic and social elites suggest that any
political bias will be in the direction of a more conservative and traditionalist
court.

A research project based on a series of in-depth interviews of non-judicial
officers in the courts of Córdoba city indicates that this arrangement produced a largely conservative, hierarchical, rule-oriented judiciary, free from
direct political interference in individual cases but attuned to prevailing
political winds and the interests of powerful social and economic actors
(Scarponetti et al. 2000b). The researchers conclude, in part, with a description that will be familiar to students of even the better-functioning judiciaries
in Latin America:

> Córdoba's tribunals show a conservative structure, with bureaucratic features that
> are visible in the organizational culture. The dominant features are the emphasis on
> administrative functions, a pyramidal working structure and the priority of formalism
> in procedures. (2000b: p. 394)

Despite the emphasis on formalism and hierarchy, judicial staff told
researchers that "complicated" cases were handled directly by the judge,
with less intervention by the staff. They defined "complicated" sometimes
in legal terms (white-collar crimes and complex financial cases) but more
often in political terms: having to do with important interests, having public
prominence, or otherwise being in the public eye.

Importantly, judicial employees unanimously denied the presence of overt
corruption or favoritism, or direct political meddling in case outcomes
(Scarponetti et al. 2000b: 405–06, 409). But, they noted, judges acknowledge
they owe their jobs to the politicians who appointed them, so that political
influence is more implicit than explicit and filters down primarily from the
Supreme Court, by way of the judicial hierarchy. They agreed that public
opinion and social pressures could affect how a case was treated (p. 410),

and that prominent cases are treated with special care. Judges, they argued, are more technocratic and rule-oriented, devoted to preserving the existing order, than interested in doing "justice" by exercising their discretion (p. 410). Judges in Córdoba, they said,

exercise extreme care not to differentiate themselves too much one from another in their rulings, getting rid of complicated cases by recusing themselves, or filling files with rulings and judgments "taken from a mold." One might infer that judges' principal preoccupation lies in reinforcing the "predictability" of their decisions, a characteristic that is indispensable if one seeks to give the justice system a more democratic bent than it has had in other times. (pp. 411–12)

The overwhelming impression is of a cautious, conservative judiciary, drawn primarily from elite families (p. 411).

Thus, the institutional and political configuration in Córdoba in the end produced a judiciary that is not above reproach but is at least technically proficient and rule oriented, placing a premium on predictability. Of all the judiciaries studied, despite its political system of appointments, this one perhaps comes closest to the model of civil law judges described in Merryman (1985) in its commitment to an apolitical application of the law that is not devoid of deference to political powers. Courts are not open to corruption or direct manipulation, although they do have an ear for public opinion. Importantly for the results we observed, their legal-technocratic propensity is often manifested as an obsession with legal formalities.

F. SUMMARY

From this discussion of the various actors we can extract the key characteristics of the legal system in Córdoba that lead to both high effectiveness and high inequality. The executive is not likely to actively resist (or actively promote) the prosecution of police officers in the absence of public pressure. As a result, neither will prosecutors, who are highly sensitive to political currents and dependent on the police for much of their work. The courts are rule oriented and have a strongly formalistic propensity; judges are largely free from endogenous pressures to favor the police but not insensitive to broad political currents. As a result, the judiciary is, by and large, willing to convict a police officer of homicide, especially in cases that garner public attention. Because of their legalistic orientation and non-investigative role, however, judges will demand and expect adherence to formal rules and a high standard of evidence. For the same reasons, judges depend entirely on prosecutors or claimants to build the record on which they will judge the case. And these actors are often the weakest link in the prosecution.

When claimants – either on their own or through the prosecutor – can supply the high-quality evidence the courts demand, convictions result. Prosecutors themselves are likely to use their own resources to generate this information only in cases that have media and public attention – the quantitative analysis in Chapter 2 shows very clearly the positive impact of public attention to a case. Prosecutors are also more likely to get good information in cases in which the claimants have their own social, political, and economic resources – again, the impact of social class and retaining a Private Prosecutor on outcomes in Córdoba comes across clearly in Chapter 2. Moreover, even when witnesses from the *villa* are willing to testify, the quality of the information these rough, uneducated witnesses supply is, by the standards of an elite, conservative judiciary, insufficiently "high quality." And so we get a high percentage of convictions – driven by a judiciary that is interested in enforcing the law – coupled with abysmal failures in cases that involve the lower classes and do not garner public attention.

8

Salvador da Bahia

Social Cleansing Under Political and Judicial Indifference

[Segunda-feira:] Um homem de cor parda, 1,70 m de altura, aparentando 28 anos, sem camisa, bermuda azul-clara e chinelos de couro de cor preta, foi mais uma vítima de grupos de extermínio que agem na periferia de Salvador. . . . A vítima estava com as mãos amarradas para as costas e foi atingida por vários tiros de pistola na cabeça . . .

Nas primeiras horas da manhã de quinta-feira, seis homens, dois deles usando camisa preta com o escudo da Polícia Civil, mataram, com vários tiros na cabeça, o desempregado Edvan Nascimento Silva, 26 anos, na estrada Cia/Aeroporto, após ser espancado na presença da mulher e filhos.

Na madrugada de domingo, na Invasão Nova Constituinte, subúrbio de Paripe, dois homens usando capuzes, após arrancarem de dentro de casa o biscateiro Arivaldo Conceição Santos, 37 anos, executaram-no na frente do seu barraco.

A Tarde Online (March 16, 2004)

A black man, an unemployed man, and a shantytown resident making a living from odd jobs: three executions in the course of one week in Salvador da Bahia, each targeting the poor and the marginalized. The odds of being killed by the police in Salvador are at least three times higher than in São Paulo. More than in any other city in this study, in Salvador the laws have been pushed aside to make way for killing the socially undesirable. Investigators with the Public Health Department found that in 1991 21% of all homicides were attributed to police activity in the death certificate.[1] A review of all

[1] Interview with Dra. Adriana, sociologist with Bahia's Public Health Department, Salvador, May 22, 2001.

the major newspapers from 1996 through 1999 by the Justice and Peace
Commission found that 15% of all homicides in those years were attributed
to the police. If to this we add another 8% attributed to extermination groups
engaged in social cleansing – and there is abundant evidence of extensive
police participation in these groups (Oiticica 2001) – more than 20% of the
homicides in Salvador are committed in the name of public order.

The courts, for the most part, simply stand aside. Despite hundreds of
cases every year, it is difficult to find a single instance in which a police
officer is convicted of murder. As reported in Chapter 2, I searched newspaper
archives, talked to prosecutors, interviewed activists, but was unable to find
any convictions except in a few cases involving children and in a couple of
cases included in the witness protection program.

How to account for this level of violence and impunity? In Chapter 3
I present evidence that the source of impunity in Salvador is a normative
rather than an informational failure; that impunity results from the application of an effective rule of decision that permits the use of deadly force
to control crime. Information is not typically the problem. Indeed, information about these crimes is generally available so long as the police are
assured of impunity. This gives these cases a distinctly different feel than the
prosecutions in São Paulo, for example. The killings are open and casual,
and investigations, when they start at all, disappear with barely a ripple into
the legal system. In São Paulo I heard the phrase "*formalismo igual, jeito
diferente*"; in Salvador even the formalities are not observed. Only when it
appears that the courts are about to overcome this normative failure does an
informational failure develop. As soon as the rules appear to shift in favor
of accountability, the police take violent measures to control the flow of
information, reverting to the pattern visible in São Paulo, Buenos Aires, and
Córdoba. In this chapter I describe the political context that leads to this
normative failure and the socio-economic conditions that make it possible,
as well as the institutional framework in which this dynamic plays out.

Both the Code of Criminal Procedure and the structure of the judiciary
in Salvador are essentially identical to what we saw in São Paulo, where
they contribute to establishing a relatively independent judiciary. In contrast, in Bahia decades of political dominance of state institutions by a single
far-right party left the state with a controlled and subservient judiciary, at
least through the end of the 1990s. In Salvador, as in São Paulo but to an
even greater extent, a high level of crime and popular tolerance for repressive measures combine with political pressure to turn a blind eye to police
abuses. Politically compromised judges, and prosecutors to a lesser extent,

are exposed to direct and indirect pressure to look the other way. And juries, should any case get that far, are unlikely to protect the rights of individuals who are represented as the source of the violence that affects Salvador.

Given this political and institutional background, at every level of the system and in case after case, the rule of decision is set to such a lenient standard that the police are virtually assured of impunity. Since the case is classified as non-murder from the very beginning, investigations never even get off the ground, and it almost makes no sense to speak of the construction of a biased procedural reality. If a quixotic judge or prosecutor should attempt to carry out an investigation, he or she faces two obstacles. In the first place, there is resistance from within the institution itself – prosecutors who go after the police have seen their careers suffer in consequence. And in addition, if it looks like an investigation might get under way, the police use their control over the streets to impose a near informational blackout, by threatening or killing witnesses and complainants.

Both the routine political construction of these cases as welcome social cleansing and the remedial informational blackouts when the policy of impunity seems to slip are facilitated by socio-economic conditions. Income distribution is as bad as or worse than in São Paulo; poverty, unemployment, and the proportion of the population that lives in shantytowns and works in the informal economy are higher. The police, unaccountable and accustomed to making their own rules, brutally repress all who might be tempted to assert their rights. The marginalized population from which victims are primarily taken is ill prepared to contend with the police in the struggle to frame these cases as violations of fundamental rights, rather than as welcome and needed social cleansing.

As mentioned, the Code of Criminal Procedure, the structure of the Polícia Militar and the Polícia Civil, the Ministério Público (the prosecutor's office), and the structure of the courts are identical to São Paulo's. In the case of São Paulo, this institutional background produced a judiciary and a prosecutorial corps that are politically independent, if somewhat conservative in the case of the former and divided in defining their social role in the case of the latter. I argued further that the weakness of the Civil Police and the importance of the Military Police to the entire legal system, coupled with deep social inequalities, made judges and prosecutors dependent on the Military Police for information. The fundamental problem, then, is not that judges in São Paulo enforce rules guaranteeing impunity. Rather, the problem is that the police can enforce a strict rationing of the information judges need to make good decisions, and that, given the political context, prosecutors are not likely to expend the resources required to overcome this information gap.

Given the near identity of institutional design between Salvador and São Paulo, then, the main question for this chapter is this: how is it that the same institutional configuration produces an independent and relatively insulated judiciary in São Paulo and its near opposite in the state of Bahia? A judiciary that applies the formal rules (albeit in a cautious manner) with informational failures at the root of judicial ineffectiveness in São Paulo, and one that is rife with normative failures in Salvador, applying permissive informal rules to legitimize the arbitrary use of force?

A. THE CODE OF CRIMINAL PROCEDURE

Full details on the Code of Criminal Procedure are discussed in connection with São Paulo and so will not be repeated here. To briefly summarize: if the accused is a Military Police officer, the Military Police itself investigates the crime. The Civil Police, which does not carry out the initial investigation, in any event depends on the Military Police to carry out its work. The Ministério Público is charged with bringing the results of the police investigation (*Inquérito Policial Militar*) to the court, where the judge technically controls the judicial phase of the investigation. After an oral trial, a jury makes the final decision on guilt or innocence.

This allocation of roles and responsibilities gives the Military Police considerable control over the supply of information in cases in which one of its own is the defendant. But the fact that the Civil Police is the primary investigative force in ordinary crimes frees judges and prosecutors from direct pressure from the Military Police, as it does in São Paulo and Córdoba. As in those cases, however, the weakness of the Judicial Police gives the Military Police more ascendance than the formal institutional framework might suggest. Indeed, this repeated pattern is not likely to be coincidental. It appears to be extraordinarily difficult to create a truly independent Judicial Police. At minimum, this repeated experience suggests the need for a separate investigative force to address police cases.[2] The Military Police, then, continue to control the investigation in these cases but have an arms-length relationship to judges and prosecutors.

---

[2] This is directly contrary to the advice given by Skolnick and Fyfe (1993). As should be clear from the results discussed in this book, at least in the context of systems with a more tenuous hold on the rule of law, the idea of turning all responsibility for policing the police to internal mechanisms of control seems ill advised, to say the least.

The end result of this institutional arrangement is a set of endogenous incentives that suggests a line-up of preferences identical to São Paulo's, with the judge, the prosecutor, and the police all either neutral or hostile to the prosecution of police officers. In the rest of this chapter I will examine the exogenous pressures on the various actors that shift them further toward preferring impunity.

B. SOCIAL CONTEXT

1. Socio-economic Context

As with the procedural environment, on most socio-economic measures Salvador is like São Paulo but more so. The population resident in *favelas* in the municipality of Salvador alone numbers 835,000, more than 35% of the total population of the municipality (IBAM [Instituto Brasileiro de Administração Municipal] 2002). This is nearly three times the percentage of São Paulo's *favelados*, who make up approximately 12% of the population. The percentage of residents who live below the line of indigence in the state of Bahia (the equivalent of Argentina's Unmet Basic Needs category) is 54.8% overall and 40.5% in the metro region (Fundação Getúlio Vargas 2001). This level of poverty has drastic implications. A study of mortality rate differences across different neighborhoods in Salvador shows geographic inequalities in mortality rates that are twice as great as the inequalities present in São Paulo (da Silva, Paim, and Costa 1999). In short, Brazil as a whole struggles with poverty and inequality, and Bahia and the Salvador metropolitan region, while not at the very bottom, are considerably worse off than São Paulo on these variables.

At the same time, note that São Paulo scores worse than Salvador on violent crime and homicide rates. The critical variable, therefore, is not the (perhaps) more objective level of threat posed by violent criminals, but the marginalization of the population from which victims are taken.

2. Socio-political Context

As Ames notes, "For many years, Bahia has been the strongest bailiwick of the Brazilian Right" (Ames 2001: 129). It is impossible to speak of politics in Bahia without placing the figure of Antônio Carlos Magalhães (commonly known by his initials ACM), of the Liberal Front Party (PFL), at the center: "For the last two decades politics in Bahia has moved around ACM. Loved by many, hated by others, rewarded and betrayed by the electorate, ACM is at the center of the state's events" (Souza 1997). ACM was first elected state deputy in 1954, and in 1967, during the military period, was appointed mayor of Salvador by the appointed governor of Bahia, Luis Vianna Filho. In 1975 he was himself appointed governor of Bahia by the military regime for an initial four-year term, then re-appointed in 1979 for another four years. After the transition to democracy, he held a series of national appointed posts under President Sarney and was the elected governor of Bahia from 1991 through 1995. With the exception of the 1987–91 term, which belonged to a PMDB (Partido do Movimento Democrático Brasileiro) governor, either ACM or his hand-picked candidates have controlled the executive in Bahia from 1971 through the end of the 1990s.

Moreover, although he was not born a *coronel* in the old style of Brazil's Northeast, ACM has a reputation for an authoritarian and controlling style. He is widely credited with saying, for example, "I win elections with a bag of money in one hand and a whip in the other." Souza (1997: 127–28) recounts interviews with other politicians in which they say, among other things, "ACM's style is violent: he attacks his opponents in their private lives. To confront him you must have nothing to hide or to fear." This verdict was confirmed recently in a case labeled by the media "*o caso dos grampos*" (the case of the wiretaps). The Bahian Ministry of Public Safety, in conjunction with the Civil Police, tapped the cell phones of a number of personal and political opponents of ACM, ranging from national political leaders such as Senator Nelson Pellegrino of the Workers' Party to ACM's former girlfriend and her new boyfriend. This case vividly demonstrates the control ACM continues to exercise over the state, since the wiretaps were approved and carried out – apparently at his behest – while he was a senator in Brasilia.

Authoritarian and repressive tendencies are visible among the top leaders of the state, and reflected also in public opinion polls. The background for this is a very real problem with violent crime. Salvador suffers from high rates of violent crime, although there is conflicting information on just where Salvador ranks in homicide rates. One study based on newspaper reviews places the Salvador metro region's murder rate at more than 40 per 100,000, compared to the United States at 6.3, and Berlin at 2.8 (de Oliveira, Sousa Ribeiro, and Zanetti 2000: center insert). This study finds that four murders take place in the city every day, on average. Excluding deaths from illness, 55% of all deaths in the city are homicides. The Instituto de Pesquisa Econômica Aplicada (IPEA) (Institute of Applied Economic Research), on the other hand, shows a homicide rate for the Salvador metro region of about 23.5 per 100,000 during the 1990s, though that may understate the figure by at least 30%.[3] In any event, what is interesting is precisely the fact that Salvador's violent crime rate is actually lower than São Paulo's, though it is not clear by how much.[4]

The combination of high crime and low trust in the justice system leads to a high level of support for vigilante measures, including police killings, lynching (a term used for any instance of popular justice, in which a group attacks and sometimes kills a suspect of a crime), and extermination groups.[5] More than 41% of men and 38% of women in a 1997 survey agreed with the practice of "social cleansing" (*limpeza social*) (*A Tarde*, June 29, 2003). The unidentified killers who make up the extermination groups that execute *marginais* are known as *justiceiros*, a word that could be translated as vigilante, but carries an obvious connotation of meting out "justice." In interviews, people, especially those of lower socio-economic standing, say *"marginal tem que morrer mesmo"* – the criminals must simply die (de Oliveira, Sousa Ribeiro, and Zanetti 2000: 35). The official crime reports for 1999 include sixty-six lynchings with injuries (i.e., some but not all the lynchings ended in the death of the victim), while a yearlong study of the major newspapers finds nine deaths attributed to lynching in 1999 alone (Carvalho 2001).

A three-year study in a large shantytown, Novos Alagados, in Salvador paints a stark picture of the ambivalent attitudes toward police violence among the residents (Machado and Noronha 2002). On the one hand, these *favelados* understand that the Military Police is violent, brutal, and indiscriminate in its actions. Police tactics in the *favela* consist of periods of indifference alternating with periods in which they enter the *favela* in force, raiding, shooting, and killing. Summarizing the beliefs of the *favelados*, the researchers say, "Obeying orders or acting on their own, the police shoot

---

[3] See IPEA's Radar Social, p. 114, available from http://www.ipea.gov.br/Destaques/livroradar. htm (last visited August 31, 2006). IPEA's numbers are based on official figures, reported by each state. IPEA flags one problem with its homicide figures: whenever there is not conclusive evidence of the intent to kill, the death is classified as "an event with indeterminate intentionality." Including all the "indeterminate intention" acts committed with firearms in the homicide category would increase Bahia's homicide rate by approximately 30% (p. 112).

[4] Salvador's violent crime rates are one-third those of Rio de Janeiro and Espírito Santo, the Brazilian leaders in homicide rates, and lower than São Paulo's. Clearly, then, the relationship between violent crime and support for violent police tactics, and between violent crime and a violent police response, is by no means linear.

[5] *A Tarde*, Salvador's major daily paper, reviewed some of the studies to this effect, including surveys done by Projeto Ativa that show a lack of confidence in the police and high levels of approval of self-help mechanisms, including lynching. "População Armada Amplia a Violência," *A Tarde*, June 29, 2003.

without major precautions, applying the death sentence against lawbreakers, suspects and innocent persons, without punishment." But residents also live in fear of crime, so they continue to support the extra-judicial execution of those they consider "*marginais*," or criminals. One inhabitant of Novos Alagados voiced this ambiguous relationship to police brutality:

> I find it's all right [killing criminals], because there are people who run in, rob, rape, commit crimes, these people must be eliminated... captured or just finished off already [*dar fim mesmo*], quickly, there is no other remedy. I am totally against violence, but in this case I am in favor. (Machado and Noronha 2002: 217)

The practice of leaving the bodies of those killed in the *favela* out in the sun for many hours before sending the coroner to pick them up prompts a similar comment from another inhabitant: "Ah! The death of a good-for-nothing is left moldering and mocking there, by the time they come pick it up it's even stinking. Everybody is in favor of their death – they died, leave them there."[6] The only censure this resident voices concerns the impact of this sight on children: "They shouldn't kill those good-for-nothings in the neighborhood, it's very ugly... the children see it. They [the police] kill them right in front of everyone. They should take them somewhere else and there the police can do us this favor" (Machado and Noronha 2002: 217).

One result of this social context is that those who have lost loved ones to police violence labor under the presumption that the victim was a criminal and thus that the killing was justified. This leaves those who are seeking justice from an unresponsive system very much alone in their quest. Wandering from office to office insisting that their child was not a criminal, repeating again and again that their son or daughter worked and helped the family: one mother's pilgrimage through government offices and media venues (described in de Oliveira, Sousa Ribeiro, and Zanetti 2000) provides a vivid illustration of how the victims of police violence are de-legitimized and stripped of citizenship.

The lack of interest in a prompt punitive response to police killings extends to the political class, according to Nelson Pellegrino. He blames the governing party, the PFL, for a complete lack of interest in the problem, to the point of refusing to approve bills that would simply have required the police to compile more detailed information on these killings.[7] Even the media is

---

[6] The translation cannot do justice to this statement, so I include it here, in its original Portuguese: "Ah, morte de vagabundo fica mofando aí, quando vem apanhar está até fedendo, todo mundo apoia a morte deles, morreu fica aí."

[7] This statement is taken from an unpublished dossier by Assunção and Sousa Ribeiro 1998 (on file with the author).

to some degree complicit. Commenting on the newspapers' persistent habit of noting the criminal history of victims (even if unrelated to the incident), Espinheira says "it's as if there is a tacit understanding that someone with a record *can be eliminated*, while another, who has never been arrested was, in fact, *murdered*, with the full moral and legal import society assigns to such an event" (de Oliveira, Sousa Ribeiro, and Zanetti 2000: 35). The clear implication is that the death of a criminal constitutes not a crime, murder, but rather a positive social function, elimination.

In sum, of all the places examined so far, Salvador appears to be the one in which exogenous pressures in favor of impunity for police killings are the strongest. The population of the *favelas* – that is, the very population most affected by the problem of police violence – feels sufficiently unprotected by the criminal justice system that they condone the practice of social cleansing. There is evidence that this attitude pervades politics, at least on the part of the ruling party. And ACM's control over not only the courts but even radio and television in the state (Ames 2001: 131) permits the government to present these killings as the legitimate use of police powers against an out-of-control criminal class. In the next several sections, I examine the institutional context that conditions the extent to which the investigative police, judges, and prosecutors participate in this permissive attitude. At a minimum, the evidence so far is clear that any aggressive attempts to prosecute Military Police officers who kill perceived *marginais* will be met with hostility.

C. THE INVESTIGATIVE POLICE

The Military Police, which is the relevant investigative force in Salvador, operates under an equally permissive rule of decision. The frequency of the killings is already evidence that police killings are tolerated and encouraged within the corporation. But there is additional evidence as well. Lemos-Nelson undertook an in-depth investigation of the response by the internal disciplinary agency of the police to a series of killings committed by the police in Salvador. She finds that these killings are covered up, the perpetrators go unpunished, and the investigators do not pass the investigative report (the *Inquérito Policial*) on to the prosecutor's office. Without the *Inquérito*, prosecutors never initiate legal proceedings. The police force's own disciplinary body, therefore, ensures that these cases never come to the attention of the legal system (Lemos-Nelson 2001).

An unpublished dossier completed in December of 1998 by twenty-seven Bahian human rights organizations (on file with the author) presents several interviews that shed additional light on police attitudes toward the killings

(Assunção and Sousa Ribeiro 1998). Nelson Pellegrino, then a state deputy from the Workers' Party (PT) and chair of the Human Rights Commission of the state legislature, claims in the dossier that police supervisors in the Military Police offer incentives to police officers who kill suspects, "because it's cheaper to kill than to capture." The investigator in charge of the homicide division in Salvador relates that when he arrives at a police station to investigate the killing of someone who had a criminal record "they say 'we have better things to do than to clear up the death of a criminal.'" Leo Ornéllas, the head of an Afro-Brazilian civil rights group, agrees: "In Bahia, before investigating, [police investigators] first check to see if the deceased victim had a criminal record, and then they decide whether or not to investigate." A priest who works in one of the most violent neighborhoods in Salvador relates a similar response by Civil Police investigators. In one case, the *delegado* refused to investigate the shooting of a young girl simply because the girl's *mother* was involved with drugs.

Even when the Civil Police attempt to investigate, they are clearly overpowered by the Military Police. The latter not only fail to cooperate, they actively – sometimes violently – resist these investigations. In one particularly egregious case, the Homicide Division of the Civil Police went to a Military Police precinct to carry out an arrest warrant against several police officers accused of having killed three minors by burning them alive. They were met with active resistance, as the entire police outpost rallied to the defense of the accused and forcibly blocked the investigative police who came to arrest the suspects. The incident nearly led to an armed confrontation between the Civil and the Military Police (Assunção and Sousa Ribeiro 1998: 25–26).

Nilton José Costa Ferreiro, the former police investigator who relates the story of this near confrontation between Civil and Military Police, eventually quit his position with the Civil Police. Costa Ferreiro was actively pursuing an investigation into Military Police participation in extermination groups. He had weathered various death threats and other forms of intimidation in the course of the investigation; his decision to quit came after Bahian prosecutors threatened to prosecute him for abuse of power if he continued tilting at windmills.

As we have seen, in only a few cases is there any effort to hold the police accountable. This occurs either when the case is politically sensitive or when it appears that the murder was committed in furtherance of a police officer's own crime rather than in furtherance of public safety. But even when an investigation appears to head in the direction of accountability, complainants are intimidated and witnesses are harassed or killed, as we will see in the next section.

D. CIVIL SOCIETY ACTORS

As in São Paulo, Buenos Aires, and Córdoba, affected individuals in Salvador have the legal standing to participate in the investigation and trial. Moreover, there are civil society actors in Salvador – the Human Rights Commission of the Brazilian Bar Association and the Justice and Peace Commission of the Salvador archdiocese, primarily – who assist claimants in this respect. But these actors face a difficult task, struggling against both violent police resistance to a complaint and investigation, detailed in this section, and the apparent futility of bringing these cases to the courts, detailed in the next section.

One organization that is dedicated to reducing violence against children, including police violence, is the Centro de Atendimento à Criança e Adolescente (CEDECA). In an interview, the director of CEDECA elucidated the hurdles facing claimants in these cases.[8] Initially, he said, it was impossible to find anyone – Civil Police, prosecutors, or judges – who was interested in investigating and prosecuting cases of police violence against children. In the 1980s parents would come in and CEDECA would attempt to assist them, but their claims would dead-end in a non-responsive legal system. Early in the 1990s, however, a federally initiated procedural reform (the details of which are more fully explained in Chapter 3) led the system to become more aggressive in protecting the rights of children. In other words, after the change it became apparent that, at least in the case of children murdered by the police, judicial operators were willing to enforce the law.

However, this change produced a new problem, described already in Chapter 2. Once the police felt that a real investigation was likely, they began to take the complaints seriously and stepped up their threats and violence against family members. The danger to parents is now so serious, CEDECA's director told me, that even the families that initially come in with complaints eventually ask CEDECA to back away, fearing for their lives or the lives of their remaining children. Prosecutors have a difficult time getting witnesses to cooperate and witnesses withdraw their initial accusations against the police.[9] An attempt to enforce one piece of the law, in the context of a weak and compromised justice system, triggers instead an increase in violence and intimidation.

It is not only CEDECA that has difficulty in protecting claimants and witnesses. Chapter 2 details the case of Heloísa, who was murdered with her

[8] Interview with Valdemar Oliveira, director, Centro de Atendimento à Criança e Adolescente, Salvador, May 22, 2001.
[9] Interview with Valdemar Oliveira, director, CEDECA, Salvador, May 22, 2001.

partner for becoming actively involved in human rights organizations in the course of seeking justice for her stepson's murder. Heloísa and her partner had met high levels of resistance from the police, and the investigation was languishing when they began a highly public campaign to bring the killers to justice. It appeared, for a while, that the Ministério Público would take an active role in the case, illustrating the limits of permissiveness – even in Bahia, prosecutors and judges are not willing to protect police officers who kill to enforce or protect extortion schemes, especially when public attention is focused on the case. All the attention could not, however, prevent the confirmed murders of Heloísa, her partner, and one other witness, or the disappearance and presumed murder of a fourth witness. The deaths brought the investigation to an end.

Christiane Gurgel, then the head of the Bahian Bar Association's Human Rights Committee, summarized the control that police exercise over the affected population: "What is hard is bringing the facts to light. There is a lot of violence against witnesses, their colleagues protect [the killers], *and the victims have to continue living in close contact with the police*" (emphasis mine).[10] She related one story in which the police took two youths suspected of minor crimes from their home and shot them. One of them died, but the other pretended to be dead and made his way to safety after the police had left the scene. The survivor refuses to testify against the police, fearing for his life.

Even when judges and prosecutors might respond, then, the overwhelming imbalance of power between the police and claimants makes it impossible for the latter to succeed in an attempt to hold the police accountable. The flow of information is stifled at the very outset. Feeding the vicious circle, the lack of information about these cases contributes to the general perception that the victims are simply criminals killed by the police in the fight against crime.

E. PROSECUTORS

If any institution might redress this imbalance of power between claimants and the police, it should be the Ministério Público, with its impressive constitutional attributions including "the legal control of the police function." Recall from the discussion of the São Paulo prosecutor's office that the institution is designed so as to have considerable independence from the other

---

[10] Interview with Christiane Gurgel, President, Commissão Direitos Humanos OAB-Bahia, May 2001.

branches of government. The head of the Ministério Público is selected by the governor, but from a slate of three candidates chosen by secret ballot by all active prosecutors. Prosecutors have life tenure and all the protections afforded judges. Moreover, the organization's organic law decrees that individual prosecutors have independence of judgment. And yet, despite powerful methods for enforcing orthodoxy through the hierarchy, the conclusion from the São Paulo case, at least, was that organizational politics are somewhat divorced from the politics of the other branches of government, as evidenced by the institution's struggles to assert itself as the defender of a democratic legal order.

In Bahia, however, there is evidence that the upper reaches of the institution are, at minimum, open to pressures on the part of ACM and his allies. Frontline prosecutors in Salvador complain that the governor ignored their wishes in selecting a candidate to head the organization. In fact, the governor chose from the list approved by prosecutors, but he passed over the candidate with the most votes in favor of a candidate who was more sympathetic to the executive. Prosecutors argue that politicians are always able to ensure that at least one candidate in the top three is amenable to their control, and they select that candidate, whether or not he or she is the top vote getter.

In a confidential interview, a prosecutor who was in charge of coordinating criminal prosecutions in Salvador suggested that prosecutors were largely political animals, although perhaps subject to less pressure than were judges. "Since we are not a deciding entity [*orgão decisório*], we are ignored more than judges are." He blamed many of the problems on investigative failures – *inquéritos* full of defects and cases that never even reach the prosecutors. But he also noted that cases involving the police, a politician, or an executive are all "difficult" for the Bahian system. In these cases, he said, justice is partial. "The problem is that the *Procurador* [the head of the Ministério Público] is political. If there is social mobilization, sometimes a prosecutor will act, but without pressure, nothing will happen [*sem pressão, não passa nada*]."[11] Christiane Gurgel also confirmed that the Bahian Ministério Público would not "mess" with politically sensitive cases, in which she included police homicides.[12]

The problem, the prosecutor said, starts at the IPM stage. This report prepared by the Military Police forms the basis for the prosecutors' decision in a case and is typically exculpatory. "If the prosecutor does not take control,

[11] Interview with anonymous prosecutor, Salvador, Bahia, May 2001.
[12] Interview with Christiane Gurgel, President, Commissão Direitos Humanos OAB-Bahia, May 2001.

it all ends there." There are, of course, investigators and prosecutors in Bahia who are serious about investigating police violence – including those who would talk to me about the difficulties they encounter in trying to do their job. But in a context in which impunity is the norm, they are themselves often punished and end up outside the system. Marília Veloso was a prosecutor in the military justice system before jurisdiction over intentional homicide cases was transferred to the civilian courts in 1996 (see discussion of São Paulo for details). She related that her attempts to pursue violent police officers were continually impeded by her superiors, until she quit out of frustration.[13]

In sum, the prosecutorial structures in both Salvador and São Paulo channel the leadership's priorities, but in Salvador external interference is more direct and pressures are greater because of the extraordinary dominance of the political right over all the state institutions. In São Paulo the Ministério Público is caught between a hostile public and a relatively supportive political leadership. Its actions in assigning resources to these cases reflect this ambivalence – it will not go too far out of its way to prosecute them, but it will treat them according to law if the facts are easily accessible. In Salvador, there is an unambiguous social and political directive to leave these cases alone as far as possible, whether the facts are accessible or not. This affects the organization's priorities and individual prosecutors' decisions in individual prosecutions. In these "difficult" cases, prosecutors know to leave well enough alone, even when the facts are staring them in the face, and simply ask the courts to validate the judgment of the IPM that the killing was justified. Moreover, this is a rational decision even if we assume a good faith, routine prosecutorial likelihood-of-conviction calculus. As we will see in the following section, the occasional prosecutor who is tempted to take on one of these cases will find a chilly reception in the courts, in addition to jeopardizing his or her career.

F. THE COURTS

One interview that I conducted with a judge in Salvador perhaps best captures the flavor of this state's judiciary. A judge in São Paulo communicated with a Salvadoran judge on my behalf and arranged a contact. After a few days in Salvador, and quite a few attempts to set up an interview in the courthouse, this judge finally called me and asked for a more private meeting. We met in a small neighborhood restaurant, some twenty minutes from the city center, the evening of May 9, 2001. As soon as the conversation began, the

---

[13] Interviews with Marília Veloso, Salvador, Bahia, multiple dates in April–May 2001.

judge insisted on anonymity.[14] He repeatedly asked if I was carrying any recording devices. I assured him that he could speak in confidence and that I was not recording the conversation. Still, he was so anxious to maintain the secrecy of our conversation that he would not speak when waiters were near, and continually checked to see if anyone could overhear. He said he feared for his safety – and certainly for his career – if it was known that he had discussed issues of judicial independence and political interference with me.

The air of intrigue continued throughout the dinner, while he explained in detail the selection, advancement, and career incentives he claimed were used by ACM and his allies to produce a judiciary that would do their bidding. The first mechanism is the appointment procedure. My informant claimed that the committee that conducts the extensive personal interviews of judicial candidates (also described in the discussion of São Paulo) is packed with ACM's supporters. The interview is used to screen out any candidates who appear to be problematic: known political opponents, the children of political opponents, potential troublemakers, or anyone suspected of political unorthodoxy is simply kept off the bench. This mechanism subverts the ostensible purpose of establishing an independent body to handle judicial selection and appointment.

Even after the appointment, and despite legal and constitutional protections, there are several mid-career ways to discipline judges, rewarding or punishing them to induce compliance. The system of transfers and promotions is quite openly used to reward judges who are politically compliant. Judges who fail to obey directives will be relegated to tiny courts of general jurisdiction deep in the interior of Bahia, or transferred from place to place, never quite making it to the more prestigious appointments in the capital or the courts of appeal. While the Constitution prevents salary reductions, there are other ways to use remuneration as a disciplining tool. The base monthly pay for judges was, at the time of the interview, about R$4,500. An appointment to the electoral court would add another R$2,000, and becoming an on-call substitute judge can add another R$1,500, nearly doubling a judge's base pay without adding too onerously to a judge's duties. Judges who are politically unpopular, according to my informant, will not be named to either of these positions. The result is a near constant monitoring and direction of individual judges' decision making any time there is a case of interest to dominant political actors.

---

[14] Given the informant's insistence on anonymity, I flipped a coin to determine whether I would use a masculine or feminine pronoun in this narrative.

My informant supplemented this general discussion with a couple of anecdotes. On one occasion in particular, in a criminal case, he issued a ruling
that was adverse to a close associate of ACM. The next day he received
a phone call from a person who is highly placed in state government, but
whom he did not identify. The caller demanded that he reverse his ruling.
When my informant did not, he was taken off the rolls of electoral judges.
He also related at some length the story of a colleague who had incurred
the displeasure of political elites and had been repeatedly passed over for
promotion. When I followed up on this information, however, this colleague
(who will also remain anonymous) would not enter into a discussion of the
topic. Any question leading in that direction – I was forced to be circumspect,
to protect the identity of my first informant – prompted an evasive answer.
I was given a detailed rendition of judicial statistics, the number of cases
handled, and the like, but no information regarding the courts' relationship
to political powers.

In short, the potential disciplining power of the mechanisms for selection and advancement identified in the discussion of São Paulo's judiciary is,
according to one judge at least, consciously employed in Bahia to create a
pliable judicial corps.[15] Of course, the opinion of one judge is not conclusive
proof, and it is entirely possible that this is all the fabrication of one mal-
content. But the story this judge tells is perfectly congruent with the public
consensus in Bahia on the relationship between ACM and the state's courts.
Opposition state legislators such as Moema Gramacho and Yulo Oiticica
agreed that the courts are subject to political interference by ACM and his
faction. The prosecutor quoted in the previous section echoed the concern
that the judiciary in Bahia is controlled by ACM. Souza (1997: 131) says
that one of the ways ACM controls "the state's political and economic life is
through the judiciary." It is no surprise, then, that ACM is widely believed
when he himself says "In Bahia we don't need [a formal mechanism for]
external control of the judiciary; I control it already!"[16]

---

[15] In addition to the obviously deleterious consequences for the rule of law of having a judiciary that is so directly manipulated, this tale is troubling from a purely electoral perspective:
if serving as an electoral judge is a reward for political compliance, then a crucial institution guarding electoral integrity is compromised; and if advancement is conditioned on
subservience, then the highest courts will be the most compromised. All the elements for
interfering with the democratic process are, therefore, in place.

[16] ACM is widely credited with making this observation in the course of a debate in the federal
legislature over the need for formal mechanisms of external control over the legislature. See,
for example, the discussion in the recent book by João Carlos Teixeira Gomes, a Bahian
journalist who had many confrontations with ACM (Teixeira Gomes 2001).

But what does this mean for police prosecutions in particular? As we have seen, there is considerable popular demand for a violent response to violent crime. The executive, responsible for public safety, is exposed to this demand. Moreover, the *caso dos grampos* illustrates the extent to which the police are tied to political leaders, even in furtherance of personalistic political interests. Kátia Alves, the civilian head of public safety in the late 1990s, has made it abundantly clear that her sympathies lay with the police, not human rights organizations. It is all too likely, then, that the executive, monolithic and controlled by the right, will pass on the weight of popular demands for a lethal police to judges. All the lawyers I interviewed agreed: as we saw in connection with the discussion of the prosecutor's office, police cases are always included in the list of "difficult" or politically sensitive cases.

G. SUMMARY

In conclusion, then, the legal system in Salvador is wide open to exogenous pressures. Moreover, given the high level of social demand for swift and draconian responses to crime, political demands tend strongly toward impunity for police officers who kill. These demands affect all the actors in the legal system, to a greater or lesser degree. If anything, judges are exposed to greater pressures than prosecutors, so that Salvador may be the one location in this study in which the latter take a stronger stand in these cases than do judges. This shifting of the normative standard at every level of the legal system produces a top-to-bottom normative failure in the system – what I have labeled elsewhere an informal institution that incorporates the legal system itself as the mechanism of enforcement (Brinks 2003, 2006). The problem, then, is not primarily a failure of information. Informational failures appear only when police behavior exceeds the limits of permissiveness, as in the case of Heloísa and her partner or the murder of street children. In general, however, even when the facts are fully known, the rule of decision legitimizes the killing so long as the victim can be portrayed as socially undesirable.

The high level of violence practiced by the police in Salvador is no surprise when the effective standard of behavior is consistently shifted so far away from the standards we might expect in a democracy. This arrangement leaves victims of police violence and those who claim on their behalf completely unprotected by the legal system. The effective rule in Salvador becomes, quite simply, that the police may kill so long as they appear to be killing good-for-nothing vagabonds in the interest of social cleansing. What is worse, their actions are de facto legitimized by the legal system, so that it becomes a part of their job to kill those suspected of crimes. As an inhabitant of Novos Alagados said: "The police, I know their profession is to commit abuses [*fazer ignorância*] but not against people, it should be against the thieves! And sometimes they kill many innocent people . . . they run around killing people, they are very violent. They're shooting all over, right? I find sometimes that they're right" (Machado and Noronha 2002: 214).

The very language used by this seventeen-year-old girl is indicative. Violence should not be employed against "persons" but may be employed against thieves: "*não é com as pessoas, é com ladrão.*" And that is how these cases are judged in Salvador by the population, the police, the prosecutors, and the courts: the victims are not citizens, who might therefore fall under the protection of the social contract; they are presumptively thieves and therefore not entitled to the protection of the law.

One of the principal lessons to be learned from Salvador is just how difficult it is for the legal system to overcome an inhospitable political environment. Even when the judiciary is formally designed to be meritocratic and independent, the formal and informal connections between the legal system and the social context are vast and varied. Ostensibly merit-based judicial appointment commissions are staffed with members of what Dahl (1957) might have called the dominant lawmaking coalition. Judicial careers can be molded and shaped by powerful political actors and the judicial elites that belong to that same coalition. Frontline prosecutors respond, willingly or not, to political appointees who determine institutional priorities. The police respond directly to political directives and protect their discretionary action with semi-sanctioned violence. Moreover, this dominant political coalition does not arise in a vacuum. Victims and witnesses too are immersed in a social context that challenges and questions them if they take a position that is contrary to the dominant one. There is not one but a myriad of pressures on all the actors in the legal system to conform to hegemonic norms.

Social change through institutional engineering, then, is a little like paddling a raft down a river. When the current is strong, in white water, paddling hard might help navigate but it will not send the raft back against the current. What are the limits to institutional engineering? This case illustrates an especially dramatic limit, in an overwhelmingly hostile social and political context. The rules are essentially irrelevant when even the operators of the institution cannot be persuaded to take a course that is anything but compliant with dominant patterns of behavior. But half-hearted change is dangerous. When claimants and operators take the institution seriously, setting a course that runs too sharply against the dominant current, and seek to engage institutional tools that are too weak, they are likely to suffer worse consequences. When parents of murdered children seek to impose some degree of accountability, but do not have the support of effective legal and social networks to resist violence and intimidation, they suffer the violence directly. When police investigators or prosecutors seek to dig too deeply into what their colleagues are doing, they pay with their careers. Whether context always trumps institutional design is a somewhat misleading question. The answer depends on how great a shift from "normative" behavior those institutions are attempting, and how deeply entrenched that behavior is in the overlapping and mutually reinforcing patterns of social power.

The importance of context is more and more often highlighted in comparative institutional analyses outside the developed world (see, e.g., Moser 2001 on how context conditions the effect of electoral institutions; or Weyland 2002, on the failure of weak institutions to produce the desired outcome). Other authors have begun to raise the question of institutional weakness in Latin America and its consequences (Levitsky and Murillo 2006). At the same time, political scientists rightly resist the easy "cultural" answer to difficult questions, opting for institutional explanations instead. And it is typically easier to accomplish institutional change than "contextual" change, either in the sense of changing the political construction of these cases or redressing socio-economic inequality. And so, all too often, the first and only prescription is to create or reform yet another institution, ignoring all that needs to be done to undergird the assertion of new rights.

9

Binding Leviathan

> Sir Thomas More: . . . What would you do? Cut a great road through the law to get after the Devil? William Roper: I'd cut down every law in England to do that! More: Oh! And when the last law was down, and the Devil turned on you – where would you hide, Roper, the laws all being flat! This country's planted thick with laws from coast to coast – man's laws, not God's – and if you cut them down . . . do you really think you could stand upright in the winds that would blow then?
>
> Robert Bolt, *A Man for All Seasons* (1962)

In Latin America, states have often responded to the felt need to "cut a great road through the law to get after the Devil" of the hour. The last devil was communism; the new devil (one of them, anyway) is crime, and vulnerable citizens are once again left struggling to stand upright in the winds that blow when immediate results trump legal processes. From iron-handed law-and-order efforts like "super *mano dura*" criminal reform proposals in Central America, to illegal ones like extra-judicial executions, lynchings, and extermination groups, due process protections take a back seat to citizen security. When this happens, as the experience of victims of police violence makes clear, it is very difficult for courts alone to stand up to those winds, even if legal protections have not been formally abolished.

This book tackles a fundamental question for today's developing democracies: under what conditions can individuals effectively engage the machinery of justice in defense of their rights? Moreover, it asks that question in the context of a right that is frequently presented as trading off protections for law-abiding citizens in exchange for the protection of criminals. The results highlighted here demonstrate that the answer to this individual-level question has much to do with aggregate political choices. Policy makers decide which claims to back with institutional development and which to leave at the mercy of individual resources. They decide which problems have become intolerable and which can be borne a while longer. These decisions in large measure determine who will find it easier and who more difficult to claim rights or vindicate a violation. And even in minimally democratic states, these choices are likely to reflect broad political currents.

In this concluding chapter, I gather the results from the empirical material, going from the more specific to the more general. I begin by summarizing the findings on each of the systems. From these comparative analyses, I extract more general conclusions applicable to legal systems and some lessons for the enforcement of civil rights laws; and on those conclusions I base some observations that are pertinent to the rule of law more generally. In the final section I present some reflections on institutions, politics, and the implications of my research for institutional analysis.

A. THE EMPIRICAL FINDINGS

In the opening chapter I argued that the ability to make an effective claim of right depends on overcoming the resistance of those on whom that right places a burden. This relatively vague observation leads directly to tallying the resources the system demands, the mechanisms available for supplying or blocking those resources, and the venues in which the clash of interests takes place. I argued that where the government does not actively intervene on behalf of the claimants we would likely see responses tied to the personal resources of a claimant and therefore greater levels of outcome inequality tied to the composition of the victim population. On the other hand, where state actors actively intervene in cooperation with more capable claimants there should be both greater effectiveness and greater equality in the outcomes.

To make this general observation more concrete, I applied the model to the prosecution of homicide charges against police officers. I argued that the endogenous and exogenous incentives that impinge on decision makers within the legal system determine their general orientation toward these claims and therefore the position they take when faced with a claim of right. Specifically, I argued that, since the police are an essential part of the criminal justice process, the system gives violators a systematic advantage in the struggle to apply the law and is therefore predisposed toward failure in cases involving alleged police misconduct. Internal actors would feel pressure to apply lenient standards to police conduct, the production of information would be curtailed, and the victim's representatives, the claimants, would be isolated in their quest for a conviction. This sets the stage for a straightforward contest between victims' relatives and the police. Claimants' resources, I anticipated, would crucially determine the success of the process, leading to an inequality of results that mirrors the inequality of resources in the victim pool.

Strong exogenous pressures from the political arena could, however, interrupt this direct translation of resource inequalities into outcome inequalities. But politics cuts both ways, and some systems are more open to political direction than others. Depending on their orientation, such political incentives could induce prosecutors and judges either to ignore these cases altogether or to adopt a more pro-claimant stance and engage more of their own resources in pursuit of the claim. Positive political incentives would flatten the inequalities present in the victim pool and produce more uniformly positive outcomes, while negative ones would render the system non-responsive to anyone's claims. Whichever way the winds blow, in more open systems, results should be tied not so much to material inequalities as to political inequalities. In such systems, results would follow the politics of police violence at least as much as they follow the socio-economic condition of the victims.

The results broadly reflect these predictions. Internal pressures to favor the police and the potential for informational failures in these prosecutions are evident in each of the systems studied. Institutional arrangements that should ameliorate these pressures, such as the separate investigative police forces of Córdoba and São Paulo, however, have less effect than I would have predicted. The Judicial Police continue to be co-opted by the ordinary police and continue to depend on the latter for operational assistance, perpetuating the informational failures. Prosecutors everywhere remain relatively indifferent to these cases, finding more common ground with police officers than with the typical victim. The victims' survivors, meanwhile, do not have sufficient resources to make up the systematic investigative deficiencies that result. Worse, the more socially excluded the victim pool, the easier it is for the police to engage in sabotage ranging from the destruction of evidence to the murder of witnesses. In short, there is ample evidence of a structural imbalance that favors the police in these cases, it is clear that this imbalance disfavors the already underprivileged, and there is more than enough reason to believe it will not be easy to overcome this imbalance solely through institutional design.

But, as expected, the political context strongly conditions these outcomes, and the right context can overcome these internal dynamics. In Uruguay, institutional design gives the police a great advantage, but a supportive political climate leads judges and prosecutors to adopt a rule of decision that is favorable to the victim. This in turn leads to often extraordinary measures to overcome the systemic imbalance and secure a conviction. At the same time, the fact that claimants are not buried deep in a context of mass social exclusion, as *favelados* might be in São Paulo or Salvador, makes it much easier for these state actors to engage the claimants in dialogue and harder for the police to squelch their involvement. In the conclusion to the chapter on Uruguay, I discuss the many ways in which politics affects legal outcomes and social inequality in turn affects politics. In more general terms, then, politics directs when and whether the state will invest resources in the form of judicial and prosecutorial investigations into allegations of violations. A population that is more engaged with the state makes it more likely that the state will make the effort and that the effort will succeed. The result is that, when the politics are right, as in Uruguay, outcomes are not dependent on the resources of individual claimants and the legal system acts with more effectiveness and less inequality.

When the political climate is hostile, on the other hand, the effectiveness of the system declines dramatically. Judges and prosecutors are, if anything, pulled closer to the police's preferences. They do not invest resources in an independent investigation and often refuse to convict even in situations in which it is evident that a violation has taken place. When the situation is sufficiently extreme, as in Salvador, inequality tends to disappear under a blanket rule of impunity. Attempts to challenge the hegemonic position are often met with violence. Again, the conclusion to the Salvador chapter discusses in some detail just how difficult it is for institutions to overcome context.

When the situation is less extreme but the system is still open to political influence, as in Buenos Aires, effectiveness rises moderately as results tend to track the political circumstances of the case. Thus, in Buenos Aires, it is nearly impossible to secure a conviction if the victim is "tainted" by violent crime. But case-specific politics can produce quite different results. In particular, cases in which the police exceed certain political (but not necessarily legal) boundaries can lead to convictions. One example is the killing of middle-class bystanders. Another is when they use tactics such as torture and disappearances that are reminiscent of the last dictatorship. When public sensibilities are offended, public demonstrations can turn acquittals into convictions.

Where the political influence is neutral, as in Córdoba, or neutralized, as in São Paulo, the results are, as predicted, largely driven by private resources. In Córdoba, political leaders did not, in the 1990s, use harsh law-and-order rhetoric or advocate violent policing, but neither did they distinguish themselves with strong human rights rhetoric. Here, the courts tend to judge these cases with a certain dispassionate equanimity that produces very positive results for those who have the resources to engage them effectively and very poor results for those with fewer resources. Moreover, the claimant pool includes both marginalized shantytown and immigrant victims as well as significant numbers of middle-class victims. The poor results occur in part because the police are able to impose silence on the underprivileged victims but not (as often) on the middle-class victims, and in part because of the disparate ability of the former to engage with the formal system. Thus a claim can be doomed by witnesses' uncultured accents and appearance, and by their silence or nervousness in the face of threats and in the unfamiliar environment of the courts. Córdoba's high-quality courts, therefore, produce moderately high levels of effectiveness and the highest levels of inequality of any of the courts examined here by relying on private resources and engaging with a diverse claimant population.

Meanwhile, in São Paulo, an autonomous court filters out popular and police pressures but leaves ample room for the police to carefully shape the record to meet the normative requirements of judges and prosecutors. In a context of broad popular support for violent police practices, the rightly celebrated public prosecutors take on these cases reluctantly and with less enthusiasm than they have for, say, consumer protection or environmental claims. The lack of state action and the nearly uniform lack of resources among victims and claimants make it unlikely that many will manage to overcome police resistance and present their own version of events. Judges then carefully apply legal standards to a procedural reality that is constructed almost exclusively out of biased police information. The result is a uniformly low level of effectiveness. The almost complete absence of high-resource victims means we cannot observe high levels of inequality, but the strong impact of NGO assistance and a Private Prosecutor on conviction rates strongly suggests a latent potential for severe inequality.

We can trace these general conclusions to findings on specific variables to support both the analysis of the normative preferences of the various actors and the emphasis on litigant resources where the political environment is neither actively supportive nor overwhelmingly hostile. In Córdoba, lacking a private attorney to accompany the prosecution reduces that system to levels of effectiveness roughly equal to São Paulo's average effectiveness. The similarity in outcomes once we control for the presence of a private attorney suggests similar dynamics at work in both places: courts will judge effectively but this requires an investment of personal resources on the part of claimants. On the other hand, lacking a lawyer in Buenos Aires, where judges and prosecutors are exposed to greater endogenous and exogenous pressures to acquit, reduces the likelihood of a conviction to near zero. In Uruguay, where the politics of police violence generate sufficient incentives to become actively supportive of the claimant's position, prosecutors and investigative judges stand in for this private attorney, producing results independent of victims' resources.

Membership in the middle class has the most dramatic impact in Córdoba, where a functioning justice system meets inequality and lukewarm political support. Having middle-class resources there more than doubles the courts' response rate, from under 35% to almost 80%. São Paulo shows very little socio-economic inequality within the courts, and the low impact of race on convictions might suggest that the courts are more egalitarian here than in Córdoba. However, the strong impact of a Private Prosecutor on outcomes in São Paulo suggests that the police would be less able to monopolize the information available about a case involving a middle-class victim and therefore that inequalities would manifest if the police were more indiscriminate in their selection of victims.

Social class is partially neutralized in Buenos Aires by a lenient standard of conduct for the police that reduces effectiveness for everyone, and by the presence of free non-state legal assistance (in the form of NGOs like CORREPI) that increases effectiveness for the underprivileged. In this more politicized system, other tolls matter more. In particular, popular mobilization around the case in what Smulovitz and Peruzzotti (Mainwaring and Welna 2003) have called societal accountability seems to matter a great deal. Note, however, that the more elaborate manifestations of societal accountability imply a breathtaking investment of personal and community resources, including marches involving thousands of people and claimants who drop everything to become almost full-time leaders of the effort. Clearly, Buenos Aires' political tolls indirectly place great demands on claimants' personal resources as well.

B. GENERAL CONCLUSIONS FROM THE EMPIRICAL FINDINGS

Efforts to improve the functioning of legal systems have typically focused on one institution at a time, rather than looking at the entire system, and have been criticized for exactly this reason (Prillaman 2000). My research suggests an even more complicated scenario than the usual prescription to focus on all aspects of internal judicial functioning at once. In order to improve results, legal reform will have to take into consideration both the rule-crafting and the fact-finding dimensions of legal decision making, recognizing that both require an examination of the relationship among the various actors in the legal system, within the broader social context. At the same time, this research suggests a particular focus for reform. In particular, effective reform requires special attention to those on whom the law imposes a duty and to the methods exercised by them to resist enforcement of that duty, and thus on the mechanisms needed to enable the beneficiaries of rights to overcome that resistance.

A couple of examples make this point most clearly. The Carandiru massacre, the Candelárias killings, the videotaped abuses in Favela Naval, the massacres in Vigário Geral or Baixada Fluminense made it clear that something had to be done to address the high levels of violence employed by the Brazilian Military Police. Reformers concerned with human rights and police violence correctly concluded that military judges were applying an overly lenient rule to decide the cases. Indeed, the only systematic study of its kind (Cano 1999) confirms that the police enjoyed a high level of impunity in the military justice system, documenting a 3 percent conviction rate in the military courts of Rio de Janeiro for police officers accused of homicide. Again correctly, reformers concluded that civilian judges would be less likely to use such a lenient standard. The solution was relatively obvious, then: the reformers pushed and ultimately managed to pass the *Lei Bicudo*, transferring jurisdiction in cases of intentional murders to the civilian justice system.

If the actual rule of decision had been the only problem, this would have produced a dramatic improvement in conviction rates. But according to my figures, it did not. The conviction rate went from perhaps 3 percent (São Paulo's conviction rate may or may not match Cano's figure for Rio but it cannot be much lower in any event) to roughly 6 percent (my figure for São Paulo). Six percent is twice as much, to be sure, but it is still a dismal success rate, given the level of violence employed by the police. Reformers failed to address the gross disparity of resources between competing claimants in the construction of the case. They (incorrectly) assumed that the Ministério Público could and would handle the investigation of these crimes and properly prepare the cases for trial. In fact, prosecutors rely too heavily on the police for the facts of these cases, receiving biased and incomplete information. And given Brazil's social reality, individual claimants are unable to resist police violence and intimidation. Fixing the rule of decision was not enough.

To improve results in actual cases, the *Lei Bicudo* needed also to redress this imbalance in the production of procedural truth. One not very satisfactory solution would have been to lessen or reverse the burden of proof in these cases, as happens in many of the civil cases arising out of the same events. In cases involving inmates killed while in custody, for example, many trial judges in São Paulo have reversed the burden of proof, requiring the state to demonstrate that the killing was justified. The result is a dramatic improvement in the outcomes. Civil awards in favor of a victim's survivors are by far more common than convictions, even in cases arising out of the same facts.[1] But in a criminal prosecution, this would be a rather egregious violation of conventional standards of due process, at least if applied to the prosecution for murder of the individuals allegedly pulling the trigger. A broader rule holding superiors responsible for the levels of violence employed by subordinates (a sort of *res ipsa loquitur* presumption that high levels of violence are evidence of improper supervision) may tend in the same direction with fewer due process implications.

A better solution would be to improve the investigative capacity of the prosecutors in this category of cases, simultaneously increasing their incentives to make use of that capacity. The number of killings of this nature in São Paulo and elsewhere, often far more than 10 percent of all homicides in a given year, to say nothing of the hundreds of other police abuses that take place on a daily basis, clearly justifies the creation of a specialized prosecutorial corps for police misconduct, with independent investigative capacity. If these prosecutors were evaluated on the strength of their performance in prosecuting police officers who commit abuses, they would also have the incentive to aggressively pursue these cases. This corps should remain in the regular prosecutor's office rather than inside the police force, as the *corregedorias* (police disciplinary bodies) currently are, or in a separate military justice system, as was the case before the *Lei Bicudo*. This would enroll the considerable talent and resources of that institution and help avoid endogenous pressures toward leniency. I do not mean to suggest that these prosecutions would ever be easy. In São Paulo, Salvador, and Córdoba we have seen just how difficult it is to wrest control of the facts from the frontline police forces, even with an investigative police force in place.

In addition, of course, Salvador's experience with the murder of street children teaches us that witnesses and complainants have to be protected

---

[1] This discussion is based on two sources: (1) conversations with the *Promotora* (the public defender from the prosecutor's office in São Paulo) in charge of assisting relatives of the victims of the Carandiru massacre, and an examination of judicial opinions and records tracking judgments in the several dozen civil cases that arose from that incident; and (2) a review of the files of the Centro Santo Dias, in São Paulo, in which the Centro pursued both a criminal and a civil claim based on the same events.

throughout the process. There must be effective and proactive mechanisms in place to prevent stricter enforcement from leading to more violence against witnesses and complainants. A witness protection program is one component; speedy trials another. And prosecutors and judges, as in Córdoba, must more aggressively prosecute obstruction of justice cases. Another measure, more problematic from a due process perspective, is erring on the side of caution in pre-trial detention rulings. Only in Uruguay is it standard practice to jail accused police officers pending trial. Although this clearly raises due process issues, the counterpart, as we saw in every other case, is the tendency of the accused to terrorize the claimants. The courts need to acknowledge this danger and balance these two concerns in deciding pre-trial release issues, rather than simply assume that if the accused is a police officer there is no reason to invoke pre-trial detention.

In short, if every incident of lethal use of force by the police triggered immediate oversight by a specialized task force, a prompt examination of the crime scene, access to federal forensic scientists, a witness protection plan when necessary, and accelerated trial times, the proportion of successful prosecutions would almost certainly increase. It would then not be too much to hope that the incidence of violations might also drop. But consider the political change that would be required in a province like Buenos Aires for such institutional change to take place. Institutional change is a political process, a point to which I will return at the end of this chapter.

This focus on the struggle among competing claimants leads to the second general point: many of the proposed fixes for legal systems follow universal prescriptions, often applying them not only across areas of the law but across countries. However, my results strongly caution that different categories of cases require different enforcement structures, again driven by differences in the capabilities of competing claimants. For instance, land disputes in Northeastern Brazil often pit wealthy landowners with dubious ownership claims against small-plot peasant farmers with possession-based claims. Courts resolving these disputes need to take into consideration the disparate capacity of each of these claimants to produce evidence, real and concocted, in support of their competing demands. The very nickname for the wealthy claimants to land occupied by poor peasants is indicative of this: they have become known as *grilheiros* (cricketers) for the alleged practice of having crickets nibble on forged land titles to simulate antiquity. Meanwhile, the claims of low-income occupiers of rural or urban plots often fail for lack of legal titles and other formal documents.

One obvious response to this imbalance in legal resources is improving the capabilities of claimants. This was, for example, the first prong of the legal strategy undertaken by CECOPAL,[2] in a land titling and ownership dispute (Ré and Taquela 1998). CECOPAL lawyers organized low-income homeowners into groups for mutual support and the exchange of information, held meetings at which they educated their clients on their legal rights, and supplied lawyers to pursue a defense in foreclosure proceedings. The homeowners used political mobilization to affect the socio-political context and petitioned the government for a change in the rules that governed their cases. The results were quite positive for the claimants, with homeowners largely retaining title to their property.

But these claimants were easy to identify and mobilize. Much more often, victims/claimants are plucked from a much larger population, and improving capabilities means reducing social inequality generally, a daunting task. In the meantime, then, the solution is to create institutional ties to the affected population that take into consideration their special circumstances. In the *grilheiro* cases, for example, an independent, state-sponsored fact-finding agent[3] might produce a more adequate record than a strictly adversarial process heavily dependent on formal legal documents. Short of bringing an entire class of claimants into greater contact with the state and improving their capacity to engage that machinery, reformers can extend an arm of the state toward this class of claimants, taking into consideration the special difficulties they face in interacting with legal instances. The Supreme Court of India, for example, has taken great steps in this direction, with its custom of appointing a senior attorney as *amicus curiae* in public interest litigation cases and appointing experts to ascertain and independently verify the facts alleged by the litigants (Muralidhar 2002).

Next, consider the importance of identifying the source of resistance to a particular right. In his *The Sociology of Law*, Evan notes that we can envision a continuum of social resistance to the policies embodied in the law. If no one resists the law, it is unnecessary since all will comply voluntarily. If everyone resists, the law is unenforceable because there will be no one to staff enforcement instances (Evan 1980). Between these two extremes, of

---

[2] Centro de Comunicación Popular y Asesoramiento Legal (CECOPAL; the Center for Popular Communication and Legal Advising), a Córdoba legal services NGO. CECOPAL works with a group of people who bought homes on installment plans that, for some of its clients, became impossible to meet as a result of inflation and other changes in the economic circumstances in Argentina. Other clients were victims of schemes in which the same home was sold multiple times. All of them faced the loss of their homes.

[3] The courts in the United States, for example, have sometimes appointed Special Masters to oversee compliance with a court-ordered remedy, in desegregation and other cases, or experts to provide an impartial opinion on a technical issue.

course, the more resistance there is, the stronger the institutional mechanisms of enforcement need to be, if the law is to have any effect at all. But it is not simply a matter of polling the population to determine the percentage of resistance to a certain law. We must pay especially close attention to the legal and extra-legal resources that can be brought to bear on the legal process by those benefited and those burdened by the law. Assuming we can minimally populate enforcement mechanisms with individuals willing to enforce the law, it is that balance of power that affects the enforcement capacity of the system more than the opinion polls Evan's comment might suggest.

Compared to more oligarchic systems, democracy has the potential to shift the balance of power at the lawmaking stage in favor of the generally underprivileged. Indeed, this is the premise for T. H. Marshall's (1950) account of how political rights breed social and economic rights. But passing narrowly tailored individual rights protections without addressing the broader context leaves undisturbed the balance of power at the enforcement stage. So long as a new law (or newly enforced law) does not attempt to shift the balance of power in the social and political system too far from the current equilibrium, it can, over time, exert its attraction and produce a change in behavior. The further the law seeks to shift that balance, however, the more coercive and pervasive the enforcement structure must be, and the more ancillary changes in the overall legal framework will be required to make it effective. In the end, if the law sets the goal too far from the current center of gravity for the strength of the available enforcement institutions to exert their attraction, it will at best have no effect at all on actual practices, and at worst create additional difficulties for any claimant foolish enough to take its promises seriously.

The case of juvenile justice reform in Salvador, discussed earlier, is one example. There the police have historically ruled the streets of low-income neighborhoods with almost unbounded discretion. The casual and unpunished shooting of a child who throws a stone at a bus makes this point abundantly. The new enforcement structure created after the *Estatuto da Criança e do Adolescente* sought to radically shift the balance of power between these children and police officers by improving enforcement of children's rights. But without improved capabilities on the part of potential claimants, and without a strong state presence and a pervasive enforcement mechanism, the police were able to preserve the existing balance of power undisturbed. When they could no longer count on the courts to look the other way, they simply used their coercive power to enforce acquiescence on the part of the victims and their families. To truly shift the balance, the state will have to invest resources in shoring up the capacity of claimants to exercise their rights and resist coercion.

Parents of murdered children in Salvador have this experience in common with many other underprivileged groups. Violent attacks against those who presume to claim land rights are all too frequent in Brazil's rural areas (Piovesan et al. 2001). This was brought home to me when one of my interviews in Salvador, with the head of an Afro-Brazilian land-rights group, was interrupted by a phone call alerting him that a gang of thugs was violently attacking a group of farmers pursuing a land claim. One report identifies nearly 1,600 murders of rural workers, indigenous people, religious workers, and others associated with the struggle for land rights from 1964 to 1989. Only 8 of those murders led to a conviction. Despite the advent of democracy, the violence (or its reporting) has escalated, with another 1,700 murdered between 1988 and 2000 and similar patterns of impunity (Piovesan et al. 2001: 22, citing a 1991 America's Watch report and a 2000 Comissão Pastoral da Terra report on rural violence). If the criminal justice system cannot protect claimants from violence and intimidation, any new rights that seek to shift power from those who control the means of coercion will be ineffective.

In short, while the law is never a seamless, uncontradictory whole, it is clear that we cannot use new cloth to patch an old garment, to borrow a biblical metaphor. A strong claim to equality in the context of overall legal inequality will simply tear the fabric of law and justice. Legislating stronger rights for a dispossessed group – rights that purport to, in Weber's words, give power to the "hitherto powerless" – without attending to the imbalance of power in the process of claiming those rights, simply exposes claimants to new violence.

And it is by no means a trivial observation that these means of coercion are often supported and maintained by the state itself, so that the left hand is tearing down what the right would build up. As is clear in the case of violent police officers, the balance of power that precedes the creation of a new right is not a Hobbesian, pre-legal state of nature, but rather the result of where both the state and the market, working together, have allocated power resources. Thus, while the focus of this book has often been on what Amartya Sen (1999) calls individual capabilities, it should be clear by now that it is the state, in response to political choices, that in large measure constitutes differential citizen capabilities.

What I have chronicled in this book, then, is one of many eddies in the current of democracy, though perhaps an extreme one. Dotted throughout societies are localized power relations where the current runs in the opposite direction and individuals are subject to an alternative legal order (O'Donnell 1993). We could come up with dozens of examples in addition to the relationship between the police and young, unemployed, low-income urban males: abusive employment relationships in rural settings, many of them approaching slavery; voters and political bosses in many rural districts across Latin America; women in many different contexts but especially in those places where domestic abuse is still tolerated; children in state institutions; petitioners in obscure government offices across Latin America, reduced to the condition of supplicants. The critical obstructions causing these eddies are social inequalities. So long as the locally powerful can use these inequalities to deny information or access to the structures that are supposed to impose liberal democracy, they can comfortably maintain their dominant position, regardless of changes in the broader context.

As we have seen throughout, one of the crucial preconditions for an effective rule of law is the presence of multiple alternative sources of information concerning the conduct of lower level actors in the system, including ordinary citizens. An actor that monopolizes information, or any other crucial resource for the system for that matter, can impose its normative preferences on outcomes all the way up the ladder. The result is a localized bottom-up normative homogeneity, the creation of authoritarian enclaves in which the binding rules applied at all levels are those imposed by non-democratic actors. This situation violates even the basic procedural aspects of the rule of law: the minimal requirement that publicly binding decisions, and most especially the decisions of actors within the legal system, be made in accordance with properly enacted laws of universal application. The counterpart of the rule of law, then, is not always normative *heterogeneity*. The rule of *law* requires, in addition, that the dominant rules of decision be laws enacted by a legitimate lawgiver, or individual rules that lie within the bounds of discretion set forth in legitimately enacted laws.

The disparate results across social classes in Córdoba, and among Violent Victim, Routine Policing, and Private Violence cases in both Buenos Aires and São Paulo, clearly illustrate that there can be different degrees of normative homogeneity within the same system for different classes of citizens. I have described Uruguay as having a generally egalitarian and effective legal system. But even in Uruguay, lawyers who work with street children describe a condition of arbitrary power on the part of the police who interact with these children. The capability of these children to access the legal system and claim its protection is dramatically low, perhaps lower than that of any other group in Uruguay. Different classes of claimants, different social and political pressures on decision makers, produce different combinations of normative and informational shifts that subdivide society into groups with more and less effective rights. Broad statements that begin "The rule of law in Latin America is..." or even "The rule of law in Argentina (or Brazil, or wherever) is..." miss as much as they describe.

Top-down normative homogeneity is not, obviously, a guarantee of the rule of *democratic* law, but it is an essential building block to that end. One inescapable conclusion from this comparative analysis is how adept judicial systems are at maintaining internal normative consistency when they wish to do so (even when they completely fail to impose normative standards on other legal actors). This book analyzes six very different judicial and prosecutorial institutions with very different mechanisms for appointment, discipline, advancement, and promotion of judges and prosecutors. Some officially eschew binding precedent; others proclaim on their official Web sites that the judicial system is not hierarchical. And yet in every one of them, no matter how independent the institutions are meant to be, there are means of enforcing orthodoxy to one degree or another. To different degrees, judges in all six judiciaries are sensitive to their hierarchical superiors, whether they are subject to binding precedent or not, and to political currents, whether they are politically appointed or not. Even the most autonomous judges (the ones in São Paulo come closest to deserving that distinction among my cases) are not autarchic. In one way or another, directly or indirectly, courts are subject to top-down control and are deeply embedded in their political context, so that politics bleeds into everyday judicial decision making.

A certain measure of this is a good thing. A completely autarchic judiciary would be uncontrolled and uncontrollable and would erode the democratic nature of a regime which is, after all, supposed to respond to the *demos*. This is not the place for a discussion of the proper role of courts in a democracy, a debate that has gone on for decades (see, e.g., Dahl 1957; Bickel 1962; Dahl 1989; Friedman 1998). Hilbink's (2003, forthcoming) analysis of the Chilean courts' actions leading up to the Pinochet coup amply demonstrates the dangers of an overly insular, purportedly apolitical judiciary. At minimum, on the basis of my findings in the course of this project, it is clear that something like "embedded autonomy" (Evans 1995) is a good thing for a democracy. Courts should be autonomous in the sense that they follow a core discipline that produces its own logic, especially a national-level logic rooted in a democratic constitution and laws. And they should be embedded in the sense of retaining extensive links to society, through appointment or disciplinary mechanisms, broad-based recruiting, and multiple institutional links to potential claimants. Such a judiciary will never be completely out of step with its own society.

I have emphasized the need for multiple connections, and others have argued the democratic deficiencies of an overly autonomous judiciary (Dahl 1957; Fiss 1993; Hilbink 2003, forthcoming), but we also saw here some less positive aspects of judicial responsiveness. In Argentina and Brazil, and increasingly in Uruguay, fear of violent crime has become pervasive and corrosive. The discussion in this book shows how, in a context of fear, more democracy, understood as more attention to majority demands, may undermine respect for basic rights guaranteed in a constitutional legal order, thus eroding the core logic of a rights-protective judiciary. To put it another way, these findings highlight the recurring tension between the *demos*-responsive and the liberal-constitutionalist elements of modern democracy. Increased *demos* responsiveness at the expense of the judiciary's core discipline and logic may well imply less capacity to defend core democratic principles embodied in constitutions, and thus less "rule of law," in the broader, more substantive meaning of that term (Raz 1979; O'Donnell 2001).

C. INSTITUTIONAL THEORY REVISITED

I conclude with some general reflections on institutionalist research. My findings present two challenges to much of the institutionalist literature. The first challenge is to pay more attention to the gap between formal rules and actual practices. Far too often researchers begin and end institutional analyses with the formal rules, without too much attention to the way these rules are worked out in practice. Often, if the discrepancy is noted, it is excused on the basis of resource constraints on research or the lack of data. Certainly, focusing on formal rules is a more efficient way to conduct research, and on occasion it may be the only practical way to proceed. The gain in efficiency, however, is more often than not outweighed by the loss of information. In the discussion of reforms to the Code of Criminal Procedure in Buenos Aires, for example, I described how lawyers and judges resist, qualify, and modify the rules that have the effrontery to tell them how they should now ply their trade. A researcher who assumes that changes in the practice of law track changes in the formal rules will miss an important part of the story.

The second challenge is to theorize and explore the gap between expected institutional outcomes and actual outcomes. Discussions of the formal attributes of Supreme Courts across Latin America may well end up placing countries like Uruguay and Costa Rica at the bottom in terms of the institutional attributes theoretically necessary for an independent judiciary. If we stop there, without noting that these same two courts are likely the most independent of all the Supreme Courts in Latin America, we have missed the most interesting and important part of the puzzle. The answer may be that we have simply miscalculated and misunderstood the institutional requisites for judicial independence. In that case, our institutional theory is simply wrong. But it is more often the case that our theories rest on unspoken and unexamined assumptions about the social, political, and economic context in which these institutions operate; on the assumption that the formal rules are the (only) ones actually applied; and on the premise that all the intended beneficiaries have the capacity to exercise their newly established rights. What we need is a more contextual institutionalism.

This gap between expected and actual outcomes generally describes the set of puzzles of which the questions raised in this project are a subset – why does a particular institution or rule ostensibly designed to produce a certain outcome actually produce a completely different one? The Uruguayan case contradicts the expectation that a more modern legal and procedural structure will produce better results. The Uruguay to São Paulo comparison confounds expectations about the relative effect of institutional strength, conventionally understood. The identical judicial institutions in São Paulo and Salvador produce radically different levels of political independence. Rather than crafting ad hoc solutions to these puzzles, political scientists need to theorize these differences and account for them.

In this book, I have argued that a contextual approach to institutionalism helps us understand two basic kinds of failures – normative and informational – that might cause legal outcomes to vary from what the formal rules prescribe. These two failures are particular instances of what we might more generally call input failures and processing failures. Institutional theory needs to account for the ways in which institutions perform both functions: first gathering inputs and then processing them according to the actual rules of decision (formal or informal).

There are, of course, examples of this kind of institutionalist research already. Recent work on informal institutions (O'Donnell 1994; Helmke and Levitsky 2006) is focused on the processing aspect of this problem, the source and nature of informal rules. The observation that the broader partisan context affects the impact of presidentialism on regime survival (Mainwaring and Shugart 1997) or of electoral design on party-system characteristics (Moser 2001) draws attention to the effect of inputs on institutional performance. Since Montesquieu we have understood that a division of functions without a division of interests will not accomplish an effective separation of powers (Bellamy 1996). The law-and-development scholars in particular criticized the wholesale transplantation of legal systems to other contexts. It is not that social scientists have failed to notice this simple fact, but that we have largely failed to translate this commonsensical observation into a better theorized and more intentional research agenda. We are all too often content to undertake an acontextual institutional analysis. Perhaps the general framework presented here can guide additional research on the effect of institutions across political and social contexts.

This project in particular demonstrates the importance of adopting a contextual institutionalist approach. Establishing an effective rule of law continues to be a central challenge for Latin America and the developing world. In this book I examined an especially significant failure of the rule of law: the impunity with which the police kill hundreds of people in some of the most important democracies of Latin America. And variations in institutional design, time and again, do not seem to produce the expected results. The legal systems in Buenos Aires, São Paulo, and Salvador are unable to effectively oversee the actions of the police because the institutions that compose them are too dependent on the police for information, or too willing to accept the popular verdict that these deaths are the acceptable price of an ongoing war against crime. Institutional design seems to have failed.

This is not because institutional design cannot, in the abstract, overcome contextual factors, although this entire project demonstrates the difficulties involved. New institutions that proactively reach out to overcome social and legal disadvantages between rights bearers and those who owe them a duty could address the problem more successfully than what we have seen to date. I described some of these possible institutional arrangements earlier in this chapter. But it is far more difficult for institutions to bridge political than social chasms. The institutions described earlier have not materialized so far, and the prospects for their appearance seem quite dim. The reason, of course, is that institutions do not spring up out of thin air; they are the product of negotiation and struggle, in a political context. Given the current politics of crime and police violence, the rising crime rates and ineffective criminal justice systems, the massive urbanization and informalization of the poor, failing institutions will be allowed to continue to fail. Under these conditions, institutional variations will continue to be half-hearted and not truly designed to reduce and punish arbitrary police violence.

Standing behind the institutional failure, then, is a social and political dynamic. Violent crime is emphasized and politicized for electoral advantage, and as a result the electorate in cities like Buenos Aires, São Paulo, or Salvador has not presented an uncompromising demand for an end to the virtual civil war declared against marginal youths. In turn, this socio-political failure rests uneasily on a new socio-economic reality, in which increasing levels of violent crime and growing dispossessed urban masses terrify all sectors of society. This is arid ground for political movements that might seek to strengthen due process and other protections by limiting the discretionary actions of the police.

In the end, faced with the failure of governments to offer any other solution to the problem of crime, the citizens of these and other cities experiencing high levels of police violence appear to have made a Hobbesian contract with the state: take any measures you wish, Leviathan, so long as you protect our persons and our property from our neighbors. The necessary institutional changes will not take place, the requisite judicial and prosecutorial willingness will not materialize, police conduct will not improve, Leviathan will not be bound, until voters in these cities begin to write some binding conditions into their social contract, election by election. This is the lesson Sir Thomas More was trying to bring home to Roper, in the well-known quote with which I began this final chapter. Due process and the law are not merely "rights for criminals," a phrase that is familiar to many Brazilians; ultimately, they keep the devil of arbitrary state conduct from turning on all of us. And it is up to all of us to demand a more restrained, accountable state.

Appendix

Methods, Case Selection, and Sampling

The fieldwork for this project took place during the course of an exploratory one-month trip to Argentina and Brazil in the summer of 1999, a much longer research trip to Argentina, Uruguay, and Brazil in 2000–01, and brief follow-up trips to Argentina and Brazil in 2004 and 2005. During the main research trip I spent four months in Buenos Aires, about three in São Paulo, and approximately a month each in Córdoba, Montevideo, and Salvador da Bahia.

The book works at three levels of analysis: countries, judicial districts, and individual legal cases. At the very outset, I chose three countries that, by reputation at least, promised some variation on the dependent variable: Argentina, Brazil, and Uruguay. As the data more or less confirmed, I expected Uruguay to be a "positive" case, Brazil to be the "negative" case, and Argentina to fall somewhere in the middle. What I did not expect was the magnitude of the cross-national variation or the important sub-national differences.

At the sub-national level, in each of the two federal countries (Brazil and Argentina), I selected two different legal environments – in each case, I compared the largest and most economically important city in the country to a more remote provincial capital, with similar populations (just over and just under two million) and a solid industrial base. These were in part selected for their similarities and differences with each other and the major city, and in part chosen because I had enough contacts and leads to suggest that I might be able to obtain sufficient information in a reasonable amount of time.

I compared each of these to each other and to Uruguay, which, as a unitary country, has a single national legal system. In terms of the size of the population covered, Uruguay is comparable to the smaller cities in each of the other two countries. Thus, though it is at times awkward to compare a country to a state or city, a direct comparison is valid for most purposes. When it is not – for example, in comparing the amount spent on the judiciary in Uruguay (with its single unitary system) to the amount spent on the judiciary in São Paulo (with a state and federal system operating side by side) – I made the necessary adjustments, as noted in the text.

Within each legal environment, I analyzed individual case outcomes. For this level of analysis, I selected the investigation and prosecution of homicides committed by the police.[1] While homicides are certainly not the most common form of violence perpetrated by the police, they offer some advantages that outweigh their drawbacks. In the first place, since the end of the dictatorships at least, when the police kill someone in the course of their duties, they typically acknowledge the killing or it comes to light very quickly. There continue to be deaths that the police do not claim, of course. These are more common in Brazil, as a result of police involvement in so-called extermination groups (Oiticica 2001). But in comparison to, for example, the practically researchable percentage of the total universe of torture incidents, beginning with a list of those who were killed by the police is likely to capture a much greater percentage of the universe of potential disputes.

In addition, as mentioned earlier, homicides are governed by less complex, less contested, and more discrete rules than "higher law" disputes concerning the separation of powers, presidential authority, and the like. Once the facts are clear, the judgment is more likely to be clear in homicide cases. We can be certain, for example, that executing someone with a shot to the back of the head is murder, whether or not the shooter is wearing a badge. There are close cases, as there are in any area of the law, but by and large research in this area involves fewer indeterminate cases than issues of decree authority, freedom of speech, or even torture. Finally, these cases are also more visible to the legal system, so the conviction rate in cases of homicide almost surely exceeds by a significant amount the conviction rate in torture cases, for example. This means that my conclusions about the failure of various systems are, if anything, conservative.

The nested research design allows for comparisons within legal systems, holding constant system-level variables; within metropolitan areas, holding constant city-specific variables; within countries, holding constant

---

[1] A note here about terminology: a homicide is simply a case involving the killing of a human being, whether intentional or not, justified or not, illegal or not. Thus when I speak of homicide cases, I do not mean to suggest that all these cases are murder – though, as we will see, I did take care to exclude those cases that quite clearly were not.

national-level variables; and ultimately across countries. The result is a rich and varied view of the dependent and independent variables, multiplying the cases and contributing to the resolution of the typical small *N*–too many variables problem. Further variation comes from diachronic comparisons in places that have experimented with different procedural codes and institutional arrangements, as, for example, Buenos Aires city, Buenos Aires province, and Córdoba, or even different judicial systems in the same location, as did Brazil, before and after the *Lei Bicudo*.

Much, though not all, of the analysis relies on a comparison of aggregate conviction rates across social groups, across time, across legal systems, and across countries to come to conclusions about legal effectiveness and inequality. One problem with using conviction rates is that they may reflect differences in the underlying distribution of cases rather than shortcomings in the legal systems. If in São Paulo the police only shoot when shot at, while in Montevideo the police execute suspects at will, we would expect radically different conviction rates, especially if both systems are working correctly and applying identical rules of decision. Moreover, the use of conviction rates as a measure of success might suggest that all the cases should end in a conviction. On this measure, Stalin's judiciary was almost certainly among the most effective in history.

In fact, however, the necessary assumption is only that the underlying distribution of legally relevant characteristics is more or less the same across the classes of cases being compared. This way the differences in conviction rates are attributable to differences in the more interesting features – the effective rule of decision, or the success in carrying out investigations – not to differences in the distribution of legally relevant factual patterns across samples. If I have adequately selected the cases, then, the rate of convictions should be higher where the investigative, prosecutorial, and judicial functions are most effective (so long as the system is not simply rubber-stamping political decisions). I will return to the sampling method shortly.

There are some rough external checks on the validity of the measure. We know, for example, that extra-judicial executions are exceedingly common in Brazil and in São Paulo in particular (Ouvidoria da Polícia 1999; Amnesty International 2005). We can be fairly certain, then, that the reason the courts in São Paulo fail to convict in 94% of the cases is not because the police are acting in self-defense 94% of the time. It is not stochastic error that produces a doubling of conviction rates across social classes in Córdoba. And it is certainly not the case that Uruguay has a higher conviction rate because its police are more violent and prone to human rights violations than the police of, say, Salvador.

Still, where the conclusions are necessarily tentative, as happens more often than I would like, I did not hesitate to indicate my uncertainty and to describe in detail the shortcomings of the data on which the conclusions are based. The problem is especially acute at both ends of the spectrum, precisely because these cases are at the extreme. In Uruguay, the research "problem" is that the low number of cases prevents stating results with statistical certainty. Clearly, there is no normatively acceptable solution to this problem. In Salvador, on the other hand, the difficulty is that police violence is so prevalent and so protected by a diversity of mechanisms that it stifles the production of information about the phenomenon. I have done my best to be explicit about these research obstacles, and the reader will have to judge whether my conclusions are sufficiently trustworthy.

One of the many difficulties in conducting a study of the problem of police homicides in any environment is obtaining accurate information about the overall universe of cases. To piece together the sample in Uruguay I carried out a detailed search of the available online databases of two major Uruguayan newspapers, *El País* and *La Brecha*, and reviewed all the available human rights reports produced both internally and externally.[2] This list of cases is surely not exhaustive. Egregious cases are more likely to receive press coverage and attention. Uncontroversial self-defense cases may not even be reported by SERPAJ or in the press. But Uruguay is a small country, shootings are uncommon, and SERPAJ receives complaints in addition to its daily search of newspapers. It is unlikely that a very large number of cases that are actually rights violations would go undetected. Moreover, as we will see, uncontroversial uses of police power are excluded from the sample in Argentina and Brazil as well, and so the samples for the different countries are comparable in this respect. Finally, because I suspect the other samples also include some confrontations, I included all the reported cases without any additional screening, although at least two of them were bona fide armed confrontations.

In Argentina, as in Uruguay, the government does not publish official figures detailing how many people die at the hands of the police. The CELS has been combing the newspapers in the Metropolitan Buenos Aires area since 1985 to glean all reported fatal and non-fatal shootings, torture, and deaths that result from ill treatment at the hands of the police, and other

---

[2] I reviewed the U.S. State Department and Freedom House reports, and all the available reports from SERPAJ, for 1990 through 2000. I also talked to lawyers from SERPAJ and IELSUR (Instituto de Estudios Legales y Sociales del Uruguay), and independent lawyers working in the area of human rights, and they were unable to point out any cases not captured by these methods.

violent acts by the police. I used the CELS annual reports (see, e.g., CELS 2000, 2001) only to measure overall levels of police homicides in Buenos Aires.

CORREPI has been gathering similar information since 1996, and it publishes a cumulative list of cases (e.g., CORREPI 2001). CORREPI relies on a daily survey of major periodicals, plus the complaints of friends and relatives of victims, and on a network of affiliated organizations around the country. CORREPI's list benefits from the organization's ever-greater insertion into many of the *villas* around the capital, and the likelihood that someone will report incidents to CORREPI even if the media do not pick them up. In Buenos Aires I used the CORREPI list of victims whose deaths occurred between 1990 and the end of 2000 as the starting point for the sample.

CORREPI imposes a filter that is mostly consistent with the purposes of this study. They include only deaths caused by members or former members of the security forces, and, they say, "We only include those cases in which, without any doubt, the death occurred in circumstances in which the victim posed absolutely no danger to third parties or the slayer. In other words, we do not include true armed confrontations" (CORREPI 2001, translation mine). The difficulty, of course, is that the police often stage a confrontation, so it seems unlikely that CORREPI will in every case be able to successfully distinguish "true" confrontations from staged ones. CORREPI compensates by being exceedingly skeptical of police accounts. Moreover, in many cases, CORREPI comes to know the friends or relatives of the victim, so its informal investigation relies on those who are most likely to be sympathetic to the victim. This, in the end, reintroduces some cases in which the illegality of the police action may not be susceptible to proof or otherwise clear-cut to an impartial adjudicator. Still, CORREPI would insist (and my examination of the cases confirms this) that the tendency is to include only those cases that are actual violations.

In Córdoba, CORREPI has a sister organization that monitors police violence and reports back, based on both individual complaints and journalistic reports (primarily in *La Voz del Interior*, the largest newspaper in Córdoba). The cases on their list come from both the capital city and other areas of Córdoba, but I limited my sample to cases from the Córdoba metropolitan area. CORREPI's Córdoba list was the beginning point for selecting a sample of cases to study in more detail, supplemented by interviews of CORREPI personnel in Córdoba.

In both Buenos Aires and Córdoba I interviewed lawyers and other members of CORREPI to identify all those cases on their list in which they knew the lawyers or other interested parties who were involved and to fill in as much information about the cases as possible. In addition, I contacted the lawyers and others they mentioned to gather additional information about the cases, and to review and copy the legal documents involved, if any were available. Upon my return to the United States, I also undertook searches in *La Nación*'s and *La Voz del Interior*'s online archives to update and complete the available information.

The final sample from Argentina consists of 227 cases from the Buenos Aires provincial courts located in the Greater Buenos Aires area (including a very small number from La Plata), 49 cases pending or decided in the federal courts of the Autonomous City of Buenos Aires (also known as Capital Federal), 90 cases from the provincial courts of Córdoba, and 2 from the federal courts in Córdoba.[3] Some of these cases still have incomplete information on a number of variables, of course, but the basic information regarding judicial treatment is there for all of them.

The sample selection in Argentina is likely to incorporate some biases that must be noted. In the first place, to the extent that results are affected by the involvement of civil society groups, lawyers, and concerned friends and relatives of the victims, the results of the sample are biased in favor of a higher conviction rate. In fact, the complete set of cases for which CORREPI has outcome information produces a 16% conviction rate, while in the more detailed sample the rate rises to 29.35%. At least half of the difference is the result of updating and completing information once the initial selection was made, but the rest, about 6 percentage points, is surely due to CORREPI's greater involvement in cases for which I have more information. In short, the results likely overstate to some degree the responsiveness of the system, but, given the lack of official data on police killings and the failure of the judiciary to generate, centralize, and disclose information on these cases, these are likely to be the best data available. Importantly, no matter what group of cases I compare, the conviction rate is higher in Buenos Aires than in São Paulo.

Fortunately, official data on the subject of police violence is available in São Paulo. Since 1990, the São Paulo state government has issued information on the number of deaths attributable to police action. These are the numbers I used to estimate the total number of police killings in São Paulo. Moreover, since 1996, the Ouvidoria da Polícia, a state ombudsman, has monitored the Civil and Military Police of the state of São Paulo. It receives

---

[3] As in Uruguay, because the information about the victim or the suspect may be different, and the results may vary according to the individual defendant or the individual victim, a case is counted as each victim in relation to each defendant.

complaints through a hotline, reviews the principal journals daily, and in addition receives an official telex whenever a police officer is involved in a fatal incident. The cases found in the Ouvidoria's files include primarily cases that take place in the course of official police functions, together with a smattering of homicides committed by police in the course of private security functions, domestic violence cases, and other crimes of passion in which the killer is identified as a police officer. The ombudsman appears to be informed in about 60 percent of the cases of homicide (the agency monitored 1,190 cases from 1996 through 2000, while police figures show a total of 2,838 deaths).

The main source of missing data in São Paulo will be those cases in which the police do not acknowledge participation. Unfortunately, given Brazil's history of police involvement in extermination groups (Lemos-Nelson 2001; Oiticica 2001), this is likely to be a greater problem here than in Argentina. Systematic information about this is, at present at least, beyond the reach of social science investigators. The Ouvidoria is also less likely than CORREPI to include instances of the private use of deadly force by members of the security forces, such as in cases of domestic violence. On the other hand, the Ouvidoria's list will include all cases of which it is informed, even those that are patently and credibly the result of armed confrontations.

The conviction rates for São Paulo are based on a sample selected from among the Ouvidoria cases. The information gathered by the Ouvidoria is organized in an electronic database. The agency opens a file on each incident report, and gathers certain documents in every case, including, where they exist, (a) the results of the *Inquérito Policial* (the basic criminal investigation carried out by the Civil Police, if there is one), (b) the *Inquérito Policial Militar* (carried out by the Military Police), and (c) the prosecutor's request either to dismiss or to indict. In addition, they often request additional documents such as autopsy reports or other forensic test results. Copies of these documents are included in each file. The final action of the prosecutor, recommending prosecution or dismissal, closes the file for the Ouvidoria. Crucially, this last document lists the prosecutor, court, and judge to which the case is assigned, the name of the individual defendants, and the case number.

I obtained a list from the Ouvidoria of all the files opened to investigate a homicide committed by the police from 1996 through 1998, in which the prosecutor's office had taken a position. I cut off the period at 1998, to give the courts a chance to act. I further limited the search to cases falling within the jurisdiction of the courts in the São Paulo metro area, to avoid having to range into the interior of the state for additional information. The final list included 158 cases in which the prosecutor requested dismissal of the case and 30 cases in which the prosecutor sought an indictment of the police officer(s) suspected in the killing. The cases that are not dismissed are both more interesting for purposes of this study and drastically fewer in number. As a result, I included all 30 of these cases in my sample, then used a computer program to randomly select just over 20% of the (128) dismissed cases to complete the sample. By weighting the 20% appropriately in the statistical analyses, I generated valid comparisons between the two groups. The final sample also includes about 60 cases that, from a review of all the documents in the file plus additional press reports where available, appeared to be cases of true armed confrontations. I excluded these cases from the analysis to maintain comparability to Argentina and Uruguay.

To complete information about the cases, I interviewed prosecutors and reviewed court records. For this last task, I was fortunate enough to have the cooperation of one of the judges from the jury division, who gave me a desk inside the clerk's office and instructed a secretary to bring me any files I requested. I also had the assistance of the staff at the Ouvidoria, who ran all over São Paulo obtaining information from prosecutors and various trial and appellate courts.

In addition, I reviewed the files kept by the Santo Dias Center for Human Rights, of the São Paulo archdiocese. Their files yielded another 37 cases, only 8% of which were dismissed outright. As discussed in the main text, and as with the CORREPI cases, the conviction rate is higher in this group than in the Ouvidoria sample, probably reflecting both the involvement of the center at all stages of the case and some bias in the selection of cases. This introduces some distortion to the overall sample of cases from São Paulo, but, on the other hand, it compensates for the higher degree of civil society involvement in the sample from Buenos Aires. As in Buenos Aires, these sampling criteria will cause any conclusions to be more conservative (i.e., based on a higher conviction rate) than a purely random sample of police homicide cases would produce.

The information on judicial responses to police homicides is much less reliable in Salvador. There is no Ouvidoria da Polícia, and the relevant NGOs do not collect systematic information on the victims of police violence. Without these starting points, it would have been very difficult to create a comprehensive and systematic list of victims and resulting judicial proceedings. Instead, as detailed in the main text, I worked with a few civil society organizations such as CEDECA, Tortura Nunca Mais, Comissão de Justiça e Paz, and the state witness protection program (PROVITA). In addition, I obtained two unpublished "dossiers," produced by local PT legislators, collecting information about police homicides and extermination groups in Salvador.

Using their lists of cases as a starting point, I interviewed their members about the circumstances of each incident and the judicial follow up to it. I spoke to prosecutors, human rights activists, and private lawyers with personal experience in police homicides. I also interviewed state legislators, principally from the Workers' Party (PT), who have been trying to address the problem of police violence for years. Finally, I carried out a series of searches in the local daily's online archive, using victim names as search terms, and in addition searching for stories involving the police, stories describing shootings of all kinds, and stories involving homicide prosecutions of any kind. The result is a non-representative list of cases that I used to estimate conviction rates and to explore the dynamics leading to convictions or acquittals in Salvador.

This book shines a light into some rather dark corners of Latin American democracy. Surely, the lens is imperfect. Generating representative information about police violence is a difficult and imprecise task. While the police themselves are usually more than willing to acknowledge the killing of a person, the details are, from their perspective, best left unexplored. In some of the places I studied, the police take this seriously enough to kill witnesses and others who look too closely. Even the prosecutorial and judicial response is difficult to discuss openly, as most of those interviewed assume from the beginning that the goal of the research is to show just how badly they are failing in their duties. Still, in each of the locations studied there were individuals who were willing to discuss this problem candidly, and some who were willing to open the doors of state agencies, courthouses, and prosecutors' offices so I could review files and data. The result is, I think, a fairly complete and relatively accurate picture of a shadowy and difficult phenomenon.

References

Adorno, Sérgio. 1994. Crime, Justiça Penal E Desigualdade Jurídica: As Mortes Que Se Contam No Tribunal Do Júri. *Revista USP* 21:132–51.

—— 1995. Discriminação Racial E Justiça Criminal Em São Paulo. *Novos Estudos – CEBRAP* No. 43 (November): 26–44.

—— 1998. O Gerenciamento Público Da Violência Urbana: A Justiça Em Ação. In *São Paulo Sem Medo: Um Diagnóstico Da Violência Urbana*, edited by P. S. Pinheiro. São Paulo: Garamond.

Ames, Barry. 2001. *The Deadlock of Democracy in Brazil.* Ann Arbor: University of Michigan Press.

Amnesty International. 2005. *"They Come in Shooting": Policing Socially Excluded Communities.* New York: Amnesty International.

Associação Juízes para a Democracia. 1999. *Propostas Da Associação Juízes Para a Democracia Para a Reforma Do Judiciário.* São Luis: Associação Juízes para a Democracia.

Assunção, Marília, and Lutz Mulert Sousa Ribeiro. 1998. *Violência Policial E a Relação Com Os Homicídios Em Salvador (1996 a Outubro 1998).* Salvador, Bahia: Movimento Nacional de Direitos Humanos.

Barahona de Brito, Alexandra. 1997. *Human Rights and Democratization in Latin America: Uruguay and Chile.* Edited by L. Whitehead. Oxford Studies in Democratization. New York: Oxford University Press.

Barcellos, Caco. 1992. *Rota 66: A História Da Polícia Que Mata.* São Paulo: Editora Globo.

Bastos Arantes, Rogério. 1999. Direito E Política: O Ministério Público E a Defesa Dos Direitos Coletivos. *Revista Brasileira de Ciencias Sociais* 14 (39): 83–102.

—— 2000. Ministério Público E Corrupção Política Em São Paulo. In *Justiça E Cidadania No Brasil*, edited by M. T. Sadek. São Paulo: Editora Sumaré.

—— 2002. *Ministério Público E Política No Brasil.* São Paulo: Editora Sumaré.

Batista Cavalcanti, Rosângela. 1999. *Cidadania E Acesso À Justiça.* São Paulo: Editora Sumaré.

Bayce, Rafael. 1996. *Informe Final Sobre Acceso a La Justicia.* Montevideo: Corte Suprema de la Nación.

Bellamy, Richard. 1996. The Political Form of the Constitution: The Separation of Powers, Rights and Representative Democracy. *Political Studies* 64: 436–56.

Bergoglio, María Inés. 1997. Acceso a La Justicia Civil: Diferencias De Clase. *Universidad Nacional de Córdoba, Centro de Investigaciones Jurídicas y Sociales, Anuario* 3:93–103.

———. 2003. Argentina: Los Efectos De La Institucionalización Democrática. In *Culturas Jurídicas Latinas De Europa Y América En Tiempos De Globalización*, edited by H. Fix-Fierro, L. Friedman, and R. Pérez Perdomo. México: Instituto de Investigaciones Jurídica, UNAM.

Bergoglio, María Inés, and Julio Carballo. 1997. Actitudes Hacia La Litigación Civil En Argentina: Diferencias Por Clase. *Universidad Nacional de Córdoba, Centro de Investigaciones Jurídicas y Sociales, Anuario* 3:41–57.

Berizonce, Roberto O. 1987. *Efectivo Acceso a La Justicia*. La Plata: Libreria Editora Platense S.R.L.

Bickel, Alexander. 1962. *The Least Dangerous Branch: The Supreme Court at the Bar of Politics*. Indianapolis: Bobbs-Merrill.

Bittencourt, Gustavo. 1997. *Informe De Consultoría Sobre Análisis Del Sistema De Financiamiento Del Poder Judicial*. Montevideo, Uruguay: Suprema Corte de Justicia.

Blaustein, Eduardo. 2003. *Villas Miseria* [four-part report on shantytowns in Buenos Aires]. Piketes, 2001 [cited May 14, 2003]. Available from http://www.piketes.com.ar/documentos.htm.

Bressan, Juan Carlos, Silvana Fernández, and Daniela Atea. 2003. Desigualdad Urbana En La Región Metropolitana Córdoba: Un Desafío De Gestión. Unpublished manuscript presented at V Seminario Nacional: "La Reforma Municipal Pendiente: Para Qué y Por Qué – Perspectivas y Prospectivas," October 9–10, 2003. Mendoza, Argentina. On file with author.

Brinks, Daniel M. 2003. Informal Institutions and the Rule of Law: The Judicial Response to State Killings in Buenos Aires and São Paulo in the 1990s. *Comparative Politics* 36 (1): 1–19.

———. 2005. Judicial Reform and Independence in Brazil and Argentina: The Beginning of a New Millennium? *Texas International Law Journal* 40 (3 [Spring]): 595–622.

———. 2006. The Rule of (Non)Law: Prosecuting Police Killings in Brazil and Argentina. In *Informal Institutions and Democracy: Lessons from Latin America*, edited by S. Levitsky and G. Helmke. Baltimore: Johns Hopkins University Press.

Bueno de Mesquita, Ethan, and Matthew Stephenson. 2002. Informative Precedent and Intrajudicial Communication. *American Political Science Review* 96 (4): 755–66.

Buscaglia, Edgardo, Maria Dakolias, and William Ratliff, eds. 1995. *Judicial Reform in Latin America: A Framework for National Development*. Stanford, Calif.: Stanford University Press.

Caldeira, Gregory. 1986. Neither the Purse nor the Sword: Dynamics of Public Confidence in the Supreme Court. *American Political Science Review* 80 (4): 1209–26.

Caldeira, Teresa Pires do Rio. 2000. *City of Walls: Crime, Segregation and Citizenship in São Paulo*. Berkeley: University of California Press.

Cano, Ignacio. 1999. O Papel Da Justiça Militar Na Investigação Das Mortes De Civis Pela Polícia No Rio De Janeiro. *Polícia e Sociedade Democrática* 1 (1): 1.

Cappelletti, Mauro, and Bryant Garth, eds. 1978–79. *Access to Justice*. 4 vols. Milan: A. Giuffrè.

Cardia, Nancy, Sérgio Adorno, and Paulo Sérgio Pinheiro. 1998. *Pesquisa Direitos Humanos E Democracia: Proposta De Intervenção Na Formação De Profissionais Do Judiciário, Do Ministério Público E Da Polícia No Estado De São Paulo, Brasil (Relatório Final)*. São Paulo: Núcleo de Estudos da Violência.

Carvalho, José Antonio de, ed. 2001. *Salvador: Cidade Repartida – Violência: Diagnóstico E O Fortalecimento Da Cidadania*. Salvador: Gráfica do Sindicato dos Bancários.

Castiglioni, Rossana. 2005. *The Politics of Social Policy Change in Chile and Uruguay: Retrenchment Versus Maintenance, 1973–1998*. New York and London: Routledge.

CELS (Centro de Estudios Legales y Sociales), ed. 1997. *Control Democrático De Los Organismos De Seguridad Interior En La República Argentina*. Buenos Aires: CELS.

——— 2000. *Derechos Humanos En Argentina: Informe Anual 2000*. Buenos Aires: Eudeba.

——— 2001. *Derechos Humanos: Argentina 2001*. Buenos Aires: Siglo XXI Editores/ Catálogos Editora.

——— 2001. *La Continuidad De Los Patrones De Violencia Policial*. Buenos Aires: CELS, Archivos de Hoy.

——— 2004. *Human Rights in Argentina: Annual Report* [Derechos Humanos En Argentina: Informe Anual]. Buenos Aires: CELS.

CELS/HRW (Centro de Estudios Legales y Sociales / Human Rights Watch). 1998. *La Inseguridad Policial: Violencia De Las Fuerzas De Seguridad En La Argentina*. Buenos Aires: Editorial Universitaria de Buenos Aires.

Centro de Estudios y Proyectos Judiciales. 2005. *Gobierno, Independencia Y Control Institucional*. Córdoba: Centro de Estudios y Proyectos Judiciales del Tribunal Superior de Justicia.

CEPAL (Comisión Económica para América Latina y el Caribe). 2003. *Panorama Social De América Latina, 2002–2003*. Santiago, Chile: United Nations.

Chevigny, Paul. 1995. *Edge of the Knife: Police Violence in the Americas*. New York: The New Press.

Cisa, Agustín. 1994. *Reforma Judicial En El Uruguay: Análisis Institucional, Actores Y Perspectivas*. Montevideo: Fundación de Cultura Universitaria.

Coase, Ronald H. 1988. *The Firm, the Market and the Law*. Chicago: University of Chicago Press.

Correa Sutil, Jorge. 1998. Modernization, Democratization and Judicial Systems. In *Justice Delayed: Judicial Reform in Latin America*, edited by F. Carrillo Flores and E. Jarquín. Washington, D.C.: Inter-American Development Bank.

——— 2001. *Acceso a La Justicia Y Reformas Judiciales En America Latina ¿Alguna Esperanza De Mayor Igualdad?* [Online paper.] Conference on Law and Society at Washington University, Washington University at St. Louis, 2001 (accessed 2001).

CORREPI (Coordinadora Contra la Represión Policial e Institucional). 2001. *Archivo De Casos, 1983–2001*. Buenos Aires: CORREPI. On file with author.

———. 2004. Carta Abierta De Los Familiares De Víctimas De La Represión Policial (January 28, 2004). Open letter from the relatives of victims of police repression, available from http://www.correpi.lahaine.org/articulo.php?p=7&more=1&c=1 (accessed May 16, 2007).

da Silva, Lígia M. Vieira, Jairnilson S. Paim, and Maria da C. N. Costa. 1999. Desigualdades Na Mortalidade, Espaço E Estratos Sociais. *Revista de Saúde Pública* 33 (2): 187–97.

Dahl, Robert. 1957. Decision-Making in a Democracy: The Supreme Court as a National Policy-Maker. *Journal of Public Law* 6 (2): 279–95.

———. 1989. *Democracy and Its Critics*. New Haven, Conn.: Yale University Press.

Dakolias, Maria. 1995. A Strategy for Judicial Reform: The Experience in Latin America. *Virginia Journal of International Law* 36 (1): 167–231.

Davis, K. E., and M. J. Trebilcock. 2001. Legal Reforms and Development. *Third World Quarterly* 22 (1): 21–36.

de Castro, Marcus Faro. 1997. The Courts, Law and Democracy in Brazil. *International Social Science Journal* 152 (June): 241–52.

de Oliveira, Nelson, Lutz Mulert Sousa Ribeiro, and Jose Carlos Zanetti, eds. 2000. *A Outra Face Da Moeda*. Salvador, Bahia: Commissão de Justiça e Paz da Arquidiocese de Salvador.

Di Federico, Giuseppe. 1998. El Consejo De La Magistratura: Cuestiones Seleccionadas Desde Una Perspectiva Comparada. In *Jornadas Internacionales Sobre El Consejo De La Magistratura*, edited by Ministerio de Justicia de la Nación. Buenos Aires: Programa de Reforma del Sistema de Justicia (PROJUS).

Diamond, Larry Jay. 1996. Democracy in Latin America: Degrees, Illusions, and Directions for Consolidation. In *Beyond Sovereignty: Collectively Defending Democracy in the Americas*, edited by T. Farer. Baltimore: Johns Hopkins University Press.

———. 1997. *Is the Third Wave of Democratization Over? An Empirical Assessment*. Notre Dame, Ind.: The Helen Kellogg Institute for International Studies.

———. ed. 1999. *Democracy in Developing Countries: Latin America*. 2nd ed. Boulder, Colo.: Lynne Rienner Publishers.

Domingo, Pilar. 2001. *Rule of Law in Latin America: The International Promotion of Judicial Reform*. Austin, Tex.: Institute of Latin American Studies.

Dutil, Carlos, and Ricardo Ragendorfer. 1997. *La Bonaerense: Historia Criminal De La Policía De La Provincia De Buenos Aires*. Buenos Aires: Editorial Planeta.

Epp, Charles. 2003. *The Rights Revolution*. Chicago: University of Chicago Press.

Epstein, Lee, and Jack Knight. 1998. *The Choices Justices Make*. Washington, D.C.: Congressional Quarterly Press.

———. 2000. Toward a Strategic Revolution in Judicial Politics: A Look Back, a Look Ahead. *Political Research Quarterly* 53 (September): 625–61.

Espinheira, Gey. 2005. *Crime without Punishment: Violence against Human Rights in Bahia* [Crime Sem Castigo: Violência Contra Os Direitos Humanos Na Bahia]. Salvador, Bahia: Centro de Defesa da Criança e do Adolescente da Bahia (on file with author).

Evan, William M. 1980. *The Sociology of Law: A Social-Cultural Perspective*. New York: The Free Press.

Evans, Peter B. 1995. *Embedded Autonomy: States and Industrial Transformation*. Princeton, N.J.: Princeton University Press.

Faria, José Eduardo, ed. 1988. *A Crise Do Direito Numa Sociedade Em Mudança*. Brasília: Editora Universidade de Brasilia.

———. 1996. A Crise Do Poder Judiciário No Brasil. *Justiça e Democracia* 3 (1): 18–64.

Felstiner, William L. F., Richard L. Abel, and Austin Sarat. 1980–81. The Emergence and Transformation of Disputes: Naming, Blaming, Claiming. *Law & Society Review* 15 (3–4): 631–54.

Ferreira Antunes, José Leopoldo, and Eliseu Alves Waldman. 2002. Trends and Spatial Distribution of Deaths of Children Aged 12–60 Months in São Paulo, Brazil, 1980–1998. *Bulletin of the World Health Organization* 80 (5): 391–98.

Fischer, Brodwyn. 2004. *Quase Pretos De Tão Pobres?* Race and Social Discrimination in Rio De Janeiro's Twentieth-Century Criminal Courts. *Latin American Research Review* 39 (1): 31–59.

Fiss, Owen. 1993. The Right Degree of Independence. In *Transition to Democracy in Latin America: The Role of the Judiciary*, edited by I. Stotzky. Boulder, Colo.: Westview Press.

FORES, and Colegio de Abogados de Buenos Aires. 1999. *Justicia Y Desarrollo Económico*. Buenos Aires: Consejo Empresario Argentino.

———. 1999. *Justicia Y Desarrollo Económico (Trabajo Completo)*. CD-ROM with full report of investigation. Buenos Aires: Consejo Empresario Argentino.

Foucault, Michel. 1980. The Eye of Power. In *Power/Knowledge: Selected Interviews and Other Writings, 1972–1977*, by Michel Foucault, edited by C. Gordon. New York: Pantheon Books.

France, Anatole. 1922 [1894]. *Le Lys Rouge* [The Red Lily]. Nouv. éd, rev. et corr. ed. Paris: Calmann-Lévy.

Friedman, Barry. 1998. The History of the Countermajoritarian Difficulty, Part One: The Road to Judicial Supremacy. *New York University Law Review* 73:333–433.

Frühling, Hugo. 1998. Judicial Reform and Democratization in Latin America. In *Fault Lines of Democracy in Post-Transition Latin America*, edited by F. Agüero and J. Stark. Miami, Fla.: North-South Center Press.

Fucito, Felipe. 1997. El Perfil Del Abogado En Ejercicio Profesional. *La Ley* 1997-E:1568–90.

———. 1999a. Abogados: La Opinión Pública Vinculada a La Profesión Jurídica. *La Ley* 1999-F:868–74.

———. 1999b. Abogados: Un Estudio Cuantitativo Sobre Los Abogados. *La Ley* 1999-E:1032–41.

Fundação Getúlio Vargas. 2001. *Mapa Do Fim Da Fome: Metas Sociais Contra Miséria Nos Municípios Baianos*. Rio de Janeiro: Fundação Getúlio Vargas.

Fundación para el Debido Proceso Legal. 2002. *Iniciativas De La Sociedad Civil Para La Transparencia En El Sector Judicial*, edited by M. Popkin. Washington, D.C.: Due Process of Law Foundation.

Galanter, Marc. 1974. Why the "Haves" Come Out Ahead: Speculations on the Limits of Legal Change. *Law & Society Review* 9 (1): 95–160.

Galleguillos, Nibaldo H. 2001. Judicial and Legal Reforms in the Democratic Transition: An Assessment of the Changing Roles of the Judiciary in Chile. Paper presented at the Annual Conference of the Latin American Studies Association, Washington, D.C.

García Lema, Alberto M. 1998. La Eficacia En La Administración De Justicia Como Valor Constitucional. In *Jornadas Internacionales Sobre El Consejo De La Magistratura*, edited by Ministerio de Justicia de la Nación. Buenos Aires: Programa de Reforma del Sistema de Justicia (PROJUS).

Gargarella, Roberto. 1996. *La Justicia Frente Al Gobierno: Sobre El Carácter Contra-Mayoritario Del Poder Judicial*. Barcelona: Editorial Ariel.

Garro, Alejandro. 1997. Access to Justice for the Poor in Latin America. In *Transitional Justice and the Rule of Law in New Democracies*, edited by A. J. McAdams. Notre Dame, Ind.: Notre Dame University Press.

Geller, William A., and Kevin J. Karales. 1981. *Split-Second Decisions: Shootings of and by Chicago Police*. Chicago: Chicago Law Enforcement Study Group.

Geller, William A., and Hans Toch. 1995. *And Justice for All: Understanding and Controlling Police Abuse of Force*. Washington, D.C.: Police Executive Research Forum.

Gibson, James L., Gregory Caldeira, and Vanessa A. Baird. 1998. On the Legitimacy of National High Courts. *American Political Science Review* 92:348–58.

González, José Luis. 2003. *La Policía En El Estado De Derecho Latinoamericano: Uruguay-Informe Preliminar*. Freiburg, Germany: Max Planck Institute for Foreign and International Criminal Law.

Gunn, Philipp. 1998. Uma Geografia Da Violência Na Periferia Metropolitana De São Paulo Nos Anos 80. In *São Paulo Sem Medo: Um Diagnóstico Da Violência Urbana*, edited by P. S. Pinheiro and J. Falcão. São Paulo: Editora Garamond.

Hamilton, Alexander, James Madison, and John Jay. 1961. *The Federalist Papers*. Edited by C. Rossiter. New York: Mentor (Penguin Books).

Hammergren, Linn. 1999. Fifteen Years of Justice and Justice Reform in Latin America: Where We Are and Why We Haven't Made More Progress. http://darkwing.uoregon.edu/~caguirre/papers.htm.

Hart, H. L. A. 1961. *The Concept of Law*. Oxford: Clarendon Press.

Hartlyn, Johnathan. 1998. *The Struggle for Democratic Politics in the Dominican Republic*. Chapel Hill: University of North Carolina Press.

Helmke, Gretchen. 2002. The Logic of Strategic Defection: Court–Executive Relations in Argentina under Dictatorship and Democracy. *American Political Science Review* 96 (2): 291–303.

———. 2005. *Courts under Constraints: Judges, Generals and Presidents in Argentina*. New York: Cambridge University Press.

Helmke, Gretchen, and Steven Levitsky, eds. 2006. *Informal Institutions and Democracy: Lessons from Latin America*. Baltimore: Johns Hopkins University Press.

Herron, E. S., and K. A. Randazzo. 2003. The Relationship between Independence and Judicial Review in Post-Communist Courts. *Journal of Politics* 65 (2): 422–38.

Hilbink, Elisabeth C. 2003. An Exception to Chilean Exceptionalism? The Historical Role of Chile's Judiciary. In *What Justice? Whose Justice? Fighting for Fairness in Latin America*, edited by S. E. Eckstein and T. Wickham-Crowley. Berkeley: University of California Press.

Forthcoming. *The Politics of Judicial Apoliticism: Chile in Comparative Perspective*. New York: Cambridge University Press.

Hinton, Mercedes. 2006. *The State on the Streets: Police and Politics in Argentina and Brazil*. London: Lynne Rienner Publishers.

Hirschl, Ran. 2004. *Towards Juristocracy – the Origins and Consequences of the New Constitutionalism*. Cambridge, Mass.: Harvard University Press.

Hobbes, Thomas. 1964 [1651]. *Leviathan*. Edited by F. B. Randall. New York: Washington Square Press.

Holmes, Stephen. 2003. Lineages of the Rule of Law. In *Democracy and the Rule of Law*, edited by J. M. Maravall and A. Przeworski. Cambridge: Cambridge University Press.

Holmes, Stephen, and Cass R. Sunstein. 1999. *The Cost of Rights: Why Liberty Depends on Taxes*. New York: W.W. Norton & Co.

Holston, James, and Teresa P. R. Caldeira. 1998. Democracy, Law and Violence: Disjunctions of Brazilian Citizenship. In *Fault Lines of Democracy in Post-Transition Latin America*, edited by F. Agüero and J. Stark. Miami, Fla.: North-South Center Press.

Iaryczower, Matías, Pablo Spiller, and Mariano Tommasi. 2002. Judicial Decision-Making in Unstable Environments. *American Journal of Political Science* 46 (4): 699–716.

2006. Judicial Lobbying: The Politics of Labor Law Constitutional Interpretation. *American Political Science Review* 100 (1): 85–97.

IBAM (Instituto Brasileiro de Administração Municipal). 2002. *Estudo De Avaliação Da Experiência Brasileira Sobre Urbanização De Favelas E Regularização Fundiária*. Rio de Janeiro: IBAM.

Inter-American Development Bank, Office of Evaluation and Oversight. 2003. *Justice Reform in Latin America: The Role of the Inter-American Development Bank*. Washington, D.C.: Inter-American Development Bank.

Jahangir, Asma. 2001. *Report of the Special Rapporteur on Civil and Political Rights, Including Questions of Disappearances and Summary Executions*. New York: United Nations Commission on Human Rights.

Jannuzzi, Paulo de Martino. 2001. Income and Poverty Levels of Vulnerable Groups in the Nineties in São Paulo Metropolitan Area. Paper presented at the 24th International Union for the Scientific Study of Population General Conference. Salvador, Brazil: IUSSP (available from http://www.iussp.org/Brazil2001/s40/S48_P02_Jannuzzi.pdf).

Jarquín, Edmundo, and Fernando Carrillo Flores, eds. 1998. *Justice Delayed: Judicial Reform in Latin America*. New York: Inter-American Development Bank.

Karl, Terry Lynn. 1995. The Hybrid Regimes of Central America. *Journal of Democracy* 6 (3): 72–86.

Kaztman, Rubén. 1997. Marginalidad E Integración Social En Uruguay. *Revista de la CEPAL* 62 (August), available from http://www.eclac.org/cgi-bin/getProd.asp?xml=/publicaciones/xml/5/10575/P10575.xml&xsl=/uruguay/tpl/p9f.xsl&base=/uruguay/tpl/top-bottom.xsl (accessed May 16, 2007).

Kiewiet, D. Roderick, and Mathew D. McCubbins. 1991. *The Logic of Delegation: Congressional Parties and the Appropriations Process*. Chicago and London: University of Chicago Press.

Kritzer, Herbert M. 1990. *The Justice Broker: Lawyers and Ordinary Litigation*. New York: Oxford University Press.

Larkins, Christopher M. 1996. Judicial Independence and Democratization: A Theoretical and Conceptual Analysis. *American Journal of Comparative Law* 44 (4 [Fall]): 605–26.

    1998. The Judiciary and Delegative Democracy in Argentina. *Comparative Politics* 31 (July): 423–42.

Lemos-Nelson, Ana Tereza. 2001. Judiciary Police Accountability for Gross Human Rights Violations: The Case of Bahia, Brazil. Ph.D. diss., Government and International Studies, University of Notre Dame, Notre Dame, Ind.

Lempert, Richard. 1987. The Autonomy of Law: Two Visions Compared. In *Autopoietic Law: A New Approach to Law and Society*, edited by G. Teubner. Berlin: Walter de Gruyter.

Levitsky, Steven, and María Victoria Murillo. 2006. Variation in Institutional Strength in Latin America: Causes and Implications. Paper presented at the 26th International Congress of the Latin American Studies Association, March 15–18, 2006, San Juan, Puerto Rico.

Linz, Juan J., and Alfred Stepan, eds. 1978. *The Breakdown of Democratic Regimes: Crisis, Breakdown, and Reequilibration*. Baltimore: Johns Hopkins University Press.

Lista, Carlos A., and Silvana Begala. 2000. Pobreza, Marginalidad Jurídica Y Acceso a La Justicia: Condicionamientos Objetivos Y Subjetivos. *Universidad Nacional de Córdoba, Centro de Investigaciones Jurídicas y Sociales, Anuario* 5:407–32.

Lopes de Souza, Marcelo. 2001. Metropolitan Deconcentration, Socio-Political Fragmentation and Extended Suburbanization: Brazilian Urbanization in the 1980s and 1990s. *Geoforum* 32:437–47.

Luhmann, Niklas. 1985. *A Sociological Theory of Law*. London: Routledge & Kegan Paul.

    1988. Closure and Openness: On Reality in the World of Law. In *Autopoietic Law: A New Approach to Law and Society*, edited by G. Teubner. Berlin: Walter de Gruyter.

Macaulay, Stewart. 1979. Lawyers and Consumer Protection Laws. *Law & Society Review* 14 (1): 115–71.

Machado, Eduardo Paes, and Ceci Vilar Noronha. 2002. A Polícia Dos Pobres: Violência Policial Em Classes Populares Urbanas. *Sociologias* 7 (January/June): 188–221.

Mahiques, Carlos, ed. 2002. Optimización De La Implementación De La Reforma Del Sistema De Enjuiciamiento Penal De La Provincia De Buenos Aires. *CEJA* 1 (2): 1–12.

Mainwaring, Scott. 2006. The Crisis of Democratic Representation in the Andes. *Journal of Democracy* 17 (3): 13–27.

Mainwaring, Scott, Daniel Brinks, and Anibal Pérez-Liñán. 2001. Classifying Political Regimes in Latin America, 1945–1999. *Studies in Comparative Development* 36 (1 [Spring]): 37–65.

Mainwaring, Scott, and Matthew Soberg Shugart, eds. 1997. *Presidentialism and Democracy in Latin America*. New York: Cambridge University Press.

Mainwaring, Scott, and Christopher Welna, eds. 2003. *Democratic Accountability in Latin America*. Oxford: Oxford University Press.

Mann, Michael. 1993. *The Sources of Social Power: The Rise of Classes and Nation-States, 1760–1914*. Vol. 2. Cambridge: Cambridge University Press.

Mantovani, Bráulio. 2002. *City of God [Cidade De Deus]*, edited by F. Meirelles and K. Lund. Burbank, Calif.: Miramax Home Entertainment.

Maravall, José María, and Adam Przeworski, eds. 2003. *Democracy and the Rule of Law*. Cambridge: Cambridge University Press.

Mariano, Benedito D., and Bernadete Toneto. 2000. *Centro Santo Dias De Direitos Humanos Da Arquidiocese De São Paulo*. São Paulo: Gráfica e Editora Peres.

Marshall, T. H. 1950. *Citizenship and Social Class, and Other Essays*. Cambridge: Cambridge University Press.

McCann, Michael. 1994. *Rights at Work: Pay Equity Reform and the Politics of Legal Mobilization*. Chicago: University of Chicago Press.

Mello de Camargo Ferraz, Antonio Augusto, ed. 1997. *Ministério Público: Instituição E Processo*. São Paulo: Editora Atlas.

Méndez, Juan E., Guillermo A. O'Donnell, and Paulo Sérgio Pinheiro, eds. 1999. *The (Un)Rule of Law and the Underprivileged in Latin America*. Notre Dame, Ind.: University of Notre Dame Press.

Merryman, John Henry. 1985. *The Civil Law Tradition: An Introduction to the Legal Systems of Western Europe and Latin America*. 2nd ed. Stanford, Calif.: Stanford University Press.

Milanovic, Branko. 2005. *Worlds Apart: Measuring International and Global Inequality*. Princeton, N.J.: Princeton University Press.

Milanovic, Branko, and Shlomo Yitzhaki. 2002. Decomposing World Income Distribution: Does the World Have a Middle Class? *Review of Income and Wealth* 48(2): 155–78.

Miller, Jonathan. 2000. Evaluating the Argentine Supreme Court under Presidents Alfonsín and Menem (1983–1999). *Southwestern Journal of Law and Trade in the Americas* 7 (Fall): 369–433.

Moser, Robert G. 2001. *Unexpected Outcomes: Electoral Systems, Political Parties, and Representation in Russia*. Pittsburgh: University of Pittsburgh Press.

Muralidhar, S. 2002. Implementation of Court Orders in the Area of Economic, Social and Cultural Rights: An Overview of the Experience of the Indian Judiciary. Paper presented at *First South Asian Regional Judicial Colloquium on Access to Justice*. New Delhi: International Environmental Law Research Centre. Available from http://www.ielrc.org/content/wo202.pdf (accessed May 17, 2007).

Murilo de Carvalho, José. 1997. *Lei, Justiça E Cidadania: Direitos, Vitimização E Cultura Política Na Região Metropolitana Do Rio De Janeiro*. Rio de Janeiro: Centro de Pesquisa e Documentação de História Contemporânea do Brasil – Fundação Getúlio Vargas.

O'Brien, David M., and Yasuo Ohkoshi. 2001. Stifling Judicial Independence from Within: The Japanese Judiciary. In *Judicial Independence in the Age of*

Democracy, edited by P. H. Russell and D. M. O'Brien. Charlottesville: University Press of Virginia.

O'Donnell, Guillermo A. 1979. *Modernization and Bureaucratic-Authoritarianism: Studies in South American Politics*. Berkeley: Institute of International Studies, University of California.

———. 1993. On the State, Democratization, and Some Conceptual Problems: A Latin American View with Glances at Some Postcommunist Countries. *World Development* 21 (8): 1355–69.

———. 1994. Delegative Democracy. *Journal of Democracy* 5 (1): 55–69.

———. 1999. Polyarchies and the (Un)Rule of Law in Latin America: A Partial Conclusion. In *The (Un)Rule of Law and the Underprivileged in Latin America*, edited by J. E. Mendez, G. O'Donnell, and P. S. Pinheiro. Notre Dame, Ind.: University of Notre Dame Press.

———. 2001. Democracy, Law and Comparative Politics. *Studies in Comparative International Development* 36 (1 [Spring]): 7–36.

———. 2004. Why the Rule of Law Matters. *Journal of Democracy* 15 (4): 32–46.

O'Donnell, Guillermo A., Philippe Schmitter, and Laurence Whitehead, eds. 1986. *Transitions from Authoritarian Rule*. Baltimore: Johns Hopkins University Press.

Oiticica, Yulo. 2001. Dossiê Grupos De Extermínio. Salvador, Bahia. Unpublished legislative briefing materials. On file with author.

Ortiz, Esteban Rafael. 1991. El Proceso Penal En Córdoba: Reforma Y Realidad. Ponencia Presentada al 7th Encuentro Panamericano de Derecho Procesal, Córdoba.

Ouvidoria da Polícia. 1999. *Pesquisa Sobre O Uso Da Forca Letal Por Policiais De São Paulo No Ano De 1999*. Available from www.ouvidoria-policia.sp.gov.br and on file with author.

Palmieri, Gustavo, Rodrigo Borda, and Cecilia Ales. *Justice Facing Police Violence*. CELS (Centro de Estudios Legales y Sociales), 2004. Available from http://www.cels.org.ar/english/index.html (accessed November 11, 2006).

Paulina, Iracy. 1999. Queixe-Se Ao Promotor. *Veja*, 16–22.

Pereira da Silva, Cátia Aida. 1999. Novas Facetas Da Atuação Dos Promotores De Justiça: Um Estudo Sobre O Ministério Público E a Defesa Dos Interesses Sociais. Ph.D. diss., Political Science, Universidade de São Paulo, São Paulo.

Peruzzotti, Enrique, and Catalina Smulovitz, eds. 2006. *Enforcing the Rule of Law: Social Accountability in New Latin American Democracies*. Pittsburgh: University of Pittsburgh Press.

Piovesan, Flávia, James Louis Cavallaro, Jaime Benvenuto Lima, Jr., José Fernando da Silva, and Valdênia Brito. 2001. *Execuções Sumárias, Arbitrárias Ou Extrajudiciais*. Recife, Brazil: Companhia Editora de Pernambuco.

Poder Judicial, República Oriental del Uruguay. Various years. *Anuario Estadístico*. Montevideo: Poder Judicial del Uruguay.

Poe-Yamagata, Eileen, and Michael Jones. 2000. *And Justice for Some*. Building Blocks for Youth. Available from http://www.buildingblocksforyouth.org/justiceforsome/jfs.html (accessed May 17, 2007).

Popkin, Margaret. 2000. *Peace without Justice: Obstacles to Building the Rule of Law in El Salvador*. Philadelphia: Penn State University Press.

Portal de la Justicia Argentina. 2003. *Estadísticas* [Web site]. Ministerio de Justicia, 2003 [cited 2003]. Available from www.justiciaargentina.gov.ar.

Poulantzas, Nicos A. 1978. *State, Power, Socialism.* London: NLB.

Prillaman, William C. 2000. *The Judiciary and Democratic Decay in Latin America: Declining Confidence in the Rule of Law.* Westport, CT: Praeger Publishers.

Ramos, Lauro. 2003. *A Informalidade Das Relações De Trabalho: 1991–2001* [paper posted online]. Instituto de Estudos do Trabalho e Sociedade, 2003. Available from http://www.iets.org.br/biblioteca/A_informalidade_das_relacoes_de_trabalho.PDF (accessed May 17, 2007).

Raz, Joseph. 1979. The Rule of Law and Its Virtue. In *Liberty and the Rule of Law*, edited by R. L. Cunningham. College Station, Tex.: Texas A&M University Press.

Ré, María Cecilia, and Maria Eugenia Taquela. 1998. *Acceso a La Tierra Y Construcción Ciudadana.* Córdoba: Ediciones CECOPAL.

Renó do Prado, Amauri, and José Carlos Mascari Bonilha. 2000. *Manual De Processo Penal: Conhecimento E Execução Penal.* São Paulo: Editora Juarez de Oliveira.

Rhenan-Segura, Jorge. 1990. *La Clase Política Y El Poder Judicial En Costa Rica.* San Jose, Costa Rica: Editorial Universidad Estatal a Distancia.

Rolnik, Raquel. 2001. Territorial Exclusion and Violence: The Case of the State of São Paulo, Brazil. *Geoforum* 32:471–82.

Rosenberg, Gerald N. 1991. *The Hollow Hope: Can Courts Bring About Social Change?* Chicago: University of Chicago Press.

Ross, H. Laurence. 1980. *Settled out of Court: The Social Process of Insurance Claim Adjustment.* 2nd ed. New York: Aldine.

Sadek, Maria Tereza, ed. 1999. *O Sistema De Justiça.* São Paulo: Editora Sumaré.

Sadek, Maria Tereza, and Rosângela Batista Cavalcanti. 2003. The New Brazilian Public Prosecution: An Agent of Accountability. In *Democratic Accountability in Latin America*, edited by S. Mainwaring and C. Welna. Oxford: Oxford University Press.

Sadek, Maria Tereza, Kazuo Watanabe, Caetano Lagrasta Neto, and Fernão Dias de Lima. 2000. *Perfil Do Réu Nos Delitos Contra O Patrimônio (Furto E Roubo).* São Paulo, SP: Centro Brasileiro de Estudos e Pesquisas Judiciais.

Salas, Luis. 2001. From Law and Development to Rule of Law: New and Old Issues in Justice Reform in Latin America. In *Rule of Law in Latin America: The International Promotion of Judicial Reform*, edited by P. Domingo and R. Sieder. London: Institute of Latin American Studies.

Santos, Boaventura de Sousa. 1977. The Law of the Oppressed: The Construction and Reproduction of Legality in Pasargada. *Law & Society Review* 12 (1):5–126.

Scarponetti, P., Z. Garay, M. Méndez, A. Vivanco, and P. Sorribas. 2000a. Desde La Ineptitud a La Corrupción ¿Qué Pasa Con La Independencia Del Poder Judicial? In *Ponencias Del Congreso Nacional De Sociología Jurídica, 2–4 Noviembre De 2000.* La Plata, Buenos Aires: Universidad Nacional de La Plata.

———. 2000b. La Cultura Jurídica Interna Y Sus Posibilidades De Cambio, Frente a Las Propuestas De Cambio Organizacional. In *Ponencias Del Congreso Nacional De Sociología Jurídica, 2–4 Noviembre De 2000.* La Plata: Buenos Aires: Universidad Nacional de La Plata.

Scheingold, Stuart A. 2004. *The Politics of Rights: Lawyers, Public Policy and Political Change.* 2nd ed. Ann Arbor: University of Michigan Press.

Schmitter, Philippe, and Terry Lynn Karl. 1991. What Democracy Is. And Is Not. *Journal of Democracy* 2:75–88.

Scott, James C. 1986. *Weapons of the Weak: Everyday Forms of Peasant Resistance.* New Haven, Conn.: Yale University Press.

Segal, Jeffrey, and Harold Spaeth. 2002. *The Supreme Court and the Attitudinal Model Revisited.* Cambridge: Cambridge University Press.

Seligson, Amber. 2002. When Democracies Elect Dictators: Motivations for and Impact of the Election of Former Authoritarians in Argentina and Bolivia. Ph.D. diss., Political Science, Cornell University, Ithaca, N.Y.

Sen, Amartya. 1999. *Development as Freedom.* New York: Random House.

Servicio Paz y Justicia (SERPAJ). 1998. Informe, Derechos Humanos en Uruguay. Montevideo, Uruguay: El Servicio.

Shapiro, Martin. 1981. *Courts: A Comparative and Political Analysis.* Chicago and London: University of Chicago Press.

Shifter, Michael. 1997. Tensions and Trade-Offs in Latin America. *Journal of Democracy* 8 (2): 114–28.

Skaar, Elin. 2002. Judicial Independence: A Key to Justice – an Analysis of Latin America in the 1990s. Ph.D. diss., Political Science, University of California–Los Angeles.

Skolnick, Jerome H., and James J. Fyfe. 1993. *Above the Law: Police and the Excessive Use of Force.* New York: The Free Press.

Smulovitz, Catalina, and Enrique Peruzzotti. 2003. Societal and Horizontal Controls: Two Cases of a Fruitful Relationship. In *Democratic Accountability in Latin America*, edited by S. Mainwaring and C. Welna. Notre Dame, Ind.: University of Notre Dame Press.

Souza, Celina. 1997. *Constitutional Engineering in Brazil.* New York: St. Martin's Press.

Staats, Joseph L., Shaun Bowler, and Jonathan T. Hiskey. 2005. Measuring Judicial Performance in Latin America. *Latin American Politics & Society* 47 (4): 77–106.

Stanley, Ruth. 2004. Law and Order Talk. Unpublished manuscript. On file with author.

Stotzky, Irwin P., ed. 1993. *Transition to Democracy in Latin America: The Role of the Judiciary.* Boulder, Colo.: Westview Press.

Teixeira Gomes, João Carlos. 2001. *Memórias Das Trevas – Uma Devassa Na Vida De Antonio Carlos Magalhães.* São Paulo: Geração Editorial.

UNDP. 1998. *Política Macroeconómica Y Pobreza En América Latina Y El Caribe.* Madrid: Mundi-Prensa Libros.

Ungar, Mark. 2001. *Elusive Reform: Democracy and the Rule of Law in Latin America.* Boulder, Colo.: Lynne Rienner Publishers.

Valenzuela, J. Samuel. 1992. Democratic Consolidation in Post-Transitional Settings: Notion, Process, and Facilitating Conditions. In *Issues in Democratic Consolidation: The New South American Democracies in Comparative Perspective*, edited by S. Mainwaring, G. O'Donnell, and J. S. Valenzuela. Notre Dame, Ind.: University of Notre Dame Press.

Vanberg, Georg. 2001. Legislative-Judicial Relations: A Game-Theoretic Approach to Constitutional Review. *American Journal of Political Science* 45 (2): 346–61.

Vanderscheuren, Franz, and Enrique Oviedo, eds. 1995. *Acceso De Los Pobres a La Justicia En Países De Latinoamérica*. Santiago, Chile: Ediciones SUR.

Vega, Juan Carlos. 1998. *La Justicia En La Transición Democrática Argentina*. Córdoba: Marcos Lerner Editora.

Ventura, Adrián, Adriana Scoccia, and Juan José Arámburu. 1999. *Cómo Se Elige a Un Juez: Reglamentos Del Consejo De La Magistratura Y Del Jurado De Enjuiciamiento*. Buenos Aires: Ediciones Depalma.

Vilanova, José Lucas. 2000. El Asesoramiento Legal Gratuito En El Marco De Las Políticas Sociales. In *Ponencias Del Congreso Nacional De Sociología Jurídica, 2–4 Noviembre De 2000*. La Plata, Buenos Aires: Universidad Nacional de La Plata.

Virgolini, Julio E. S. 1988. Tribunales Y Sociedad: El Pueblo Y La Justicia. In *La Independencia De Jueces Y Abogados En Argentina, Brasil, Paraguay Y Uruguay*, edited by Comisión Internacional de Juristas. Geneva and Montevideo: Centro Para la Independencia de Jueces y Abogados & IELSUR.

Weber, Max. 1978 [1921]. *Economy and Society: An Outline of Interpretive Sociology*. Translated by E. Fischoff, H. Gerth, A. M. Henderson, F. Kolegar, C. W. Mills, T. Parsons, M. Rheinstein, G. Roth, E. Shills, and C. Wittich. Edited by G. Roth and C. Wittich. 2 vols. Vol. 2. Berkeley: University of California Press.

Weyland, Kurt G. 2002. *The Politics of Market Reform in Fragile Democracies: Argentina, Brazil, Peru and Venezuela*. Princeton, N.J.: Princeton University Press.

Worden, Robert E. 1995. The "Causes" of Police Brutality: Theory and Evidence on Police Use of Force. In *And Justice for All: Understanding and Controlling Police Abuse of Force*, edited by W. A. Geller and H. Toch. Washington, D.C.: Police Executive Research Forum.

Zaffaroni, Eugenio Raúl. 1994. *Estructuras Judiciales*. Buenos Aires: Ediar.

Zaverucha, Jorge. 1999. Military Justice in the State of Pernambuco after the Brazilian Military Regime: An Authoritarian Legacy. *Latin American Research Review* 34 (2): 43–73.

Index